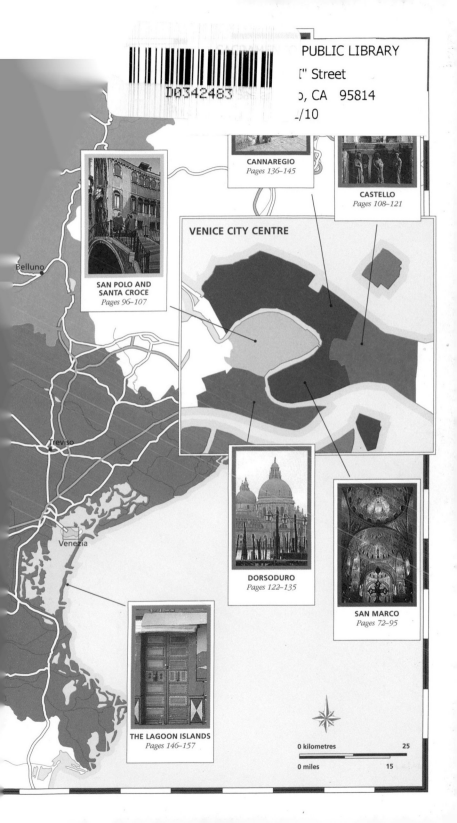

CANNAREGIO
Pages 136–145

CASTELLO
Pages 108–121

SAN POLO AND
SANTA CROCE
Pages 96–107

VENICE CITY CENTRE

Belluno

Treviso

Venezia

DORSODURO
Pages 122–135

SAN MARCO
Pages 72–95

THE LAGOON ISLANDS
Pages 146–157

0 kilometres   25

0 miles   15

EYEWITNESS TRAVEL

VENICE
& THE VENETO

EYEWITNESS TRAVEL

VENICE
& THE VENETO

MAIN CONTRIBUTORS:
SUSIE BOULTON
CHRISTOPHER CATLING

DK

LONDON, NEW YORK,
MELBOURNE, MUNICH AND DELHI
www.dk.com

PRODUCED BY Pardoe Blacker Publishing Limited, Lingfield, Surrey
PROJECT Editor Caroline Ball
ART EDITOR Simon Blacker
EDITORS Jo Bourne, Molly Perham, Linda Williams
DESIGNERS Kelvin Barratt, Dawn Brend, Jon Eland,
Nick Raven, Steve Rowling
MAP CO-ORDINATORS Simon Farbrother, David Pugh
PICTURE RESEARCH Jill De Cet

CONTRIBUTOR (TRAVELLERS' NEEDS) Sally Roy

MAPS
Phil Rose, Jennifer Skelley, Jane Hanson
(Lovell Johns Ltd, Oxford UK)
Street Finder maps based upon digital data, adapted
with permission from L.A.C. (Italy)

PHOTOGRAPHERS
John Heseltine (Venice), Roger Moss (Veneto)

ILLUSTRATORS
Arcana Studios, Donati Giudici Associati srl,
Robbie Polley, Simon Roulstone

Reproduced by Colourscan, Singapore
Printed and bound in China by L. Rex Printing Co. Ltd

First American edition 1995
10 11 12 13 10 9 8 7 6 5 4 3 2 1

Published in the United States by DK Publishing,
375 Hudson Street, New York, New York 10014

Reprinted with revisions 1995, 1997 (twice), 1998, 1999,
2000, 2001, 2002, 2003, 2004, 2006, 2008, 2010

Copyright 1995, 2010 © Dorling Kindersley Limited, London
A Penguin Company

ISSN: 1542–1554
ISBN: 978-0-75666-132-8

FLOORS ARE REFERRED TO THROUGHOUT IN ACCORDANCE WITH AMERICAN
USAGE; IE THE "FIRST FLOOR" IS THE FLOOR AT GROUND LEVEL.

*Front cover main image: Gondolas opposite
San Giorgio Maggiore, Venice*

We're trying to be cleaner and greener:

- we recycle waste and switch things off
- we use paper from responsibly managed
forests whenever possible
- we ask our printers to actively reduce
water and energy consumption
- we check out our suppliers' working
conditions – they never use child labour

**Find out more about our values and
best practices at www.dk.com**

**The information in this
Dorling Kindersley Travel Guide is checked regularly.**
Every effort has been made to ensure that this book is as up-to-date
as possible at the time of going to press. Some details, however,
such as telephone numbers, opening hours, prices, gallery hanging
arrangements and travel information are liable to change. The
publishers cannot accept responsibility for any consequences arising
from the use of this book, nor for any material on third party
websites, and cannot guarantee that any website address in this
book will be a suitable source of travel information. We value the
views and suggestions of our readers very highly. Please write to:
Publisher, DK Eyewitness Travel Guides, Dorling Kindersley,
80 Strand, London, WC2R 0RL, Great Britain.

CONTENTS

The Venetian explorer Marco Polo

INTRODUCING
VENICE AND
THE VENETO

Palazzo Pisani Moretta on
the Grand Canal

◁ View across the Grand Canal

The Rialto Bridge, on the
Grand Canal

Veronese's *Passion and Virtue* in
the Villa Barbaro at Masèr

The medieval Palio dei Dieci Comuni at Montagnana

Asparagus stalks

The Doge's Palace
in Piazza San Marco

HOW TO USE THIS GUIDE

This guide helps you get the most from your stay in Venice and the Veneto. It provides both expert recommendations and detailed practical information. *Introducing Venice and the Veneto* maps the region and sets it in its historical and cultural context. *Venice Area by Area* and *The Veneto*

Area by Area describe the important sights, with maps, pictures and detailed illustrations. Suggestions for food, drink, accommodation, shopping and entertainment are in *Travellers' Needs*, and the *Survival Guide* has tips on everything from the Italian telephone system to travelling around Venice by *vaporetto*.

VENICE AREA BY AREA

The city has been divided into five sightseeing areas. The lagoon islands make up a sixth area. Each area has its own chapter, which opens with a list of the sights described. All the sights are numbered and plotted on an *Area Map*. The detailed information for each sight is presented in numerical order, making it easy to locate within the chapter.

Each area of Venice can be quickly identified by its colour coding.

A locator map shows where you are in relation to other areas of the city.

1 Area Map
For easy reference, the sights are numbered and located on a map. The sights are also shown on the Venice Street Finder *on pages 288–97.*

Sights at a Glance lists the chapter's sights by category: Churches; Museums and Galleries; Historic Buildings; Palaces; Streets, Bridges and Squares.

2 Street-by-Street Map
This gives a bird's eye view of the heart of each sightseeing area.

Stars indicate the sights that no visitor should miss.

A suggested route for a walk covers the more interesting streets in the area.

3 Detailed information on each sight
All the sights in Venice are described individually. Addresses, telephone numbers, nearest vaporetto *stop, opening hours and information on admission charges are also provided.*

1 Introduction
The landscape, history and character of each region is described here, showing how the area has developed over the centuries and what it offers to the visitor today.

THE VENETO AREA BY AREA
In this book, the Veneto has been divided into three regions, each of which has a separate chapter. The most interesting sights to visit have been numbered on a *Regional Map*.

Each area of the Veneto can be quickly identified by its colour coding.

2 Regional Map
This shows the road network and gives an illustrated overview of the whole region. All the sights are numbered and there are also useful tips on getting around the region by car, bus and train.

3 Detailed information on each sight
All the important towns and other places to visit are described individually. They are listed in order, following the numbering on the Regional Map. Within each town or city, there is detailed information on important buildings and other sights.

Stars indicate the best features and works of art.

For all the top sights, a Visitors' Checklist provides the practical information you will need to plan your visit.

4 The top sights
These are given two or more full pages. Historic buildings are dissected to reveal their interiors; museums and galleries have colour-coded floorplans to help you locate the most interesting exhibits.

INTRODUCING VENICE AND THE VENETO

FOUR GREAT DAYS IN VENICE AND THE VENETO

Visitors are simply spoiled for choice in this part of Italy. There are scores of museums, churches and art galleries in Venice which demand attention, preferably with stops along the way for a meal at a waterside café or a ride on a gondola. Then there are the historic towns of the Veneto, each with its own special story to tell, dotted across the beautiful hinterland. The four itineraries outlined here are designed to show the variety of activities this region has to offer. The Venice and Verona days can be enjoyed using public transport alone, whereas Lake Garda is best explored by car and ferry. The price guides give an indication of the overall cost, including travel, food and admission charges.

Gondola, Venice

THE TREASURES AND STYLE OF ST. MARK'S

- Early morning in the Basilica
- See how the Doges lived
- Fashion shopping along the Calle XXII Marzo
- View from a gondola

TWO ADULTS allow at least €120

Morning
It is worth getting to the **Basilica** *(see pp78–83)* as early as possible to enjoy the glittering mosaics and solemn Byzantine interior in the morning light. Don't forget to climb the narrow steps to the balconies that overlook St Mark's Square. Once back at ground level, wander around the busy *piazza*, bustling with people and pigeons, before taking a (pre-booked) guided tour of the recently restored **Torre dell'Orologio** *(see p76)*, with its magnificent astronomical clock, or the adjoining **Museo Correr** *(see p77)*. Nearby is the **Doge's Palace** *(see pp84–9)*, which offers the chance to visit the

Rooftop view of Santa Maria della Salute and Dogana di Mare

state apartments for a glimpse into how the city's former rulers once lived. A light lunch in the converted stables below is a good way to round off the morning.

Afternoon
A five-minute walk away is the exclusive shopping street **Calle XXII Marzo** *(see p91)*, lined with top fashion boutiques with enticing window displays. A perfect, if expensive, way to end the day is with a relaxing **gondola ride** *(see p284)* over St Mark's basin and along the labyrinth of quiet back canals. Another option is to visit the historic **Caffè Florian** *(see p250)* and watch the world go by while sipping an aperitif to the sounds of its lively orchestra.

Feeding the pigeons in front of the Basilica on St Mark's Square

ART AND WATERBUSES

- Art at the Accademia
- A lunchtime *gelato*
- Get caught up in modern art
- Relax on a *vaporetto*

TWO ADULTS allow at least €120

Morning
The renowned **Accademia** art gallery *(see pp130–33)* is crammed with paintings illustrating Venice's glorious history as the Serenissima Republic. Canvases by great masters such as Titian, Bellini and Veronese adorn this converted monastery, and an audio gallery guide is a great help in navigating your way around. When you

◁ Perspective view of Venice by Bernard von Breydenbach, 1486 have had your fill, walk over to the broad, sun-blessed **Zattere** waterfront *(see pp128–9)* for views of the Giudecca and passing waterborne traffic. Lunch can be enjoyed at any one of the outdoor restaurants here, finished off with a classic Italian *gelato* (ice cream) *(see pp250–51)*.

Afternoon
The afternoon can be well spent at the nearby **Peggy Guggenheim Collection** *(see p134)*, a landmark collection of Modern art. The works by Miró, Picasso and Pollock, to name but a few, occupy a light-filled single-storey *palazzo* on the Grand Canal. A pleasant place to stop for a drink is the lovely terrace café. Once outside wander back to the Zattere and catch *vaporetto* **n.52** *(see pp282–3)*, which circumnavigates the city giving a panoramic conclusion to the day.

THE ROMANCE OF VERONA

- A visit to Juliet's house
- The awe-inspiring Arena
- Sightseeing from a horse-drawn carriage
- A walk around the tranquil Giardini Giusti gardens

TWO ADULTS allow at least €150

Morning
One of the most romantic cities in the world, Verona is the setting of the tragic tale of Romeo and Juliet.

The perfect way to start your visit is at the **Casa di Giulietta** (Juliet's house) *(see p199)*, although the building is not authentic it is still atmospheric. A short stroll away is the beautiful Piazza Brà, home to the awe-inspiring **Roman Arena** *(see pp194–5)*, where opera is performed outdoors in the summer months. It is well worth taking the time to climb up the immense tiers of stone seats to admire the massive structure and views of the surrounding city. A great place to stop for lunch is the family-run **Ristorante Greppia** *(see p249)*, the menu features plenty of delicious local specialities.

Afternoon
Returning to Piazza Brà, a nice way to view the sights, while resting your feet, is a gently paced horse-drawn carriage ride, which takes in many of the sights of the town, including the spectacular **Castelvecchio** museum *(see p193)* and the photogenic Pontevecchio bridge. Across the river is the **Giardino Giusti** *(see p203)*, a lovely example of a Renaissance garden dotted with aged cedar trees and clipped hedges. A lovely way to spend the early evening is with an aperitif in **Piazza delle Erbe** *(see p198)*. Try a glass of Valpolicella wine while watching the square empty of its daytime clutter, allowing the central fountain to once again make its presence felt.

The pretty town of Malcésine overlooks Lake Garda

A FAMILY DAY ON GLORIOUS LAKE GARDA

- The tunnels of Gardesana
- View from the water
- Ride the revolving cable-car to Monte Baldo
- An evening swim off the rocks at Sirmione

FAMILY OF 4 allow at least €150

Morning
From Desenzano drive up the western side of the lake on the exciting **Gardesana** *(see p205)*. This road hugs the shore and passes through numerous rock tunnels. For a more relaxing ride choose one of the ferries that ply these waters. Take a break at **Riva del Garda** *(see p209)* to enjoy the beautiful views of the lake. On the way back down the eastern shore **Malcésine** *(see p209)*, with its castle sitting proudly on a rocky promontory, is a good place to stop for lunch.

Afternoon
From Malcésine you can take a spectacular revolving cable car up the side of Monte Baldo, a haven for lovers of wild flowers and spectacular views. Back down at lake level proceed south towards the beautiful **Sirmione Peninsula** *(see pp206–7)*. Park at the entrance and explore the photogenic Roca Scaligera. Nearby is the lakeside walk; the vast slabs of rock are a stunning place to take a swim.

The maze of carefully-clipped hedges in Giardini Giusti

Putting Venice and the Veneto on the Map

The Veneto lies in the northernmost sector of Italy, and stretches from the Dolomite mountains in the north to the flatlands of the Venetian lagoon in the south. One of the most prosperous regions of Italy, the Veneto covers an area of 47,562 sq km (18,364 sq miles), and has a population of 4.5 million. Rail and road links with the rest of Europe are excellent, and three international airports serve the region: Valerio Catullo in Verona, Marco Polo on the edge of the lagoon, and Treviso.

EUROPE

NORWAY
FINLAND
SWEDEN
ESTONIA
RUSSIAN FEDERATION
UNITED KINGDOM
DENMARK
LATVIA
REP OF IRELAND
LITHUANIA
NETHERLANDS
BELORUSSIA
BELGIUM
GERMANY
POLAND
LUXEMBOURG
CZECH REP.
UKRAINE
FRANCE
SLOVAKIA
SWITZERLAND
AUSTRIA
HUNGARY
SLOVENIA
ITALY
CROATIA
ROMANIA
Venezia (Venice)
SERBIA
BULGARIA
SPAIN
MONTENEGRO
MACEDONIA
ALBANIA
GREECE

Mulhouse
Basel (Basle)
Bodens
Zurich
BERNE
LIECHTENST.
SWITZERLAND
Genève (Geneva)
L. Maggiore
Mt Blanc
Milano (Milan)
Torino (Turin)
Genova (Genoa)
Savona
Nice
Marseille
Toulon

Doubs
Rhône
A5
N12
10
N9
N6-E70
E70
A5
A4
A26
A7
A21
A6
A1-E35
A12-L
A10
A9
A54
A8-E80
A57

Ligurian Sea

Bastia
Calvi
C O R S I C A
Porto Torres
Olbia
S A R D I N I A
S131

Satellite image of the Veneto, with the Venetian lagoon bottom right

Piazza San Marco in Venice

KEY

☐	The Veneto
✈	Airport
⛴	Ferry port
▬	Motorway
▬	Major road
—	Railway Line

0 kilometres · 100
0 miles · 100

Central Venice

Venice is divided into six ancient administrative districts or *sestieri*. The areas described in this book for the most part follow the *sestieri* boundaries, with San Polo and Santa Croce combined. Visitors usually start with the Piazza San Marco, heading for the Doge's Palace and the breathtaking basilica, but each district has its own distinct character, and time spent exploring each will be fully rewarded.

San Polo and Santa Croce: a pretty stone bridge by the Fondamenta del Megio linking streets unchanged for centuries

Dorsoduro: the mouth of the Grand Canal

| 0 metres | 250 |
| 0 yards | 250 |

Cannaregio: view
along the picturesque
Rio Madonna
dell'Orto

Castello: façade
detail of the
Scuola Grande di
San Marco

San Marco: the
Campanile in Piazza
San Marco

KEY

	Major sight
	Ferry boarding point
	Vaporetto boarding point
	Traghetto crossing
	Gondola waiting point
	Tourist information
	Hospital
	Church
	Police station
	Synagogue
	Post office

A PORTRAIT OF THE VENETO

*V*enice and the Veneto form, on the face of it, an unlikely partnership. Venice is a romantic tourist city frozen in time, the Veneto a forward-thinking and cosmopolitan part of the new Europe. Yet the commercial dynamism of the mainland cities is a direct legacy of the Old Lady of the Lagoon who, in her prime, ruled much of the Mediterranean.

Venice is one of the few cities in the world that can truly be described as unique. It survives against all the odds, built on a series of low mud banks amid the tidal waters of the Adriatic and regularly subject to floods. Once a powerful commercial and naval force in the Mediterranean, Venice has found a new role. Her *palazzi* have become shops, hotels and apartments, her warehouses have been transformed into museums and her convents have been turned into centres for art restoration. Yet little of the essential fabric of Venice has altered in 200 years. A prewar guide to the city is just as useful today as when it was published, a rare occurrence on a continent scarred by the aerial bombing of World War II and the demands of postwar development. More than 14 million visitors a year succumb to the magic of this improbable city whose streets are full of water and where the past has more meaning than the present.

For all this Venice has had a price to pay. So desirable is a Venetian apartment that rents are beyond the means of the Venetians themselves. Many of the city's apartments are owned by wealthy foreigners who use them perhaps for two or three weeks a year – unlit windows at night are indicative of absent owners.

The lion of St Mark, symbol of imperial Venice

Children attending their first communion at Monte Berico, outside Vicenza

◁ A traditional Carnival clown takes a break from the celebrations

An elderly Venetian in an ageing Venice

In 1997 the population of the city was 68,600 (compared with 150,000 in 1950), but in 2001 the numbers rose for the first time since the 1950s. The average age of the Venetian population is nearly 50. One reason the city shuts down so early at night is that the waiters, cooks and shop assistants all have to catch the last train home across the causeway to Mestre.

Mestre, by contrast, is a bustling city of 180,000 inhabitants, with a busy oil terminal and an expanding industrial base, as well as some of the liveliest discos in Italy. Governed by the same mayor and city council, Mestre and Venice have been described as the ugliest city in the world married to the most beautiful. Yet Mestre, founded by Venetians who foresaw a day when development land would run out in the lagoon, is simply an extension of the same entrepreneurial spirit that characterized mercantile Venice in her heyday, a spirit that is now typical of the region as a whole.

Fruit seller in Sirmione, on Lake Garda

One move to inject new life into Venice entails reconverting former industrial sites such as the abattoir and the cotton mill, which have become university premises. A flour mill is currently being transformed into a convention centre.

THE INDUSTRIOUS NORTH

The creativity and industry of the people of the Veneto contradict all the clichés about the irrationality and indolence of the Italian character. For a tiny area, with a population of 4.5 million, the Veneto is remarkably productive. Many world-renowned companies have manufacturing bases in the area, from Jacuzzi Europe and Zanussi, to

Benetton shop in Treviso

Benetton, Olivetti and Iveco Ford. As a result, poverty is rare, and the region has progressed from its prewar agricultural base to a modern manufacturing and distribution economy.

Unencumbered by the rest of Italy, the three northern regions of Piedmont, Lombardy and Veneto alone would qualify for membership of the G10 group of the world's richest nations, a fact exploited by the region's politicians in separatist calls for independence from Rome. Coldshouldering the rest of the Italian peninsula, the Veneto looks east to Slovenia for an example of a small state that has recently achieved independence, and north to Germany as a model of political federalism and sound economic management.

Valle di Cadore in the Dolomites, close to the Austrian border

Despite the ferocity of battles fought against them down the ages, the people in the north of the Veneto have a close relationship with their Teutonic neighbours. Today, German signs, food and language can be easily found in the towns around Lake Garda and the Dolomites. Here, the pretty Tyrolean farmsteads and onion-domed churches are a marked contrast to the isolated fishing communities of the lagoon, where Venice's maritime heritage is still evident. Between these two extremes, however, the cities of the Veneto plain, with their wealth of culture, provide a more typical view of Italian life.

ITALIAN TRADITION

Padua is a perfect example of the *città salotto*, a city built like a salon on a human scale, where the streets are an extension of the home and where the doorless Caffè Pedrocchi is treated like the city's main square. Here Paduans come to drink coffee or write a letter, read a newspaper or talk to friends. Just like the salons of old, the café provides a meeting place for intellectual discourse and entertainment.

It is not just the Paduans who treat their streets and squares like so many corridors and rooms in one vast communal palace. After 5pm crowds throng Verona's Via Mazzini, taking part in the evening stroll, the *passeggiata*. Against the backdrop of the Roman arena or medieval *palazzi* they argue, swap gossip, forge alliances and strike deals. Younger strollers dress to impress, while young mothers bring their babies out to be admired. For all their modernity, the people of the Veneto still understand the powerful part played by ancient rituals such as this in cementing a strong sense of community.

Traditional Venetian rowing

Wedding Ferrari decorated with typical Italian style

The Building of Venice

Venice is built on a patchwork of more than 100 low-lying islands in the middle of a swampy lagoon. To overcome these extremely challenging conditions, early Venetian builders evolved construction techniques unique to the city, building with impermeable stone supported by larchwood rafts and timber piles. This method proved effective and most Venetian buildings are remarkably robust, many having stood for at least 400 years. By 1500 the city had taken on much of its present shape and only since the 20th century has further building begun to alter the outline.

Campo Santa Maria Mater Domini *is a typical medieval square, with its central wellhead and its business-like landward façades – decoration on buildings was usually reserved for the canal façades.*

Campaniles often lean because of compaction of the underlying subsoil.

Pinewood piles *were driven 7.5 m (25 ft) into the ground before building work could begin. They rest on the solid caranto (compressed clay) layer at the bottom of the lagoon.*

Istrian stone, a type of marble, was used to create damp-proof foundations.

Bricks

Closely packed piles do not rot in the waterlogged subsoil because there is no free oxygen, vital for microbes that cause decay.

Water grilles

Sand acting as a filter

The well was the source of the fresh water supply. Rainwater was channelled through pavement grilles into a clay-lined cistern filled with sand to act as a filter.

Ornate wellheads, *such as this one in the Doge's Palace courtyard photographed in the late 19th century, indicate the importance of a reliable water supply for the survival of the community. Strict laws protected the purity of the source, prohibiting "beasts, unwashed pots and unclean hands".*

THE CAMPANILE FOUNDATIONS

When the Campanile in the Piazza San Marco *(see p76)* collapsed in 1902, the ancient pilings, underpinning the 98.5-m high (323-ft) landmark, were found to be in excellent condition, after 1,000 years in the ground. Like the Campanile, all buildings in Venice are supported on slender oak and pine piles, harvested in the forests of the northern Veneto and floated downriver to the Venetian lagoon. Once driven through the lagoon subsoil, they create an immensely strong and flexible foundation. Even so, there is a limit to how much weight the piles can carry – the Campanile, its height having been increased several times, simply grew too tall and collapsed. When the tower was rebuilt, timber foundations were again used, but this time more than double the size.

Strengthening the Campanile foundations

Palazzo roofs, built of light, glazed tiles, had gutters to channel rainwater to the well.

Façades were built of light-weight rose-coloured bricks, sometimes left bare, sometimes weatherproofed with plaster.

Bridges *were often privately owned and tolls were charged for their use. Originally, none had railings, creating a night-time hazard for the unwary in the dark streets.*

High water level

Low water level

Accumulated rubbish is regularly removed by dredging to prevent the canal silting up.

Sand and clay

Caranto is compacted clay and sand in alternate layers, which provides a stable base for building.

THE CAMPO (SANTA MARIA MATER DOMINI)

The fabric of Venice is made up of scores of self-contained island communities, linked by bridges to neighbouring islands. Each has its own water supply, church and belltower, centred on a *campo* (square), once the focus of commercial life. *Palazzi*, with shops and warehouses at ground floor level, border the *campo* which is connected to workshops and humbler houses by a maze of side alleys.

The Venetian Palazzo

Baroque statue

Venetian houses evolved to meet the needs of a city without roads. Visitors usually arrived by boat, so the façade facing the canal was given lavish architectural treatment, while the landward side, which was accessible from a square or alley, was rarely so ornate. Most Venetian houses were built with three storeys, with kitchens located on the ground floor for ready access to water, or in the attic to enable cooking smells to escape. Typically, a *palazzo* served as a warehouse and business premises, as well as a family home, reflecting the city's mercantile character.

Renaissance doorcase with lion

BYZANTINE (12TH AND 13TH CENTURIES)

The earliest surviving private *palazzi* in Venice date from the 13th century and reflect the architectural influence of the Byzantine world. Façades are recognizable by their ground-floor arcades and arched open galleries which run the entire length of the first floor. Simple motifs feature leaves or palm trees.

Byzantine roundel, Fondaco dei Turchi

The Byzantine arcades of the Fondaco dei Turchi (built 1225)

Façade carvings feature the owner's coat of arms and the Lion of St Mark.

Byzantine horseshoe-shaped arches

Cushion capitals have only simple motifs.

Palazzo Loredan (see p64) *has an elegant ground floor arcade and first floor gallery typical of a 13th-century Byzantine palace.*

GOTHIC (13TH TO MID-15TH CENTURIES)

Elaborate Gothic *palazzi* are more numerous than any other style in Venice. Most famous of all is the Doge's Palace *(see pp82–3)*, with elegant arches in Istrian stone and fine tracery which give the façade a delicate, lace-like appearance. This style, emulated throughout the city, can be identified through its use of pointed arches and carved window heads.

Palazzo Foscari (see p66) *is a fine example of the 15th-century Venetian Gothic style, with its finely carved white Istrian stone façade and pointed arches.*

The interlacing ribs of pointed ogee arches create a delicate tracery.

Trefoil "three leaved" window heads are typically Gothic.

Quatrefoil patterns on elegant gallery windows

Gothic capitals are adorned with foliage, animals and faces.

Gothic capitals (Doge's Palace)

RENAISSANCE (15TH AND 16TH CENTURIES)

Houses of the Renaissance period were often built in sandstone rather than traditional Venetian brick. The new style was based on Classical architecture, with emphasis on harmonious proportions and symmetry. The new decorative language, borrowing motifs from ancient Rome and Greece, typically incorporated fluted columns, Corinthian capitals and semi-circular arches.

Palazzo Grimani (see p64) *has lavish stone carving which none but the wealthy could afford; massive foundations were constructed to bear the incredible weight.*

Bold projecting roof cornices are a feature of Renaissance architecture.

Theatrical masks serve as keystones to window arches.

Corinthian pilasters on the portal to San Giovanni Evangelista

The Venetian door, a very popular Renaissance motif, has a rounded central arch flanked by narrower side openings. This combination was also used for windows.

BAROQUE (17TH CENTURY)

Venetian Baroque has its roots in the Renaissance Classical style but is far more exuberant. Revelling in bold ornamentation that leaves no surface uncarved, garlands, swags, cherubs, grotesque masks and rosettes animate the main façades of buildings such as the 17th-century Ca' Pesaro.

Cherubs and plumed heads are carved into Baroque stone window heads

Recessed windows and column clusters create an interesting play of light and shadow.

Semi-circular window head of Palazzo Balbi with two lights and spandrel decorated with a circle.

Massive blocks with deep ridges give solidity to the lower walls

Ca' Pesaro (see p62) *is an example of Baroque experimentation, with its flat façade broken into a three-dimensional stone pattern of deep recesses and strong projections.*

Baroque cartouche

THE VENETIAN HOUSE

The layout of a typical *palazzo* (often called Ca', short for *casa*, or house) has changed little over the centuries, despite the very different styles of external decoration.

Attic rooms were reserved for servants.

Courtyards took the place of gardens.

The upper floor housed the family.

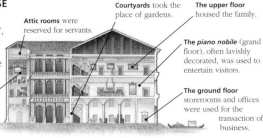

The *piano nobile* (grand floor), often lavishly decorated, was used to entertain visitors.

The ground floor storerooms and offices were used for the transaction of business.

Offices, used for storing business records, evolved into libraries.

The Villas of Palladio

Andrea Palladio

When it became fashionable in the 16th century for wealthy Venetians to acquire rural estates on the mainland, many turned to the prolific architect, Andrea Palladio (1508–80) for the design of their villas. Inspired by ancient Roman prototypes, described by authors such as Vitruvius and Virgil, Palladio provided his clients with elegant buildings in which the pursuit of pleasure could be combined with the functions of a working farm.

Palladio's designs were widely imitated and continue to inspire architects to this day.

The façade *is symmetrical; dovecotes and stables in the wings balance the central block.*

The Room of the Little Dog *is ornate and lavishly decorated with frescoes by Veronese. Look closely to see the detail of a spaniel in one of the panels.*

The Nymphaeum *combines utility with art; the same spring that feeds the statue-lined pool also supplies water to the villa.*

KEY

- ☐ Crociera
- ☐ Bacchus Room
- ☐ Room of the Tribunal of Love
- ☐ Hall of Olympus
- ☐ Room of the Little Dog
- ☐ Room of the Oil Lamp
- ☐ Nymphaeum
- ☐ Non-exhibition space

THE VILLA BARBARO

Palladio and Veronese worked closely to create this splendid villa (commissioned in 1555, *see p167*). Lively frescoes of false balconies, doors, windows and rural views create the illusion of greater space, perfectly complementing Palladio's light, airy rooms.

DEVELOPMENT OF THE VILLA

Palladio experimented with many different designs which he published in his influential *Quattro Libri (Four Books)* in 1570, illustrating the astonishing fertility of his mind and his ability to create endless variations on the Classical Roman style.

The portico statues reflect Palladio's study of ancient Roman buildings.

The pedimented pavilion is all that survives of Palladio's ambitious design; the main residence was never built.

Stables and storerooms

Villa Thiene (1546), now the town hall, Quinto Vicentino

The Hall of Olympus *shows Giustiniana, mistress of the house and wife of Venetian ambassador Marcantonio Barbaro, with her youngest son, wetnurse and family pets.*

In the Crociera, *the cross-shaped central hall, servants peer round false doors, while imaginary landscapes blur the boundary between the house interior and the garden.*

The Room of the Oil Lamp *symbolizes virtuous behaviour; here Strength, with the club, leans on Truth, with the mirror.*

The Bacchus Room, *with its winemaking scenes and chimneypiece carved with the figure of Abundance, reflects the bucolic ideal of the villa as a place of good living and plenty.*

Arcades resemble triumphal arches.

Palazzo-style central hall

Service wing

The domed cross plan was adapted by Palladio from church architecture.

The façades face the four points of the compass.

Villa Pisani (1555), Montagnana *(see p184)*

Villa Capra "La Rotonda" (1569), Vicenza *(see p171)*

Styles in Venetian Art

Venetian art grew out of the Byzantine tradition of iconographic art, designed to inspire religious awe. Because of the trade links between Venice and Constantinople, capital of Byzantium, the Eastern influence lasted longer here than elsewhere in Italy. Andrea Mantegna introduced the Renaissance style to the Veneto in the 1460s, and his brother-in-law Giovanni Bellini became Venice's leading painter. In the early 16th century Venetian artists began to develop their own style, in which soft shading and dramatic use of light distinguishes the works of Venetian masters Titian, Giorgione, Tintoretto and Veronese. The development of this characteristic Venetian style, which the prolific but lesser known artists of the Baroque and Rococo periods continued, can be seen in the chronological arrangement of the Accademia (see p130–33).

Detail from Veneziano's Coronation of the Virgin

The Last Judgment (12th century) from Torcello: in the damp climate, mosaics, not frescoes, were used to decorate Venetian churches.

BYZANTINE GOTHIC

Paolo Veneziano is credited with the move from grand-scale mosaics to more intimate altarpieces. His painting mixes idealized figures with the hairstyles, costumes and textiles familiar to 14th-century Venetians. The typically lavish use of jewel colours and gold, symbol of purity, can also be seen in the work of Veneziano's pupil (and namesake) Lorenzo, and in the gilded warrior angels of Guariento (see p179).

Veneziano's entire dazzling polyptych (1325) of which this is the centrepiece, is in the Accademia (see p132).

Paolo Veneziano's Coronation of the Virgin

The Madonna's gentle face reinforces the courtly refinement of Veneziano's work.

The composition and colours reflect the style of the early Byzantine icons which influenced the artist.

Arabesque patterns on the tunics reflect Moorish influence.

Musicians like these played at grand ceremonies in San Marco.

TIMELINE OF VENETIAN ARTISTS

	1300	1350	1400	1450
		1356–72 (active) Lorenzo Veneziano	**1430–1516** Giovanni Bellini	**1483–1539** Giovanni Pordenone
			1431–1506 Andrea Mantegna	**1450–1526** Vittore Carpaccio
		1338–c.1368 Guariento	**1415–84** Antonio Vivarini	**1480–1528** Palma il Vecchio
				1480–1556 Lorenzo Lotto
		1395–1455 Antonio Pisanello	**1429–1507** Gentile Bellini	**1467–1510** "Il Morto da Feltre"
		1400–71 Jacopo Bellini		**1477–1510** Giorgione
		1321–62 (active) Paolo Veneziano	**1432–99** Bartolomeo Vivarini	
			1441–1507 Alvise Vivarini	**1487–1576** Titian

EARLY RENAISSANCE

Renaissance artists were fascinated by Classical sculpture and developed new techniques of perspective and shading to give their figures a three-dimensional look. Using egg-based tempera gave crisp lines and bold blocks of colour, but with little tonal gradation. The Bellini family dominated art in Renaissance Venice, and Giovanni, who studied anatomy for greater accuracy in his work, portrays the feelings of his subjects through their facial expressions.

In Bellini's 1488 Frari altarpiece, the Madonna is flanked by Saints Peter, Nicholas, Benedict and Mark (see p102).

Illusionistic details *fool the eye: the real moulding copies the painted one.*

St Benedict carries the Benedictine book of monastic rule.

Musical cherubs playing at the feet of the Virgin are a Bellini trademark; music was a symbol of order and harmony.

Giovanni Bellini's *Madonna and Child with Saints*

HIGH RENAISSANCE

Oil-based paints, developed in the late 15th century, liberated artists. This new medium enabled them to create more fluid effects, an advantage Titian exploited fully. The increasingly expressive use of light by Titian and contemporaries resulted in a distinctive Venetian style, leading to Tintoretto's masterly combination of light and shade *(see p106–7).*

Titian began this Madonna in 1519 for the Pesaro family altar in the great Frari church (see p102), after his Assumption was hung above the high altar.

The Virgin is placed off centre, contrary to a centuries-old rule, but Titian's theatrical use of light ensures that she remains the focus of attention.

Saint Peter looks down at Venetian nobleman Jacopo Pesaro, who kneels to give thanks to the Virgin.

Members of the Pesaro family, *Titian's patrons, attend the Virgin; Lunardo Pesaro, gazing outwards, was heir to the family fortune.*

Titian's *Madonna di Ca' Pesaro*

1500	1550	1600	1650	1700
1500–71 Paris Bordone		**1600–38** Francesco Maffei	**1712–93** Francesco Guardi	
			1707–88 Francesco Zuccarelli	
1518–94 Tintoretto			**1708–85** Pietro Longhi	
			1696–1770 Giambattista Tiepolo	
	1548–1628 Palma il Giovane		**1675–1758** Rosalba Carriera	
			1676–1729 Marco Ricci	
	1528–88 Paolo Veronese	**1581–1644** Bernardo Strozzi	**1697–1768** Canaletto	
1517–92 Jacopo Bassano			**1727–1804** Giandomenico Tiepolo	

Gondolas and Gondoliers

Hippocampus (sea horse) ornament

Gondoliers are part of the symbolism and mythology of Venice. Local legend has it that they are born with webbed feet to help them walk on water. Their intimate knowledge of the city's waterways is passed down from father to son (this is still very much a male preserve). The gondola, with its slim hull and flat underside, is perfectly adapted to negotiating narrow, shallow canals. Once essential for the transport of goods from the markets to the *palazzi*, gondolas today are largely pleasure craft and a trip on one is an essential part of the Venetian experience *(see p284)*. It gives an entirely different perspective on the city, gliding past grand palatial homes, using a form of transport that dates back over 1,000 years.

Squero San Trovaso (see p129) *is the oldest of Venice's five surviving* squeri *(boatyards). Here, new wood is seasoned, while skilled craftsmen build new gondolas and repair some of the 400 craft in use.*

Traditional dress for a gondolier is a beribboned straw hat, striped vest and black trousers.

The gondolier, unusually for an oarsman, stands upright and pushes on the oar to row the boat in the direction he is facing.

Passengers sit on upholstered cushions and low stools.

The rowlock *(forcola)* can hold the oar in eight different positions for steering the craft.

The oar has a ribbed blade.

The asymmetrical shape *of the gondola counteracts the force of the oar. Without the leftward curve to the prow, 24 cm (9.5 inches) wider on the left than the right, the boat would go round in circles.*

CONTINUING A TRADITION

Gondolas are hand-crafted from nine woods – beech, cherry, elm, fir, larch, lime, mahogany, oak and walnut – using techniques established in the 1880s. A new gondola takes three months to build and costs £10,000.

GONDOLA DECORATION

Black pitch, or tar, was originally used to make gondolas watertight. In time this sombre colour gave way to bright paint-work and rich carpets, but such displays of wealth were banned in 1562. Today all except ceremonial gondolas are black, ornamented only with their *ferro*, and a golden hippocampus on either side. For special occasions such as weddings, the *felze* (the traditional black canopy) and garlands of flowers appear, while funeral craft, now seldom seen, have gilded angels.

Ceremonial gondolas

Upper Reaches of the Grand Canal *(c.1738) is one of many paintings by Canaletto to capture the everyday life of gondoliers and their craft. Since they were first recorded in 1094, gondolas have been a Venetian institution, inspiring writers, artists and musicians.*

Races and parades *are part of the fun during Venice regattas. Professional gondoliers race in pairs or in teams of six, using boats specially designed for competition. Many amateur gondoliers also participate in the events.*

The *ferro* serves to balance the weight of the rower. Its metal teeth symbolize the six *sestieri* of Venice, beneath a doge's cap.

Seven layers of black lacquer give the gondola its gloss.

The main frame is built of oak.

More than 280 separate pieces of wood are used in constructing a gondola.

Mooring posts *and channel markers feature prominently in the crowded waterways of Venice. The posts may be topped with a family crest, to indicate a private mooring.*

Funeral gondola approaching S Michele *(see p149)*

Wedding gondola

Venetian Masks and the Carnival

The Venetian gift for intrigue comes into its own during the Carnival, a vibrant, playful festival preceding the abstinence of Lent *(see p32)*. Masks and costume play a key role in this anonymous world; social divisions are dissolved, participants delight in playing practical jokes, and anything goes. The tradition of Carnival in Venice began in the 11th century and reached its peak of popularity and outrageousness in the 18th century. Industrialization left little leisure time and Carnival fell into decline, but was successfully revived in 1979.

Flamboyant Carnival costume

Modern Carnival Revellers
Since 1979, each year sees more lavish costumes and impromptu celebrations.

Laws forbidding the wearing of costly lace were suspended at Carnival.

The high spirits of Venetian women scandalized many foreign observers.

The Plague Doctor
This sinister Carnival garb is based on the medieval doctor's beaked face-protector and black gown, worn as a precaution against plague.

TRADITIONAL MASK CELEBRATION

Carnival in the 18th century began with a series of balls in the Piazza San Marco, as in this fresco on the walls of Quadri's famous café in the square *(see p74)*.

Gambling at the Ridotto
Fortunes were squandered every night of Carnival at the state-run casino depicted in Guardi's painting (c.1768).

Street Entertainers
Musicians and comedians attract the crowds in the piazza San Marco.

The **satyr-like** profile of this dancer hints that he is the devil in disguise.

Columbine
A classic Carnival figure, Columbine wears lace and an apron, but no mask.

MAKING A MASK

Many masks, and the characters they represent, are deeply rooted in Venetian history. Though instantly recognizable by such features as the beaked nose of the Plague Doctor, each character can be interpreted in a style that is unique to its maker, making each piece a true work of art.

① **The form of the mask** *is first modelled out of clay. Then a plaster of Paris mould is made using the fired clay sculpture as a pattern.*

② **Papier mâché paste,** *made from a pulpy fibrous mixture of rags and paper dipped in glue, is used to make the mask itself.*

③ **To shape the mask,** *papier mâché paste is pushed into the plaster mould, then put aside to set. It becomes hard yet flexible as it dries.*

④ **The size, or glue,** *used to make the papier mâché gives the mask a smooth, shiny surface, similar to porcelain, when it is extracted.*

⑤ **An abrasive polish** *is used to buff the surface of the mask, which is then ready to receive the white base coat.*

⑥ **Cutting the eye holes** *and other features requires the mask maker to have a steady hand.*

⑦ **The features** *are painted on the mask and the final touches are added with a few clever brushstrokes.*

⑧ **The finished mask** *is ready to wear at the Carnival or to hang on a wall – the perfect Venetian souvenir.*

VENICE AND THE VENETO THROUGH THE YEAR

Venice is a city that can be enjoyed at all times of the year. Even winter's mists add to the city's romantic appeal, though clear blue skies and balmy weather make spring and autumn the best times to go. This is especially true if you combine a visit to Venice with a tour of the Veneto, where villa gardens and alpine meadows put on a colourful

Festive flag throwers in Feltre

display from the beginning of April. Autumn sees the beech, birch and chestnut trees of the region turn every shade of red and gold. In summer the waters of Lake Garda, fed by melted snow from the Alps, serve to moderate the heat. Winters are mild, allowing some of the crops typical of the southern Mediterranean, like lemons and oranges, to grow.

Winter in the delta of the River Po

WINTER

Once a quiet time of year, winter now brings an increasing number of visitors to the city of Venice, especially over Christmas, New Year and Carnival. Many a day that begins wet and overcast ends in a blaze of colour – the kind of sunset reflected off rain-washed buildings that Canaletto liked to paint. In the resorts of the Venetian Dolomites, popular for winter sports, the conditions are perfect for skiing from early December throughout the winter months.

DECEMBER

Nativity. Churches all over Venice and the Veneto mount elaborate Nativity scenes in the days leading up to Christmas. Attending mass is a moving experience at this time, even for non-Christians.

Canto della Stella. In Desenzano, on Lake Garda *(see p204)*, Christmas is marked by open-air processions called *Canto della Stella*, literally "singing to the stars".

JANUARY

Epiphany *(6 Jan)*. Children of the Veneto get another stocking full of presents at Epiphany, supposedly brought by the old witch Befania (also known as Befana, Refana or Berolon). She forgot about Christmas, according to the story, because she was too busy cleaning her house. Good children traditionally get sweets, but naughty children get cinders from her hearth. Images of the witch appear in cake-shop windows, along with evil-looking biscuits made to resemble charcoal.

FEBRUARY

Carnival *(ten days up to Shrove Tuesday)*. The pre-Lent festival of Carnevale *(see p30)*, which means "farewell to meat", is celebrated throughout the Veneto. First held in Venice in the 11th century, it consisted of two months of revelry every year. Carnival fell into decline during the 18th century, but was revived in 1979 with such success that the causeway has to be closed at times to prevent overcrowding in the city.

Today the ten-day festival is mainly an excuse for donning a mask and costume and parading around the city. Various events are organized for which the Tourist Board will have details, but anyone can buy a mask and participate while watching the gorgeous costumes on show in the Piazza San Marco *(see pp74–5)*.

Bacanal del Gnoco *(last Fri of Carnival)*. Traditional masked procession in Verona, with groups from foreign countries and allegorical floats from the Verona area. Masked balls are held in the town's squares.

Masked revellers at the Carnival

AVERAGE DAILY HOURS OF SUNSHINE

Hours
10
8
6
4
2
0
Jan Feb Mar Apr May Jun Jul Aug Sep Oct Nov Dec

Sunshine Chart
Few days are entirely without sunshine in Venice and the Veneto. The amount of sunshine progressively builds up to mid-summer, when it is dangerous to venture out without adequate skin protection.

Spring wisteria in Verona's Giardini Giusti *(see p203)*

La Sensa *(Sun after Ascension Day)*. The ceremony of Venice's Marriage with the Sea draws huge crowds, as it has every year since Doge Pietro Orseolo established the custom in AD 1000. Once the ceremony was marked with all the pomp that the doge and his courtiers could muster. Today the words "We wed thee, O Sea, in token of true and lasting dominion" are spoken by a local dignitary who then casts a laurel crown and ring into the sea.

Celebrating La Sensa, Venice's annual Marriage with the Sea

SPRING

This is the season when many fine gardens all over the Veneto and round Lake Garda come into their own. As the snow melts, there is time to catch the brief glory of the alpine meadows and the region's nature reserves, renowned for rare orchids and gentians. Verona holds its annual cherry market and many other towns celebrate the arrival of early crops.

MARCH

La Vecia *(mid-Lent)*. Gardone and Gargnano, villages on Lake Garda *(see p204)*, play host to festivals of great antiquity, when the effigy of an old woman is burnt on a bonfire. The so-called Hag's Trials are an echo of the darker side of medieval life.
Su e zo per i ponti *(second Sun in Mar)*. A marathon-style race in Venice. Participants run or walk through the city's streets *su e zo per i ponti* (up and down the bridges).

APRIL

Festa di San Marco *(25 Apr)*. The feast of St Mark, patron saint of Venice, is marked by a gondola race across St Mark's Basin between Sant' Elena *(see p121)* and Punta della Dogana *(see p135)*. On this occasion, it is traditional for Venetian men to give their wives or lovers a red rose.

MAY

Festa della Sparesea *(1 May)*. A delightful festival and regatta for the new season's asparagus is held on Cavallino, in the lagoon, where the crop is grown.

Spring produce in the Rialto's vegetable market

Vogalonga *(Sun following La Sensa)*. Hundreds of boats take part in the Vogalonga (the "Long Row") from the Piazza San Marco to Burano *(see p150)* and back – a distance of 32 km (20 miles).
Festa Medioevale del vino Soave Bianco Soave *(16 May)*. Sumptuous medieval-style celebration of the investiture of the Castillian of Suavia. There is a procession with a historical theme, music in the town square, theatrical performances and displays of various sports.
Valpollicellore *(9 May)*. Festival of local wine, with exhibitions, in Cellore d'Illasi.

AVERAGE MONTHLY TEMPERATURE (VENICE)

Temperature Chart
Summers in Venice can be unbearably humid, while winters can bring the occasional snowfall. Temperatures in the Dolomites are considerably lower, with snow and freezing conditions from November to March.

SUMMER

Summer brings the crowds to Venice. Queues for museums and popular sites are long, and hotels are frequently fully booked. Avoid visiting the city during the school holidays (mid-Jul–end Aug). Verona, too, will be full of opera lovers attending the famous festival, but elsewhere in the Veneto it is possible to escape the crowds and enjoy the spectacular countryside.

JUNE

Sagra di Sant'Antonio *(13 Jun).* The Feast of St Anthony has been celebrated in Padua for centuries. The day is marked by a lively fair in Prato della Valle *(see p183).*
Biennale *(Jun–Oct).* The world's biggest contemporary art exhibition takes place in Venice in odd-numbered years *(see p260).*
Festa di Santi Pietro e Paolo *(end Jun).* The feast day of Saints Peter and Paul is celebrated in many towns with fairs and musical festivals.
Regata dei 500 x 2 *(third Sun in Jun).* Adriatic Classic sailing regatta starting from Caorle *(see p175).*

Exhibit by Japanese artist Yayoi Kusama at the Biennale

Boats for hire at Sirmione on Lake Garda

JULY

Opera Festival *(Jul–Sep).* Verona's renowned opera festival overlaps with the equally famous **Shakespeare Festival**, providing culture lovers with a feast of music, drama, opera and dance in the stimulating setting of the Roman Arena and the city's churches *(see pp260–61).*
Festa del Redentore *(third Sun in Jul).* The city of Venice commemorates its deliverance from the plague of 1576. An impressive bridge of boats stretches across the Giudecca Canal so that people can walk to the Redentore church to attend mass. On the Saturday night, crowds line the Zattere or row their boats into the lagoon to watch a spectacular firework display *(see p154).*
Sardellata al Pal del Vo *(late Jul).* Moonlit sardine fishing displays on Lake Garda at Pal del Vo. Boats are illuminated and decorated, and the catch is cooked and distributed to guests and participants.

AUGUST

Village Festivals. The official holiday month is marked by local festivals throughout the Veneto, giving visitors the chance to sample food and wines and see local costume and dance. Around Lake Garda these are often accompanied by firework displays and races in boats like large gondolas.
Palio di Feltre *(first weekend in Aug).* Medieval games, horse-racing and feasts commemorate Feltre's inclusion in the Venetian empire *(see p219).*
Festa dell'Assunta *(8–16 Aug).* Spectacular nine-day celebration in Vittorio Veneto *(see p219).* The colourful festivities feature dance, poetry, cabaret and music competitions.

AVERAGE MONTHLY RAINFALL

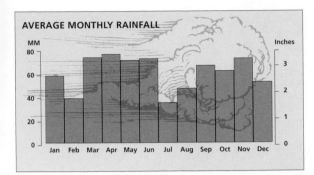

Rainfall Chart
The mountains and sea combine to give Venice and the Veneto higher rainfall than is normal in the rest of Italy, with the possibility of rain on just about any day of the year. The driest months are February and July.

AUTUMN

Expect to see a profusion of market stalls selling a huge range of wild fungi as soon as the climatic conditions are right for them to grow. Local people go on expeditions to harvest them, and mushroom dishes will also feature high on the restaurant menus along with game. Another feature of autumn is the grape harvest, a busy time of year in the wine-producing regions of Soave, Bardolino and Valpolicella *(see pp208–9).*

Grapes ripening in the Bardolino area

Medieval costume at Montagnana's Palio dei Dieci Comuni

SEPTEMBER

Venice Film Festival *(early Sep).* The International Film Festival attracts an array of filmstars and paparazzi to the Lido *(see p157).*
Regata Storica *(first Sun in Sep).* Gondoliers and other boatsmen compete in a regatta which starts with an historic pageant down the Grand Canal.

Partita a Scacchi *(second weekend in Sep, in even-numbered years).* Maròstica's chequerboard main square hosts a human chess game in medieval costume *(see p166).*
Palio dei Dieci Comuni *(first Sun in Sep).* The liberation of the town of Montagnana is celebrated with a pageant and horse race *(see p184).*

OCTOBER

Bardolino Grape Festival *(first weekend in Oct).* A festival that celebrates the completion of the harvest.
Festa del Mosto *(first weekend in Oct).* The Feast of the Must on Sant'Erasmo, the market-garden island in the lagoon *(see p149).*
Venice Marathon *(mid-Oct).* This run starts on the Brenta Riviera and finishes in Venice.

NOVEMBER

Festa della Salute *(21 Nov).* Deliverance from the plague is celebrated with the erection of a pontoon bridge across the Grand Canal to La Salute *(see p135).* Venetians light candles in the church to give thanks for a year's good health.

PUBLIC HOLIDAYS

New Year (1 Jan)
Epiphany (6 Jan)
Easter Monday (variable)
Liberation Day (25 Apr)
Labour Day (1 May)
Assumption (15 Aug)
All Saints (1 Nov)
Immaculate Conception (8 Dec)
Christmas Day (25 Dec)
Santo Stefano (26 Dec)

Rowers practising for the Regata Storica

THE HISTORY OF VENICE AND THE VENETO

The winged lion of St Mark is a familiar sight to anyone travelling in the Veneto. Mounted on top of tall columns in the central square of Vicenza, Verona, Chioggia and elsewhere, it is a sign that these cities were once part of the proud Venetian empire. The fact that the lion was never torn down as a hated symbol of oppression is a credit to the benign nature of Venetian authority.

In the 6th century AD, Venice had been no more than a collection of small villages in a swampy lagoon. By the 13th century she ruled Byzantium and, in 1508, the pope, the kings of France and Spain and the Holy Roman Emperor felt compelled to join forces to stop the advances of this powerful empire. As the League of Cambrai, their combined armies sacked the cities of the Veneto, including those such as Vicenza which had initially

Doge Giovanni Mocenigo (1478–85)

sided with the League. Venetian territorial expansion was halted, but she continued to dominate the Eastern Mediterranean for another 200 years.

The Venetian system of government came as close to democracy as anyone was to devise until the 19th century, and it stood the city and its empire in good stead until the bumptious figure of Napoleon Bonaparte dared to intrude in 1797. But by then Venice had become a byword for decadence and decline, the essential mercantile instinct that had created and sustained the Serene Republic for so long having been extinguished. As though exhausted by 1,376 years of independent existence, the ruling doge and his Grand Council simply resigned, but their legacy lives on, to fascinate visitors with its extraordinary beauty and remarkable history.

A map dated 1550, showing how little Venice has changed in nearly 500 years

◁ Tintoretto's *Triumph of Doge Nicolò da Ponte* (1580–84), Sala del Maggior Consiglio, Doge's Palace

Roman Veneto

The Veneto takes its name from the Veneti, the pre-Roman inhabitants of the region, whose territory fell to the superior military might of the Romans in the 3rd century BC. Verona was then built as a base for the thrusting and ambitious Roman army which swept northwards over the Alps to conquer much of modern France and Germany. While the Roman empire remained intact the Veneto prospered, but the region bore the brunt of fierce and destructive barbarian attacks that began in the 4th century AD. Riddled by in-fighting and the split between Rome and Constantinople, the imperial administration began to crumble.

A Roman bust in Vicenza

Horsemen in Roman Army
Goths, Huns and Vandals served as mercenaries in the Roman cavalry but later turned to plunder.

Horse-Drawn Carriage
Finds from the region show the technological skills and luxurious lifestyles of the inhabitants.

The Forum (market square)

The Arena was completed in AD 30 to entertain the troops stationed in Verona. It could hold 30,000 spectators.

Chariot Racing
A pre-Roman chariot in Adria's museum (see p185) suggests the Romans adopted the sport from their predecessors.

VERONA
Securely fortified and moated by the River Adige, Roman Verona was divided into square blocks (*insulae* or "islands"). The Forum has since been filled in by medieval palaces, but several landmarks are still discernible today (*see p192*).

TIMELINE

6th century BC Veneto region occupied by the Euganei and the Veneti

89 BC The citizens of Verona, Padua, Vicenza, Este and Treviso granted full rights of Roman citizenship

87 BC Catullus, Roman love poet, born in Verona

600 BC	500	400	300	200	100

3rd century BC Veneto conquered by the Romans. The Veneti and Euganei adopt Roman culture and lose their separate identities

Catullus (87–c.54 BC)

Hunting in the Lagoon

The wild lagoon, future site of Venice, attracted fishermen and huntsmen in pursuit of game and wildfowl. It also became a place of refuge during raids by Huns and Goths.

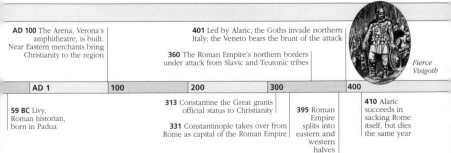

The theatre, built in the 1st century BC, is still used for open-air performances *(see p260).*

Two arches of the Ponte Romano *(see p202)* survive intact.

Gladiators

Bloodthirsty citizens flocked to the gladiatorial contests in which prisoners of war, criminals and Christian martyrs were put to the sword.

WHERE TO SEE ROMAN VENETO

Verona *(p192)* has the highest concentration of Roman sites in the region; the archaeological museum *(p202)* is full of fine mosaics and sculptures, and Castelvecchio *(p193)* has some very rare early Christian glass and silver. Good museums can also be found at Este *(p184)*, Adria, Treviso *(p174)* and Portogruaro, situated near Concordia *(p175)*.

This fine mosaic *of a nightingale in Treviso Museum is from Trevisium, the town's Roman predecessor.*

Verona's Arena *is an awe-inspiring home for the city's opera festival, despite the loss of its outer wall to earthquakes.*

AD 100 The Arena, Verona's amphitheatre, is built. Near Eastern merchants bring Christianity to the region		**401** Led by Alaric, the Goths invade northern Italy; the Veneto bears the brunt of the attack **360** The Roman Empire's northern borders under attack from Slavic and Teutonic tribes		*Fierce Visigoth*

AD 1	100	200	300	400
59 BC Livy, Roman historian, born in Padua		**313** Constantine the Great grants official status to Christianity **331** Constantinople takes over from Rome as capital of the Roman Empire	**395** Roman Empire splits into eastern and western halves	**410** Alaric succeeds in sacking Rome itself, but dies the same year

The Birth of Venice

9th-century Venetian coin

Fleeing the Goths, who were systematically looting and burning their way southwards to Rome, the people of the Veneto sought refuge among the wild and uninhabited islands of their marshy coast. There they formed villages, and from the ashes of the Roman past rose the city of Venice (founded, as tradition has it, in AD 421). Exploiting its easily defended maritime position, important trade links with Byzantium were created. Venice proclaimed its brash self-confidence by brazenly stealing the relics of St Mark the Evangelist from Alexandria, in Egypt.

Early Venetian Settlements
The Rialto Bridge (from Rivo Alto, or "high bank") marks the spot of one of many early settlements.

San Marco as it was before 14th-century rebuilding.

The First Crusade *(1095–9)*
Venice cunningly used the Crusades to her advantage, gaining valuable trading rights in captured cities such as Antioch and Tripoli.

The Bishop of Altino
The cathedral at Torcello was founded in AD 639, when Altino's bishop led a mass exodus to the lagoon island, fleeing Lombardic invaders.

THE ARRIVAL OF THE RELICS

This 13th-century mosaic from the façade of San Marco depicts the body of St Mark being carried into the newly built basilica for reburial in AD 832. By securing the relics of such an important saint, Venice signalled its ambition to be considered one of the foremost cities in Christendom, on a par with Rome.

TIMELINE

421 Venice founded, traditionally – and conveniently – on St Mark's Day, 25 April

452 Attila the Hun invades Italy and plunders the Veneto

570 The Lombards' first invasion of northern Italy; beginning of mass migration from the cities of the Veneto to lagoon islands

Charlemagne (742–814)

726 First documented doge, Orso Ipato

400	500	600	700	800

So-called "Attila's throne" in Torcello

552 Totila the Goth invades Italy and destroys many towns in the Veneto

639 Torcello cathedral founded

697 According to legend, Paoluccio Anafesta is elected first doge

774 Charlemagne invited to drive Lombards from Italy

800 Charlemagne is crowned first Holy Roman Emperor by Pope Leo III

Diplomacy
Strategically placed between the powers of Rome and Byzantium, Venice was continually exerting her powers of diplomacy. Here, Doge Ziani receives Holy Roman Emperor Frederick I, whom he reconciled with Pope Alexander III in 1177.

WHERE TO SEE EARLY VENICE

The cathedral at Torcello *(pp152–3)* is the oldest surviving building in Venice, and the Basilica San Marco *(pp78–83)* has many period treasures. Early Venetian coins are in the Correr Museum *(p77)*. The original statue of St Theodore is in the Doge's Palace courtyard.

Looting the remains of St Mark from Alexandria was seen as an act of anti-Moslem piety.

Torcello cathedral's *jewel-like mosaics (11th century) are masterpieces of Byzantine art, probably the work of craftsmen from Constantinople.*

The doge and his entourage are wearing Byzantine-style caps and robes.

St Theodore
The Byzantine emperor nominated Theodore as the patron saint of Venice. Venice chose St Mark instead, an act of defiance against Byzantine rule.

The Pala d'Oro, *St Mark's 10th-century altarpiece, shows merchants bringing St Mark's plundered relics to Venice.*

---

814 First Venetian coins minted; work begins on first Doge's Palace

832 First Basilica San Marco completed

1171 Six districts *(sestieri)* of Venice established

1095 First Crusade; Venice provides ships and supplies

1120 Verona's San Zeno church begun

1173 First Rialto Bridge built

1177 Emperor Frederick I Barbarossa agrees to peace terms with Pope Alexander III

900	1000	1100	1200

888 King Berengar I of Italy chooses Verona as his seat

828 Venetian merchants steal body of St Mark from Alexandria

1128 First street lighting in Venice

1000 Doge Pietro Orseolo rids the Adriatic of pirates, commemorated by the first Marriage of Venice to the Sea ceremony

1202 Venice diverts the Fourth Crusade to its own ends, the conquest of Byzantium

The Growth of the Empire

During the middle ages, Venice expanded in power and influence throughout the eastern Mediterranean, culminating in the conquest of Byzantium in 1204. At home, in contrast to the fractional strife of most of the area, Venice enjoyed a uniquely ordered administration head-ed by the doge, an elected leader

The doge's hat, the zogia

whose powers were carefully defined by the Venetian constitution. Real power lay with the Council of Ten and the 2,000 or so members of the Grand Council, from whose number the doge and his advisers were elected.

Bocca di Leone
Such letterboxes were used to report crimes anonymously and were often abused (p89).

Doge Enrico Dandolo boldly led the attack on Constantinople, despite being over 90 and completely blind.

Cangrande I
Founder of the Veronese Scaligeri dynasty (see p207), Cangrande I ("Big Dog") typified the totalitarian rule of most Italian cities.

Marco Polo in China
Renowned Venetian merchant, Marco Polo (see p143) spent over 20 years at the court of Kublai Khan.

SIEGE OF CONSTANTINOPLE
Facing financial difficulties, the leaders of the Fourth Crusade agreed to attack the capital of Byzantium, as payment for warships supplied by Venice. The city fell in 1204, leaving Venice ruler of Byzantium.

TIMELINE

1204 Conquest of Constantinople; Venice's plunder includes four bronze horses	**1260** Scaligeri family rules Verona	**1309** Present Doge's Palace begun
1222 University of Padua founded	**1271–95** Marco Polo's journey to China	**1325** The names of Venice's ruling families are fixed and inscribed in the Golden Book
1200	**1250**	**1300**	**1350**
	1284 Gold ducats first minted in Venice	**1310** The Venetian Constitution is passed; Council of Ten formed	**1348–9** Black Death plague kills half Venice's population
The Four Horses of San Marco	**1301** Dante, exiled from his native Florence, is welcomed to Verona by the Scaligeri rulers	**1304–13** Giotto paints the Scrovegni Chapel frescoes (pp180–81) in Padua	

Decapitation
Doge Marin Falier was beheaded in 1355 for plotting to become absolute ruler of Venice. His execution was a warning to future doges.

WHERE TO SEE IMPERIAL VENICE

The Doge's Palace combines ceremonial splendour and the grimmer business of imprisonment and torture (pp84–9). Aspects of the constitution are on display in the Correr Museum (p77). A *bocca di leone* survives on the Zattere (p129).

Imperial treasures and ancient buildings were lost when the 900-year-old city was looted and burned.

Electing the Doge
This pointer was used for counting votes during dogal elections, using a convoluted system designed to prevent candidates bribing their way to power.

Troops scaled the fortifications from galleys moored against the city walls.

Many doges *are commemorated by Renaissance-style monuments in the church of Santi Giovanni e Paolo (pp116–17).*

Queen of Cyprus
Venice shamelessly gained Cyprus in 1489 by arranging for Caterina Cornaro, from one of Venice's noblest families, to marry the island's king, then poisoning him.

Meetings of the Grand Council, *dominated by the merchant class, were held in the Sala del Maggior Consiglio (p87) in the Doge's Palace.*

Battle of Chioggia

1489 Cyprus ceded to Venice by Queen Caterina Cornaro

1518 Titian's *Assumption* hung in Frari (p102)

1400	1450	1500

1380 Battle of Chioggia: Venice defeats Genoa to win undisputed maritime supremacy in the Adriatic and Mediterranean

1453 Constantinople falls to the Turks; Venice's empire reaches its zenith

1508 Andrea Palladio, architect, born in Padua

1430 Giovanni Bellini born, greatest of the artistic family

Titian (1487–1576)

The Queen of the Adriatic

By the 16th century, Venice held a monopoly on Mediterranean trade and had colonized the whole of northeastern Italy, from the Adriatic to the Alps. Keeping hold of such a vast empire meant being in a constant state of war. The League of Cambrai, dedicated to destroying Venice, was formed in 1508 by the most powerful men in Europe, Pope Julius II and the Holy Roman Emperor Maximilian. Their troops sacked the cities of the Veneto, but the region remained loyal to Venice's relatively benign rule. Far more of a threat were the Turks. They carved out the Ottoman Empire from 1522, driving Venice from the eastern Mediterranean and eventually taking Cyprus in 1570.

16th-century armour from the Doge's Palace

Sails were a hazard in battle, but could be utilized for a swift escape.

Oarsmen sat in cramped conditions with less than 60 cm (2 ft) of space; each team was led by a foreman.

Galileo's Telescope
Galileo, professor at Padua University from 1592 to 1610, demonstrated his telescope to Doge Leonardo Donà in 1609.

Battle of Lepanto
Venice led the combined forces of the Christian world in this bloody victory over the Turks, fought in 1571.

TIMELINE

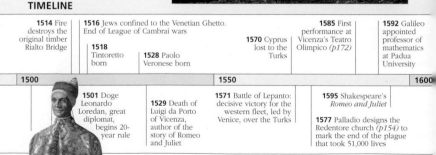

1514 Fire destroys the original timber Rialto Bridge	**1516** Jews confined to the Venetian Ghetto. End of League of Cambrai wars	**1585** First performance at Vicenza's Teatro Olimpico *(p172)*	**1592** Galileo appointed professor of mathematics at Padua University
	1518 Tintoretto born	**1528** Paolo Veronese born	**1570** Cyprus lost to the Turks	

1500	1550	1600

1501 Doge Leonardo Loredan, great diplomat, begins 20-year rule	**1529** Death of Luigi da Porto of Vicenza, author of the story of Romeo and Juliet	**1571** Battle of Lepanto: decisive victory for the western fleet, led by Venice, over the Turks	**1595** Shakespeare's *Romeo and Juliet*
			1577 Palladio designs the Redentore church *(p154)* to mark the end of the plague that took 51,000 lives

Celebrating the End of the Plague

More deadly than any opposing army, plague hit Venice in 1575 and again in 1630, carrying off Titian among its 100,000 victims.

The Venice Arsenale

Venice was at the forefront of maritime construction. Her heavily defended shipyards were capable of turning out warships at the rate of one a day.

To synchronize the oarsmen, a drummer beat time at the stern.

The trireme was so named because the oars were grouped in threes. Each trireme had up to 150 oars.

VENETIAN TRIREME

Venetian naval supremacy was based on the swift and highly manoeuvrable trireme, used to sink enemy ships by means of its pointed battering ram and its bow-mounted cannon.

WHERE TO SEE MARITIME VENICE

The triumph of Venice over the sea is celebrated in the Museo Storico Navale *(p118)*. For a glimpse of the extensive and disused Arsenale shipyard in Castello, take a trip on *vaporetto* route No. 41, 42, 51 or 52 *(p283)*.

Arsenale lions, *plundered from Piraeus in 1687, guard the forbidding gates of the Arsenale shipyard* (p119).

Santa Maria della Salute *was built in thanksgiving for deliverance from the 1630 plague* (p135).

ntverdi
(1567–
643)

1678 Elena Piscopia receives doctorate from Padua University, the first woman in the world ever to be awarded a degree *(p178)*

1703 Vivaldi joins La Pietà as musical director

1718 Venetian maritime empire ends with the surrender of Morea to the Turks

1650 — 1700

Elena Piscopia (1646–84)

1613 Monteverdi appointed choirmaster at Basilica San Marco

1630 Plague strikes Venice again, reducing the city's population to 102,243, its smallest for 250 years

1669 Venice loses Crete to the Turks

1708 In a bitter winter, the lagoon freezes over and Venetians can walk to the mainland

Glorious Decadence

Casanova, the Venetian libertine

No longer a major power, 18th-century Venice became a byword for decadence, as aristocratic Venetians frittered away their inherited wealth in lavish parties and gambling. All this crumbled in 1797 when the city was besieged by Napoleon, who demanded the abdication of the doge. Napoleon granted the city to his opponents, the Austrians, whose often authoritarian rule drove many people of the Veneto to join the vanguard of the revolutionary Risorgimento. This movement, led in Venice by Daniele Manin, was dedicated to creating a free and united Italy, a dream not fully realized until 1870, four years after Venice was freed from Austrian rule.

The State-Run Casino
The notorious Ridotto, open to anyone wearing a mask, closed in 1774 as many Venetians had bankrupted themselves.

Gambling fever so gripped the city that gaming tables were set up between the columns in the Piazza.

Caffè Pedrocchi
Several intellectuals who had used this lavishly decorated café (see p178) in Padua as their base, were executed for leading a revolt against Austrian rule in 1831.

The Horses of St Mark
Among the art treasures looted by Napoleon were the Four Horses of St Mark, symbols of Venetian liberty. The horses were returned in 1815.

IMPERIAL RITUAL
Canaletto's *St Mark's Basin on Ascension Day* (c.1733) captures the empty splendour of Venice on the eve of her demise. The doge's gold and scarlet barge has been launched for the annual ceremony of Venice's Marriage to the Sea.

TIMELINE

1720 Caffè Florian opens in Venice *(p250)*	**1752** Completion of sea walls protecting the lagoon entrances	**1755** Casanova imprisoned in Doge's Palace	**1789** The Dolomites named after Déodat Dolomieu (1750–1801)	
1725 Casanova born in Venice		**1775** Caffè Quadri *(p250)* opens in Venice		
1720		**1770**		
	1757 Canova, Neo-Classical sculptor, born in Venice	**1790** Venetian opera house, La Fenice, opens		
		1797 Napoleon invades the Veneto; Doge Lodovico Manin abdicates; Venetian Republic ends		
	Café Florian	**1798** Napoleon grants Venice and its territories to his Austrian allies in return for Lombardy		

Antonio Vivaldi
(1678–1741)
Fashionable Venetians flocked to hear the red-haired priest's latest compositions, performed by the orphan girls of La Pietà. Vivaldi's most famous work, The Four Seasons *(1725), was a great success throughout Europe.*

WHERE TO SEE 18TH-CENTURY VENICE

The Museo Storico Navale *(p118)* displays a beautifully crafted model of the Bucintoro and its original banner. Vivaldi concerts are a regular feature at La Pietà church *(p112)*. Paintings by Guardi, Canaletto and Longhi capture the spirit of the age and are found in the Accademia *(pp130–3)*, Correr Museum and Ca' Rezzonico *(p126)*.

The Bucintoro, the doge's ceremonial barge

Sumptuary laws, passed in 1562, decreed that all Venetian gondolas must be black to prevent lavish displays of wealth.

Fortunes were spent *on opulent wigs, jewels and clothing for costume balls and the theatre. This high-heeled shoe is in the Correr Museum (p77).*

The comic antics *of Harlequin and Pantaloon at La Fenice (p93) ensured the popularity of the theatre with Venetians.*

No Longer an Island
Venice lost its isolation in 1846 when a causeway joined the city to the mainland and the Italian rail network.

1804 Napoleon crowned King of Italy and takes back Venice

Daniele Manin (1804–57)

1859 Second War of Italian Independence; after Battle of Solferino, Red Cross founded

1814–15 Austrians drive French from Venice; Congress of Vienna returns the Veneto to Austria

1861 Vittorio Emanuele crowned King of Italy

1820

1870

1818 Byron swims up the Grand Canal

1846 Venetian rail causeway links the city to the mainland for the first time

1853 Ruskin publishes *The Stones of Venice*

1848 First Italian War of Independence. Venice revolts against Austrian rule

1849 Hunger and disease force Venetian rebels, led by Daniele Manin, to surrender

1866 Venice and Veneto freed from Austrian rule

Venice in Vogue

From being an introverted and unchanging city, Venice developed with remarkable speed. The opening of the Suez Canal in 1869 brought new prosperity; a new harbour was built for ocean-going ships and Venice became a favourite embarkation point for colonial administrators and rich Europeans travelling east. The fashion for sea-bathing and patronage by wealthy socialites reawakened interest in the city, and the founding of the Biennale attracted Europe's leading artists, who expressed their enthusiasm for the city in novels, paintings and music.

Peggy Guggenheim *(1898–1979) Patron of the avant garde, Peggy Guggenheim brought her outstanding art collection (see p134) to Venice in 1949.*

The Hotel Excelsior's Moorish exterior is distinctive.

Bathing huts, designed for modesty in the 1920s, are still a feature of the Lido.

Igor Stravinsky *(1882–1971) Along with Turgenev, Diaghilev and Ezra Pound, Stravinsky was one of many émigrés enchanted by the magic of Venice.*

Hotel Excelsior *When it was built in 1907, the Hotel Excelsior (see p233) was the world's largest hotel.*

THE LIDO

From the turn of the century, grand hotel developments along the sandy Adriatic shore turned the Lido into Europe's most stylish seaside resort. The island has since given its name to bathing establishments the world over.

TIMELINE

Richard Wagner (1813–83)

1883 Wagner dies in Palazzo Vendramin-Calergi

1902 Collapse of campanile in Piazza San Marco

1912 Opening of rebuilt campanile; Thomas Mann writes *Death in Venice*

1870	1880	1890	1900	1910

1881 Venice becomes second largest port in Italy after Genoa

1889 Poet Robert Browning dies in Ca' Rezzonico

1895 First Biennale art exhibition

1903 Patriarch Sarto of Venice becomes Pope Pius X

The International Exhibition of Modern Art

Venice became a showcase for all that was new in world art and architecture when the Biennale was launched. The first exhibition, in 1895, showed work by Renoir and Monet.

The manicured beaches of the Lido became a catwalk for style-conscious holidaymakers.

WHERE TO SEE TURN-OF-THE-CENTURY VENICE

Regular *vaporetto* services link Venice to the Lido *(p156)*, with its deluxe hotels, sports facilities and beaches. The pavilions of the Biennale *(p121)* are usually only open during the exhibition. A lift carries visitors to the top of the rebuilt Campanile *(p76)* for panoramic views of Venice.

San Michele, *the cemetery isle* (p151), *is the last resting place of eminent foreigners, such as Serge Diaghilev, Igor Stravinsky and Ezra Pound.*

The exclusive *Grand Hôtel des Bains* (p233) *on the Lido has retained its Art Deco style and private section of beach.*

The Campanile

After the appearance of ominous warning cracks, the 1,000-year-old bell tower crashed to the ground in 1902. It was rebuilt within a decade (see p76).

1917 Work starts on constructing the port of Marghera

1926 Mestre is formally granted town status

German travel poster from 1936

1954 Britten's *Turn of the Screw* premièred in Venice

1943–5 Mussolini rules a puppet state, the Salò Republic

1959 Patriarch Roncalli elected Pope John XXIII

1920	1930	1940	1950	1960

1918 Fierce fighting in mountain passes of the Veneto in the last weeks of World War I

1932 First Venice Film Festival

1931 Venice is linked to the mainland by a road causeway

1951 Stravinsky's *The Rake's Progress* premièred in Venice

1956 Cortina d'Ampezzo hosts Winter Olympics

1960 Venice airport opens

Venice Preserved

In November 1966 Venice was hit by the worst floods in its history, sparking worldwide concern for the future of the city's delicate and decaying fabric. Major steps have since been taken to protect Venice and its unique heritage, though some difficult issues remain, including the erosion and wave damage caused by public and private waterborne craft, and pollution from the mainland. However, the allure of Venice, set in its watery lagoon, is as compelling as ever.

Pink Floyd in Venice
Pink Floyd's 1989 rock concert threatened the city's equilibrium.

Venice as Film Set
Venice has served as the backdrop to countless films, including Fellini's Casanova *(1976) and* Indiana Jones and the Last Crusade *(1989).*

The Regata Storica, held in September, is an annual trial of strength and skill for gondoliers.

After the Flood
During the 1966 floods, the waters rose nearly 2 m (6 ft). Great damage was done by fuel oil, washed out of broken tanks. It is now banned from the city in favour of gas.

TOURISM

Venetian regattas are part of a rich tradition that enhances the city's attraction to tourists, providing employment for many on the mainland as well as in Venice itself. Even so, some complain that tourism has turned Venice from a living city into one vast museum.

TIMELINE

1966 Floods cause devastation in Venice. UNESCO launches its Save Venice appeal

1973 Laws passed to reduce pollution, subsidence and flooding

1978 Patriarch Luciani of Venice elected Pope John Paul I, but dies 33 days later

Carnival reveller

1988 First experimental stage of MOSE, the lagoon flood barrier, is completed

1960	1970	1980

1968 Protestors prevent part of the lagoon being drained to extend Marghera's industrial zone

1970 Luchino Visconti's film, *Death in Venice*

1979 Venetian Carnival is revived

Visconti and Dirk Bogarde on the set of Death in Venice

1983 Venice officially stops sinking after extraction of underground water prohibited

Benetton
The famous clothing firm, originating in Treviso, represents the modern face of Veneto industry.

Venice plays host to over 14 million visitors every year.

Glass Blowing
This age-old tradition still contributes to the economy.

Subsidence, caused by water extraction for use in Marghera, is being remedied by piping water into Venice.

The Acqua Alta
High tides can cause floods and paralyze the city. Plans for a flood barrier across the lagoon are subject to controversy.

RESTORATION IN VENICE

One positive result of the 1966 floods was a major international appeal for funds to pay for the cleaning of historic buildings, statues and paintings. Funds raised are coordinated under the auspices of UNESCO, with offices in Venice.

Restorers *learn how to repair and conserve fragile works of art at a European centre for conservation on San Servolo (p154).*

Madonna dell'Orto (p140) *was restored by the Italian Art and Archives Rescue Fund (later renamed Venice in Peril).*

1992 Venice rocked by corruption scandals. Metro network beneath lagoon proposed

1994 Voters decide against a divorce between Venice and Mestre, which share a mayor and city council

1995 Centenary of Biennale Exhibition

2006 Romano Prodi approves construction of the lagoon flood barrier, which is due to be completed by 2012

| 1990 | 2000 | 2010 | 2020 |

1992 Venice Film Festival celebrates 60 years

1932–1992 Venice Film Festival poster

2002 Construction begins on the fourth bridge over the Grand Canal

2008 The fourth bridge over the Grand Canal opens

A *traghetto* crossing the Grand Canal ▷

VENICE AREA
BY AREA

Venice at a Glance

Venice is small and most of the sights can be comfortably visited on foot. The heart of the city is the Piazza San Marco, which is overlooked by the great Basilica and the Doge's Palace. For many, these are attractions enough, but there are delights worth exploring beyond the Piazza, such as the galleries of the Accademia, Ca' Rezzonico and the imposing Frari church. Unique to Venice are the naval Arsenale to the east and the Ghetto in the north.

Ghetto
Established in the early 16th century, this fascinating quarter was the world's first ghetto (see p145).

Santa Maria Gloriosa dei Frari
This soaring Gothic edifice, founded by the Franciscans in 1340, is a rich repository of Venetian painting and sculpture (see pp102–3).

CANNAREGIO
Pages 136–45

SAN POLO AND SANTA CROCE
Pages 96–107

DORSODURO
Pages 122–35

SAN MAR
Pages 72–

0 metres	500
0 yards	500

Ca' Rezzonico
The splendid rooms of this palace, overlooking the Grand Canal, are decorated with 18th-century furniture and paintings (see p126).

Accademia
Carpaccio's St Ursula cycle (1490–5) is one of the treasures of the Accademia, which has a comprehensive collection of Venetian art (see pp130–3).

Rialto Bridge
The bustling Rialto Bridge (see p100) was named after the ancient commercial seat of Venice, where the first inhabitants settled.

Ca' d'Oro
This ornate palace is the finest example of Venetian Gothic style (see p142).

Basilica San Marco
Magnificent mosaics sheathe the domes, walls and floor of the Byzantine Basilica (see pp78–83).

Arsenale
The great dockyard, first of its kind in Europe, was the naval nerve centre of the Venetian Empire (see p119).

CASTELLO
Pages 108–21

Doge's Palace
The colonnaded Gothic palace was the seat of government as well as home to the doge and his family (see pp84–89).

Santa Maria della Salute
Marking the southern end of the Grand Canal, this great Baroque church is one of the city's landmarks (see p135).

A VIEW OF
THE GRAND CANAL

Known to the Venetians as the *Canalazzo*, the Grand Canal sweeps through the heart of Venice, following the course of an ancient river bed. Since the founding days of the empire it has served as the city's main thoroughfare. Once used by great galleys or trading vessels making their stately way to the Rialto, it is nowadays teeming with *vaporetti*, launches, barges and gondolas. Glimpses of its glorious past, however, are never far away. The annual re-enactment of historic pageants, preserving the traditions of the Venetian Republic, brings a blaze of colour to the canal. The most spectacular is the Regata Storica held in September *(see p35)*,

Venetian gondolier

a huge procession of historic craft packed with crews in traditional costumes, followed by boat and gondola races down the Grand Canal.

The parade of palaces bordering the winding waterway, built over a span of around 500 years, presents some of the finest architecture of the Republic. Historically it is like a roll-call of the old Venetian aristocracy, with almost every *palazzo* bearing the name of a once-grand family. Bright frescoes may have faded, precious marbles worn, and foundations frayed with the tides, but the Grand Canal is still, to quote Charles VIII of France's ambassador in 1495, "the most beautiful street in the world".

See pages 60–61

See pages 58–9

See pages 62–3

See pages 64–5

See pages 66–7

See pages 70–71

See pages 68–9

0 metres 250

0 yards 250

◁ **The Grand Canal at its most colourful, during the Regata Storica**

Santa Lucia to Palazzo Flangini

Vaporetto ticket office, Grand Canal

The Grand Canal is best admired from a gondola or a *vaporetto*. Several lines travel the length of the canal *(see p283)* but only the No. 1 goes slowly enough for you to take in any of the palaces. The journey from the station to San Zaccaria takes about 40 minutes. Nearly 4 km (2½ miles) long, the canal varies in width from 30 to 70 m (98 to 230 ft) and is spanned by four bridges, the Scalzi, the Rialto, the Accademia and the Constituzione. The modern Constituzione bridge links Piazzale Roma and Santa Lucia station.

LOCATOR MAP

Santa Maria di Nazareth *is known today as the Scalzi, after the supposedly "shoeless" Carmelites who founded it (see p145). Within is the tomb of Ludovico Manin, last of the doges.*

Santa Lucia railway station (see p280), *built in the mid-19th century and remodelled in the 1950s, links the city with the mainland.*

Ferro

La Direzione Compartimentale, *the administration offices for the railway, was built at the same time as the station, on the site of the church of Santa Lucia and other ancient buildings.*

Ferrovia

Palazzo Diedo, *also known as Palazzo Emo, is a Neo-Classical palace of the late 18th century. It is believed to be the birthplace of Angelo Emo (1731–92), the last admiral of the Venetian fleet. The palace was built by Andrea Tirali, an engineer who worked on the restoration of San Marco.*

Palazzo Calbo Crotta *is now the 4-star Hotel Principe. Fine antiques and fabrics which once decorated the palace are now in Ca' Rezzonico (see p126).*

Palazzo Flangini *was designed by Giuseppe Sardi, a leading 17th-century architect.*

Ferrovia

Palazzo Gritti *was built in the 16th century. The Grittis were a wealthy family who produced one of the most intelligent doges, Andrea Gritti (reigned 1523–38).*

The Scalzi Bridge was built in 1934, replacing the original wrought-iron bridge.

Campo San Simeone Grande, *named after the nearby church (otherwise called San Simeone Profeta), is one of the few campi overlooking the canal.*

Casa Adoldo and Palazzo Foscari-Contarini *were both rebuilt in the 16th century. According to local tradition, the great Doge Francesco Foscari (ruled 1423–57) was born in the original Foscari-Contarini palace.*

San Simeone Piccolo *is a large church, in spite of its name (*piccolo *means small). Built in 1738, its design was based partly on the Pantheon in Rome. It is open for worship only.*

San Geremia to San Stae

This stretch sees the start of the great palaces. The most remarkable is the Vendramin Calergi, which became a model for other Venetian palaces.

LOCATOR MAP

San Geremia houses the relics of St Lucy, formerly preserved in Santa Lucia where the station now stands.

Palazzo Labia, *frescoed with Tiepolo's Venetian-style Story of Cleopatra, is open to the public (see p143).*

Palazzo Querini has the family coat of arms on the façade.

Ca' dei Cuori (House of Hearts) was named after the hearts in the family coat of arms.

Riva di Biasio

Palazzo Giovanelli, *a restored Gothic palace, was acquired by the Giovanellis in 1755. This titled non-Venetian family had been admitted into the Great Council in 1668 for a fee of 100,000 ducats.*

Fondaco dei Turchi *was a splendid Veneto-Byzantine building before last century's brutal restoration. Today it houses the Natural History Museum (see p105).*

Palazzo Donà Balbi, *built in the 17th century, is named after two great Venetian families who intermarried. The Donà family produced four doges.*

Deposito del Megio, *a crenellated building with a reconstructed Lion of St Mark, was a granary in the 15th century.*

San Marcuola, *dedicated to St Ermagora and St Fortunatus, was built in 1728–36 by Giorgio Massari, but the façade was never completed.*

Palazzo Vendramin Calergi, *an early Renaissance palace, was designed by Mauro Coducci. The composer Richard Wagner died here in 1883. Today, Venice's casino is housed in the palace.*

Palazzo Marcello, rebuilt in the early 18th century, was the birthplace of composer Benedetto Marcello in 1686.

Palazzo Erizzo has two huge paintings depicting the feats of Paolo Erizzo, who died heroically fighting the Turks in 1469.

Palazzo Emo belonged to the family of a famous Venetian admiral *(see p58)*.

San Marcuola

San Stae

Palazzo Belloni Battagia, *with its distinctive pinnacles, was built by Longhena in the mid-17th century for the Belloni family, who had bought their way into Venetian aristocracy.*

Palazzo Tron, *built in the late 16th century, hosted a famous ball in 1775 in honour of Emperor Joseph II of Austria.*

San Stae *is striking for its Baroque façade, graced by marble statues. It was funded by a legacy left by Doge Alvise Mocenigo in 1709 (see p105).*

Palazzo Barbarigo to the Markets

Here the canal is flanked by stately palaces, built over a
period of five centuries. The most spectacular is the
Gothic Ca' d'Oro, whose façade once glittered
with gold.

LOCATOR MAP

Palazzo Barbarigo retains
the vestiges of its 16th-
century frescoed
façade paintings.

Palazzo Gussoni-Grimani's
façade once had frescoes by
Tintoretto. It was home to the
English ambassador in 1614–18.

Palazzo Fontana Rezzonico
was the birthplace of
Count Rezzonico
(1693), the fifth
Venetian
pope

⚓ **San Stae**

Ca' Foscarini,
a Gothic building
of the 15th century,
belonged to the Foscari
family before it became
the residence of the Duke
of Mantua in 1520.

Ca' Pesaro, *a huge and stately
Baroque palace designed by
Longhena (see p23), today houses
the Gallery of Modern Art and
the Oriental Museum (see p105).
It was built for Leonardo Pesaro,
a Procurator of San Marco.*

Casa Favretto
(Hotel San Cassiano)
was the home of the
painter Giacomo
Favretto (1849–87).

**Palazzo Morosini
Brandolin** *belonged to
the Morosini family, one
of the Case Vecchie
families, deemed to be
noble before the 9th
century.*

**Ca' Corner della
Regina** *is
named after
Caterina
Cornaro, Queen
of Cyprus, who
was born here
in 1454. The
present building
(1724–7) was
designed by
Domenico Rossi.*

The Pescheria *has been the site of a busy fish
market for six centuries. Today it takes place in the
striking mock-Gothic market hall, built in 1907.*

Ca' d'Oro, *the most famous of Venetian Gothic palaces (see p144), houses paintings, frescoes and sculpture from the collection of Baron Giorgio Franchetti, who bequeathed the palace and all its contents to the State.*

CANALETTO

Antonio Canale (Canaletto) (1697–1768) is best known for his *vedute* or views of Venice. He studied in Rome, but lived here for most of his life. One of his patrons was Joseph Smith *(see below)*. Sadly there are very few of his paintings left on view in the city.

Palazzo Sagredo *passed from the Morosini to the Sagredo family in the early 18th century. The façade shows characteristics of both Veneto-Byzantine and Gothic styles.*

Palazzo Foscarini *was the home of Marco Foscarini, a diplomat, orator and scholar who rose to the position of doge in 1762.*

Palazzo Michiel dalle Colonne was named after its distinctive colonnade.

Palazzo Mangili Valmarana *was designed by Antonio Visentini (above) in Classical style for Joseph Smith, who became the English consul in Venice. Smith (1682–1770) was a patron of both Visentini and Canaletto.*

Palazzo Michiel del Brusà was rebuilt and named after the great fire *(brusà)* that swept the city in 1774.

Oro

Ca' da Mosto *is a good example of 13th-century Veneto-Byzantine style. Alvise da Mosto, the 15th-century navigator, was born here in 1432.*

Rialto Mercato

Tribunale Fabbriche Nuove, Sansovino's market building (1555), is now the seat of the Assize Court.

The Rialto Quarter

The area around the rialto bridge is the oldest and busiest quarter of the city. Traditionally a centre of trade, crowded quaysides and colourful food markets still border the canal south of the bridge.

LOCATOR MAP

Palazzo Papadopoli, *formerly known as Coccina-Tiepolo, was built in 1560. Its splendid hall of mirrors has been preserved.*

Riva del Vin *is one of the few spots where you can sit and relax on the banks of the Grand Canal (see p98).*

Ca' Corner-Martinengo-Ravà *became the Leon Bianco Hotel in the 19th century. The American writer, James Fenimore Cooper, stayed here in 1838.*

Palazzo Barzizza, rebuilt in the 17th century, still preserves its early 13th-century façade.

San Silvestro

Palazzo Grimani, *a fine, if somewhat austere looking, Renaissance palace (see p23), was built in 1556 by Michele Sanmicheli for the Procurator, Girolamo Grimani. The State purchased the palace in 1807 and it is now occupied by the city's Court of Appeal.*

Palazzo Farsetti and Palazzo Loredan, *both occupied by the City Council, were built around 1200 and finally merged in 1868. Palazzo Farsetti became an academy for young artists, one of whom was Canova.*

Fondaco dei Tedeschi, *originally used as a warehouse and lodgings for German traders, is now the main post office.*

Palazzo Camerlenghi, built in 1528, was once the offices of the city treasurers *(camerlenghi)*. The ground floor was the State prison.

Rialto

Riva del Ferro is the quayside where German trading barges offloaded iron *(ferro)*.

The Rialto Bridge (see p100) *was built to span the Grand Canal in what was, and still is, the most commercial quarter of the city.*

Palazzo Manin-Dolfin *was built by Sansovino in 1538–40 but only his Classical stone façade survives. The interior was completely transformed for Ludovico Manin, last doge of Venice (died 1797). He intended to turn the house into a magnificent palace extending as far as Campo San Salvatore.*

Casetta Dandolo's predecessor is said to have been the birthplace of Doge Enrico Dandolo (ruled 1192–1205).

Palazzo Bembo, *a 15th-century Gothic palace, was the birthplace of the Renaissance cardinal and scholar, Pietro Bembo, who wrote one of the earliest Italian grammars.*

THE DANDOLO FAMILY

The illustrious Dandolo family produced four doges, 12 procurators of San Marco, a patriarch of Grado and a queen of Serbia. The first of the doges was Enrico who, despite being old and blind, was the principal driving force in the Crusaders' plan to take Constantinople in 1204 (see p42). The other remarkable doge in the family was the humanist and historian, Andrea Dandolo (died 1354).

Doge Enrico Dandolo

La Volta del Canal

The point where the canal doubles back sharply on itself is known as La Volta – the bend. This splendid curve was long ago established as the finishing stretch for the annual Regata Storica *(see p35).*

LOCATOR MAP

Palazzo Marcello, *which belonged to an old Venetian family, is also called "dei Leoni" because of the lions either side of the doorway.*

Palazzo Persico, on the corner of Rio San Polo, is a 16th-century house in Lombardesque style.

Palazzo Civran-Grimani is a Classical building of the early 17th century.

Palazzo Balbi, *seat of the regional government, was built for Nicolò Balbi, who is said to have died of a chill surveying its construction. From here, Napoleon viewed the 1807 regatta, held in his honour.*

Ca' Foscari *was built for Doge Francesco Foscari in 1437* (see p22). *It is now part of the University of Venice.*

Palazzo Giustinian was the residence of Wagner in 1858–9, when he was composing the second act of *Tristan and Isolde.*

San Toma

San Samuele

Ca' Rezzonico

Ca' Rezzonico, *now the museum of 18th-century Venice* (see p126), *became the home of the poet Robert Browning and his son, Pen, in 1888.*

Palazzo Barbarigo della Terrazza, built in the 1560s, was known for its roof terrace. It now houses the German Institute.

Palazzo Capello-Layard was the home of Sir Austen Henry Layard, excavator of Nineveh.

Sant' Angelo 🚏

Palazzo Corner Spinelli, Mauro Coducci's outstanding Renaissance palace, built in 1490–1510, became a proto-type for other mansions in Venice.

Palazzo Garzoni, *a renovated Gothic palace, is now part of the university. The* traghetto *service, which links the neighbouring Calle Garzoni to San Tomà on the other side of the canal, is one of the oldest in Venice.*

Palazzo Mocenigo, *formed by four palaces linked together, has a plaque to the poet Byron who stayed here in 1818.*

Palazzo Moro Lin, *also known as the "palace of the 13 windows", was created in the 17th century for the painter Pietro Liberi by merging two Gothic houses.*

Palazzo Grassi, *built in the 1730s, was bought by Fiat in 1984 and turned into a venue for art exhibitions.*

Palazzo Capello Malipiero, *a Gothic palace, was reconstructed in 1622. Beside it, in Campo di San Samuele, stands the church of San Samuele which has a 12th-century Veneto-Byzantine campanile.*

Ca' Rezzonico

Ca' Rezzonico to the Guggenheim

This southern stretch of the canal, widening after the Accademia, is lined by a rich and varied parade of palaces.

Palazzo del Duca, planned in the 15th century as a sumptuous palace but never finished, houses a collection of porcelain

Palazzo Falier *was said to have been home to Doge Marin Falier, who was beheaded for treason in 135 (see p43).*

Palazzo degli Scrigni, built in 1609, acquired its name from the coffers *(scrigni)* inherited by the Contarini in 1418.

Accademia

Palazzo Loredan, *home of Doge Francesco Loredan (1752–62), is one of many belonging to that family.*

The wooden Accademia Bridge *was built in 1932 as a temporary structure to replace a 19th-century iron bridge. By popular demand it has been retained.*

The Accademia *galleries, within the former church, monastery and Scuola della Carità, house the world's greatest collection of Venetian paintings (see pp130–33).*

Palazzo Contarini del Zaffo, *a magnificent Renaissance palace of the late 1400s, was built for a branch of the ubiquitous Contarini family. Early this century it was acquired by the Polignac family.*

LOCATOR MAP

Ca' Grande, *a huge Classical palace, was designed in 1545 by Sansovino for Giacomo Cornaro, nephew of the Queen of Cyprus. The family was one of the richest in Venice and spared no expense in the palace's decoration. This family tree illustrates the extent of the Cornaro's wealth and influence in Venice.*

Palazzo Franchetti Cavalli belonged to Archduke Frederick of Austria, who died here in 1836.

Palazzo Barbaro *comprises two palaces, one of which was bought by the Curtis family in 1885. Monet and Whistler painted here and Henry James (right) wrote* The Aspern Papers.

Casetta delle Rose, *one of the smallest houses on the canal, was the home of Italian poet Gabriele d'Annunzio during World War I. Canova (above) had his studio here in 1770.*

Palazzo Barbarigo, *beside the Campo San Vio, stands out for the harsh mosaics, added in 1887.*

Peggy Guggenheim *established her collection of modern art in Venice in 1951 (see p134). She chose as her venue the Palazzo Venier dei Leoni, which had been built in 1749 and never finished.*

Palazzo Dario, *built in 1487, is a charming but strangely ill-fated palace (see p135).*

To La Salute and San Marco

The view along the final stretch of the canal is one of the finest – and most familiar – in Venice. Near the mouth rises the magnificent church of La Salute with busy St Mark's Basin beyond.

LOCATOR MAP

Palazzo Contarini Fasan, *a tiny 15th-century palace with an elegant façade, is popularly known as the House of Desdemona from Shakespeare's* Othello.

The Palazzo Gritti-Pisani, *where Ruskin stayed in 1851, is better known today as the luxurious 5-star Hotel Gritti Palace (see p228).*

Santa Maria Del Giglio

Salute

The mock-Gothic mansion, Ca' Genovese, was built in 1892 in the place of the second Gothic cloister of the San Gregorio monastery.

The deconsecrated Gothic brick church *of Abbazia San Gregorio and a little cloister are all that survive of what was for centuries a powerful monastic centre. The church is now used as a laboratory for the renovation of large-scale paintings.*

Palazzo Salviati *was the head-quarters of the Salviati glass-producing company, hence the glass mosaics on the façade.*

Palazzo Tiepolo, *the Hotel Europa and Regina, was formerly owned by the Tiepolo family, associated with an unsuccessful uprising in 1310.*

Harry's Bar (see p92) *was popular with Hemingway and other writers. This was the very first Harry's Bar in the world.*

Palazzo Giustinian, headquarters of the Biennale, used to be a hotel, where Turner, Verdi and Proust stayed.

San Marco Vallaressa

Giardinetti Reali, the Royal Gardens, were created by Napoleon to improve his view from the Procuratie Nuove.

Palazzo Treves Bonfili, a Classical building of the 17th century, is decorated with Neo-Classical frescoes, paintings and statuary.

The view from the Dogana, *taking in the Doge's Palace, the Campanile of San Marco and the Zecca, is one of the most memorable in Venice.*

Santa Maria della Salute, *a Baroque church of monumental proportions, is supported by over a million timber piles. Built to commemorate the end of the 1630 plague, it was the work of Baldassare Longhena (see p135).*

Dogana di Mare, *the customs house, is topped by a weathervane figure of Fortune (see p135).*

SAN MARCO

Home of the political and judicial nerve centres of Venice, the *sestiere* of San Marco has been the heart of Venetian life since the early days of the Republic. The great showpiece of the Serenissima was the Piazza San Marco, conceived as a vista for the Doge's Palace and the Basilica. The square, described by Napoleon as "the most elegant drawing room in Europe",

Adam and Eve on the corner of the Doge's Palace

was the only one deemed fit to be called a piazza – the others were merely *campi*, or fields.

The San Marco area has the bulk of luxury hotels, restaurants and shops. It is also home to several imposing churches, three theatres, including the famous Fenice, and a wealth of handsome *palazzi*. Many of these line the sweeping southern curve of the Grand Canal which borders the *sestiere*.

SIGHTS AT A GLANCE

Churches
Basilica San Marco
   pp78–83 ❸
San Moisè ⓫
San Salvatore ⓲
Santa Maria Zobenigo ⓭
Santo Stefano ⓰
San Zulian ㉑

Museums and Galleries
Libreria Sansoviniana ❺
Museo Archeologico ❻
Museo Correr ❽
Museo Fortuny ⓱

Palaces
Doge's Palace pp84–9 ❹
Palazzo Contarini
   del Bovolo ⓬

Historic Buildings and Monuments
Campanile ❶
Columns of San Marco
   and San Teodoro ❼
San Giorgio Maggiore ㉒
Torre dell'Orologio ❷

Streets and Squares
Campo San Bartolomeo ⓳
Campo Santo Stefano ⓯
Mercerie ⓴

Bars
Harry's Bar ❾

Theatres
La Fenice ⓮
Ridotto ❿

KEY

█ Street-by-Street map
   See pp74–5

█ Street-by-Street map
   See pp90–91

🛥 Vaporetto boarding point

🚣 Traghetto crossing

0 metres   250

0 yards   250

SAN GIORGIO MAGGIORE

◁ Central dome of the Basilica San Marco

Street-by-Street: Piazza San Marco

Lion of St Mark

Throughout its long history the Piazza San Marco has witnessed pageants, processions, political activities and countless Carnival festivities. Tourists flock here in their thousands, for the Piazza's eastern end is dominated by two of the city's most important historical sights – the Basilica and the Doge's Palace. In addition to these magnificent buildings there is plenty to entertain, with elegant cafés, open-air orchestras and smart boutiques beneath the arcades of the Procuratie.

So close to the waters of the lagoon, the Piazza is one of the first points in the city to suffer at *acqua alta* (high tide). Tourists and Venetians alike can then be seen picking their way across the duckboards which are set up to crisscross the flooded square.

Gondolas
Traditionally gondolas have moored in the Bacino Orseolo, named after Doge Orseolo.

Quadri's café was the favourite haunt of Austrian troops during the Occupation (*see p48*).

Museo Correr
Giovanni Bellini's Pietà *(1455–60) is one of many Renaissance masterpieces hanging in the picture galleries of the Correr* ⑧

The Ala Napoleonica is the most recent wing enclosing the square, built by Napoleon to create a new ballroom.

PROCURATIE VECCHIE

PIAZZA SAN MAR

PROCURATIE NUOVE

| 0 metres | 75 |
| 0 yards | 75 |

Caffè Florian
(see p250) was the favourite haunt of 19th-century literary figures such as Byron, Dickens and Proust.

The Giardinetti Reali (royal gardens) were laid out in the early 19th century.

San Marco Vallaresso

STAR SIGHTS

★ Basilica San Marco

★ Doge's Palace

★ Campanile

Torre dell'Orologio
The Madonna on the clock tower is greeted each Epiphany and Ascension by clockwork figures of the Magi ❷

Piazzetta dei Leoncini was named after the pair of porphyry lions which stand in the square.

LOCATOR MAP
See Street Finder, map 7

★ Basilica San Marco
The remarkable Basilica of St Mark is a glorious reflection of the city's Byzantine connection ❸

★ Doge's Palace
Once the Republic's seat of power and home to its rulers, the Doge's Palace, beside the Basilica, is a triumph of Gothic architecture ❹

★ Campanile
Today's tower replaced the one that collapsed in 1902. The top provides spectacular views of the city ❶

Museo Archeologico
The museum sculptures had a marked influence on Venetian Renaissance artists ❻

Columns of San Marco and San Teodoro
The columns marked the main entrance to Venice when the city could be reached only by sea ❼

San Marco Giardinetti

The Zecca, designed by Sansovino, was the city mint until 1870, and gave its name to the *zecchino* or Venetian ducat. It houses the Biblioteca Marciana.

Libreria Sansoviniana
The ornate vaulting of the magnificent library stairway is decorated with frescoes and gilded stucco ❺

CALLE LARGA SAN MARCO

RIO DEL PALAZZO

PIAZZETTA

MOLO SAN MARCO

Campanile ❶

Piazza San Marco. **Map** 7 B2. **Tel** 041 522 40 64. 🚤 San Marco. ◯ call ahead to check opening times. 🦽 ♿

From the top of St Mark's campanile, high above the Piazza, visitors can enjoy sublime views of the city, the lagoon and, visibility permitting, the peaks of the Alps. It was from this viewpoint that Galileo demonstrated his

The spire, 98.5 m (323 ft) high, is topped with a golden weathervane which was designed by Bartolomeo Bon.

The five bells in the tower each had their role during the Republic. The *marangona* tolled the start and end of the working day; the *malefico* warned of an execution; the *nona* rang at noon; the *mezza terza* summoned senators to the Doge's Palace; and the *trottiera* announced a session of the Great Council.

An internal lift, installed in 1962, provides visitors with access to one of the most spectacular views across Venice.

The Loggetta was built in the 16th century by Jacopo Sansovino. Its Classical sculptures celebrate the glory of the Republic.

The allegorical reliefs from Verona depict Justice representing Venice, Jupiter as Crete and Venus as Cyprus. All were carefully rebuilt after the campanile's collapse in 1902.

telescope to Doge Leonardo Donà in 1609. To do so he would have climbed the internal ramp. Access today is via a lift that can carry 14 people. Nevertheless there is almost always a queue. Visitors at the top of the tower on the hour should note that the five bells ring quite loudly.

The first tower, completed in 1173, was built as a lighthouse to assist navigators in the lagoon. In the Middle Ages, it took on a less benevolent role as the support for a torture cage where offenders were imprisoned and in some cases left to die. The tower's present appearance dates from the early 16th century, when it was restored by Bartolomeo Bon after an earthquake.

The tower survived the vicissitudes of time until 14 July 1902 when its foundations gave way and it suddenly collapsed. The only casualties were the Loggetta at the foot of the tower and the custodian's cat. The following year, with the help of many donations, the foundation stone was laid for a campanile *"dov'era e com'era"* ("where it was and how it was"). The new tower was opened on 25 April (St Mark's Day) 1912. Due to small structural shifts, work has begun to reinforce the foundations. There is no known end date for the work.

The highly ornamented clock face of the Torre dell'Orologio

Torre dell'Orologio ❷

Piazza San Marco. **Map** 7 B2. **Tel** 041 520 90 70 🚤 San Marco. ◯ 9am–4pm for pre-booked tours only. 🦽

The richly decorated Renaissance clock tower stands on the north side of the Piazza, over the archway leading to the Mercerie (see p95). It was built in the late 15th century, and the central section is thought to have been designed by Mauro Coducci. Displaying the phases of the moon and the zodiac, the gilt and blue enamel clock was originally designed with seafarers in mind. A story was spread by scandalmongers that once the clock was complete, the two inventors of the complex clock mechanism had their eyes gouged out to prevent them creating a replica.

The clock mechanism is currently on display in the Doge's Palace, awaiting the completion of restoration work at the tower. During Ascension Week, when working, the clock draws large crowds who watch the figures of the Magi emerge from side doors to pay their respects to the Virgin and Child, whose figures are set above the clock. At the very top two huge bronze figures, known as the *Mori*, or Moors, strike the bell on the hour.

Basilica San Marco ❸

See pp78–83.

Doge's Palace ❹

See pp84–9.

Libreria Sansoviniana ❺

Piazzetta (entrance Ala Napoleonica). **Map** 7 B3. *Tel 041 240 72 11 (Biblioteca Marciana).* San Marco. 9am–7pm daily. public hols.

Praised by Andrea Palladio as the finest building since antiquity, the library was designed in the Classical style by the architect Jacopo Sansovino. During construction (1537–88) the vaulting collapsed: Sansovino was blamed and imprisoned. He was freed after appeals from eminent acquaintances, but had to reconstruct the building at his own expense.

At the top of the monumental stairway (*see p75*), behind a booth, is a rare example of Jacopo de' Barbari's bird's-eye map of Venice dating to 1500.

The salon is sumptuously decorated and features two fine ceiling paintings by Paolo Veronese, *Arithmetic and Geometry* and *Music*.

Museo Archeologico ❻

Piazzetta (9am–7pm: entrance Ala Napoleonica). **Map** 7 B3. *Tel 041 522 59 78.* San Marco. Nov–Mar: 9am–5pm; Apr–Oct: 9am–7pm. 1 Jan, 25 Dec.

Housed in rooms in both the Libreria Sansoviniana and the Procuratie Nuove, the museum provides a quiet retreat from the bustle of San Marco. The collection owes its existence to the generosity of Domenico Grimani, son of Doge Antonio Grimani, who bequeathed all his Greek, Roman and Roman sculpture, together with his library, to the state in 1523.

Columns of San Marco and San Teodoro ❼

Piazzetta. **Map** 7 C3. San Marco.

Along with all the bounty from Constantinople came the two huge granite columns which now tower above the Piazzetta. These were said to have been erected in 1172 by the engineer Nicolò Barattieri, architect of the very first Rialto Bridge. For his efforts he was granted the right to set up gambling tables between the columns. A more gruesome spectacle on the same spot was the execution of criminals, which took place here until the mid-18th century. Even today, superstitious Venetians will not be seen walking between the columns.

Columns of San Marco and San Teodoro

The western column is crowned by a marble statue of St Theodore, who was the patron saint of Venice before St Mark's relics were smuggled from Alexandria in AD 828. The statue is a modern copy – the original is kept for safety in the Doge's Palace (*see p88*).

The second column is surmounted by a huge bronze of the Lion of St Mark. Its origin remains a mystery, though it is thought to be a Chinese chimera with wings added to make it look like a Venetian lion. In September 1990 the 3,000-kg (3-ton) beast went to the British Museum in London for extensive restoration, and was returned with great ceremony and skill to the top of the column.

Fragment from a monumental statue, in the Museo Archeologico

A Portrait of a Young Man in a Red Hat by Carpaccio (c.1490)

Museo Correr ❽

Procuratie Nuove (entrance Ala Napoleonica). **Map** 7 B2. *Tel 041 240 52 11.* San Marco. 9am–7pm daily (to 5pm Nov–Mar). 1 Jan, 25 Dec. allows access to Libreria Sansoviniana & Museo Archeologico.

The wealthy Abbot Teodoro Correr's extensive collection of works of art and documents forms the nucleus of the civic museum.

The first rooms form a suitably Neo-Classical backdrop for early statues by Antonio Canova (1757–1822). The rest of the floor covers the history of the Venetian Republic, with maps, coins, armour and a host of doge-related exhibits.

On the second floor, the Museo del Risorgimento is devoted to the history of the city, until Venice became part of unified Italy in 1866. Also here is the Quadreria, or picture gallery. The paintings are hung chronologically and the rooms have the bonus of explanations in English. The collection enables you to trace the evolution of Venetian painting, and to see the influence that Ferrarese, Paduan and Flemish artists had on the Venetian school. The most famous works in the gallery are the Carpaccios: *A Portrait of a Young Man in a Red Hat* (c.1490), and *Two Venetian Ladies* (c.1507). The latter is traditionally, but probably incorrectly, known as *The Courtesans* because of the ladies' décolleté dresses.

Basilica San Marco ❸

This awesome Basilica, built on a Greek cross plan and crowned with five huge domes, is the third church to stand on this site. The first, built to enshrine the body of St Mark in the 9th century, was destroyed by fire. The second was pulled down in the 11th century in order to make way for a more spectacular edifice designed by an unknown architect (1063–94), reflecting the escalating power of the Republic. The basilica continued to be remodelled over the following centuries, and in 1807 it succeeded San Pietro in the *sestiere* of Castello *(see p120)* as the cathedral of Venice; it had until then served as the doge's private chapel for State ceremonies.

The Pentecost Dome, showing the Descent of the Holy Ghost as a dove, was probably the first dome to be decorated with mosaics.

St Mark and Angels
The statues crowning the central arch are additions from the early 15th century.

★ **Horses of St Mark**
The four horses are replicas of the gilded bronze originals (see p80), now protected inside the Basilica.

★ **Central Doorway Carvings**
The central arch features 13th-century carvings of the Labours of the Month. The grape harvester represents September.

★ **Façade Mosaics**
A 17th-century mosaic shows the smuggling out of Alexandria of St Mark's body, reputedly under slices of pork to deter prying Muslims.

Ciborium

The fine alabaster columns of the altar canopy, or ciborium, are adorned with scenes from the New Testament.

The Ascension Dome features a magnificent 13th-century mosaic of Christ surrounded by angels, the 12 Apostles and the Virgin Mary.

St Mark's body, believed lost in the fire of AD 976, supposedly reappeared when the new church was consecrated in 1094. The remains are housed in the altar.

Allegorical mosaics

St Mark's Treasury

Baptistry

Baptistry Mosaics

Herod's Banquet (1343–54) is one of the mosaics in a cycle of scenes from the life of St John the Baptist.

VISITORS' CHECKLIST

Piazza San Marco. **Map** 7 B2. **Tel** *041 270 83 11.* 🚤 *San Marco.* **Basilica, Treasury and Pala d'Oro** ◯ *Apr–Sep: 9:45am–5pm Mon–Sat, 2–4pm Sun; Oct–Mar: 9.45am–4.45pm Mon–Sat, 2–4pm Sun.* 🔓 *for Treasury only.* **Museum** ◯ *10am–4pm daily.* 📷 *Museum, Treasury and Pala d'Oro only.* ✝ *9 times a day. Sightseeing is limited during services.* 🎧 *in English twice a week in season.* 🚫 📷 ♿ 🏛

★ The Tetrarchs

This charming sculptured group in porphyry (4th-century Egyptian) is thought to represent Diocletian, Maximian, Valerian and Constance. Collectively they were the tetrarchs, appointed by Diocletian to help rule the Roman Empire.

The so-called Pilasters of Acre in fact came from a 6th-century church in Constantinople.

STAR FEATURES

★ Façade Mosaics

★ Central Doorway Carvings

★ Horses of St Mark

★ The Tetrarchs

Inside the Basilica

Dark, mysterious and enriched with the spoils of conquest, the Basilica is a unique blend of Eastern and Western influences. This oriental extravaganza, embellished over a period of six centuries with fabulous mosaics, marble and carvings, made a fitting location for the ceremonies of the Serene Republic. It was here that the doge was presented to the city following his election, that heads of State, popes, princes and ambassadors were received, and where sea captains came to pray for protection before embarking on epic voyages.

Mascoli Chapel
Formerly called the "New Chapel", this is named after an all-male confraternity, or mascoli.

The Porta dei Fiori or Gate of Flowers is decorated with 13th-century reliefs.

North Aisle
The gallery leading off the museum affords visitors a splendid overall view of the mosaics.

The columns of the inner façade are thought to be fragments of the first basilica.

★ **Pentecost Dome**
Showing the Apostles touched by tongues of flame, the Pentecost Dome was decorated in the 12th century.

Main entrance

★ **Atrium Mosaics**
In the glittering Genesis Cupola the Creation of the World is described in concentric circles. Here, God creates the fish and birds.

The baptistry is also called Chiesa dei Putti (church of the cherubs).

The Altar of the Virgin has a 10th-century icon of the Madonna of Nicopeia, which came with the spoils of war in 1204 (see p42).

The Chapel of St Peter has a 14th-century altar screen relief of St Peter worshipped by two Procurators.

★ Pala d'Oro

The magnificent altarpiece, created in the 10th century by medieval goldsmiths, is made up of 250 panels such as this one, each adorned with enamels and precious stones.

The sacristy door (always locked) has fine bronze panels by Sansovino, including portraits of himself with Titian and Aretino.

★ Ascension Dome

A mosaic of Christ in Glory decorates the enormous central dome. This masterpiece was created by 13th-century Venetian craftsmen, who were strongly influenced by the art and architecture of Byzantium.

South aisle

The Altar of the Sacrament is surrounded by mosaics of the parables and miracles of Christ dating from the late 12th or early 13th century.

★ Treasury

A repository for precious booty from Constantinople, the Treasury also houses ancient Italian works of art, such as this 12th- or 13th-century incense burner.

STAR FEATURES

- ★ Atrium Mosaics
- ★ Ascension and Pentecost Domes
- ★ Pala d'Oro
- ★ Treasury

Exploring the Basilica

The Basilica cannot comfortably be covered in one visit. The mosaics, the rich store of eastern bounty, the mysterious lighting and the sheer size of the place create a feeling of confusion for first-time visitors. Make several visits, ideally at different times of the day. The mosaics look especially splendid when the church is fully illuminated (11:30am–12:30pm Mon–Fri, 11:30am–4pm Sat, 2–4pm Sun). Visitors with organized tours are often led towards the Pala d'Oro and Treasury and miss out on other sections of the church. Avoid the crowds by visiting early in the morning or in the evening. If a mass is in progress visitors are expected to be silent and will only be able to visit certain areas.

The Genesis Cupola of the atrium

Stories of Joseph and of Moses in the domes at the north end. The figures of saints on either side of the main doorway date from the 11th century and are among the earliest mosaics in the church. Just in front of the central doorway there is a lozenge of porphyry to mark the spot where the Emperor Frederick Barbarossa was obliged to make peace with Pope Alexander III in 1177 *(see p41)*.

MUSEO MARCIANO

A precarious stairway from the atrium, marked *Loggia dei Cavalli*, takes you up to the recently restored church museum. The gallery gives a splendid view into the basilica, while from the exterior loggia visitors can survey the Piazza San Marco and take a closer look at the replica horses on the church façade. It was from this panoramic balcony that doges and dignitaries once looked down on ceremonies taking place in the square. The original gilded bronze horses, housed in a room at the far end of the museum, were stolen from the top of the Hippodrome (ancient racecourse) in Constantinople in 1204 but their origin, either Roman or Hellenistic, remains a mystery. In the same room is Paolo Veneziano's 14th-century *pala feriale*, painted with stories of St Mark, which once covered the Pala d'Oro. Also on show are medieval

MOSAICS

Clothing the domes, walls and floor of the basilica are over 4,000 sq m (40,000 sq ft) of gleaming golden mosaics. The earliest, dating from the 12th century, were the work of mosaicists from the east. Their techniques were adopted by Venetian craftsmen who gradually took over the decoration, combining Byzantine inspiration with western influences. During the 16th century, sketches and cartoons by Tintoretto, Titian, Veronese, and other leading artists were reproduced in mosaic. The original iconographical scheme, depicting stories from the Testaments, has more or less been preserved by careful restoration.

Among the finest mosaics in the basilica are those decorating the 13th-century central Dome of the Ascension and the 12th-century Dome of the Pentecost over the nave.

The *pavimento*, or basilica floor, spreads out like an undulating Turkish carpet. Mosaics, made of marble, porphyry and glass are used to create complex and colourful geometric

patterns and beautiful scenes of beasts and birds. Some of these scenes are allegorical. The one in the left transept of two cocks carrying a fox on a stick was designed to symbolize cunning vanquished by vigilance.

ATRIUM (VESTIBULE)

The 13th-century mosaics decorating the cupolas, vaults and lunettes of the atrium are among the finest in the basilica. The scenes depict Old Testament stories, starting at the southern end with the Genesis Cupola (showing 26 detailed episodes of the Creation), to the

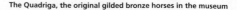

The Quadriga, the original gilded bronze horses in the museum

Noah and the Flood – atrium mosaics from the 13th century

illuminated manuscripts, fragments of ancient mosaics and antique tapestries.

SANCTUARY AND PALA D'ORO

Beyond the Chapel of St Clement, tickets are sold to view the most valuable treasure of San Marco: the Pala d'Oro. This jewel-spangled altarpiece situated behind the high altar consists of 250 enamel paintings on gold foil, enclosed within a gilded silver Gothic frame. Originally commissioned in Byzantium in AD 976, the altarpiece was embellished over the centuries.

Statue of St Mark on the iconostasis

Following the fall of the Republic, Napoleon helped himself to some of the precious stones, but the screen still gleams with pearls, rubies, sapphires and amethysts.

The iconostasis, the screen dividing nave from chancel, is adorned with marble Gothic statues of the Virgin and Apostles, and was carved in 1394 by the Dalle Masegne brothers. Above the high altar the imposing green marble baldacchino is supported by finely carved alabaster columns featuring scenes from the New Testament.

BAPTISTRY AND CHAPELS

The Baptistry (closed to the public) was added in the 14th century by Doge Andrea Dandolo (1343–54) who is buried here. Under his direction the baptistry was decorated with outstanding mosaics depicting scenes from the lives of Christ and John the Baptist. Sansovino, who designed the font, is buried by the altar.

The adjoining Zen Chapel (currently closed to the public) originally formed part of the atrium. It became a funeral chapel for Cardinal Zen in 1504 in return for his bequest to the State.

In the left transept of the basilica the Chapel of St Isidore, normally accessible only for worship, was also built by Dandolo. Mosaics in the barrel vault ceiling tell the tale of the saint, whose body

The archangel Michael, a Byzantine icon from the 11th century in the Treasury

was stolen from the island of Chios and transported to Venice in 1125. To its left the Mascoli Chapel, used in the early 17th century by the confraternity of Mascoli (men), is decorated with scenes from the life of the Virgin Mary. The altarpiece has statues depicting the Virgin and Child between St Mark and St John.

The third chapel in the left transept is home to the icon of the Madonna of Nicopeia. Looted in 1204, she was formerly carried into battle at the head of the Byzantine army.

The revered icon of the Nicopeia Madonna, once a war insignia

TREASURY

Although plundered after the fall of the Republic and much depleted by the fundraising sale of jewels in the early 19th century, the treasury nevertheless has a precious collection of Byzantine silver, gold and glasswork. Today, most of the treasures are housed in a room whose remarkably thick walls are believed to have been a 9th-century tower of the Doge's Palace. Exhibits include chalices, goblets, reliquaries, two intricate icons of the archangel Michael and an 11th-century silver-gilt reliquary made in the form of a five-domed basilica (see p81). The sanctuary, with over 100 reliquaries, is normally open to the public.

Doge's Palace ❹

The Palazzo Ducale started life in the 9th century as a fortified castle, but this and several subsequent buildings were destroyed by a series of fires. The existing palace owes its external appearance to the building work of the 14th and early 15th centuries. The designers broke with tradition by perching the bulk of the pink Verona marble palace on lace-like Istrian stone arcades, with a portico supported by columns below. The result is a light and airy masterpiece of Gothic architecture.

Arco Foscari
The Adam and Eve figures on this triumphal arch in the courtyard are copies of the 15th-century originals by Antonio Rizzo.

★ Porta della Carta
This 15th-century Gothic gate was the principal entrance to the palace. From it, a vaulted passageway leads to the Arco Foscari and the internal courtyard.

Exit

STAR FEATURES

★ Giants' Staircase

★ Porta della Carta

The balcony on the west façade was added in 1536 to mirror the early 15th-century balcony looking on to the quay.

★ Giants' Staircase
This late 15th-century staircase by Antonio Rizzo was used for ceremonial purposes. It was on the landing at the top that the doges were crowned with the glittering zogia.

Torture Chamber
"The court of the room of the Cord" recalls the practice of interrogating suspects as they hung by their wrists.

Sala dei Tre Capi
(Chamber of the Three Heads of the Council of Ten)

Bridge of Sighs
The famous bridge once crossed by offenders on their way to the State interrogators.

Sala della Bussola
(Compass Room)

Drunkenness of Noah
This early 15th-century sculpture, symbolic of the frailty of man, is set on the corner of the palace.

Ponte della Paglia *(see p113)*

Main entrance

Adam and Eve
with the serpent are depicted in stone on the corner of the Piazzetta.

Sala del Maggior Consiglio
An entire wall of the Great Council Hall is taken up by Domenico and Jacopo Tintoretto's Paradise (1588–92).

Inside the Doge's Palace

Intricate carved Gothic capital

From the early days of the Republic, the Doge's Palace was the seat of the government, the Palace of Justice and the home of the doge. For centuries this was the only building in Venice entitled to the name palazzo (the others were merely called Ca', short for Casa). The power of the Serenissima is ever present in the large and allegorical historical paintings which embellish the walls and ceilings of the splendid halls and chambers. These ornate rooms are testament to the glory of the Venetian Republic, and were designed to impress and overawe visiting ambassadors and dignitaries.

Colonnade
Sunlight streams through the arches of the Loggia on the first floor of the palace.

STAR FEATURES

★ Collegiate Rooms

★ Sala del Maggior Consiglio

★ Prisons

Mars
The Giants' Staircase is named after Sansovino's monumental figures, statues of Mars and Neptune, sculpted in 1567.

Ground floor

Scala d'Oro
Sansovino's lavish staircase was built between 1554 and 1558. The arched ceiling is embellished with gilded stucco by Alessandro Vittoria.

Exit through Porta della Carta

KEY TO FLOORPLAN

▢	State Apartments
▢	Collegium and Senate Rooms
▢	Council of Ten and Armoury
▢	Great Council Rooms
▢	Prisons
▢	Non-exhibition space

Wellhead
The two 16th-century bronze wellheads in the courtyard are considered to be the finest in Venice.

★ **Collegiate Rooms**
Bacchus and Ariadne Crowned by Venus is the finest of four mythological scenes by Tintoretto in the Anticollegio.

Third floor

The Sala del Consiglio dei Dieci has a ceiling decorated with paintings by Veronese (1553–4).

Sala dello Scudo
The walls of this room are covered with maps of the world. In the centre are two huge 18th-century globes.

First floor

Second floor

★ **Sala del Maggior Consiglio**
The first 76 doges, with the exception of the traitor Marin Falier, are portrayed on a frieze round the upper walls of the room.

★ **Prisons**
These 16th-century cells were mainly used for petty offenders. Serious criminals were lodged in the dank pozzi (wells).

nce

THE SECRET ITINERARY

The fascinating, though poorly publicized, Secret Itinerary (Itinerari Segreti) tour *(see Visitors' Checklist p85)* takes visitors behind the scenes in the palace to the offices and Hall of the Chancellery, the State Inquisitors' room, the Torture Chamber and the prisons. It was from these cells that Casanova made his spectacular escape in 1755. Tours are available in Italian, English and French. Each is limited to 25 people and lasts for 75 minutes.

Casanova's cell door

Exploring the Doge's Palace

A tour of the palace takes visitors through a succession of richly decorated chambers and halls. The rooms are on four levels, and they all have name boards carrying an explanation of their function in Italian and English. The latest equipment available is an up-to-date infrared audioguide, which can be hired for a commentary on the whole palace or just the areas that are of particular interest.

Allow plenty of time for the visit, and try to take a break at the coffee shop. Located at water level, it affords evocative views of gondolas gliding past in the canal.

St Theodore in the palace courtyard

COURTYARD

The courtyard is reached via a vaulted passage from the Porta del Frumento. At the top of the Giants' Staircase, on the opposite side of the courtyard, new doges were crowned with the *zogia* or dogal cap.

SCALA D'ORO AND STATE APARTMENTS

The sumptuous Scala d'Oro (golden staircase), built between 1538 and 1559, was designed by Jacopo Sansovino. It takes its name, however, from the elaborate gilt stucco vault, which was added by Alessandro Vittoria (1554–8). The doge's private apartments on the second floor were built after the fire of 1483 and later looted on the orders of Napoleon. They are bare of furnishings, but the lavish ceilings and colossal carved chimney-pieces in some of the rooms give an idea of the doges' lifestyle. The most ornate is the Sala degli Scarlatti, with a richly carved gilt ceiling, a fireplace (c.1501) designed by Antonio and Tullio Lombardo and a relief (1501–21) by Pietro Lombardo of Doge Leonardo Loredan at the feet of the Virgin.

The Sala dello Scudo, or map room, contains maps and charts. The picture gallery further on features works by Vittore Carpaccio and Giovanni Bellini, and some incongruous wooden demoniac panels by Hieronymous Bosch.

A bocca di leone used for denouncing tax evaders

SALA DELLE QUATTRO PORTE TO SALA DEL SENATO

The second flight of the Scala d'Oro leads to the third floor and its council chambers. The first room, the Sala delle Quattro Porte, was completely rebuilt after the 1574 fire, its ceiling designed by Andrea Palladio and frescoed by Tintoretto.

The next room, the Anticollegio, was the waiting room. The end walls are decorated with mythological scenes by Tintoretto: *Vulcan's Forge; Mercury and the Graces; Bacchus and Ariadne* and *Minerva Dismissing Mars*, all painted in 1578. Veronese's masterly *Rape of Europa* (1580), opposite the window, is one of the most eyecatching works in the palace.

Off the Anticollegio, the Sala del Collegio was the hall where the doge and his counsellors met to receive ambassadors and discuss matters of State. Embellishing the magnificent ceiling are 11 paintings by Veronese (c.1577), of which the most notable – in the centre, far end – is *Justice and Peace Offering Sword, Scales and Olive Branch to Venice*.

It was in the next room, the Sala del Senato, that the doge would sit with some 200 senators to discuss matters such as foreign affairs or nominations of ambassadors. The wall and ceiling paintings, by pupils of Tintoretto or the master himself, are further propaganda for the Republic.

SALA DEL CONSIGLIO DEI DIECI TO THE ARMERIA

The route returns through the Sala delle Quattro Porte to the Sala del Consiglio dei Dieci. This was the meeting room of the awesomely powerful Council of Ten, founded in

Veronese's *Dialectic* (c.1577), Sala del Collegio

1310 to investigate and prosecute crimes concerning the security of the State. Napoleon pilfered some of the Veroneses from the ceiling but two of the finest found their way back here in 1920: *Age and Youth and Juno Offering the Ducal Crown to Venice* (both 1553–54).

In the next room, the Sala della Bussola, offenders awaited their fate in front of the Council of Ten. The room's *bocca di leone* (lion's mouth), used to post secret denunciations, was just one of several within the palace. The wooden door here leads to the rooms of the Heads of the Ten, the State Inquisitors' Room and thence to the torture chamber and prisons. This is the route taken by those on the Secret Itinerary.

Age and Youth (1553–54) by Veronese

Others follow the flow to the Armoury – one of the finest collections in Europe, thanks in part to bequests by European monarchs.

SALA DEL MAGGIOR CONSIGLIO

Another staircase, the Scala dei Censori, leads down to the second floor, along the hallway and past the Sala del Guariento with fresco fragments of *The Coronation of the Virgin* by Guariento (1365–67). From the *liagò*, or veranda, where Antonio Rizzo's marble statues of Adam and Eve (1480s) are displayed, visitors pass into the magnificent Sala del Maggior Consiglio or Hall of the Great Council. A chamber of monumental proportions, it was here that the Great Council convened to vote on constitutional questions, to pass laws and elect the top officials of the Serene Republic. The hall was also used for State banquets. When Henry III of France paid a royal visit, 3,000 guests were entertained in this spectacular room.

By the mid-16th century the Great Council had around 2,000 members. Any Venetian of high birth over 25 was entitled to a seat – with the exception of those married to a commoner. From 1646, by which time the Turkish wars had depleted state coffers, nobility from the *terra firma* or those from merchant or professional classes with 100,000 ducats to spare could purchase their way in.

Tintoretto's huge, highly restored work called *Paradise* (1587–90) occupies the eastern wall. Measuring 7.45 by 24.65 m (25 by 81 ft) it is one of the largest paintings in the world. For a man in his late seventies, albeit assisted by his son, it is a remarkably vigorous composition.

The ceiling of the hall is decorated with panels glorifying the Republic. One of the finest is Veronese's *Apotheosis of Venice* (1583). A frieze along the walls illustrates 76 doges by Tintoretto's pupils. The portrait covered by a curtain is Marin Falier, beheaded for treason in 1355. The other 42 doges are portrayed in the Sala dello Scrutinio, where new doges were nominated.

PRISONS

View of the lagoon through a grille on the Bridge of Sighs

From the Sala del Maggior Consiglio a series of passageways and stairways leads to the Bridge of Sighs *(see p113)* which links the palace to what were known as the New Prisons, built between 1556 and 1595.

Situated at the top of the palace, just below the leaded roof, are the *piombi* cells (*piombo* means lead). These cells are hardly inviting but prisoners here were far more comfortable than the criminals who were left to fester in the *pozzi* – the dark dank dungeons at ground level. The windowless cells of these ancient prisons are still covered with the graffiti of the convicts. Visitors on the Secret Itinerary tour are shown Casanova's cell in the *piombi* and told of how he made his daring escape from the palace through a hole in the roof.

Visits end with the offices of the Avogaria, where the state prosecutors *(avogadori)* prepared the trials.

The splendid Sala del Maggior Consiglio, the hall of the Great Council

Street-by-Street: Around La Fenice

West of the huge expanse of the ever-crowded Piazza San Marco there is a labyrinth of alleys to explore. At the centre of this part of the *sestiere* is Campo San Fantin, flanked by the Renaissance church of San Fantin. Nearby is the Ateneo Veneto, formerly a *scuola* whose members had the unenviable role of escorting prisoners to the scaffold. The narrow streets around these sights have some wonderfully exotic little shops, while the more recent Calle Larga XXII Marzo further south boasts big names in Italian fashion. The quarter in general has some excellent restaurants but, being San Marco, the prices in the majority of establishments are fairly steep.

Campo San Fantin has a late Renaissance church, San Fantin, with a particularly beautiful apse designed by Jacopo Sansovino.

★ La Fenice
The opera house gained its name (the phoenix) after a fire in 1836. Destroyed by fire again in 1996, it is now beautifully restored **14**

The Rio delle Veste
leads past the rear of the theatre. This is the route taken by those fortunate enough to arrive for their night out by gondola.

KEY

– – – Suggested route

0 metres	75
0 yards	75

Santa Maria Zobenigo
The carvings feature the Barbaro family who paid for the church façade. Ground-level reliefs show towns where the family held high ranking posts **13**

STAR SIGHTS

★ La Fenice

★ San Moisè

LOCATOR MAP
See Street Finder, map 7

The statue of Daniele Manin, *leader of the 1848 uprising, stands on Campo Manin gazing towards the house where he once lived.*

Palazzo Contarini del Bovolo
This palazzo is often difficult to find, but worth seeking out for its fairy-tale external stairway (c.1499) ⑫

Frezzeria, *in medieval times, was the street where citizens went to purchase their arrows (frecce). Its shops now sell exotic clothes.*

Calle Larga XXII Marzo *was named after 22 March 1848, the day of Manin's rebellion. Today the street is best known for its trendy designer boutiques.*

★ San Moisè
The exuberant Baroque façade of San Moisè (c.1668) was funded by a legacy from the patrician Vincenzo Fini, whose bust features above a side door ⑪

Harry's Bar ❾

Calle Vallaresso 1323. **Map** 7 B3.
🚤 San Marco. See also **Restaurants, Cafés and Bars** pp250–51.

Celebrated for cocktails, *carpaccio* and American clientèle, Harry's Bar is famous throughout Venice. Founded in 1931 by the late Giuseppe Cipriani, it was financed by a Bostonian called Harry who thought Venice had a dearth of decent bars. They chose a storeroom at the Grand Canal end of the Calle Vallaresso as their location, conveniently close to the Piazza San Marco. Since then, the bar has seen a steady stream of American visitors, among them Ernest Hemingway who used to come here after shooting in the lagoon. The bar became the most popular venue in Venice, patronized by royalty, film stars and heads of state.

Ernest Hemingway, a regular at Harry's Bar

These days there are far more American tourists than famous figures, often there to sample the Bellini cocktail that Cipriani invented *(see p241)*. Aesthetically, the place is unremarkable and there is no terrace for meals alfresco.

Ridotto ❿

Calle del Ridotto, 1332 San Marco. **Map** 7 B3. **Tel** 041 520 02 11. 🚤 San Marco. ⬤ to hotel guests and on request.

In an effort to control the gambling mania that swept Venice in the 1600s, the State allowed Marco Dandolo to use his palace as the first public gaming house in Europe. In 1638 the Ridotto was opened, with the proviso that players came disguised in a mask. In 1774 the Great Council closed the casino's doors on account of the number of Venetians ruined at its tables.

In 1947 the old Palazzo Dandolo was converted into a theatre. Now restored, it is part of the Hotel Monaco and Grand Canal *(see p229)*.

San Moisè ⓫

Campo San Moisè. **Map** 7 A3. **Tel** 041 296 06 30. 🚤 San Marco. ⬤ 9:30am–12:30pm, 4–6:30pm daily.

One of the churches in Venice that people love to hate, San Moisè displays a ponderous Baroque façade. Completed in 1668, it is covered in grimy statues, swags and busts. John Ruskin, in a characteristic anti-Baroque outrage, described it as the clumsiest church in Venice. The interior has a mixed collection of paintings and sculpture from the 17th and 18th centuries. In the nave is the tombstone of John Law, a financier from Scotland who founded the Compagnie d'Occident to develop the Mississippi Valley. His shares collapsed in 1770 in the notorious South Sea Bubble, and he fled to Venice, surviving on his winnings at the Ridotto.

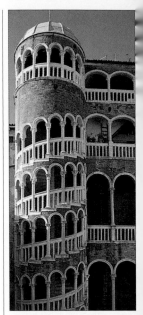

Façade of San Moisè, encrusted with Baroque ornamentation

Palazzo Contarini del Bovolo ⓬

Corte Contarini del Bovolo, 4299 San Marco. **Map** 7 A2. **Tel** 041 271 90 12. 🚤 Rialto or Sant'Angelo. ⬤ Apr–Oct: 10am–6pm daily; Nov–Feb: 10am–4pm Sat & Sun.

Tucked away in a maze of alleys (follow signs from Campo Manin), this *palazzo* is best known for its graceful

The external stairway of the Palazzo Contarini del Bovolo

external stairway, which is currently closed for renovation. In Venetian dialect *bovolo* means snail shell, appropriate to the spiral shape of the stairway. The Contarini, a learned family who had the 15th-century palace built, were known as "the philosophers". There is also a collection of Byzantine well-heads.

Santa Maria Zobenigo ⓭

Campo Santa Maria del Giglio. **Map** 6 F3. **Tel** 041 275 0462. 🚤 Santa Maria del Giglio. ⬤ 10am–5pm daily (from 1pm Sun & public hols). ⬤ Sun (Jul & Aug); 1 Jan, 25 Dec. 🈂️ 🚫 📷 🛗

Named after the Jubanico family who are said to have founded it in the 9th century, this church is also referred to as "del Giglio" ("of the lily"). The exuberant Baroque façade was financed by the affluent Barbaro family and was used to glorify their naval and diplomatic achievements.

Inside is a tiny museum of church ornaments and paintings including *The Sacred Family* attributed to Rubens and two works by Tintoretto.

La Fenice 🅮

Campo San Fantin. **Map** 7 A3. **Box office** *Tel* 041 24 24. 🚤 *San Marco.* 🖸 www.teatrolafenice.it

Theatre houses were enormously popular in the 18th century and La Fenice, the city's oldest theatre, was no exception. Built in 1792 in Classical style, it was one of several privately owned theatres showing plays and operas to audiences from all strata of society. In December 1836 a fire destroyed the interior but a year later it was resurrected, just like the mythical bird, the phoenix *(fenice)* which is said to have arisen from its ashes.

Another fire in early 1996 again destroyed the theatre, except for its façade. Now beautifully rebuilt, La Fenice shares the concert and opera season with the Malibran Theatre near Rialto.

Throughout the 19th century the name of La Fenice was linked with great Italian composers. The many operatic premières that took place here include Verdi's *La Traviata* (1853) and Rossini's *Tancredi* (1813) and *Semiramide* (1823). During the Austrian Occupation *(see p48)* red, white and green flowers, symbolizing the Italian flag, were thrown on stage, to shouts of "Viva Verdi" – the letters of the composer's name standing for Vittorio Emanuele Re d'Italia. More recently, the theatre saw premières of Stravinsky's *The Rake's Progress* (1951) and Britten's *Turn of the Screw* (1954).

Shop in Campo Santo Stefano selling antiques and masks

Campo Santo Stefano 🅯

Map 6 F3. 🚤 *Accademia or Sant'Angelo.*

Also known as Campo Francesco Morosini after the 17th-century doge who once lived here, this *campo* is one of the most spacious in the city. Bullfights were staged until 1802, when a stand fell and killed some of the spectators. It was also a venue for balls and Carnival festivities. Today it is a pleasantly informal square where children play and visitors drink coffee in open-air cafés.

The central statue is Nicolò Tommaseo (1802–74), a Dalmatian scholar who was a central figure in the 1848 rebellion against the Austrians.

At the southern end of the square the austere-looking Palazzo Pisani, overlooking the Campiello Pisani, has been the Conservatory of Music since the end of the 19th century. Music wafts from its open windows all through the year. On the opposite

side of the square No. 2945, Palazzo Loredan, is the home of the Venetian Institute of Sciences, Letters and Arts.

The ceiling of Santo Stefano, in the form of a ship's keel

Santo Stefano 🅰

Campo Santo Stefano. **Map** 6 F2. *Tel* 041 275 04 62. 🚤 *Accademia or Sant'Angelo.* ⬜ *10am–5pm daily (from 1pm Sun & public hols).* ⬤ *Sun (Jul & Aug); 1 Jan, 25 Dec.* 🖸 *Sacristy only.* 🔊 🚫 🖸

Deconsecrated six times on account of the violence that took place within its walls, Santo Stefano today is remarkably serene. Built in the 14th century and radically altered in the 15th, the church has a notable carved portal by Bartolomeo Bon and a campanile with a typical Venetian tilt. The interior has a splendid ship's keel ceiling, carved tiebeams and tall pillars of Veronese marble. The most notable works of art, including some paintings by Tintoretto, are housed in the damp sacristy.

La Fenice, rebuilt after it was destroyed by fire in 1996

Courtyard of the Palazzo Pesaro, where Fortuny lived

Museo Fortuny ⑰

Palazzo Pesaro degli Orfei,
Campo San Beneto, San Marco 3780.
Map 6 F2. **Tel** 041 520 09 95.
🚤 Sant'Angelo. ◻ 10am–6pm
Wed–Mon. 🈂 ⌀

Known principally for his
fantastic pleated silk dresses,
Fortuny was also a painter,
sculptor, set designer,
photographer, and scientist.
One of his inventions was the
Fortuny Dome which is used
in theatre performances to
create the illusion of sky.

Mariano Fortuny y Madrazo,
or Don Mariano as he liked
to be called, was born in
1871 in Granada and moved
to Venice in 1889. In the early
20th century he purchased
the Palazzo Pesaro, a late
Gothic *palazzo* that had
originally been owned by
the fabulously rich and
influential Pesaro family.
Fortuny spent the remainder
of his life here and both the
house and its contents were
bequeathed to the city by
his wife in 1956.

The large rooms and *portego*
make a splendid and appropriate setting for the precious
Fortuny fabrics. Woven with
gold and silver threads, these
were created by Fortuny's
reintroduction of Renaissance
techniques and use of ancient
dyes. The collection also
includes paintings by Fortuny
(less impressive than the
fabrics), decorative panels and
a few of the finely pleated,
clinging silk dresses regarded
as a milestone in early 20th-
century women's fashion.

San Salvatore ⑱

Campo San Salvatore. **Map** 7 B1.
Tel 041 270 24 64. 🚤 Rialto.
◻ 9am–noon, 3–7pm Mon–Sat.

The interior of this church is
an excellent example of
Venetian Renaissance
architecture. If the main door
is closed visitors can enter by
the side entrance, which is
squeezed between shops
along the Mercerie. The
present church was designed
by Giorgio Spavento in the
early 16th century, and continued by Tullio Lombardo
and Jacopo Sansovino. The
pictorial highlight is Titian's
Annunciation (1566) over the
third altar on the right. Nearby,
Sansovino's monument to
Doge Francesco Venier
(1556–61) is one of several
Mannerist tombs in the church.

On the high altar is Titian's
Transfiguration of Christ
(1560). The end of the right
transept is dominated by a
vast monument to Caterina
Cornaro, Queen of Cyprus
(see p43). Executed by the
sculptor Bernardino Contino
in 1580–84, the tomb shows
the queen handing over her
kingdom to the doge.

Campo San Bartolomeo ⑲

Map 7 B1. 🚤 Rialto.

Close to the Rialto, the
square of San Bartolomeo
bustles with life, particularly
in the early evening when
young Venetians rendezvous
here. They meet at cafés, bars
or by the statue of Carlo
Goldoni (1707–93), Venice's
prolific and most celebrated
playwright. His statue, in a
fitting spot for a writer who
drew his inspiration from
daily social intercourse, is by
Antonio del Zotto (1883).

The beautiful Renaissance interior
of the church of San Salvatore

St George and Dragon bas-relief on a corner of the Mercerie

Mercerie ⑳

Map 7 B2. 🚤 *San Marco or Rialto.*

Divided into the Merceria dell'Orologio, Merceria di San Zulian and Merceria di San Salvatore, this is, and always has been, a principal shopping thoroughfare. Linking Piazza San Marco with the Rialto, it is made from a string of narrow, bustling alleys, lined by small shops and boutiques. The 17th-century English author John Evelyn described it as "the most delicious streete in the World for the sweetnesse of it … tapisstry'd as it were, with Cloth of Gold, rich Damasks & other silk." He wrote of perfumers, apothecary shops and nightingales in cages. Today all this has been replaced with fashions, footwear and glass.

At the southern end, the relief over the first archway on the left portrays the woman who in 1310 accidentally stopped a revolt. She dropped her pestle out of the window, killing the standard-bearer of a rebel army. They retreated, and the woman was given a guarantee that her rent would never be raised.

San Zulian ㉑

Campo San Zulian. **Map** 7 B2.
Tel 041 523 53 83. 🚤 *San Marco.*
🕐 *8:30am–6:30pm daily.* 🕆 *in English: 9:30am daily and 11.30am on religious holidays.*

On the busy Mercerie, the church of San Zulian (or Giuliano) provides a refuge from the crowded alleys. Its interior features gilded woodwork, 16th- and 17th-century paintings, and sculpture. The central panel of the frescoed ceiling portrays *The Apotheosis of St Julian*, painted in 1585 by Palma il Giovane. The 16th-century church façade was designed by Sansovino and paid for by the rich and immodest physician Tommaso Rangone. His bronze statue stands out against the white Istrian stone walls.

Bronze statue of Tommaso Rangone

San Giorgio Maggiore ㉒

Map 8 D4. **Tel** 041 522 78 27. 🚤 *San Giorgio.* 🕐 *9:30am–12:30pm, 2:30–5pm (later in summer).* **Campanile** 🕐 *9:30am–12:30pm, 2:30–5.30pm (later in summer).* 🎫 **Foundation Tel** 041 524 01 19. 🕐 *Sat & Sun; Mon–Fri by appointment.* 🎫

Appearing like a stage set across the water from the Piazzetta, the little island of San Giorgio Maggiore has been captured on canvas countless times.

The church and monastery, built between 1559–80, are among Andrea Palladio's greatest architectural achievements. The church's temple front and the spacious, serene interior with its perfect proportions and cool beauty are typically Palladian in that they are modelled on the Classical style of ancient Rome. Within the church, the major works of art are the two late Tintorettos on the chancel walls: *The Last Supper* and *Gathering of the Manna* (both 1594). In the Chapel of the Dead is his last work, *The Deposition* (1592–4), finished by his son Domenico.

The top of the tall campanile, reached by a lift, affords a superb panorama of the city and lagoon.

Centuries ago Benedictine monks occupied the original monastery, which was rebuilt in the 13th century following an earthquake. It later became a centre of learning and a residence for eminent foreign visitors. Following the Fall of the Republic in 1797 (*see p48*) the monastery was suppressed and its treasures plundered.

In 1829 the island became a free port, and in 1851 the headquarters of the artillery. By this time it had changed out of recognition. The complex regained its role as an active cultural centre when the monastery, embracing Palladio's cloisters, refectory and library, was purchased in 1951 by Count Vittorio Cini (*see p134*). Today it is a thriving centre of Venetian culture with international events and exhibitions. There is also an evocative open-air theatre.

Cloisters designed by Palladio in the monastery of San Giorgio Maggiore

Palladio's church of San Giorgio Maggiore on the island of the same name

SAN POLO AND SANTA CROCE

The *sestieri* of San Polo and Santa Croce, bordered by the upper sweep of the Grand Canal, were both named after churches which stood within their boundaries. The first inhabitants are said to have settled on the cluster of small islands called *Rivus Altus* (high bank) or Rialto. When markets were established in the 11th century, the quarter became the commercial hub of Venice. San Polo is still one of the liveliest *sestieri* of the city, with its market stalls, small shops and

Shuttered window in Campo Sant'Aponal

local bars. The bustle of the market gives way to a maze of narrow alleys opening on to squares. Focal points are the spacious Campo San Polo, the Frari church and the neighbouring Scuola di San Rocco. Santa Croce for the most part is a *sestiere* of very narrow, tightly packed streets and squares where you will see the humbler side of Venetian life. Its grandest *palazzi* line the Grand Canal. Less alluring is the Piazzale Roma, the city's giant car park, lying to the west.

SIGHTS AT A GLANCE

Churches
San Cassiano ❹
San Giacomo dell'Orio ⓮
San Giacomo di Rialto ❷
San Giovanni Evangelista ⓭
San Nicolò da Tolentino ⓬
San Pantalon ⓫
San Polo ❻
San Rocco ❿
San Stae ⓰
Santa Maria Gloriosa dei Frari pp102–3 ❽

Museums and Galleries
Ca' Mocenigo ⓱
Ca' Pesaro ⓲
Casa di Goldoni ❼
Fondaco dei Turchi (Natural History Museum) ⓯
Scuola Grande di San Rocco pp106–7 ❾

Streets and Squares
Campo San Polo ❺

Bridges
Rialto Bridge ❶

Markets
Rialto Markets ❸

KEY

- ■ Street-by-Street map See pp98–9
- Vaporetto boarding point
- Traghetto crossing

0 metres 250

0 yards 250

◁ **Ponte del Megio, in a quiet corner of Santa Croce**

Street-by-Street: San Polo

The Rialto bridge and markets make
this a magnet for tourists. Traditionally
the city's commercial quarter, it was
here that bankers, brokers and
merchants conducted their affairs.
Streets are no longer lined with stalls
selling spices and fine fabrics, but the
food markets and pasta shops are a
colourful sight. The old-fashioned
standing-only bars called *bacari* are
packed with locals. In contrast, Riva
del Vin to the south, by the Grand
Canal, is strictly tourist territory.

San Cassiano
*Inside this church is
a carved altar (1696)
and a* Crucifixion
*by Tintoretto
(1568)* ❹

Ponte Storto
*is crooked, like
many bridges in
the city. It leads
under a portico to
Calle Stretta, a narrow
alley that is only 1 m (3
ft) wide in places.*

Sant'Aponal,
*founded in the 11th
century, rebuilt in
the 15th, is now
deconsecrated.
Gothic reliefs
decorate the façade.*

Riva del Vin,
*where wine was offloaded
from boats, is one of the few
accessible quaysides along
the Grand Canal.*

San Silvestro

STAR SIGHTS

★ Rialto Markets

★ Rialto Bridge

★ Rialto Markets
The Rialto markets have been in operation for centuries. The Pescheria (above) sells fresh fish and seafood, and the Erberia sells fruit and vegetables ❸

LOCATOR MAP
See Street Finder, maps 2, 3, 7

The statue of Gobbo of the Rialto, the hunchback, was sculpted in 1541 *(see p100).*

Rialto Mercato

San Giacomo di Rialto
Since its installation in 1410, the clock on this church has been a notoriously poor time-keeper ❷

KEY

– – – Suggested route

0 metres	75
0 yards	75

Calle della Madonna looks distinctly medieval with its overhanging first floors.

★ Rialto Bridge
A beloved landmark of the Grand Canal, the bridge marks the geographical centre of the city. The balustrades afford fine views of the canal ❶

Rialto Bridge ❶

Ponte di Rialto. **Map** 7 A1. 🚤 *Rialto.*

The Rialto bridge has been a busy part of the city for centuries. At any time of day you will find swarms of crowds jostling on the bridge, browsing among the souvenirs or taking a break to watch the constant swirl of activity on the Grand Canal from the bridge's balustrades.

Stone bridges were built in Venice as early as the 12th century, but it was not until 1588, after the collapse, decay or sabotage of earlier wooden structures, that a solid stone bridge was designed for the Rialto. One of the early wood crossings collapsed in 1444 under the weight of spectators at the wedding ceremony of the Marchese di Ferrara.

Vittore Carpaccio's painting *The Healing of the Madman* (1496, *see p133*) in the Accademia shows the fourth bridge – a rickety-looking structure with a drawbridge for the tall-masted galleys. By the 16th

Busy canalside restaurant near the Rialto Bridge

century this was in a sad state of decay and a competition was held for the design of a new bridge to be built in stone. Michelangelo, Andrea Palladio and Jacopo Sansovino were among the eminent contenders, but after months of deliberation it was the aptly named Antonio da Ponte who won the commission. The bridge was built between 1588 and 1591 and, until 1854, when the Accademia Bridge was constructed, this remained the only means of crossing the Grand Canal on foot.

San Giacomo di Rialto ❷

Campo San Giacomo, San Polo.
Map 3 A5. **Tel** 041 522 47 45.
🚤 *Rialto, San Silvestro.* ⬜ 9am–noon, 4–6pm daily. 🕯 *during mass.*

The first church to stand on this site was allegedly founded in the 5th century, making it the oldest church in Venice. The present building dates from the 11th–12th centuries, with major restoration in 1601. The original Gothic portico and huge 24-hour clock are the most striking features.

The crouching stone figure on the far side of the square is the so-called Gobbo (hunchback) of the Rialto. In the 16th century this was a welcome sight for minor offenders who were forced to run the gauntlet from Piazza San Marco to this square at the Rialto.

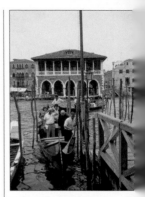

***Traghetto* ferrying passengers across to the Erberia**

Rialto Markets ❸

San Polo. **Map** 3 A5. 🚤 *Rialto.*
Erberia *(fruit and vegetable market) until noon Mon–Sat,* **Pescheria** *(fish market) until noon Tue–Sat.*

Venetians have come to the Erberia to buy fresh produce for hundreds of years. Heavily laden barges arrive at dawn and offload their crates on to the quayside by the Grand Canal. Local produce includes red radicchio from Treviso, and succulent asparagus and baby artichokes from the islands of Sant'Erasmo and Vignole *(see p149)*. In the adjoining fish market are sole, sardines, skate, squid, crabs, clams and other species of seafood and fish. To see it all in full swing you must arrive early in the morning – by noon the vendors are packing up.

RIALTO BRIDGE

Until the 19th century this was the only link between the two sides of the Grand Canal.

The central thoroughfare is lined with two rows of shops.

External balustraded footpath

The height of 7.5 m (24 ft) enabled galleys to pass below.

Single arch span of 48 m (157 ft)

San Cassiano ❹

Campo San Cassiano, San Polo.
Map 2 F5. *Tel 041 721 408.* 🚤 *San Stae.* 🕐 *9am–noon, 5–7pm Mon–Sat; 9am–noon Sun (not during mass).*

The Medieval Church of San Cassiano is a bizarre mix of architectural styles. Of the original church, which was restored in the 19th century, only the campanile survives. The highlight of the interior is Jacopo Tintoretto's immensely powerful *Crucifixion* (1568), which is in the sacristy.

The campo in which the church stands was notorious for prostitutes in the 1500s.

Campo San Polo ❺

Map 6 F1. 🚤 *San Silvestro.*

The spacious square of San Polo has traditionally been host to spectacular events. As far back as the 15th century it was the venue for festivities, masquerades, ceremonies, balls and bullbaiting

The most dramatic event was the assassination of Lorenzino de' Medici in 1548. He had taken refuge in Venice after brutally killing his cousin Alessandro, Duke of Florence. Lorenzino was stabbed in the square by two assassins who were in the service of Cosimo de' Medici, and both were handsomely rewarded by the Florentine duke.

On the eastern side of the square is the beautiful Gothic Palazzo Soranzo. This was originally two palaces – the one on the left is the older. The building is still owned by the Soranzo family.

Palazzo Corner Mocenigo, which is situated in the northwest corner (No. 2128), was once the residence of the eccentric English writer Frederick Rolfe (1860–1913), alias Baron Corvo. He was thrown out of his lodgings when his English hostess read his manuscript of *The Desire and Pursuit of the Whole* – a cruel satirization of English society in Venice.

A detail of the Gothic façade of Palazzo Soranzo, Campo San Polo

Since 1979 the square has enjoyed a revival of Carnival festivities. This wide open space is also a haven for local youngsters, who ride bikes, rollerskate or play football. Such activities would not have gone down well in the 17th century – a plaque on the apse of the church, dated 1611, forbids all games (or selling merchandise) on pain of prison, galley service or exile.

San Polo ❻

Campo San Polo. **Map** 6 F1. *Tel 041 275 04 62.* 🚤 *San Silvestro.* 🕐 *10am–5pm daily (from 1pm Sun & public hols).* 🔘 *Sun (Jul & Aug); 1 Jan, 25 Dec.* 🏛🕐❌🏛

Founded in the 9th century, rebuilt in the 15th and revamped in the early 19th in Neo-Classical style, the church of San Polo lacks any sense of homogeneity. Yet it is worth visiting for individual features such as the lovely Gothic portal and the Romanesque lions at the foot of the 14th-century campanile – one holds a serpent between its paws, the other a human head.

Inside, follow the signs for the *Via Crucis del Tiepolo* – fourteen canvases of the Stations of the

A lion at the foot of the campanile, Church of San Polo

Cross by Giandomenico Tiepolo. The church also has paintings by Veronese, Palma il Giovane (the Younger) and a dark and dramatic *Last Supper* by Tintoretto.

Carlo Goldoni 1707–93

Casa di Goldoni ❼

Palazzo Centani, Calle dei Nomboli, San Polo 2794. **Map** 6 E1. *Tel 041 244 03 17.* 🚤 *San Tomà.* 🕐 *10am–4pm Thu–Tue (5pm Apr–Oct).* 🔘 *public hols.* 🏛🏛♿

Carlo Goldoni, one of the city's favourite sons, wrote over 250 comedies, many based on Commedia dell'Arte figures. Goldoni was born in the beautiful Gothic Palazzo Centani (or Zantani) in 1707. The house, which has recently been restored, was left to the city in 1931 and is now a centre for theatrical studies and has a collection of theatrical memorabilia. The enchanting courtyard has a 15th-century open stairway and a magnificent wellhead, which features carved lions and a coat of arms bearing a hedgehog.

Santa Maria Gloriosa dei Frari 🔵

Known by all simply as the Frari (a corruption of *Frati*, meaning brothers), this huge, plain Gothic church dwarfs the eastern section of San Polo. The first church was built by Franciscan friars in 1250–1338, but was replaced by a larger building which was completed by the mid-15th century. The interior is striking for its sheer size and for the quality of its works of art. These include masterpieces by Titian and Giovanni Bellini *(see pp26–7)*, a statue by Donatello and a number of imposing monuments to famous Venetians.

Foscari Monument
Doge Foscari set a record by reigning for 34 years (1423–57).

The campanile is 80 m (262 ft) high, the tallest in the city after that of San Marco.

★ Assumption of the Virgin
Titian's glowing and spectacular work (1518) inevitably draws the eye through the monk's choir towards the altar.

Rood Screen *(1475)*
Pietro Lombardo and Bartolomeo Bon carved this and decorated it with marble figures.

Madonna di Ca' Pesaro (1526) shows Titian's mastery of light and colour.

★ Monks' Choir
This consists of three-tiered stalls (1468), carved with bas-reliefs of saints and Venetian city scenes.

FLOORPLAN

Exploration of the huge interior can be daunting. The floorplan pinpoints 12 highlights that should not be missed.

KEY TO FLOORPLAN

1 Canova's tomb
2 Monument to Titian
3 Titian's *Madonna di Ca' Pesaro*
4 Choir stalls
5 Corner Chapel
6 Tomb of Monteverdi
7 Tomb of Doge Nicolò Tron
8 High altar with Titian's *Assumption of the Virgin*
9 Tomb of Doge Francesco Foscari
10 Donatello's *John the Baptist* (c.1450)
11 B Vivarini's altar painting (1474), Bernardo Chapel
12 Giovanni Bellini's *Madonna Enthroned with Saints* (1488)

VISITORS' CHECKLIST

Campo dei Frari. **Map** 6 D1.
Tel 041 275 04 62. 🚌 San
Tomà. ⬜ 10am–6pm Mon–Sat,
1–6pm Sun & religious hols.
⬛ 1 Jan, 25 Dec. 🔗 except
for those attending mass.
🚫 📷 ⛪ frequent.

Monument to Titian *(1853)*
Canova's pupils, Luigi and Pietro Zandomeneghi, built this monument to Titian in place of the one conceived by Canova himself.

The former monastery,
which houses the State Archives, has two cloisters, one in the style of Sansovino, another designed by Palladio.

Entrance

Canova's Tomb
Canova designed, but never actually made, a Neo-Classical marble pyramid like this as a monument for Titian. After Canova's death in 1822, his pupils used a similar design for their master's tomb.

STAR FEATURES

★ Monks' Choir

★ Assumption of the Virgin by Titian

Scuola Grande di San Rocco ➒

See pp106–7.

San Rocco ➓

Campo San Rocco, San Polo. **Map** 6 D1.
Tel 041 523 48 64. ⬛ San Tomà.
◯ Apr–Oct: 8am–12:30pm, 3–5pm
daily; Nov–Mar: 8am–12:30pm Mon–
Fri, 3–5pm Sat, Sun & public hols.

Sharing the little square with the celebrated Scuola Grande di San Rocco is the church of the same name. Designed by Bartolomeo Bon in 1489 and largely rebuilt in 1725, the exterior is a mix of architectural styles. The façade was added in 1765–71.

Inside, the main interest lies in Tintoretto's paintings in the chancel, which depict scenes from the life of St Roch, patron saint of contagious diseases. Of these the most notable is *St Roch Curing the Plague Victims* (1549).

San Pantalon ⓫

Campo San Pantalon, Dorsoduro.
Map 6 D2. **Tel** 041 523 58 93. ⬛
San Tomà, Piazzale Roma. ◯
7.30am–12.30pm, 4–6pm Mon–Sat.

Fumiani's ceiling painting (1680–1704), San Pantalon

The overwhelming feature of this late 17th-century church is the painted ceiling, dark, awe-inspiring and remarkable for its illusionistic effects. The ceiling comprises a total of 40 scenes (admirers claim this makes it the world's largest work of art on canvas), depicting the martyrdom and apotheosis of the physician St Pantalon. The artist, Gian Antonio Fumiani, took 24 years (1680–1704) to achieve this masterpiece, but then he allegedly fell to his death from the scaffolding.

Paolo Veronese's emotive painting *St Pantalon Healing a Boy* (second chapel on the right) was his final work of art (1587). To see Antonio Vivarini and Giovanni d'Alemagna's *Coronation of the Virgin* (1444) and *The Annunciation* (1350), attributed to Paolo Veneziano, ask the custodian for access to the Chapel of the Holy Nail *(Cappella del Sacro Chiodo).*

San Nicolò da Tolentino ⓬

Campo dei Tolentini, Santa Croce.
Map 5 C1. **Tel** 041 522 21 60.
⬛ Piazzale Roma. ◯ 8am–noon,
4–7pm daily. 🔘 during mass.

Close to Piazzale Roma *(see p271)*, San Nicolò da Tolentino is an imposing 17th-century church with a Classical portico. The interior, decorated with 17th-century paintings, is the resting place of Francesco Morosini (d.1678), the Venetian patriarch.

A cannonball embedded in the façade is a memento of an Austrian bombardment during the siege of 1849.

San Giovanni Evangelista ⓭

Campiello de la Scuola, San Polo. **Map**
6 D1. **Tel** 041 71 82 34. ⬛ San
Tomà. ◯ phone for an appointment.

A confraternity of flagellents founded the Scuola of St John the Evangelist in 1261. The complex, just north of the Frari *(see pp102–3),* has a church, *scuola* and courtyard. Separating the square from the street is Pietro Lombardo's elegant white and grey screen and portal (1480), and in the arch crowning the portal

Lombardo's marble screen and portal, San Giovanni Evangelista

there is carved eagle, which is the symbol representing St John the Evangelist.

The main hall of the Scuola is reached via a splendid 15th-century double stairway by Mauro Coducci (1498). Large, dark canvases decorate the ceiling and walls of the 18th-century hall. The Scuola's greatest art treasure, the cycle of paintings depicting *The Stories of the Cross,* is now on display in the Accademia gallery *(see p133).* It formerly embellished the oratory (off the main hall) where the Reliquary of the True Cross is still carefully preserved.

San Giacomo dell'Orio ⓮

Campo San Giacomo dell'Orio,
Santa Croce. **Map** 2 E5. **Tel** 041
275 04 62. ⬛ Riva di Biasio or San
Stae. ◯ 10am–5pm daily (from
1pm Sun & public hols). 🔘 Sun
(Jul & Aug); 1 Jan, 25 Dec. 🖾 🔲 🚫

This church is a focal point of a quiet quarter of Santa Croce. The name "dell'Orio" (locally dall'Orio) may derive from a laurel tree *(alloro)* that once stood near the church.

Founded in the 9th century, rebuilt in 1225 and repeatedly modified, the church is a mix of architectural styles. The campanile, basilica ground plan and Byzantine columns survive from the 13th century. The ship's keel roof and the columns are from the Gothic period, and the apses are Renaissance. The sacristy ceiling was decorated by Veronese and there are some interesting altar paintings.

Fondaco dei Turchi ⑮

Canal Grande, Santa Croce 1730. **Map** 2 E4. **Tel** 041 275 02 06. *San Stae.* 9am–1pm Tue–Fri, 10am–4pm Sat–Sun.

The building that now contains Venice's natural history museum has a chequered history. In the 13th century it was one of the largest *palazzi* on the Grand Canal. In 1381 it was bought by the state for the Dukes of Ferrara and its lavishly decorated rooms were used for banquets and state functions. In 1621 the Turks set up a warehouse (*fondaco*), and the spacious portico was used for loading merchandise. As commerce with the Orient declined further, the structure fell into disrepair until, roused by Ruskin's passionate interest, the Austrians began restoration work in the 1850s.

Since 1924 the Fondaco has housed the natural history museum (Museo di Storia Naturale). There is a collection of stuffed animals, crustacea and dinosaur fossils and a section on lagoon life. Prize exhibits include a skeleton of an *Ouranosaurus nigeriensis*, 7 m (23 ft) long and 3.6 m (12 ft) tall, and a fossil of an *Sarcosuchus imperator* – an ancestor of the crocodile.

Ouranosaurus skeleton in the Fondaco dei Turchi

San Stae ⑯

Campo San Stae, Santa Croce. **Map** 2 F4. **Tel** 041 275 0462. *San Stae.* 10am–5pm (from 1pm Sun). Sun (Jul & Aug); 1 Jan, 25 Dec.

Restored in 1977–8 by the Pro Venezia Foundation, San Stae (or Sant'Eustachio) has a spick-and-span sculpted façade. It was built in 1709 by Domenico Rossi. Works by Piazzetta, Tiepolo and other 18th-century artists decorate the chancel. Near the second altar on the left is the bust of Antonio Foscarini, executed for treason in 1622 but pardoned the following year.

One of the finely furnished rooms of Ca' Mocenigo

Ca' Mocenigo ⑰

Salizzada San Stae, Santa Croce 1992. **Map** 2 F5. **Tel** 041 72 17 98. *San Stae.* 10am–5pm Tue–Sun (to 4pm Nov–Mar). 1 Jan, 1 May, 25 Dec.

One of the oldest and greatest of all Venetian families, the Mocenigos produced seven doges. There were various branches of the family, one of which resided in this handsome 17th-century mansion. Count Alvise Nicolò Mocenigo, the last of this particular branch, died in 1954, bequeathing the palace to the Comune di Venezia (city authorities).

The entrance façade is unremarkable, but the interior is elegantly furnished and gives you a rare opportunity of seeing inside a *palazzo* preserved more or less as it was in the 18th century. The frescoed ceilings and other works of art are celebrations of the family's achievements. The illustrious Mocenigos are portrayed in a frieze around the portego on the first floor.

The Museo del Tessuto e del Costume inside the house contains antique fabrics and exquisitely made costumes.

Ca' Pesaro ⑱

Canal Grande, Santa Croce 2076. **Map** 2 F5. *San Stae.* **Galleria d'Arte Moderna Tel** 041 524 06 95. **Museo Orientale Tel** 041 524 11 73. 10am–6pm Tue–Sun (Nov–Mar: to 5pm); ticket office closes one hour earlier. 1 Jan, 1 May, 25 Dec. combined ticket.

It took 58 years to complete this magnificent Baroque palace. Built for the Pesaro family, it was the masterpiece of Baldassare Longhena, who worked on it until his death in 1682. Antonio Gaspari then took over Longhena's design, eventually completing the structure in 1710.

In the 19th century the Duchess of Bevilacqua La Masa bequeathed the palace to the city for exhibiting the works of unestablished Venetian artists. The Galleria d'Arte Moderna was founded in 1897. Today this features a permanent exhibition of work by artists such as Bonnard, Matisse, Miró, Klee, Klimt and Kandinsky, in addition to works by Italian artists of the 19th and 20th centuries.

The Museo Orientale has an idiosyncratic collection of Chinese and Japanese artifacts collected by the Count of Bardi during his 19th-century travels.

Gustav Klimt's *Salome*, **Gallery of Modern Art, Ca' Pesaro**

Scuola Grande di San Rocco ⑨

Pianta's caricature of Tintoretto

Founded in honour of St Roch (San Rocco), the Scuola was set up as a charitable institution for the sick. Construction began in 1515 under Bartolomeo Bon and was completed in 1549 by Scarpagnino, financed largely by donations from Venetians who believed that St Roch, the patron saint of contagious diseases, would save them from the plague. In 1564 Tintoretto *(see p140)* was commissioned to decorate the walls and ceilings of the Scuola. His remarkable cycle of paintings starts in the Sala dell'Albergo *(see Gallery Guide)*.

Restored main entrance to the Scuola di San Rocco

SALA DELL'ALBERGO

THE CRUCIFIXION
In this panorama of Calvary, Tintoretto reached a pitch of religious feeling never hitherto achieved in Venetian art.

A self-portrait was often a feature of Tintoretto's paintings.

The subsidiary figures are full of life but do not lessen the central drama.

Figure of Christ
The crucified figure of the Redeemer is raised and leaning, accentuating His divinity and saving grace.

A competition was held in 1564 to select an artist to paint the central ceiling panel of the Sala dell'Albergo in the Scuola. To the fury of his rivals, Tintoretto pre-empted his fellow competitors by installing his painting *in situ* prior to judging. He won the commission and was later made a member of the Scuola. Over the next 23 years, Tintoretto decorated the entire building.

The series of paintings, completed in 1587, reveals Tintoretto's revolutionary use of light, mastery of foreshortening and visionary use of colour. The winning painting, *St Roch in Glory* ①, can be seen on the ceiling

of the Sala dell'Albergo. The most moving work in the cycle is the *Crucifixion* (1565) ②. Henry James wrote: "Surely no single picture contains more of human life; there is everything in it, including the most exquisite beauty." Of the paintings on the entrance wall, portraying the Passion of Christ, the most notable is *Christ Before Pilate* (1566–7) ③.

Sala dell'Albergo

UPPER HALL

Scarpagnino's great staircase (1544–6), decorated with two vast paintings commemorating the plague of 1630, leads to the Upper Hall. The biblical subjects on the walls and ceiling were painted in 1575–81. The ceiling paintings (viewed most comfortably with a hired mirror) portray scenes from the Old Testament. The three large central square paintings represent: *Moses Striking Water from the Rock* ④, *The Miracle of the Bronze Serpent* ⑤ and *The Gathering of the Manna* ⑥, all alluding to the Scuola's charitable aims in alleviating thirst, sickness and hunger respectively. All three paintings are crowded compositions with much violent movement. The vast wall paintings in the hall feature episodes from the

New Testament. The most striking paintings are *The Temptation of Christ* ⑦, which shows a handsome young Satan offering Christ two loaves of bread, and *Adoration of the Shepherds* ⑧. Like *The Temptation of Christ*, the *Adoration* is composed in two halves, with a female figure, shepherds and ox below, and the Holy Family and onlookers above.

The beautiful carvings below the paintings were added in the 17th century by Francesco Pianta. The allegorical figures include (near the altar) a caricature of Tintoretto with his palette and brushes, which is meant to represent Painting. Near the entrance to the Sala dell'Albergo you can see Titian's *Annunciation*. The easel painting *Christ Carrying the Cross* is attributed to Giorgione, though many believe it to be a Titian.

VISITORS' CHECKLIST

Campo San Rocco.
Map 6 D1. **Tel** *041 523 48 64.*
San Tomà. Apr–Oct:
9am–5:30pm daily; Nov–Mar:
10am–5pm daily. 1 Jan,
Easter, 25 Dec.

GROUND FLOOR HALL

The Flight into Egypt (1582–7)
(detail)

This final cycle, executed in 1583–7, consists of eight paintings illustrating the life of Mary. The series starts with an *Annunciation*, and ends with an *Assumption*, which was restored some years ago. The tranquil scenes of *St Mary of Egypt* ⑨, *St Mary Magdalene* ⑩ and *The Flight into Egypt* ⑪, painted when Tintoretto was in his late sixties, are remarkable for their serenity. This is portrayed most lucidly by the Virgin's isolated spiritual contemplation in the *St Mary of Egypt*. In all three paintings, the landscapes, rendered with rapid strokes, play a major role.

The Temptation of Christ, 1578–81 (detail)

GALLERY GUIDE

The paintings, which unfortunately are not well lit, have no labels, but a useful plan of the Scuola is available (in several languages) free of charge at the entrance.

To see the paintings in chronological order, start in the Sala dell'Albergo (off the Upper Hall), followed by the Upper Hall and finally the Ground Floor Hall.

Main entrance

Upper Hall

Ground Floor Hall

KEY

Wall paintings

Ceiling paintings

CASTELLO

The largest *sestiere* of the city, Castello stretches from San Marco and Cannaregio in the west to the modern blocks of Sant'Elena in the east. The area takes its name from the 8th-century fortress that once stood on what is now San Pietro, the island which for centuries was the religious focus of the city. The church here was the episcopal see from the 9th century and the city's cathedral from 1451

Water stoup, Santa Maria Formosa

to 1807. The industrial hub of Castello was the Arsenale, where the great shipyards produced Venice's indomitable fleet of warships. Castello's most popular and solidly commercial area is the Riva degli Schiavoni promenade. Behind the waterfront it is comparatively quiet, characterized by narrow alleys, elegantly faded *palazzi* and fine churches, including the great Santi Giovanni e Paolo *(see pp116–17)*.

SIGHTS AT A GLANCE

Churches
La Pietà ❸
San Francesco della Vigna ⓮
San Giorgio dei Greci ❷
San Giovanni in Bragora ⓱
San Lorenzo ⓯
Santi Giovanni e Paolo pp116–17 ⓬
San Zaccaria ❶

Historic Buildings and Monuments
Arsenale ⓳
Hotel Danieli ❹
Ospedaletto ⓭
Statue of Colleoni ❿

Streets, Bridges and Squares
Campo Santa Maria Formosa ❾
Ponte della Paglia and Bridge of Sighs ❻
Riva degli Schiavoni ❺

Walk
Exploring Eastern Castello ⓴

Museums, Galleries and Scuole
Fondazione Querini Stampalia ❽
Museo Diocesano d'Arte Sacra ❼
Museo Storico Navale ⓲
Scuola di San Giorgio degli Schiavoni ⓰
Scuola Grande di San Marco ⓫

KEY

▢ Street-by-Street map
   See pp110–11

⚓ *Vaporetto* boarding point

0 metres   250

0 yards   250

◁ **Bas relief on Rio Terrà Garibaldi, eastern Castello**

Street-by-Street: Castello

A stroll along the Riva degli Schiavoni is an integral part of a visit to Venice. Glorious views of San Giorgio Maggiore compensate for the commercialized aspects of the quayside: souvenir stalls, excursion touts and an overabundance of tourists. Associations with literary figures are legion. Petrarch lived at No. 4145, Henry James was offered "dirty" lodgings at No. 4161, and Ruskin stayed at the Hotel Danieli. Inland, the quiet, unassuming streets and squares of Castello provide a contrast to the bustling waterfront.

13th-century Madonna in the Museo Diocesano

Palazzo Trevisan-Cappello, used as a showroom for Murano glass, was the home of Bianca Cappello, wife of Francesco de' Medici.

★ Museo Diocesano
The cloisters of the ancient Benedictine monastery of Sant'Apollonia herald the museum **⑦**

CAMPO SS
FILIPPO E GIACOMO

CALLE DRIO LA CHIESA

SALIZZADA SAN PI

RIO DEL PALAZZO

CALLE DEGLI ALBANESI

CALLE DELLE RASSE

RIO DEL VIN

Ponte della Paglia and Bridge of Sighs
Crowds throng the Istrian stone Ponte della Paglia – the "straw bridge" – for the best views of the neighbouring Bridge of Sighs, the covered bridge that links the Doge's Palace to the old prisons **⑥**

Riva degli Schiavoni
This paved quayside was established over 600 years ago, and widened in 1782 **⑤**

RIVA DEGLI
SCHIAVONI

San Zaccaria
Paglia

San Zaccaria
Danieli

STAR SIGHTS

★ Museo Diocesano

★ San Zaccaria

★ La Pietà

Hotel Danieli
Joseph da Niel, after whom this hotel was named, turned the Palazzo Dandolo into a haunt for 19th-century writers and artists **④**

Palazzo Priuli,
*overlooking the quiet
Fondamenta Osmarin, is a
fine Venetian Gothic palace.
The corner window is
particularly beautiful, but the
early 16th-century façade
frescoes have long since
disappeared.*

LOCATOR MAP
See Street Finder, maps 7, 8

San Giorgio dei Greci
*Subsidence is the cause of the
city's tilting bell-towers: San
Giorgio dei Greci's looks
particularly perilous* ❷

★ **San Zaccaria**
*Coducci added Renaissance
details such as this panel to
the Gothic façade* ❶

KEY

– – – Suggested route

0 metres   75
0 yards   75

Map labels:
RIO SAN PROVOLO
FMTA DELL OSMARIN
CALLE DEI GRECI
CAMPO SAN ZACCARIA
RIO DEI GRECI
CALLE BOSELLO
CALLE DELLA PIETA
RIVA DEGLI SCHIAVONI
Zaccaria anda
MVE

Pensione Wildner
is where Henry
James completed
Portrait of a Lady
(1881).

**The Statue of
Vittorio
Emanuele II,**
*the first king
of a united Italy, was
sculpted by Ettore
Ferrari in 1887.*

★ **La Pietà**
*In Vivaldi's day, the church became
famous for the superb quality of its
musical performances* ❸

San Zaccaria ❶

Campo San Zaccaria. **Map** 8 D2. **Tel** 041 522 12 57. 🚤 San Zaccaria. ⏱ 10am–noon, 4–6pm Mon–Sat; 4–6pm Sun & public hols. 🎫 Chapels & Crypt.

Set in a quiet square just a stone's throw from the Riva degli Schiavoni, the church of San Zaccaria is a successful blend of Flamboyant Gothic and Classical Renaissance styles. Founded in the 9th century, it was completely rebuilt between 1444 and 1515. Antonio Gambello began the façade in Gothic style and, when Gambello died in 1481, Mauro Coducci completed the upper section, adding all the Classical detail.

The adjoining Benedictine convent, which had close links with the church, became quite notorious for the riotous behaviour of its nuns. The majority were from families of Venetian nobility, many of them sent to the convent to avoid the expense of a dowry.

Every Easter the doge came with his entourage to San Zaccaria – a custom which originated as an expression of gratitude to the nuns, who had relinquished part of their garden so that Piazza San Marco could be enlarged.

The artistic highlight of the interior (illuminate with coins in the meter) is Giovanni Bellini's sumptuously coloured and superbly serene *Madonna and Child with Saints* (1505) in the north aisle.

On the right of the church is a door to the Chapel of St Athanasius which leads to the Chapel of San Tarasio. The chapel is decorated with vault frescoes (1442) by Andrea del Castagno of Florence, and Gothic polyptychs painted in 1443–4 by Antonio Vivarini and Giovanni d'Alemagna. The relics of eight doges lie buried in the waterlogged crypt.

Distant view of San Giorgio dei Greci's tilting campanile

San Giorgio dei Greci ❷

Map 8 D2. **Tel** 041 523 95 69. 🚤 San Zaccaria. ⏱ 9am–12:30pm, 1:30–4:30pm Mon–Sat, 10am–5pm Sun. **Museo dell'Icone Tel** 041 522 65 81. ⏱ 9am–5pm daily. 🎫 🚫

The most remarkable feature of this 16th-century Greek church is the listing campanile, which looks as if it is about to topple into the Rio dei Greci. Inside is the *matroneo* – the gallery where, in keeping with Greek Orthodox custom, the women sat apart from the men. Note also the iconostasis separating the sanctuary from the nave. The nearby Scuola di San Nicolò dei Greci, redesigned in 1678, is now the museum of icons of the Hellenic Institute.

La Pietà ❸

Riva degli Schiavoni. **Map** 8 D2. **Tel** 041 522 21 71. 🚤 San Zaccaria. ⏱ 10am–noon, 3–5pm daily.

The church of La Pietà (or Santa Maria della Visitazione) dates from the 15th century. It was rebuilt in 1745–1760 by Giorgio Massari, and the Classical façade was added in 1906. The church has a cool, elegant interior, with an oval plan. The resplendent ceiling fresco, *Triumph of Faith* (1755), was painted by Giambattista Tiepolo.

The Pietà started its life as a foundling home for orphans. It proved so popular that a warning plaque was set up (still to be seen on the side wall), threatening damnation to parents who tried to pass off their children as orphans.

From 1703 until 1740 Antonio Vivaldi directed the musical groups and wrote numerous oratorios, cantatas and vocal pieces for the Pietà choir, and the church became famous for its performances.

Today the church is a popular venue for concerts – with a strong emphasis on the music of Vivaldi. These are held throughout the year, usually on Mondays and Thursdays.

Bas relief on La Pietà's early 20th-century façade

Hotel Danieli ❹

Riva degli Schiavoni 4196. **Map** 7 C2. 🚤 San Zaccaria. See also **Where to Stay** p231.

One of the most celebrated hotels in Europe, the Danieli's deep pink façade is a landmark on the Riva degli Schiavoni. Built in the 14th century, it became famous as the venue for the first opera performed in Venice, Monteverdi's *Proserpina Rapita*

Detail from *The Nun's Parlour at San Zaccaria* by Francesco Guardi

For hotels and restaurants in this region see pp228–33 and pp242–7

(1630). The palace became a hotel in 1822 and soon gained popularity with the literary and artistic set. Its famous guests included Balzac, Proust, Dickens, Cocteau, Ruskin, Debussy and Wagner. In the 1830s Room 10 witnessed an episode in the love affair between the French poet and dramatist Alfred de Musset, and novelist George Sand: when de Musset fell ill after a surfeit of orgies, Sand ran off with her Venetian doctor.

Riva degli Schiavoni ❺

Map 8 D2. 🚤 *San Zaccaria.*

The sweeping promenade that forms the southern quayside of Castello was named after the traders from Dalmatia (Schiavonia) who used to moor their boats and barges here. For those who arrive in Venice by water, this long curving quayside is a spectacular introduction to the charms of the city.

At its western end, close to Piazza San Marco, the broad promenade teems during the day with tourists thronging around the souvenir stalls and people hurrying to and from the *vaporetto* stops. Nothing can detract, however, from the glorious views across the lagoon to the island of San Giorgio Maggiore *(see p95)*.

The Riva degli Schiavoni has always been busy with boats. Canaletto's drawings in the 1740s and 1750s show the Riva bustling with gondolas, sailing boats and barges. The gondolas are still here, but it is also chock-a-block with water taxis, *vaporetti*, excursion boats and tugs. Naval ships and ocean liners can also often be seen.

The modern annexe of the Hotel Danieli caused a great furore when it was built in 1948. Intruding on a waterfront graced by fine Venetian palaces and mansions, its stark outline is still something of an eyesore. The annexe marks the spot where Doge Vitale Michiel II was

Riva degli Schiavoni – the city's most famous promenade

stabbed to death in 1172. Three centuries earlier, in 864, Doge Pietro Tradonico had suffered the same fate in nearby Campo San Zaccaria.

Ponte della Paglia and Bridge of Sighs ❻

Map 7 C2. 🚤 *San Zaccaria.*

The name of the Ponte della Paglia may derive from the boats that once moored here to off-load their cargoes of straw *(paglia)*. Originally built in 1360, the existing structure dates from 1847.

According to legend the Bridge of Sighs, built in 1600 to link the Doge's Palace with the new prisons, takes its name from the lamentations of the prisoners as they made their way over to the offices

Ponte della Paglia behind the Bridge of Sighs

of the feared State Inquisitors. Access to the bridge is available to the public via the Doge's Palace *(see p87)*.

Museo Diocesano d'Arte Sacra ❼

Sant'Apollonia, Ponte della Canonica, Castello 4312. **Map** 7 C2. *Tel* 041 522 91 66. 🚤 *San Zaccaria.* ⭕ 10am–6pm daily. ⬤ *public hols.* 📷 *includes entry to cloisters.*

One of the architectural gems of Venice, the cloister of Sant'Apollonia is the only Romanesque building in the city. Only a few steps from St Mark's, the cloister provides a quiet retreat from the hubbub of the Piazza.

The monastery was once the home of Benedictine monks, but its non-ecclesiastical uses have been manifold. In 1976 its cloisters became the home of the diocesan museum of sacred art, founded in order to provide a haven for works of art from closed or deconsecrated churches. The collection includes paintings, statues, crucifixes and many pieces of valuable silver. The museum has two workshops, staffed by volunteers who restore the paintings and statues. The collection is ever-changing, but among the major permanent exhibits are works by Luca Giordano (1634–1705), which came from the Church of Sant'Aponal, and a 16th-century wood and crystal tabernacle.

Fondazione Querini Stampalia **8**

Campo Santa Maria Formosa, 5252 Castello. **Map** 7 C1. **Tel** 041 271 14 11. 🚉 San Zaccaria. **Palace** ◯ 10am–8pm Tue–Sat, 10am–7pm Sun. ◉ Mon. 🖪 🖾 🖾 🖵 **Library** ◯ 10am–midnight Tue–Sat, 10am–7pm Sun.

The large Palazzo Querini Stampalia was commissioned in the 16th century by the descendants of the old Venetian Querini family. Great art lovers, they filled the palace with fine paintings.

In 1868 the last member of the dynasty bequeathed the palace and the family collection of art to the foundation that bears his name. The paintings include works by Giovanni Bellini, Giambattista Tiepolo, and some vignettes by Pietro and Alessandro Longhi. The library on the first floor, which is open to the public, contains over 200,000 books.

Campo Santa Maria Formosa **9**

Campo Santa Maria Formosa. **Map** 7 C1. 🚉 Rialto, Fondamente Nuove. **Church Tel** 041 275 04 62. ◯ 10am–5pm daily (from 1pm Sun). ◉ Sun (Jul &Aug); 1 Jan, 25 Dec. 🔔 🖾 🚫

Large, rambling, and flanked by handsome palaces, this market square is one of the most characteristic *campi* of Venice. On the southern side is the church of Santa Maria Formosa, distinctive for its swelling apses. Built on ancient foundations, the church was designed by Mauro Coducci in 1492 but took over a century to assume its current form. Unusually, it has two main façades – one over-looking the *campo*, the other the canal. The campanile was added in 1688. Its most notable feature is the truly grotesque stone face that decorates its foot.

Inside, Palma il Vecchio's polyptych *St Barbara and Saints* (*c*.1523) ranks among the great Venetian master-pieces and looks particularly splendid since its restoration

by the American Save Venice organization. Palma's por-trayal of the handsome and dignified figure of St Barbara glorifies Venice's ideal female beauty. She is surrounded by saints, with a central lunette of the *pietà* above. St Barbara was the patron saint of soldiers: in wartime they prayed to her for protection, in victory they came for thanksgiving.

Statue of Colleoni **10**

Campo Santi Giovanni e Paolo. **Map** 3 C5. 🚉 Ospedale Civile.

Bartolomeo Colleoni, the famous *condottiere* or commander of mercenaries, left his fortune to the Republic on condition that his statue was placed in front of San Marco. A prominent statue in the Piazza would have broken with precedent, so the Senate cunningly had Colleoni raised before the Scuola di San Marco instead of the basilica. A touchstone of early Renais-sance sculpture, the equestrian statue of the proud warrior (1481–8) is by the Florentine

Statue of Bartolomeo Colleoni

Andrea Verrocchio and, after his death, was cast in bronze by Alessandro Leopardi. The statue has a strong sense of power and movement which arguably ranks it alongside works of Donatello.

Scuola Grande di San Marco **11**

Campo Santi Giovanni e Paolo. **Map** 3 C5. 🚉 Ospedale Civile. **Library Tel** 041 529 43 23. ◯ 8:30am–2pm Mon–Fri (ring bell). ◉ public hols, one week in mid-Aug, 24 Dec–1 Jan. **Church Tel** 041 522 56 62. ◯ 8am–noon Mon–Sat, 9–10am Sun.

Few hospitals can boast as rich and unusual a façade as that of Venice's Ospedale Civile. It was built originally as one of the six great confra-ternities of the city (*see p127*). Their first headquarters were destroyed by fire in 1485, but the Scuola was rebuilt at the end of the 15th century.

The delightful asymmetrical façade, with its arcades, marble panels and *trompe l'oeil* effects, was the work of Pietro Lom-bardo working in conjunction with Giovanni Buora. The upper order was finished by Mauro Coducci in 1495. The interior was revamped in the 19th century and, since then, most of the artistic master-pieces have been dispersed.

The library has a fine carved 16th-century ceiling, and the hospital chapel, the Church of San Lazzaro dei Mendicanti, contains an early Tintoretto and a work by Veronese.

Palma il Vecchio's St Barbara in Santa Maria Formosa

Santi Giovanni e Paolo ⑫

See pp116–17.

Ospedaletto ⑬

Calle Barbaria delle Tole, 6691 Castello.
Map 4 D5. **Tel** 041 532 29 20. 🚤
Ospedale Civile. ⏱ 3:30–6:30pm
Thu–Sat (3–6pm Nov–Feb). 📷 🎫

Beyond the south flank of Santi Giovanni e Paolo (see pp116–17) is the façade of the Ospedaletto or, more correctly, Santa Maria dei Derelitti. The Ospedaletto was set up by the Republic in 1527 as a charitable institution to care for the sick and aged, and to educate orphans and abandoned girls. Such an education consisted largely of the study of music. The girls became leading figures in choirs and orchestras, with concerts bringing in funds for the construction in 1776 of a *sala della musica*, which became the main performance venue. This elegant room features frescoes by Jacopo Guarana.

The church, which formed part of the Ospedaletto, was built by Andrea Palladio in 1575. Its façade was added in 1674 by Baldassare Longhena. The huge, hideous heads on the façade have been described as anti-Classical abominations, likened to diseased figures and swollen fruit. The interior of the church is decorated with

Fresco by Guarana in the *sala della musica* of the Ospedaletto

less provocative works of art and notable paintings from the 18th century, including *The Sacrifice of Isaac* (1720) by Giambattista Tiepolo.

San Francesco della Vigna ⑭

Ramo San Francesco. **Map** 8 E1.
Tel 041 520 61 02. 🚤 Celestia.
⏱ 8am–12:30pm, 3–7pm daily.

The name "della Vigna" derives from a vineyard that was bequeathed to the Franciscans in 1253. The church which the order built here in the 13th century was rebuilt under Jacopo Sansovino in 1534, with a façade added in 1562–72 by Palladio.

The interior has a rich collection of works of art, including sculpture by Alessandro Vittoria, Paolo Veronese's *The Holy Family with Saints* (1562) and Antonio da Negroponte's *Virgin and Child* (c.1450). The *Madonna and Child with Saints* (1507) by Giovanni Bellini hangs near the cloister.

The decorative façade of the Scuola Grande di San Marco

San Lorenzo ⑮

Campo San Lorenzo. **Map** 8 D1.
🚤 San Zaccaria. 🔵 for restoration.

Deconsecrated and closed for restoration, the church of San Lorenzo's only claim to fame is as the alleged burial place of Marco Polo (see p143). Unfortunately there is nothing to show for it because his sarcophagus disappeared during rebuilding in 1592. A collection of paintings was dispersed, and for many years the church was abandoned.

In 1987 restorers discovered the foundations of two earlier churches, dating from AD 850 and the late 12th century. The foundations of the present medieval structure, as well as substantial remains of the marble floor, have been damaged by water seeping in from the adjacent canal. Restoration work funded by the British Venice in Peril Fund has long been at a standstill.

Marco Polo

Santi Giovanni e Paolo ⑫

Figure in left transept

More familiarly known as San Zanipolo, Santi Giovanni e Paolo vies with the Frari *(see pp102–3)* as the city's greatest Gothic church. It was built in the late 13th to early 14th centuries by the Dominican friars, and is striking for its huge dimensions and architectural austerity. Known as the Pantheon of Venice, it houses monuments to no less than 25 doges. Many of these are outstanding works, executed by the Lombardi family and other leading sculptors of the day.

★ Cappella del Rosario
The Adoration of the Shepherds *is one of many works by Paolo Veronese which decorate the Rosary Chapel.*

The sacristy has paintings that celebrate the Dominican Order.

★ Tomb of Nicolò Marcello
This magnificent Renaissance monument to Doge Nicolò Marcello (d.1474) was sculpted by Pietro Lombardo.

The doorway, which is decorated with Byzantine reliefs, is one of the earliest Renaissance architectural features in Venice. The portico carvings are attributed to Bartolomeo Bon.

The marble columns were taken from a former church on the island of Torcello.

★ Tomb of Pietro Mocenigo
Pietro Lombardo's great masterpiece (1481) commemorates the doge's military pursuits when he was Grand Captain of the Venetian forces. This west side wall is largely devoted to Mocenigo monuments.

STAR SIGHTS

- ★ Doges' Tombs
- ★ Cappella del Rosario
- ★ Cappella di San Domenico

The bronze statue is a monument to Doge Sebastiano Venier, who was Commander of the Fleet at Lepanto.

The Baroque high altar is attributed to Baldassare Longhena.

★ **Tomb of Andrea Vendramin**
The nude figures of Lombardo's masterpiece (1476–8) were considered unsuitable and replaced by St Catherine and St Mary Magdalene (side statues).

The panel by Vivarini shows *Christ Bearing the Cross* (1474).

St Catherine of Siena's foot is buried here in a precious reliquary; her relics are scattered in churches throughout Italy.

The Nave
The vast interior is cross-vaulted, held by wooden tie-beams and supported by ten huge columns of Istrian stone blocks.

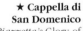

★ **Cappella di San Domenico**
Piazzetta's Glory of St Dominic for this chapel – his only ceiling painting – displays a mastery of colour, perspective and foreshortening. The artist had a profound influence on the young Tiepolo.

St George slaying the Dragon by Carpaccio, in the Scuola di San Giorgio degli Schiavoni

Scuola di San Giorgio degli Schiavoni ⓰

Calle Furlani, Castello 3959A.
Map 8 E1. **Tel** *041 522 88 28.*
🚤 *San Zaccaria.* ⃝ *Apr–Oct:
9:45am–1pm, 2:45–6pm Tue–Sun;
Nov–Mar: 10am–12:30pm, 3–6pm
Tue–Sun.* ⬤ *Sun pm, public hols &
special events.* 🎫 🚫

Within this surprisingly simple Scuola are some of the finest paintings of Vittore Carpaccio, which were commissioned by the Schiavoni community in Venice during the 15th century.

From the earliest days of the Republic, Venice forged trade links with the coastal region of Schiavonia (Dalmatia) across the Adriatic. By 1420 permanent Venetian rule was established there, and many of the Schiavoni came to live in Venice. By the mid-15th century the Slav colony in the city had grown considerably and the State gave permission for them to found their own confraternity *(see p127).*

The Scuola was established in 1451. It is a delightful spot to admire Carpaccio's exceptional works of art, and has changed very little since the rebuilding of the Scuola in 1551. The exquisite frieze, executed between 1502 and 1508, shows scenes from the lives of favourite saints: St George, St Tryphon and St Jerome. Each episode of the narrative cycle is remarkable for its vivid colouring, minutely observed detail and historic record of Venetian life. Outstanding among them

are *St George Slaying the Dragon, St Jerome Leading the Tamed Lion to the Monastery,* and *The Vision of St Jerome.*

San Giovanni in Bragora ⓱

Campo Bandiera e Moro. **Map** 8 E2.
Tel *041 296 06 30.* 🚤 *Arsenale.* ⃝
9am–noon, 3:30–5:30pm Mon–Sat.

The foundations of this simple church date back to ancient times but the existing building is essentially Gothic (1475–9). The intimate interior has major works of art which demonstrate the transition from Gothic to early Renaissance. Bartolomeo Vivarini's altarpiece, *Madonna and Child with Saints* (1478) is unmistakably Gothic. Contrasting with this is Cima da Conegliano's *Baptism of Christ* (1492–5) on the main altar. This large-scale narrative scene, in a realistic landscape, set a precedent for later Renaissance painters.

Museo Storico Navale ⓲

Campo San Biagio, Arsenale,
Castello 2148. **Map** 8 F3.
Tel *041 520 02 76.* 🚤 *Arsenale.*
⃝ *8:45am–1:30pm Mon–Fri,
8:45am–1pm Sat.* ⬤ *public hols.* 🎫

It was the Austrians who, in 1815, first had the idea of assembling the remnants of the Venetian navy and creating a historical naval museum. They began with a series of models of vessels that had been produced in the 17th century by the Arsenale, and to these added all the naval paraphernalia they could obtain. The exhibits include friezes preserved from famous galleys of the past, a variety of maritime firearms and a replica of the Doge's ceremonial barge, the *Bucintoro.*

The collection has been housed in an ex-warehouse on the waterfront since 1958, and now traces Venetian and Italian naval history to the present day.

The first exhibits you see on entering are the World War II human torpedoes or "pigs". Torpedoes such as these helped sink HMS *Valiant* and HMS *Queen Elizabeth*: they were guided to their target by naval divers who jumped off just before impact.

The rest of the museum is divided into the Venetian navy, the Italian navy from 1860 to today, Adriatic vessels and the Swedish room. The museum is well laid out and has informative explanations in English.

Model of the *Bucintoro* in the Museo Storico Navale

Arsenale ⑲

Map 8 F1. 🚤 *Arsenale*.
Limited public access.

Heart of the city's maritime-power, the Arsenale was founded in the 12th century and enlarged in the 14th to 16th centuries to become the greatest naval shipyard in the world. The word "arsenal" derives from the Arabic *darsina'a*, house of industry – which indeed it was.

At its height in the 16th century, a workforce of 16,000, the *arsenalotti*, was employed to construct, equip and repair the great Venetian galleys *(see pp44–5)*. One of the first production lines in Europe, it was like a city within a city, with its own workshops, warehouses, factories, foundries and docks.

Entrance to the Arsenale, guarded by 16th-century towers

THE ASSEMBLY-LINE SYSTEM

The *arsenalotti*, master ship-builders of the 16th century

During the Arsenale's heyday, a Venetian galley could be constructed and fully equipped with remarkable speed and efficiency. From the early 16th century the hulls, which were built in the New Arsenal, were towed past a series of buildings in the Old Arsenal to be equipped in turn with rigging, ammunition and food supplies. By 1570, when Venice was faced with the Turkish threat to take Cyprus, the Arsenale was so fast it was capable of turning out an entire galley in 24 hours. Henry III of France witnessed the system's efficiency in 1574 when the *arsenalotti* completed a galley in the time it took for him to partake in a state feast.

Surrounded by crenellated walls, the site today is largely abandoned. The huge gateway and vast site are the only evidence of its former splendour. The gateway, in the form of a triumphal arch, was built in 1460 by Antonio Gambello and is often cited as Venice's first Renaissance construction.

The two lions guarding the entrance were pillaged from Piraeus (near Athens) by Admiral Francesco Morosini in 1687. A third lion, bald and sitting upright, bears runic inscriptions on his haunches, thought to have been carved by Scandinavian mercenaries who in 1040 fought for the Byzantine emperor against some Greek rebels.

By the 17th century, when the seeds of Venetian decline were well and truly sown, the number of *arsenalotti* plummeted to 1,000. Following the Fall of the Republic in 1797,

Napoleon destroyed the docks and stripped the *Bucintoro* (the Doge's ceremonial ship) of its precious ornament. Cannons and bronzes were melted down to contribute to victory monuments celebrating the French Revolution.

Today the area is under military administration and for the most part closed to the public. The bridge by the arched gateway affords partial views of the shipyard, or try taking a scenic trip on a *vaporetto* (either route 41 or 42), which follows the perimeter of the Arsenal.

Some parts of the Arsenale, such as the Corderie, the old rope factory, are now being used as performance spaces or exhibition centres, mostly for the Biennale *(see p260)*. A research consortium developing marine and coastal technologies also operates from the Arsenale.

Lagoon entrance
Arsenale Novissimo, 15th–16th century
Old sail factory
Arsenale Vecchio, 12th–13th century
Arsenale Nove, 14th century
Corderia

Late 18th-century engraving of the Arsenale

Exploring Eastern Castello ⑳

This peaceful stroll takes you from the animated Castello quayside to the quieter eastern limits of the city. The focal point of the tour is the solitary island of San Pietro di Castello, site of the former cathedral of Venice. From here you head south to the island of Sant'Elena with its historic church and Venice's football stadium, and return via the public gardens along the scenic waterfront.

(see p119). Then take the first on the left, marked Calle San Gioachin, cross a small bridge and turn left at the "crossroads". Once you are past Campo Ruga ⑤, take the second turning on the right

The calm and leafy Giardini Pubblici ⑯

A tribute to the women fallen in World War II ⑱

Via Garibaldi

This broad, busy street ① was created by Napoleon in 1808 by filling in a canal. The first house on the right ② was the home of John Cabot and his son Sebastian, the Italian navigators who in 1497 found what they thought to be the coast of China (but in reality was the Labrador coast of Newfoundland). Near the end of the street, through a gate on the right, a bronze monument of Garibaldi ③ by Augusto Benvenuti (1885) marks the northern end of the Viale Garibaldi, which leads to the public gardens.

Returning to Via Garibaldi, take the left-hand embankment at the end of the street, pausing on the bridge ④ for distant views of the Arsenale

and cross the bridge over the broad Canale di San Pietro.

The island of San Pietro di Castello

The old church of San Pietro di Castello ⑥ and its freestanding, tilting campanile ⑦ overlook a grassy square. The island, once occupied by a fortress *(castello)*, was one of Venice's earliest settlements. The church, which was probably founded in the 7th century, became the cathedral of Venice and remained so until 1807 when San Marco took its place *(see p80).* The existing church, built to a

Palladian design in the mid-16th century, has several notable features. These include the Lando Chapel, the Vendramin Chapel and the marble throne from an Arabic tombstone, originally said to have been the Seat of St Peter.

In the south of the square, Mauro Coducci's elegant stone campanile was built in 1482–8, and the cupola was added in 1670. Beside the church, the Palazzo Patriarcale (Bishop's

KEY

•••	Walk route
✸	View point
🚏	*Vaporetto* boarding point

The busy Via Garibaldi, with John Cabot's house on the far right ②

For hotels and restaurants in this region see pp228–33 and pp242–7

Palace) ⑧ was turned into barracks by Napoleon. The old cloisters are overgrown and strung with washing and fishing nets.

From the Bishop's Palace take the Calle drio il Campanile south from the square and turn left when you come to the canal. The first turning right takes you across the Ponte di Quintavalle ⑨, a wooden bridge with good views of brightly coloured boats anchored on either side of the waterway.

The island of San Pietro, with its curious leaning campanile ⑦

San Pietro to Sant'Elena

The large and semi-derelict building at the foot of the bridge is the ex-church and monastery of Sant'Anna ⑩. Take the first left off the *fondamenta*, cross Campiello Correr and then take Calle GB Tiepolo and cross the Secco Marina. Continue straight ahead and over the bridge for the Church of San Giuseppe ⑪. On the rare occasions it is open you can see Vincenzo Scamozzi's monument to Doge Marino Grimani

(1595–1605). Cross the square beyond the church and zigzag left, right and left again for Paludo San Antonio, an uninspiring modern street that has been reclaimed from marshland (*palude*). At the far end cross the bridge over the Rio dei Giardini ⑫ and take the street ahead. A right turn along Viale 4 Novembre brings you down to the spacious gardens of Parco delle Rimembranze ⑬. At the southern end of the park, cut left at Calle Buccari ⑭, then right for the bridge over Rio di Sant'Elena. In front, the Church of Sant'Elena ⑮ is a pretty Gothic church founded in the 13th century. Retrace your steps over the bridge and turn left, following the waterfront back through the park.

Detail from Gothic façade of Sant'Elena ⑮

Giardini Pubblici and the Biennale Pavilions

At the far side of the park, the bridge across the Rio dei Giardini brings you to the public gardens and to the Biennale gate entrance ⑯. If it happens to be summer in an odd-numbered year, the gardens will be open with the Biennale pavilions ⑰ at which 40 to 50 nations exhibit many examples of contemporary art (*see p260*).

Riva dei Partigiani

Outside the public gardens on Riva dei Partigiani is a large bronze statue. Lying on the steps of the embankment, the monument can only be seen at low tide. Known as La Donna Partigiana, this is a memorial to all the women who were killed fighting in World War II ⑱.

TIPS FOR WALKERS

Starting point: The western end of Via Garibaldi.
Length: Just under 5 km (3 miles).
Getting there: Vaporetto No. 1, 41 or 42 to Arsenale.
Stopping-off points: There are a handful of simple cafés and trattorias along the route, most of them on Via Garibaldi. The waterside Caffè Paradiso at the entrance to the Giardini Pubblici has excellent views. For good seafood, try the Hostaria Da Franz (see p241) along Fondamenta San Giuseppe (No. 754). The green shady parks are a welcome retreat from the bustle of the city.

CAMPO SPORTIVO

CAMPO DELLA CHIESA

CALLE OSLAVIA

C PODGORA

VIALE PIAVE

CALLE DEL SABOTINO

C GEN CHINOTTO

CALLE ZUGNA

FONDAMENTA SANT'ELENA Rio di S. Elena

VIALE QUATTRO NOVEMBRE

VIALE SANT'ELENA

CALLE F PASSARELLA

C ROVERETO

C BUCCARI

VIALE QUATTRO NOVEMBRE

PARCO DELLE RIMEMBRANZE

VIALE VITTORIO VENETO

CAMPO SPORTIVO

Sant'Elena

0 metres 200
0 yards 200

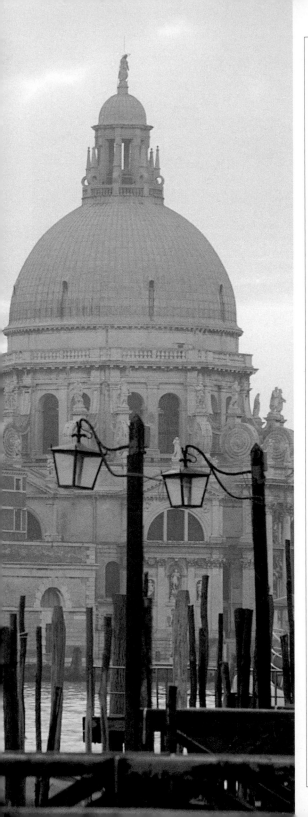

FONDAM
PRO
FONDAM
Ric

7

FMTA BARBARIGO
Rio di San Nicolò   FMTA DI PESCHERIA   R d
CORTE
LARDONA   CAMPO
ANGELO RAF   **8**

SAL SAN BA.

BANCHINA DI SAN BASE

KEY

Street-by-Street map
See pp124–5

Vaporetto boarding point

Traghetto crossing

◁ **View across the Grand Canal
to Santa Maria della Salute**

DORSODURO

orsoduro is named after the solid subsoil on which this area has been built up (the name means "hard backbone"). The western part, the island of Mendigola, was colonized centuries before the Rialto was established in AD 828 as the permanent seat of Venice. The settlement then spread eastwards, covering another six islands.

Squero di San Trovaso, the gondola boatyard

East of the Accademia, the Dorsoduro is a quiet and pretty neighbourhood with shaded squares, quiet canals and picturesque residences belonging to wealthy Venetians and foreigners. In the early 1900s the area was favoured by British expatriates who used to attend the Anglican church of St George in Campo San Vio. Among the area's attractions are the wide-embracing lagoon views,

both from the eastern tip near the Salute and from the Zattere across to the island of Giudecca. West of the Accademia, the *sestiere* is more vibrant, with the busy Campo Santa Margherita as its attractive focal point. Further west, the shabbier area around the beautiful church of San Nicolò dei Mendicoli was originally the home of fishermen and sailors. The Dorsoduro plays host to several major collections of art, notably the Accademia Gallery and the Peggy Guggenheim Collection of 20th-century art. The churches are also rich repositories of paintings and sculpture: San Sebastiano has fine paintings by Paolo Veronese; the Scuola Grande dei Carmini and the church of the Gesuati have ceilings painted by Giambattista Tiepolo.

Michele Giambono's *St Michael* (c.1450) in the Accademia

0 metres   250
0 yards   250

Street-by-Street: Dorsoduro

Between the imposing palaces on the Grand Canal and the Campo Santa Margherita lies an almost silent neighbourhood of small squares and narrow alleys. The delightful Rio San Barnaba is best appreciated from the Ponte dei Pugni, near the barge selling fruit and vegetables. The Rio Terrà, though architecturally uninspiring, has a fascinating mask shop and some cafés that are lively at night-time. All roads seem to lead to Campo Santa Margherita, the heart of Dorsoduro. The square bustles with activity, particularly in the morning when the market stalls are functioning.

Reliefs on a house at Ponte Trovaso

★ **Scuola Grande dei Carmini**
Tiepolo painted nine ceiling panels for the Scuola in 1739–44. The central panel features the Virgin and St Simeon Stock ❺

Palazzo Zenobio *has been an Armenian college since 1850. Occasionally visitors can see the sumptuous 18th-century ballroom.*

Santa Maria dei Carmini
The church's oldest feature is the Gothic side porch with fragments of decorative Byzantine reliefs ❻

KEY

– – – Suggested route

0 metres	50
0 yards	50

STAR SIGHTS

★ Scuola Grande dei Carmini

★ Ca' Rezzonico

★ San Barnaba

Fondamenta Gherardini *runs beside the Rio San Barnaba, one of the prettiest canals in the sestiere.*

Campo Santa Margherita
Open-air cafés are an integral part of the square. Causin sells particularly delicious Italian ice cream ④

LOCATOR MAP
See Street Finder, map 6

Palazzo Giustinian
is the 15th-century palace where Richard Wagner stayed while he was writing the second act of Tristan and Isolde in 1858.

Ca' Foscari, with its splendid setting, was chosen as the lodging place for Henry III of France in 1574.

Palazzo Nani is one of the fine palaces that lie on the great curve called the Volta del Canal.

Ca' Rezzonico

Ponte dei Pugni
Vicious fistfights used to take place on the top of this bridge ②

★ San Barnaba
A floating barge crammed with crates of fruit and vegetables lends a colourful note to the area ①

★ Ca' Rezzonico
The grand stairway has two putti, symbolizing winter and autumn ③

Campo San Barnaba ❶

Map 6 D3. 🚤 *Ca' Rezzonico.*

The Parish of San Barnaba, with its canalside square at the centre, was known in the 18th century as the home of impoverished Venetian patricians. They were attracted by the cheap rents, and while some relied on state support or begging, others worked in the State gambling house.

Today the square and canal, with its vegetable barge, are quietly appealing. The church (Tel: 041 296 06 30, open am Mon–Sat) is fairly unremarkable, apart from a Tiepolesque ceiling and a *Holy Family* attributed to Paolo Veronese.

Ponte dei Pugni ❷

Fondamenta Gherardini. **Map** 6 D3. 🚤 *Ca' Rezzonico.*

Venice has several Ponti dei Pugni ("bridges of fists"), but this is the most famous. Spanning the peaceful Rio San Barnaba, the small bridge is distinguished by two pairs of footprints set in white stone on top of the bridge. These mark the starting positions for the fights which traditionally took place between rival factions. Formerly there were no balustrades and contenders hurled each other straight into the water. The battles became so bloodthirsty that they were banned in 1705.

Boats and barges moored along the Rio San Barnaba

Tiepolo's *New World* fresco, part of a series in Ca' Rezzonico

Ca' Rezzonico ❸

Fondamenta Rezzonico 3136. **Map** 6 E3. **Tel** 041 241 01 00. 🚤 *Ca' Rezzonico.* ⬭ *Nov–Mar: 10am–5pm Wed–Mon; Apr–Oct: 10am–6pm Wed–Mon.* 🔴 *1 Jan, 1 May, 25 Dec.* 🖼️📷🏠🛍️♿🔲

This richly furnished Baroque palace is one of the most splendid in Venice. It is also one of the few palaces in the city, which opens its doors to the public. Since 1934 it has housed the museum of 18th-century Venice, its rooms furnished with frescoes, paintings and period pieces taken from other local palaces or museums.

The building was begun by Baldassare Longhena (architect of La Salute, *see p135*) in 1667, but the funds of the Bon family, who commissioned it, ran dry before the second floor was started. In 1712, long after Longhena's death, the unfinished palace was bought by the Rezzonicos, a family of merchants-turned-bankers from Genoa. A large portion of the Rezzonico fortune was spent on the purchase, construction and decoration of the palace. By 1758 it was in a fit state for the Rezzonicos to throw the first of the huge banquets and celebratory parties for which they later became renowned.

In 1888 the palace was bought by the poet Robert

Allegory of Strength, *Andrea Brustolon*

Browning and his son, Pen, who was married to an American heiress. Browning spoke of the "gaiety and comfort of the enormous rooms" but had little time to enjoy them. In 1889 he died of bronchitis.

The outstanding attraction in the palace today is Giorgio Massari's ballroom, which occupies the entire breadth of the building. It has been beautifully restored and is embellished with gilded chandeliers, carved furniture by Andrea Brustolon and a ceiling with *trompe l'oeil* frescoes. Three rooms between the ballroom and Grand Canal side of the palace have ceilings with frescoes by Giambattista Tiepolo including, in the Sala della Allegoria Nuziale, his lively *Nuptial Allegory* (1758).

Eighteenth-century paintings occupy the *piano nobile* (second floor). A whole room is devoted to Pietro Longhi's portrayals of everyday Venetian life. Other paintings worthy of note are Francesco Guardi's *Ridotto* (1748) and *Nuns' Parlour* (1768), and one of the few Canalettos in Venice, his *View of the Rio dei Mendicanti* (1725). Giandomenico Tiepolo's fascinating series of frescoes painted for his villa at Zianigo (1770–1800) are also to be found here. On the floor above is a reconstructed 18th-century apothecary's shop and a puppet theatre.

Campo Santa Margherita ➍

Map 6 D2. ⬛ Ca' Rezzonico.

The sprawling square of Santa Margherita, lined with houses from the 14th and 15th centuries, is the lively hub of western Dorsoduro. Market stalls, off-beat shops and cafés attract many young people. The fish stalls sell live eels and lobster, the *erborista* alternative medicine, and the bakers some of the tastiest loaves in Venice.

The former church of Santa Margherita, now an auditorium owned by the university, lies to the north of the square. Visitors can see sculptural fragments from the original 18th-century church, including gargoyles, on the truncated campanile and adjacent house. The Scuola dei Varotari (Scuola of the tanners), the isolated

A 15th-century carving of Santa Margherita and the dragon

building in the centre of the square, has a faded relief of the Madonna della Misericordia protecting the tanners.

Scuola Grande dei Carmini ➎

Campo Carmini. **Map** 5 C2. **Tel** 041 528 94 20. ⬛ Ca' Rezzonico. ⬜ 10am–5pm daily. ⬛ 1 Jan, 25 Dec. 🈺 📷

The headquarters of the Carmelite confraternity was built beside their church in 1663. In the 1740s Giambattista Tiepolo was commissioned to decorate the ceiling of the *salone* (hall) on the upper floor. The nine ceiling paintings that he produced so impressed the Carmelites that Tiepolo was promptly made an honorary member of the brotherhood.

The ceiling used to show *St Simeon Stock Receiving the Scapular of the Carmelite Order from the Virgin* but, unfortunately, in 2000 the painting crashed to the floor, its support having been eaten by woodworm. The work is currently in Bologna, where it is being restored. The Carmelites honoured St Simeon Stock because he re-established the order in Europe after its expulsion from the Holy Land in the 13th century.

Santa Maria dei Carmini ➏

Campo Carmini. **Map** 5 C3. **Tel** 041 296 06 30. ⬛ Ca' Rezzonico or San Basilio. ⬜ 2:30–5:30pm Mon–Sat.

Known also as Santa Maria del Carmelo, this church was built in the 14th century but has since undergone extensive alterations. The most prominent external feature is the lofty campanile, whose perilous tilt was skilfully rectified in 1688. The impressive interior is large, sombre and richly decorated. The arches of the nave are adorned with gilded wooden statues,

Santa Maria dei Carmini

and a series of paintings illustrating the history of the Carmelite Order.

There are two interesting paintings in the church's side altars. Cima da Conegliano's *Adoration of the Shepherds* (c.1509) is in the second altar on the right (coins in the light meter are essential). In the second altar on the left is Lorenzo Lotto's *St Nicholas of Bari with Saints Lucy and John the Baptist* (c.1529). This painting demonstrates the artist's religious devotion, personal sensitivity and his love of nature. On the right-hand side of this highly detailed, almost Dutch-style landscape, there is a tiny depiction of St George killing the dragon.

SCUOLE

The *scuole* were peculiarly Venetian institutions. Founded mainly in the 13th century, they were lay confraternities existing for the charitable benefit of the neediest groups of society, the professions or resident ethnic minorities (such as the Scuola dei Schiavoni, *see p118*). Some became extremely rich, spending large sums on buildings and paintings, often to the disadvantage of their declared beneficiaries.

Upper Hall of the Scuola Grande dei Carmini

Nave of San Nicolò dei Mendicoli, one of the oldest churches in Venice

San Nicolò dei Mendicoli ❼

Campo San Nicolò. **Map** 5 A3.
Tel 041 275 03 82. 🚤 San Basilio.
⬜ 10am–noon, 3–6pm Mon–Sat.

Contrasting with the remote and rundown area that surrounds it, this church remains one of the most charming and delightful in Venice. Originally constructed in the 12th century, it has been rebuilt extensively over the centuries; the little porch on the north flank dates from the 15th century.

   Thanks to the Venice in Peril Fund, in the 1970s the church underwent one of the most comprehensive restoration programmes since the floods of 1966 *(see p50).* The floor, which was 30 cm (1 ft) below the level of the canals, was rebuilt and raised slightly to prevent further damage, the roofs and lower walls were reconstructed, and paintings and statues restored. The

interior is richly embellished, particularly the nave with its 16th-century gilded wood statues. On the upper walls is a series of paintings of the life of Christ by Alvise dal Friso and other pupils of Veronese.

Angelo Raffaele ❽

Campo Angelo Raffaele. **Map** 5 B3.
Tel 041 522 85 48. 🚤 San Basilio.
⬜ 9am–noon, 3–5:30pm Mon–Sat;
varies on Sun & public hols.

The main attraction of this 17th-century church is the series of panel paintings on the organ balustrade. These were executed in 1749 by Antonio Guardi, brother of the more famous Francesco. They tell the tale of Tobias, the blind prophet cured by the archangel Raphael, after whom the church is named.

San Sebastiano ❾

Campo San Sebastiano. **Map** 5 C3.
Tel 041 275 04 62. 🚤 San Basilio.
⬜ 10am–5pm Mon–Sat.
⬛ 1 Jan, 25 Dec. 📷 🚫 📞

This 16th-century church has one of the most colourful and homogeneous interiors of Venice. This is thanks to the artist Veronese who, from 1555 to 1560 and again in the 1570s, was commissioned to decorate the sacristy ceiling, the nave ceiling, the frieze, the east end of the choir, the high altar, the doors of the organ panels and the chancel – in that order. The paintings, which are typical of Veronese, are rich and radiant, with sumptuous costumes and colours. Among the finest of his works are the three ceiling paintings that tell the story of Esther, Queen of Xerxes I of Persia, who brought about the deliverance of the Jewish people. Appropriately, the artist is buried in San Sebastiano, alongside the organ.

Zattere ❿

Map 5 C4. 🚤 Zattere or San Basilio.

Stretching along the southern part of the *sestiere,* the Zattere is the long quayside looking across to the island of Giudecca. The name derives from the rafts *(zattere)* made of and carrying timber from the Republic's forests. After skilful navigation along

San Sebastiano, viewed from the bridge of the same name

Café tables laid out along the Zattere

the River Piave, the rafts were dismantled on arrival in Venice. On a sunny day it is a pleasure to sit at a waterside café here, looking across to the Church of the Redentore *(see p154)* or watching the waterbuses as they cross back and forth between the shores.

Squero di San Trovaso ⓫

Rio San Trovaso. **Map** 6 D4. ⛴ Zattere. **No public access.**

This is one of the few surviving gondola workshops in Venice *(see pp28–9)* and the most picturesque. Its Tyrolean look dates from the days when craftsmen came down from the Cadore area of the Dolomites *(see p215)*.

It is not open to the public, but from the far side of the Rio San Trovaso it is possible to watch the upturned gondolas being given their scraping and tarring treatment. Nowadays, only around ten boats are made each year, but there is still plenty to see.

San Trovaso ⓬

Campo San Trovaso. **Map** 6 D4. **Tel** 041 296 06 30. ⛴ Zattere or Accademia. ⏲ 3–6pm Mon–Sat.

The church of Santi Gervasio e Protasio, which in the eccentric Venetian dialect is slurred to San Trovaso, was built in 1590. Unusually it has two identical façades, one overlooking a canal, the other a quiet square. The church stood on neutral ground between the parishes of

the rival factions of the Castellani and Nicolotti families, and tradition has it that this necessitated a separate entrance for each party.

The interior houses some late paintings by Jacopo Tintoretto, and there are two notable works of art worth seeking out. Michele Giambono's 15th-century Gothic painting, *St Chrysogonus on Horseback*, is situated in the chapel on the right of the chancel, and exquisite marble reliefs of angels with instruments ecorate the altar of the Clary chapel opposite.

Santa Maria della Visitazione ⓭

Fondamenta delle Zattere. **Map** 6 E4. **Tel** 041 522 40 77. ⛴ Zattere. ⏲ 8am–noon, 3–6pm daily (to 5pm in winter). Restoration work in progress so call before visiting.

Situated beside the Gesuati, this Renaissance church was built between 1494 and 1524 by the Order of the Gesuati. Inside the church is a fine wooden ceiling painted by 16th-century Umbrian and

Tuscan artists. The exterior *bocca di leone* to the right of the façade is one of several "lion's mouth" denunciation boxes surviving from the rule of the Council of Ten *(see p42)*; this one was used to complain about the state of the streets.

Gesuati ⓮

Fondamenta delle Zattere. **Map** 6 E4. **Tel** 041 275 04 62. ⛴ Zattere. ⏲ 10am–5pm daily (from 1pm Sun). 📷 🔊 🚫

Not to be confused with the Gesuiti *(see p142)*, this church was built by the Dominicans, who took possession of the site in the 17th century, when the Gesuati Order was suppressed. Work began in 1726 and the stately façade reflects that of Palladio's Redentore church across the Giudecca. It is the most conspicuous landmark of the long Zattere quayside. The interior of the church is richly decorated.

Gesuati façade statue

Tiepolo's frescoed ceiling, *The Life of St Dominic* (1737–39) demonstrates the artist's mastery of light and colour. Equally impressive (and far easier to see) is his *Virgin with Saints* (1740), situated in the first chapel on the right. The church also boasts two altar paintings by Sebastiano Ricci and Giambattista Piazzetta.

Squero di San Trovaso, where gondolas are given a facelift

Accademia ⑮

The largest collection of Venetian art in existence, the Gallerie dell'Accademia, is housed in three former religious buildings. The basis of the collection was the Accademia di Belle Arti, founded in 1750 by the painter Giovanni Battista Piazzetta. In 1807 Napoleon moved the academy to these premises, and the collection was greatly enlarged by works of art from churches and monasteries he suppressed.

Exterior detail of the Accademia

Ceiling Sketch
Tiepolo's The Translation of the Holy House to Loreto (c.1742) was a sketch for the ceiling of the Scalzi church (see p145).

The Apothecary's Shop
Pietro Longhi is best known for his witty, gently satirical depictions of domestic patrician life in Venice. This detail comes from a painting dated c.1752.

KEY TO FLOORPLAN

- ☐ Byzantine and International Gothic
- ☐ Early Renaissance
- ☐ High Renaissance
- ☐ Baroque, genre and landscapes
- ☐ Ceremonial paintings
- ☐ Temporary exhibitions
- ☐ Non-exhibition space

13
14
16
16a
15
17
20
18
19
21
23
22
24

Sala dell'Albergo

★ **Cycle of St Ursula** *(1495–1500) (detail)*
The Arrival of the English Ambassadors *is one of Vittore Carpaccio's eight paintings chronicling the tragic story of St Ursula.*

The former Church of Santa Maria della Carità
was rebuilt by Bartolomeo Bon in the mid-15th century.

Entrance

The inner courtyard was designed by Andrea Palladio.

11

10

The Stealing of St Mark
Jacopo Tintoretto's painting of 1562 shows the Christians of Alexandria abducting the body of St Mark, which was about to be burnt by the pagans.

6   9

5

4   8

3   7

2

★ **The Tempest** (c.1507)
In his enigmatic landscape, Giorgione was probably indulging his imagination rather than portraying a specific subject.

★ **Coronation of the Virgin**
Paolo Veneziano's polyptych (1325) has a central image of the Virgin surrounded by a panoply of religious scenes. This detail shows episodes from the Life of St Francis.

STAR SIGHTS

★ Cycle of St Ursula by Carpaccio

★ The Tempest by Giorgione

★ Coronation of the Virgin by Veneziano

GALLERY GUIDE

The current programme of restoration work is ongoing, be prepared for absent paintings or whole sections closed off. It is sensible to phone ahead for more details. The paintings are dependent on natural light, so to see them at their best try to visit on a bright morning. Upstairs, a second gallery called Quadreria contains works by artists such as Bellini and Tintoretto. Guided visits are free of charge, but it is essential to book in advance.

Exploring the Accademia's Collection

Spanning five centuries, the fascinating collection of
paintings in the Accademia provides a complete
spectrum of the Venetian school, from the medieval
Byzantine period through the Renaissance to the
Baroque and Rococo *(see pp26–7)*. The order is more
or less chronological, with the exception of the final
rooms, which take visitors back to the Renaissance.

BYZANTINE AND INTERNATIONAL GOTHIC

Room 1 shows the influence
of Byzantine art on the early
Venetian painters. Paolo Veneziano, the true founder of
the Venetian school, displays
a blend of both western and
eastern influences in his
sumptuous *Coronation of
the Virgin* (1325). The
linear rhythms are quite
unmistakably Gothic, yet
the overall effect and the
glowing gold background
are distinctly Byzantine.

In the same room,
*Coronation of the
Virgin* (1448) by
Michele Giam-
bono shows the
influence of
International
Gothic style,
which was
brought to
Venice by Gentile da Fabriano
and Pisanello. This particular
style was characterized by
delicate naturalistic detail, as
typified by the birds and
animals in the foreground of
Giambono's painting.

Coronation of the Virgin (c.1448)
by Michele Giambono

EARLY RENAISSANCE

The Renaissance came late to
Venice, but by the second
quarter of the 15th century it
had transformed the city into
an art centre rivalling those of

Florence and Rome. The Bellini
family – Jacopo, the father,
and his two sons Gentile and
Giovanni – played a dominant
role in the early Venetian
Renaissance.

Central to Venetian art in
the 15th century was the *Sacra
Conversazione*, where the
Madonna is portrayed in a
unified composition with saints.
Giovanni Bellini's altar-
piece for San Giobbe
(c.1487) in Room 2 is
one of the finest
examples. Giovanni,
the younger Bellini,
was profoundly
influenced by the
controlled
rational style
and mastery of
perspective in
the works of his
brother-in-law,
Andrea Man-
tegna, whose
work *St George*
(c.1460) is in Room 4. To
Mantegna's rationality and
harsh realism Giovanni added
humanity. This is seen in his
Madonna paintings (Rooms 4
and 5), which are masterpieces
of warmth and harmony. Outstanding examples are *The
Virgin and Child between St
Catherine and St Mary Magdalene* (c.1490) in Room 4;
Madonna of the Little Trees
(c.1487) and *Virgin and Child
with John the Baptist and a
Saint* (c.1505) in Room 5.
The inventive young artist

Portrait of a Gentleman (c.1525) by
Lorenzo Lotto (detail)

Giorgione was influenced by
Bellini, but went way beyond
his master in his development
of the landscape to create
mood. In the famous, atmospheric *Tempest* (c.1507) in
Room 5, this treatment of the
landscape and the use of the
figures to intensify that mood
was an innovation adopted in
Venetian painting of the 16th
century and beyond.

Out on a limb from the
main 16th-century Venetian
tradition was the enigmatic
Lorenzo Lotto, best known for
portraits conveying moods of
psychological unrest. His
melancholic *Portrait of a
Gentleman* (c.1525) in Room
7 is a superb example. More
in the Venetian tradition, Palma
il Vecchio's sumptuously
coloured *Sacra Conversazione*
in Room 8, painted around
the same time, shows the
unmistakable influence of the
early work of Titian.

HIGH RENAISSANCE

Occupying an entire wall of
Room 10, the monumental
Feast in the House of Levi
by Paolo Veronese (1573)
was originally commissioned

Paolo Veronese's *Feast in the House of Levi* (detail)

s *The Last Supper*. However, he hedonistic detail in the painting, such as the drunkard and the dwarfs, was not well received and Veronese found himself before the Inquisition. Ordered to eliminate the profane content of the picture, he simply changed the title.

Jacopo Tintoretto made his reputation with *The Miracle of the Slave* (1548), which is also in Room 10. The painting shows his mastery of the dramatic effects of light and movement. This was the first of a series of works painted for the Scuola Grande di San Marco *(see p114)*. In the next room, Veronese's use of rich colour is best admired in the *Mystical Marriage of St Catherine* (c.1575).

Healing of the Madman (c.1496) by Vittore Carpaccio

BAROQUE, GENRE AND LANDSCAPES

The Rape of Europa (1740–50) by Francesco Zuccarelli (detail)

Venice suffered from a lack of native Baroque painters, but a few non-Venetians kept the Venetian school alive in the 17th century. The most notable among these was the Genoese Bernardo Strozzi (1581–1644). The artist was a great admirer of the work of Veronese, as can be seen in his *Feast at the House of Simon* (1629) in Room 11. Also represented in this room is Giambattista Tiepolo, the greatest Venetian painter of the 18th century.

The long corridor (12) and the rooms which lead from it are largely devoted to light-hearted landscape and genre paintings from the 18th

century. Among them are pastoral scenes by Francesco Zuccarelli, works by Marco Ricci, scenes of Venetian society by Pietro Longhi and a view of Venice by Canaletto (1763). This was the painter's entry for admission to the Accademia, and is a fine example of his sense of perspective.

CEREMONIAL PAINTINGS

Rooms 20 and 21 return to the Renaissance, featuring two great cycles of paintings from the late 16th century. The detail in these large-scale anecdotal canvases provides a fascinating glimpse of the life, customs and appearance of Venice at the time. Room 20 houses *The Stories of the Cross* by Venice's leading artists, commissioned by the Scuola di San Giovanni Evangelista *(see p104)*. Each one depicts an episode of the relic of the Holy Cross, which the kingdom of Cyprus donated to the Scuola. In *The Procession in St Mark's Square* (1496) by Gentile Bellini, it is possible to compare the square with how it looks today.

Another, Vittore Carpaccio's *Healing of the Madman* (1496), shows the Rialto bridge which collapsed in 1524.

The second series, minutely detailed *Scenes from the Legend of St Ursula* (1490s) by Carpaccio in Room 21, provides a brilliant kaleidoscope of life. Mixing reality and imagination, Carpaccio relates the episodes from the life of St Ursula using settings and costumes of 15th-century Venice.

SALA DELL'ALBERGO

When the Scuola della Carità became the site of the Academy of Art in the early 19th century, the Scuola's *albergo* (where students lodged) retained its original panelling and 15th-century ceiling. The huge *Presentation of the Virgin* (1538) is one of the surprisingly few Titians in the gallery, and was painted for this very room. The walls are also adorned with a grandiose triptych (1446) by Antonio Vivarini and Giovanni d'Alemagna.

Detail from Titian's *Presentation of the Virgin* (1538)

Cini Collection ⑯

Palazzo Cini, San Vio 864. **Map** 6 E4.
Tel *041 521 07 55.* ▦ *Accademia.*
◻ *10am–1pm, 2–7pm Tue–Sun.*
◉ *Aug, Dec–Mar.* ▨ ▮

The Palazzo Cini belonged
to Count Vittorio Cini
(1884–1977), a collector and
patron of the arts. Between
1951 and 1956 he restored
San Giorgio Maggiore *(see
p95)* and created the Cini
Foundation as a memorial to
his son, who was killed in
an air crash in 1949.

The collection displayed here
includes china, ivories, books,
illuminated manuscripts,
miniatures, porcelain and
furniture, but the outstanding
works of art are the Tuscan
Renaissance paintings that
Cini collected. These include
works by or attributed to
Botticelli, Piero di Cosimo,
Piero della Francesca, Filippo
Lippi and Pontormo.

The Cini Collection has
been open to the public since
1984, but unfortunately, it is
only open for seven months
of the year.

Madonna col Bambino (c.1437) by
Filippo Lippi, the Cini Collection

Peggy Guggenheim Collection ⑰

Palazzo Venier dei Leoni, Dorsoduro
701. **Map** 6 F4. ***Tel*** *041 240 54 11.*
▦ *Accademia.* ◻ *10am–6pm
Wed–Mon.* ◉ *25 Dec.* ▨ ◪ ◻
▮ ▯ ⌀ ♿ *partial.*

Intended as a four-storey
palace, the 18th-century
Palazzo Venier dei Leoni in fact
never rose beyond the ground
floor – hence its nickname, *Il
Palazzo Nonfinito* (The Unfinished Palace). In 1949 the
building was bought as a home
by the American millionairess
Peggy Guggenheim (1898–
1979), a collector, dealer and
patron of the arts. A perspi-
cacious and high-spirited
woman, she befriended and
furthered the careers of many
innovative abstract and surre-
alist artists. One was her
second husband, Max Ernst.

The collection consists of
200 paintings and sculptures,
representing almost every
modern art movement. The
dining room has notable

Interno Olandese II (c.1928) by
Joan Miró

Cubist works of art including
The Poet by Pablo Picasso. An
entire room is devoted to
Jackson Pollock, who was a
Guggenheim discovery. Other
artists represented are Miró, de
Chirico, Magritte, Kandinsky,
Mondrian and Malevich.

Sculpture is laid out in the
house and garden. One of
the most elegant works is
Constantin Brancusi's *Maiastra*
(1912). The most provocative
piece is Marino Marini's *Angelo
della Città* (Angel of the City,

1948), a prominently
displayed man sitting on a
horse, erect in all respects.
Embarrassed onlookers avert
their gaze to enjoy views
of the Grand Canal.

The Guggenheim is
one of the most visited
sights of the city. The
light-filled rooms
and the modern
canvases provide a
striking contrast to
the Renaissance
paintings which are
the main attraction in
Venetian churches
and museums. The
team of interns here
are usually arts gradu-
ates from English-
speaking countries,
which is a great help
to many tourists.

In 2009, a
contemporary art
gallery opened in
the Punta della
Dogana. The Guggenheim
had planned to acquire the
site, however, the French
businessman Francois Pinault
was granted the lease.

Maiastra
by Constantin
Brancusi

Façade of the Palazzo Venier dei Leoni, the home of the Peggy Guggenheim Collection of modern art

Campiello Barbaro ⑱

Map 6 F4. 🚤 Salute.

An enchanting little square, the Campiello Barbaro is shaded by trees and flanked on one side by the wisteria-clad walls of Ca' Dario. It is hard to believe the stories of murder, bankruptcy and suicide that have befallen the owners of this Grand Canal palace. The most recent was Raul Gardini, one of Italy's best-known industrialists, who shot himself in 1992.

The ill-fated Ca' Dario, which backs on to Campiello Barbaro

Santa Maria della Salute ⑲

Campo della Salute. Map 7 A4. Tel 041 274 39 28. 🚤 Salute. ⬜ 9am–noon, 3–5:30pm daily. ◑ Sun am. 📷 for Sacristy. 📷

This great Baroque Church standing at the entrance of the Grand Canal is one of the most imposing architectural landmarks of Venice. Henry James likened it to "some great lady on the threshold of her salon… with her domes and scrolls, her scalloped buttresses and statues forming a pompous crown and her wide steps disposed on the ground like the train of a robe". The church was built in thanksgiving for the deliverance of the city from the plague of 1630, hence the name Salute, meaning health and salvation. Every 21 November, in celebration, (see p35), worshippers approach across a bridge of boats which span the mouth of the Grand Canal. Baldassare Longhena started the church in 1630. It was completed in 1687, five years after his death.

The interior is comparatively sober. It consists of a large octagonal space below the cupola and six chapels radiating from the ambulatory. The large domed chancel and high altar dominate the view from the main door. The altar's sculptural group by Giusto Le Corte represents the Virgin and Child protecting Venice from the plague. Some of the best works, such as Titian's ceiling paintings of *Cain and Abel*, *The Sacrifice of Abraham and Isaac and David and Goliath* (1540–49), are beyond the altar, where visitors

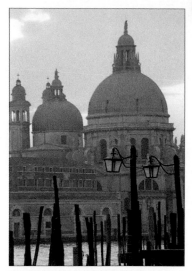

The Baroque church of Santa Maria della Salute viewed from across the Grand Canal

are not allowed. In the sacristy is Titian's early altarpiece of *St Mark Enthroned with Saints Cosmos, Damian, Roch and Sebastian* (1511–12), while on the wall opposite the entrance is *The Wedding at Cana* (1551), a major work by Tintoretto.

Next to the church, the historic Punta della Dogana building has been renovated and now houses an important collection of contemporary art.

Interior of the Salute showing the octagonal core of the church

Dogana di Mare ⑳

Map 7 A4. 🚤 Salute.

This eastern promontory of the Dorsoduro provides a panorama which embraces the Riva degli Schiavoni, the island of San Giorgio Maggiore and the eastern section of Giudecca. The *dogana di mare*, or sea customs post, was originally built in the 15th century to inspect the cargo of ships which were intending to enter Venice. The customs house visitors see today was constructed in the late 17th century and replaced a tower which originally guarded the entrance to the Grand Canal. On the corner tower of the house two bronze Atlases support a striking golden ball with a weathervane figure of Fortuna on the top.

0 metres   250

0 yards   250

◁ **The façade of
Tintoretto's house in
Fondamenta dei Mori**

CANNAREGIO

The city's most northerly *sestiere*, Cannaregio, stretches in a large arc from the 20th-century railway station in the west to one of the oldest quarters of Venice in the east. The northern quays look out towards the islands in the lagoon, while to the south the *sestiere* is bounded by the upper sweep of the Grand Canal.

The name of the quarter derives either from the Italian *canne*, meaning canes or reeds, which grew here centuries ago, or perhaps from "Canal Regio" or Royal Canal – the former name of what is now the Canale di Cannaregio. This waterway was the main entry to Venice before the advent of the rail link with the mainland. Over a third

Hanukah lamp in the Ghetto

of the city's population lives in Cannaregio. For the most part it is an unspoilt area, divided by wide canals, crisscrossed by alleys and characterized by small stores, simple bars and the artisans' workshops.

One of the prettiest and most remote quarters is in the north, near the church of Madonna dell'Orto and around Campo dei Mori.

Tourism is concentrated along two main thoroughfares: the Lista di Spagna and the wide Strada Nova, both on the well-worn route from the station to the Rialto. Just off this route lies the world's oldest ghetto. Though the Jewish community now lives all over the city, this is historically the most fascinating quarter of Cannaregio.

KEY

- Street-by-Street map *See pp138–9*
- Railway station
- *Vaporetto* boarding point
- *Traghetto* crossing

Street-by-Street: Cannaregio

Channel marker in the lagoon

Surprisingly few tourists find their way to this unspoilt quarter of northern Cannaregio. This is the more humble, peaceful side of Venice, where clean washing is strung over the waterways and the streets are flanked by the softly crumbling façades of shuttered houses. Along the wide *fondamente*, the little shops and stores stock basic groceries and the bars are always crowded with local Venetians. The quarter's cultural highlight is the lovely Gothic church of Madonna dell'Orto, Tintoretto's parish church.

To Madonna dell'Orto 🚤

★ Madonna dell'Orto
One of the finest Gothic churches in Venice, Madonna dell'Orto has a richly decorated façade and a wealth of works by Tintoretto ❶

Fondamenta della Sensa
This peaceful backwater, with its typically Venetian peeling façades, is undisturbed by tourism ❸

★ Campo dei Mori
This square is named after the stone statues of three Moors (Mori) which are carved on its walls ❷

Tintoretto *lived with his family in this house, No. 3399 Fondamenta dei Mori, from 1574 until his death in 1594.*

To Ca' d'Oro 🚤

KEY

– – – Suggested route

STAR SIGHTS

★ Madonna dell'Orto

★ Campo dei Mori

San Marziale
Ceiling paintings by Sebastiano Ricci (1700–25) and a bizarre Baroque altar adorn this Baroque church ❹

Fondamenta Gasparo Contarini *is named after the cardinal, diplomat and scholar who lived at Palazzo Contarini dal Zaffo (see p68) in the 16th century.*

LOCATOR MAP
See Street Finder, maps 2, 3

Venetian oarsmen *usually practise their technique on the lagoon, but they can also be seen on Cannaregio's quieter canals.*

La Sacca della Misericordia is a large man-made basin opening out into the lagoon, with views of the islands of San Michele and Murano.

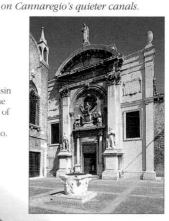

Campo dell'Abbazia, *a peaceful open square with decorative herring-bone floor tiles, is over-looked by the Scuola Vecchia della Misericordia and a deconsecrated church.*

Fondamenta della Misericordia, *named after the nearby scuola, was built in the Middle Ages.*

0 metres   50
0 yards   50

The campanile of Madonna dell'Orto, crowned by an onion-shaped cupola

Madonna dell'Orto ❶

Campo Madonna dell'Orto. **Map** 2 F2.
Tel 041 275 04 62. 🚇 Madonna dell'Orto. ⏰ 10am–5pm Mon–Sat, 1–5pm Sun. 🎫 🚫 🚫

This lovely Gothic church is frequently referred to as the English Church in Venice for it was British funds that helped restore the building after the 1966 floods *(see p50)*. The original church, founded in the mid-14th century, was dedicated to St Christopher, patron saint of travellers, to protect the boatmen who ferried passengers to the islands in the northern lagoon. The dedication was changed and the church reconstructed in the early 15th century, following the discovery, in a nearby vegetable garden *(orto)*, of a statue of the Virgin Mary said to have miraculous powers. However, a 15th-century statue of St Christopher, newly restored, still stands above the portal.

The interior, faced almost entirely in brick, is large, light and uncluttered. The greatest treasures are the works of art by Tintoretto, who was a parishioner of the church. His tomb, which is marked with a plaque, lies in the chapel to the right of the chancel. The most dramatic of his works are the towering paintings in the chancel (1562–4). On the right wall is *The Last Judgment*, whose turbulent content caused John Ruskin's wife Effie to flee the church. In the painting *The Adoration of the Golden Calf* on the left wall, the figure carrying the calf, fourth from the left, is said to depict Tintoretto himself.

Inside the chapel of San Mauro visitors can see the radically restored statue of the Madonna which inspired the reconstruction of the church.

To the right of the entrance is Cima da Conegliano's magnificent painting, *St John the Baptist and Other Saints* (c.1493). The vacant space opposite belongs to Giovanni Bellini's *Madonna with Child* (c.1478), which was stolen for the third time in 1993.

Campo dei Mori ❷

Map 2 F3. 🚇 Madonna dell'Orto.

According to popular tradition, the "Mori" were the three Mastelli brothers who came from the Morea (the Peloponnese). The brothers, who were silk merchants by trade, took refuge in Venice in 1112 and built the Palazzo Mastelli, visible from Fondamenta Gasparo Contarini and recognizable by its camel bas relief. The brothers' stone figures are embedded in the wall of the *campo* on its eastern side. The corner figure with the makeshift rusty metal nose (added in the 19th century) is "Signor Antonio Rioba" who, like the Roman Pasquino, was the focus of malicious fun and satire. A fourth oriental merchant with a large turban faces the Rio della Sensa on the façade of Tintoretto's house *(see p138)*.

One of the stone Moors which gave the Campo dei Mori its name

---

TINTORETTO (1518–94)

Jacopo Robusti, nicknamed Tintoretto because of his father's occupation of silk dyer, was born, lived and died in Cannaregio. He left Venice only once in his life. A devout Christian, volatile and unworldly, his was a highly individual and theatrical style, conveyed by vivid exaggeration of light and movement, bold fore-shortening and fiery, fluid brushstrokes. His remarkably prolific output has never been ascertained, but scores of his works survive, many still in the places for which they were painted. Examples of his canvases can be seen in the church of Madonna dell' Orto, the Accademia *(see pp130–33)*, and the Doge's Palace *(see pp84–9)* His crowning achievement, however, was the great series of works for the Scuola Grande di San Rocco *(see pp106–7)*.

The peaceful and atmospheric Fondamenta della Sensa

Fondamenta della Sensa ❸

Map 2 E2. 🚊 *Madonna dell'Orto.*

When the marshy lands of Cannaregio were drained in the Middle Ages, three long, straight canals were created, running parallel to each other. The middle of these is the Rio della Sensa, which stretches from the Sacca di Sant'Alvise at its western end to the Canale della Misericordia in the east. The Fondamenta cuts through a quiet quarter of Cannaregio, where daily life goes on undisturbed by tourism. With its small grocery shops, and simple local bars and *trattorias*, the neighbourhood feels far removed from San Marco.

This is one of the poorer areas of the city, though it is interspersed with fine (but neglected) palaces that once belonged to wealthy Venetians. Abbot Onorio Arrigoni lived at No. 3336 with his collection of antiques, and Palazzo Michiel (No. 3218) is an early Renaissance palace which became the French embassy.

San Marziale ❹

Campo San Marziale. **Map** 2 F3.
Tel 041 71 99 33. 🚊 *San Marcuola.*
⬜ *by appointment only.*

A Baroque church on medieval foundations, San Marziale was rebuilt between 1693 and 1721. The church is mainly visited for the ceiling frescoes by Sebastiano Ricci, a painter of the decorative Rococo style. Executed between 1700 and 1705, relatively early in Ricci's career, these bold, foreshortened frescoes already combine the Venetian tradition with flamboyant Rococo flourishes. Sadly though, the vivid colours for which Ricci was known have been sullied by decades of grime. The central painting shows *The Glory of Saint Martial*, while the side paintings relate to the image of the Virgin.

Fondamente Nuove ❺

Map 3 B3. 🚊 *Fondamente Nuove.*

The Fondamente Nuove or "New Quays" are actually over 400 years old. This chain

Altar of San Marziale showing a carving of the Virgin and Child

of waterside streets borders the northern lagoon for one kilometre (over half a mile), from the solitary Sacca della Misericordia to the Rio di Santa Giustina in Castello on the eastern side.

Before the construction of the quays in the 1580s, this was a desirable residential area where the air was said to be healthy and the houses had gardens sloping down to the lagoon.

One of the residents was Titian, who lived from 1531 to his death in 1576 in a now demolished house at Calle Larga dei Botteri No. 5182–3 (a plaque marks the site).

Today the quaysides are aesthetically uninspiring but they do provide splendid views of the northern lagoon and, on a clear day, the peaks of the Dolomites. The island most visible from the quays is San Michele in Isola *(see p151)*, its dark, stately cypress trees rising high above the cemetery walls.

Oratorio dei Crociferi ❻

Campo dei Gesuiti, 4905 Cannaregio.
Map 3 B3. **Tel** 041 532 29 20. 🚊
Fondamente Nuove. ⬜ *Apr–Jun & Sep–Oct: 3–6pm Fri–Sat; Jul–Aug: 4–7pm Fri–Sat.* 🈺 📷

Founded in the 13th century as a hospital for returning Crusaders, the Oratorio dei Crociferi (built for the order of the Bearers of the Cross) was turned into a charitable institution for old people in the 15th century.

Between 1583 and 1591 the artist Palma il Giovane, commissioned by the Crociferi, decorated the chapel with a glowing cycle of paintings, depicting the crucial events in the history of this religious order. The paintings suffered terrible damage in the floods of 1966 *(see p50)*, but were successfully restored and the chapel reopened in 1984.

The inscriptions on the walls of some of the surrounding houses in the square are those of art and craft guilds, such as silk weavers and tailors, whose works formerly occupied the buildings.

The sumptuous ceiling frescoes of the Gesuiti church

Gesuiti ●

Campo dei Gesuiti. **Map** 3 B4.
Tel 041 528 65 79.
🚏 Fondamente Nuove.
🕙 10am–noon, 4–6pm daily.

The Jesuits' close links with the papacy provoked Venetian hostility during the 17th century, and for 50 years they were refused entry to the city. However, in 1714 they were given permission to build this church in the north of Venice, on the site of a 12th-century church which had belonged to the Order of the Crociferi. Consecrated as Santa Maria Assunta, the church is always referred to simply as the Gesuiti; thus it is often confused with the Gesuati in Dorsoduro (*see p129*).

Domenico Rossi's imposing Baroque exterior gives only a hint of the opulence of the interior. The proliferation of green and white marble, carved in parts like great folds of fabric, gives the impression that the church is clothed in damask.

Titian's *Martyrdom of St Lawrence* (c.1555), above the first altar on the left, has been described by the art historian Hugh Honour as "the first successful nocturne in the history of art".

Santa Maria dei Miracoli ●

Campo dei Miracoli. **Map** 3 B5. **Tel** 041 275 04 62. 🚏 Fondamente Nuove or Rialto. 🕙 10am–5pm Mon–Sat, 1–5pm Sun & public hols. 💶 📷 ⌀

An exquisite masterpiece of the early Renaissance, the Miracoli is the favourite church of many Venetians and the one where they like to get married. Tucked away in a maze of alleys and waterways in eastern Cannaregio, it is small and somewhat elusive, but well worth the effort needed to find it.

Often likened to a jewel box, the façade is decorated with various shades of marble, with fine bas-reliefs and sculpture. It was built in 1481–9 by the architect Pietro Lombardo and his sons to enshrine *The Virgin and Child* (1408), a painting believed to have miraculous powers. The picture, by Nicolò di Pietro,

Decorative column, interior of Santa Maria dei Miracoli

can still be seen above the altar. The interior of the church, which ideally should be visited when pale shafts of sunlight are streaming in through the windows, is embellished by pink, white and grey marble and crowned by a barrel-vaulted ceiling (1528) which has 50 portraits of saints and prophets. The balustrade, between the nave and the chancel, is decorated by Tullio Lombardo's carved figures of St Francis, Archangel Gabriel, the Virgin and St Clare. The screen around the high altar and the medallions of the Evangelists in the cupola spandrels are also by Lombardo.

Above the main door, the choir gallery was used by the nuns from the neighbouring convent, who entered the church through an overhead gallery. The Miracoli has recently undergone a major restoration programme, which was funded by the American Save Venice organization.

SANTA MARIA DEI MIRACOLI
The façade is a harmonious tapestry of decorated panels and multi-coloured polished stone.

The semi-circular crowning lunette emphasizes the church's jewel-box appearance.

A false loggia is formed of Ionic arches, inset with windows. The marble used was reportedly left over from the building of San Marco.

The marble panels are fixed to the bricks by metal hooks. This method, which prevents the build-up of damp and salt water behind the panels, dates from the Renaissance.

For hotels and restaurants in this region see pp228–33 and pp242–7

San Giovanni Grisostomo, the last work of Mauro Coducci

San Giovanni Grisostomo ⑨

Campo S Giovanni Grisostomo.
Map 3 B5. Tel 041 523 52 93.
Rialto. 8:15am–12:15pm,
7:30pm daily No entry during
mass.

This pretty terracotta-coloured church is found near the Rialto. Built between 1479 and 1504, the church was the last work of Mauro Coducci.

The interior, built on a Greek-cross plan, is dark and intimate. Notable works of art include Giovanni Bellini's *St Jerome with Saints Christopher and Augustine* (1513), above the first altar on the right. Influenced by Giorgione, this was probably Bellini's last painting. Another artist inspired by Giorgione was Sebastiano del Piombo, whose *St John Chrysostom and Six Saints* (1509–11) hangs above the high altar. Some believe that the figures of St John the Baptist and St Liberal were painted by Giorgione himself.

Santi Apostoli ⑩

Campo Santi Apostoli. Map 3 B5.
Tel 041 523 82 97. Ca' d'Oro.
9am–noon, 4–7pm daily.

The Campo Santi Apostoli is a busy crossroads for pedestrians en route to the Rialto or the railway station. Its church is unremarkable architecturally and little

MARCO POLO

Born around 1254 in the quarter of Cannaregio near the Rialto, Marco Polo left Venice at the age of 18 for his four-year voyage to the court of the Emperor Kublai Khan. He impressed the Mongol emperor and stayed for some 20 years, working as a travelling diplomat.

Returning to Venice in 1295, he brought with him a fortune in jewels and a host of spellbinding stories about the Khan's court.

As a prisoner of war in Genoa in 1298 he compiled an account of his travels, with the cooperation of an inmate. Translated into French, this was to become *Le Livre des merveilles*. Despite the fact that many Italians disbelieved his wondrous tales of the east, the book was an instant success.

His nickname became Marco Il Milione (of the million lies); hence the name of the two little courtyards where the Polo family lived: Corte Prima del Milion and Corte Seconda del Milion.

Marco Polo leaving on his travels, from a manuscript c.1338

remains of the 16th-century building. A notable exception, however, is the enchanting late 15th-century Renaissance Corner Chapel on the right of the nave, believed to have been designed by Mauro Coducci. The chapel contains *The Communion of St Lucy* by Giambattista Tiepolo (1748), the tomb of Marco Corner, probably by Tullio Lombardo (1511), and an inscription to Corner's daughter, Caterina Cornaro, Queen of Cyprus, who was buried here before she was moved to the Church of San Salvatore *(see p94)*.

Tomb of Doge Marco Corner in Santi Apostoli (Corner Chapel)

Ca' d'Oro ⑪

See p144.

Palazzo Labia ⑫

Fondamenta Labia (entrance on Campo S Geremia). Map 2 D4.
Tel 041 781 111. Ponte Guglie.
Renovation in progress. Call ahead.

The Labias were a wealthy family of merchants from Catalonia who bought their way into the Venetian patriciate in 1646. Towards the end of the century they built their prestigious palace on the wide Cannaregio Canal, close to its junction with the Grand Canal. In 1745–50 the ballroom was frescoed by Giambattista Tiepolo. The wonderfully painted scenes are taken from the life of Cleopatra but the setting is Venice, and the queen's attire is that of a 16th-century noble lady.

Passed from one owner to another the palace gradually lost all trace of its former grandeur and variously served as a religious foundation, a school and a doss-house. Between 1964 and 1992 it was owned by the Italian broadcasting network, RAI, who undertook its restoration.

The frescoes can be seen free of charge, but only by making an appointment.

Ca' d'Oro ⓫

One of the great showpieces of the Grand Canal, the Ca' d'Oro (or House of Gold) is the finest example of Venetian Gothic architecture in the city. The façade, with its finely carved ogee windows, oriental pinnacles and exotic marble tracery, has an unmistakable flavour of the east. But this once gloriously embellished *palazzo* suffered many changes of fortune and there is now little inside to remind visitors that this was once a 15th-century palace. Since 1984 it has been home to the Giorgio Franchetti Collection.

HISTORY

In 1420 the wealthy patrician, Marino Contarini, commissioned the building of what he was determined would be the most magnificent palace in the city. The decoration and the intricate carving were executed by a team of Venetian and Lombard craftsmen, and he had the façade adorned in ultramarine, gold leaf and vermilion.

Tullio Lombardo's Double Portrait

In the course of the 16th century the house was remodelled by a succession of owners, and by the early 18th century was semi-derelict. In 1846 the Russian Prince Troubetzkoy bought it for the famous ballerina Maria Taglioni. Under her direction, the Ca' d'Oro suffered barbaric restoration. The open staircase was ripped out, the wellhead by Bartolomeo Bon (1427–8) was sold and much of the stonework removed. It was finally rescued by Baron Franchetti, a patron of the arts, who restored it to its former glory and bequeathed it to the state in 1915. A restoration programme for the façade, first put into action in the 1970s, is now finally completed, revealing the building's exotic design. The pretty paved courtyard contains Bon's beautifully carved wellhead. This was one of the pieces retrieved by Franchetti.

FIRST FLOOR

Pride of place is given to Andrea Mantegna's *St Sebastian* (1506), the artist's last painting and Franchetti's favourite work of art. The *portego* (gallery) opening on to the Grand Canal is a showroom of sculpture. Among the finest pieces are bronze relief by the Paduan sculptor, Il Riccio (1470–1532), Tullio Lombardo's marble *Double Portrait* (c.1493) and Sansovino's lunette of the Virgin and Child (c.1530). Rooms to the right of the *portego* have some fine Renaissance bronzes and, among the paintings, an *Annunciation* and *Death of the Virgin* (both c.1504) by Vittore Carpaccio and assistants. A room to the left of the *portego* is devoted to non-Venetian painting, and includes Luca Signorelli's *Flagellation* (c.1480).

SECOND FLOOR

The upper floor houses paintings by Venetian masters, including a *Venus* by Titian, two Venetian views by Guardi, and fresco fragments by Titian. Other exhibits include tapestries and ceramics. Explanatory cards in each room aid visitors.

The *Annunciation* (1504) by Vittore Carpaccio and assistants

VISITORS' CHECKLIST

Canal Grande (Calle Ca' d'Oro). **Map** 3 A4. **Tel** 041 523 87 90. Ca' d'Oro. ⏱ 8:15am–7:15pm daily (to 2pm Mon). ⏺ 1 Jan, 1 May, 25 Dec.

Scalzi ⑬

Fondamenta Scalzi. **Map** 1 C4.
Tel 041 71 51 15. Ferrovia.
◯ 7am–noon, 4–7pm daily.

Beside the modern railway station *(see p58)* stands the church of Santa Maria di Nazareth, known as the Scalzi. The *scalzi* were "barefooted" Carmelite friars who came to Venice during the 1670s and commissioned their church to be built on the Grand Canal. Designed by Baldassare Longhena, the huge Baroque interior is an over-elaboration of marble, gilded woodwork and sculptures. The ceiling painting, *The Council of Ephesus* by Ettore Tito (1934), replaced Giambattista Tiepolo's fresco of *The Translation of the Holy House to Loreto* (1743–5), which was destroyed by the Austrian bombardment of 24 October 1915.

San Giobbe ⑭

Campo San Giobbe. **Map** 1 C3. *Tel* 041 275 04 62. Ponte dei 3 Archi. ◯ 10am–5pm Mon–Sat. ∅

The church of San Giobbe stands in a remote *campo* full of cats. The early Gothic structure of the church was modified in the 1470s by Pietro Lombardo who added Renaissance elements to the design such as the saints over the portal. The Martini chapel, second on the left, is decorated with Della Robbia-style glazed terracotta. The altarpieces by Giovanni Bellini and Vittore Carpaccio were removed when Napoleon suppressed the monastery of San Giobbe, and are now in the Accademia Gallery *(pp130–33)*.

**Saint by Lombardo,
San Giobbe portal**

The Ghetto ⑮

Map 2 E3. *Tel* 041 71 53 59. Ponte Guglie. **Museo Ebraico** Campo del Ghetto Nuovo. Ponte Guglie. ◯ 10am–7pm (Oct–May: 10am–5pm) Sun–Fri. ● 1 Jan, 1 May, 25 Dec, Jewish hols.

In 1516 the Council of Ten *(see p42)* decreed that all Jews in Venice be confined to an islet of Cannaregio. The quarter was cut off by wide canals and the two watergates were manned by Christian guards. The area was named the Ghetto after a foundry – *geto* in Venetian – that formerly occupied the site. The name was subsequently given to Jewish enclaves throughout the world. By day Jews were allowed out of the Ghetto, but at all times they were made to wear identifying badges and caps. The only trades they could pursue were in textiles, money-lending and medicine.

The rising number of Jews forced the Ghetto to expand.

The wrought-iron bridge leading northwards out of the Ghetto

Buildings rose vertically (the so-called skyscrapers of Venice) and spread into the Ghetto Vecchio (1541) and the neighbouring Ghetto Novissimo (1633). By the mid-17th century the Jewish population numbered over 5,000.

In 1797 Napoleon pulled down the gates, but under the Austrians the Jews were again forced into confinement. It was not until 1866 that they were granted their freedom.

Of the 500 Jews now in Venice, only 33 live in the Ghetto. However, the quarter has not lost its ethnic character. There are kosher food shops, a Jewish baker, a Jewish library, and two synagogues where religious ceremonies still take place. There are also several shops on the large, recently restored Campo del Ghetto Nuovo, which sell items such as glass rabbis and Hanukah lamps.

Flowers in front of the Holocaust Memorial

Museo Ebraico

The small Jewish Museum in the Ghetto Nuovo houses a collection of artifacts from the 17th–19th centuries. A guided tour of the quarter's synagogues leaves from the museum daily except Saturday, every hour from 10:30am to 5:30pm (4:30pm in winter). Led by English-speaking guides, the tours give a fascinating glimpse into the past life of the Ghetto. A short history of the quarter is followed by a visit to the lavishly decorated German, Spanish and Levantine synagogues.

Campo del Ghetto Nuovo, the oldest part of the Ghetto

THE LAGOON ISLANDS

Image of the Madonna, Torcello

S hrouded in myth and superstition, the lagoon was once the preserve of fishermen and hunters. But marauders in the 5th and 6th centuries AD drove mainland dwellers to the safety of the marshy lagoon *(see p40)*. Here, they conquered their watery environment, which was protected from the open sea by thin sandbanks *(lidi)*, created from silt washed down by the rivers of the Po delta. In the 13th century the first *murazzi* were built – sea walls of angular stone which safeguard the *lidi* from erosion. Experiments with tidal barriers continue in an effort to combat the ever-present threat of flooding *(see p51)*.

The thriving communities that once lived and traded here are long gone. Many of the islands, formerly used as sites for monasteries, hospitals or powder factories, are now abandoned, but a handful of them are undergoing development – one as an international university, another as an exclusive resort.

SIGHTS AT A GLANCE

Burano ❷
Giudecca ❻
Lazzaretto Nuovo ⓬
Lido ❿
Murano ❹
Poveglia ⓭
San Clemente ⓫

San Francesco del Deserto ❸
San Lazzaro degli Armeni ❾
San Michele ❺
San Servolo ❼
Santa Maria della Grazia ❽
Torcello pp152–3 ❶

KEY

✈ Airfield

🚉 Railway station

| 0 kilometres | 5 |
| 0 miles | 3 |

◁ **Colourful houses in Burano**

Exploring the Lagoon

A trip to the Lagoon Islands makes a welcome break from the densely packed streets of the city. Murano, celebrated for its glass, can be reached in a matter of minutes. Further north, Burano, the "lace island", and ancient Torcello are well worth the longer ride. The Lido, with its sandy beaches, is an easy journey from San Marco. Some of the lesser known islands are worth exploring too, but access can sometimes be difficult.

Murano
Some of Murano's canalside porticoes survive from medieval days

Murano and San Michele
are clearly visible from the northern quaysides of Venice.

San Michele
World-famous writers and artists are buried alongside Venetians on this island ❺

VENEZIA

San Giorgio in Alga had its monastery partially destroyed by fire in 1717. It was demolished in the 19th century.

SANTA MARIA DELLA GRAZIA ❽

SAN CLEMENTE ⓫

Giudecca
Palladio's great church of the Redentore, on the waterfront, is the island's cultural highlight ❻

Sant'Angelo della Polvere, recognizable by its towers, was formerly a powder factory.

SAN SPIRITO ●

Sacca Sessola, an artificial island, was the site of a hospital until 1980.

POVEGLIA ⓭

Lido
Behind the crowded beaches and grand hotels, the Lido has some pleasantly peaceful waterways ❿

Torcello
The island's cathedral, founded in AD 639, is the oldest building in the lagoon **1**

Sant'Ariano is a former ossuary island where the bones of Venetians were taken.

Burano
Gaily painted, shuttered houses are a distinctive feature of the island's streets and quaysides **2**

MAZZORBO

e **Vignole** has
narket gardens and
an ancient fort.

MADONNA DEL MONTE

SAN GIACOMO IN PALUDE

3 SAN FRANCESCO DEL DESERTO

TREPORTI

12 LAZZARETTO NUOVO

PUNTA SABBIONI

Sant' Erasmo, once a Roman pleasure ground, is now a vegetable garden.

PORTO DI LIDO

SAN NICOLO

LIDO

GOLFO DI VENEZIA

San Servolo
This is now a centre for artisans learning restoration techniques, such as stucco and plasterwork **7**

GETTING AROUND
The main islands of the northern lagoon are well served by the *vaporetti (see pp282–3)* and the Laguna Nord boat route from Fondamente Nuove. A few of the smaller islands have a limited public service; others can only be reached by water taxi.

Lazzaretto Vecchio
is a tiny island with
a varied past. It can
be seen in the
distance from the
boat that runs
from San Marco
to the Lido.

San Lazzaro degli Armeni
Visits to this green and pretty monastery island take in the church, library, museum and printing press **9**

0 kilometres 2

0 miles 1

KEY

Major road

Minor road

Torcello **❶**

See pp152–3.

A stall selling lace and linen in Burano's main street

Burano **❷**

🚤 *LN, either from Fondamente Nuove, approx. 40–50 minutes, or from San Zaccaria via the Lido and Punta Sabbioni, approx. 1½ hours.*

Burano is the most colourful of the lagoon islands. Lying in a lonely expanse of the northern lagoon, it is distinguished from a distance by the tall, dramatically tilted tower of its church. In contrast to the desolate Torcello, the island is densely populated, its waterways lined by brightly painted houses.

A tour of the island's sights will take an hour or so. The street from the ferry stop takes visitors to the main thoroughfare, Via Baldassare Galuppi, named after the Burano-born composer (1706–85). The

street is lined with lace and linen stalls and open-air trattorias serving fresh fish.

🏛 Museo del Merletto

Piazza Baldassare Galuppi. *Tel 041 73 00 34.* ☐ *10am–5pm Wed–Mon (to 4pm Nov–Mar).* ● *1 Jan, 1 May, 25 Dec.* 📷

The Buranese are fishermen and lacemakers by trade. Visitors can still see the men scraping their boats or mending nets, but lacemakers are rare. In the 16th century the local lace was the most sought after in Europe. It was so delicate it became known as *punto in aria* ("points in the air"). Foreign competition, coupled with the Republic's decline, led to a slump in the 18th century in Burano's industry. However, the need for a new source of income led to a revival of the skill in 1872 and the founding of a lacemaking school, the Scuola dei Merletti.

Today, authentic Burano lace is hard to find. Genuine pieces take weeks of pain-staking labour, and are expensive. Original pieces can be seen at the informative Museo del Merletto. Displays of household linens and clothing feature fine antique lace, much of it created at the school.

Mazzorbo

Linked to Burano by a foot-bridge, Mazzorbo is an island of orchards and gardens. Ferries en route to Burano and Torcello pass through its canal. The only surviving church is the Romanesque-Gothic Santa Caterina.

San Francesco del Deserto **❸**

Access via water taxi from the landing stage in Burano. *Visits to the island: usually 9–11am, 3–5pm Tue–Sun, but call ahead for up-to-date information.* Monastery *Tel 041 528 68 63.*

This little Oasis of greenery, inhabited by nine friars, lies just south of Burano. There is no *vaporetto* service and to get there you must bargain with the boatmen on Burano's quayside, who will ferry you across the shallow waters and await your return.

The multilingual friars who live on the island give tours of the old church and the lovely gardens, which have a tree said to have sprouted from the staff of St Francis of Assisi.

A Buranese fisherman about to haul in the day's catch

Murano **❹**

🚤 *No. 41, 42 or LN from Fondamente Nuove; DM from Piazzale Roma.*

Like the city of Venice, Murano comprises a cluster of small islands, connected by bridges. It has been the centre of the glassmaking industry since 1291, when the furnaces and glass craftsmen were moved here from the city, prompted by the risk of fire to the buildings and the dis-agreeable effects of smoke.

Historically Murano owes its prosperity entirely to glass. From the late 13th century, when the population num-bered over 30,000, Murano enjoyed self-government, minted its own coins and had its own Golden Book *(see p42)* listing members of the aristoc-racy. In the 15th and 16th centuries it was the principal glass-producing centre in Europe. Murano's glass artisans were granted unprecedented privileges, but for those who

Brightly painted street in Burano

eft the island to found busi-
esses elsewhere there were
evere penalties – even death.
   Although a few of Murano's
palazzi bear testimony to its
former splendour, and its
basilica still survives, most
tourists visit for glass alone.
Some are enticed by offers of
free trips from factory touts in
San Marco, others go by excursion launch or independently
on the public *vaporetti*.
   Some of the factories are
now derelict, but glass is still
produced in vast quantities.
Among the plethora of kitsch
(including imports from the
Far East) are some wonderful
pieces, and it pays to seek
out the top glass factories *(see
p253)*. Many furnaces, however, close at the weekend.

⬛ Museo Vetrario

Palazzo Giustinian, Fondamenta
Giustinian. **Tel** 041 73 95 86. ⬜
10am–6pm Thu–Tue (Nov–Mar: to
5pm). ⬤ 1 Jan, 1 May, 25 Dec. ⬛ ⬜
The Museo Vetrario (glass
museum) in the huge Palazzo
Giustinian houses a splendid
collection of antique pieces.
The prize exhibit of the collection is the Barovier wedding
cup (1470–80), with enamel-
work decoration by Angelo
Barovier. There is also a section
devoted to modern glass, with
some splendid items on view.

⬛ Basilica dei Santi Maria e Donato

Fondamenta Giustinian.
Tel 041 73 90 56. ⬜ 8am–noon,
4–6pm daily. ⬤ Sun am.

The colonnaded exterior of Murano's Basilica dei Santi Maria e Donato

The island's architectural
highlight is the Basilica dei
Santi Maria e Donato, whose
magnificent colonnaded apse
is reflected in the waters of
the San Donato canal. Despite
some heavy-handed restoration undertaken in the 19th
century, this 12th-century
church still retains much of its
original beauty. Visitors
should note the Veneto-
Byzantine columns and
Gothic ship's keel roof.
An enchantingly evoca-
tive mosaic portrait of
the Madonna, seen stand-
ing alone against a gold
background, decorates
the apse.
   The church's floor, or
pavimento, dating from
1140, is equally beauti-
ful. With its medieval
mosaics of geometric
figures, exotic birds,
mythical creatures
and inexplicable symbols, it
incorporates fragments of
ancient glass from the island's
foundries into its imagery.

Diaghilev's
tombstone

San Michele ❺

🚤 No. 41 or 42 from Fondamente
Nuove.

Studded with dark cypress-
esand enclosed within high
terracotta walls, the cemetery
island of San Michele lies just
across the water from Venice's
Fondamente Nuove. The
bodies of Venetians were
traditionally buried in
church graveyards in
Venice, but for reasons of
hygiene and space, San
Michele and its neighbour
were designated cemeter-
ies in the 19th century.
   The church of San
Michele in Isola stands
by the landing stage.
Designed by Mauro
Coducci (c.1469), it
was the first church in
Venice to be faced in
white Istrian stone.
The cemetery itself rambles
over most of the island.
With its carved tombstones
and chapels it has a curious
fascination. Some graves
have suffered neglect, but
most are well-tended and
enlivened by a riot of flowers.
The most famous graves are
those of foreigners: Ezra
Pound (1885–1972), in the
Evangelisti (Protestant) section,
and Sergei Diaghilev (1872–
1929) and Igor Stravinsky
(1882–1971) in the *Greci* or
Orthodox section. These
bodies have been allowed to
rest in peace. Most others are
dug up after about ten years
to make way for new arrivals,
and the bones taken to the
ossuary island of Sant'Ariano.
Today, however, because of
increasing lack of space on
San Michele, most bodies are
buried on the mainland.

GLASS BLOWING

A main attraction of a trip to
Murano is a demonstration of
the glass-blowing technique.
Visitors can watch while a
glass blower takes a blob of
molten paste on the end of
an iron rod and, by twisting,
turning and blowing, miracu-
lously transforms it into a
vase, bird, lion, wine goblet
or similar work of art. The
display is followed by a tour
of the showroom and a certain amount of pressure from
the salespeople. There is no
obligation to buy, however.

Glass blower at work in Murano

Torcello **❶**

Established between the 5th and 6th centuries, Torcello grew into a thriving colony *(see p40)*, with palaces, churches and a population said to have reached 20,000. But with the rise of Venice the island went into decline. Today, the population is just 60 and all that remains of this once vigorous island is the Byzantine cathedral, the church of Santa Fosca and the memory of its former glory.

★ **Apse Mosaic**
The 13th-century Madonna, set against a gold background, is one of the most moving mosaics in Venice.

★ **Domesday Mosaics**
The huge and highly decorative mosaic of the Last Judgment covers the entire west wall.

Pulpit
The present basilica dates from 1008, but includes many earlier features. The marble pulpit is made of fragments from the first, 7th-century church.

The Roman sarcophagus below the altar is said to contain the relics of St Heliodorus.

★ **Iconostasis**
The exquisite Byzantine marble panels of the rood screen are carved with peacocks, lions and flowers. This detailed relief shows two peacocks drinking from the fountain of life.

Nave Columns
The finely carved capitals on the marble nave columns date from the 11th century.

Torcello's Last Canals
Silted canals and malaria hastened Torcello's decline. One of the remaining waterways runs from the vaporetto stop to the basilica.

Santa Fosca
Built in the 11th and 12th centuries on a Greek-cross plan, the church has a lovely portico and a serene Byzantine interior.

The central dome
and cross sections are supported by columns of Greek marble with fine Corinthian capitals.

Attila's Throne
It was said that the 5th-century king of the Huns used this marble seat as his throne.

To *vaporetto* boarding point →

Museo dell' Estuario
Old church treasures and archaeological fragments are housed here.

STAR FEATURES

★ Iconostasis

★ Domesday Mosaics

★ Apse Mosaic

Boats moored along the Ponte Lungo on the Giudecca

Giudecca ❻

No. 41, 42 or 82.

In the days of the Republic, the island of Giudecca was a pleasure ground of palaces and gardens. Today it is very much a suburb of the city, its dark, narrow alleys flanked by apartments, its squares overgrown and its *palazzi* neglected. Many of its old factories have been converted into modern housing. However, the long, wide quayside skirting the city side of the island makes a very pleasant promenade and provides stunning views of Venice across the water. The

island was originally named Spinalunga (long spine) on account of its shape. The name Giudecca, once thought to have referred to the Jews, or *giudei*, who lived here in the 13th century, is more likely to have originated from the word *giudicati* meaning "the judged". This referred to troublesome aristocrats who, as early as the 9th century, were banished to the island.

The Hotel Cipriani *(see p233)*, among the most luxurious places to stay in Venice, is quietly and discreetly located at the tip of the island. In contrast, at the western end of the island looms the massive Neo-Gothic ruin of the Mulino Stucky. It was built in 1895 as a flour mill by the Swiss entrepreneur Giovanni Stucky, an unpopular employer who was murdered by one of his workers in 1910. The mill ceased functioning in 1954. Following extensive renovations, it re-opened in 2007 as a luxury hotel with a rooftop pool.

✿ Il Redentore

Campo Redentore. **Tel** *041 275 04 62.* 🚤 *Redentore.* ◯ *10am–5pm daily (from 1pm Sun & public hols).* ◑ *Sun (Jul & Aug); 1 Jan, 25 Dec.* 🖼 🗌

Giudecca's principal monument is Palladio's church of Il Redentore (the Redeemer). It was built in 1577–92 in thanksgiving for the end of the 1576 plague, which wiped out a third of the city's population. Every year since its creation, the doge and his entourage would visit the church, crossing from the Zattere on a bridge of boats. The Feast of the Redeemer is still celebrated on the third weekend in July *(see p34)*.

The church of Il Redentore, styled on the architecture of ancient Rome, is a masterpiece of harmony and proportion. The Classical interior presents a marked contrast to the ornate and elaborate style of most Venetian churches. The main paintings, by Paolo Veronese and Alvise

Vivarini, are in the sacristy to the right of the choir. The most rewarding views of the Redentore are from Venice across the water. For special festivities the church is often floodlit after dark, which makes a spectacular sight.

✿ Le Zitelle

Fondamenta delle Zitelle. **Tel** *041 521 74 11.* 🚤 *Zitelle.* ◯ *Apr–Oct: 3:30–6:30pm Fri & Sat.* 🗌

Palladio's church is now the site of Venice's most up-to-date congress centre. The building adjoining the church used to be a hostel for spinsters *(zitelle)*, who occupied themselves by making fine lace.

An artisan at work at the San Servolo training centre

San Servolo ❼

No. 20 from San Zaccaria.
Venice International University Tel *041 271 95 11.*

Half-way between San Marco and the Lido is the island of San Servolo. Now a centre for teaching crafts and home to the Venice International University, it started life as one of the original monastery islands of Venice. Benedictine monks established a monastery here in the 8th century, and later added a hospital.

In 1725 the island became a lunatic asylum and a new hospital was built to house the patients. The Council of Ten *(see p42)* declared that this was to be strictly a shelter for "maniacs of noble family or comfortable circumstances". Poor maniacs were imprisoned or left to their own devices. In 1797 Napoleon scrubbed this discriminatory decree and the asylum became free to all. In 1980 this spartan island

Palladio's Redentore church, Giudecca

was taken over by The Venice European Centre for the Trades and Professions of Conservation. Later, in 1996, Venice International University opened its doors here. Extensive renovation work has restored the historic buildings, and the large park in which they are set.

Santa Maria della Grazia ❽

No public access.

Originally called La Cavana or Cavanell, the island lies just a short distance away from San Giorgio Maggiore (see p95). Formerly a shelter for pilgrims on their journey to the Holy Land, it became a monastery island in the 15th century. Its name was changed when a church was constructed to enshrine a miraculous image of the Virgin, brought from Constantinople. The religious buildings, including a Gothic church with some fine paintings, were secularized under Napoleon. The island became a military zone under his rule, but the buildings were subsequently destroyed during the 1848 revolutionary uprising (see p48).

More recently occupied by a hospital for infectious diseases, this has now been transferred to the main hospital in Venice and the island sold.

San Lazzaro degli Armeni ❾

Tel 041 526 01 04. 🚤 No. 20 from Riva degli Schiavoni. ◯ 3:30–5pm daily. 🏛 🎥

Lying just off the Lido (see p156), San Lazzaro degli Armeni is a small, very green monastery island, recognizable by the onion-shaped cupola of its white campanile. The buildings are surrounded by well-groomed gardens and dark groves of cypress trees. Since the 18th century it has been an Armenian monastery and centre of learning.

Early history

This small island served as an asylum in the 12th century and later became a hospital island for lepers, named after their patron saint, Lazarus. The lepers were then transferred to the Ospedale di San Lazzaro dei Mendicanti at Santi Giovanni e Paolo (see pp116–17). In 1717 an Armenian monk, Manug di Pietro, known as Mechitar ("the consoler"), was forced to flee his homeland, the Morea, when the Turks invaded. Venetian rulers gave him the island of San Lazzaro in the southern lagoon as a place of shelter. Here, he established a religious order. The Armenians rebuilt the island, setting up a monastery, church, library, study rooms, gardens and

Illuminated manuscript, San Lazzaro degli Armeni

Prince Nehmekhet's sarcophagus (c.1000 BC), San Lazzaro

orchards. The island became a place of study where monks taught (and still teach) young Armenians their culture.

The island today

Today, multilingual monks give visitors guided tours of the church, the art collection, the library and the museum, which houses Armenian, Greek, Indian and Egyptian artifacts. One of the most famous is an Egyptian sarcophagus complete with mummy, which is one of the best-preserved in the world. The most impressive exhibit is the printing hall where, over 200 years ago, a press produced works in 36 languages. A polyglot press is still in use, producing postcards, maps and prints for visitors.

Lord Byron

In 1816 the poet Byron would often row from Venice to absorb Armenian culture. Full of admiration for the monks, he wrote that the monastery "appears to unite all the advantages of the monastic institution without any of its vices ... the virtues of the brethren ... are well fitted to strike a man of the world with the conviction that 'there is another and a better', even in this life." The room where he studied, with mementoes, has been carefully preserved.

The garden and cloisters of San Lazzaro degli Armeni

The Lido, away from the crowds and glare of the beaches

Lido ⑩

🚤 No's 1, 51, 52, 61, 62, 82 (summer) and LN to Santa Maria Elisabetta; No. 17 from Tronchetto to San Nicolò.

The Lido is a slender sand-bank 12 km (8 miles) long, which forms a natural barrier between Venice and the open sea. It is both a residential suburb of the city and – more importantly for tourists – the city's seaside resort. The only island in the lagoon with roads, it is linked to the Tronchetto island car park by car ferry. From Venice, the Lido is served by regular

The elegant bar of the Hôtel des Bains on the Lido

vaporetti. The fastest of these (Motonave LN) takes little more than ten minutes to reach its destination.

The Lido's main season runs from June to September, the most crowded months being July and August. In winter most hotels are closed.

The world's first lido

In the 19th century, before the Lido was developed, the island was a favourite haunt of Shelley, Byron and other literary figures. Byron swam from the Lido to Santa Chiara via the Grand Canal in under four hours.

Bathing establishments were gradually opened and by the turn of the century the Lido had become one of Europe's most fashionable seaside resorts, frequented by royalty, film stars and leading lights of the literati. They stayed in the grand hotels, swam in the sea or sat in deckchairs on the sands by the striped *cabanas.* Life in the Lido's heyday was brilliantly evoked in Thomas Mann's book *Death in Venice* (1912). The Hôtel des Bains, where the melancholic Von

Aschenbach stays, features in the novel and in Visconti's 1970 film. It is still a promi-nent landmark and an elegant place to stay *(see p233).*

The Lido is no longer the prestigious resort it was in the 1930s. Beaches are crowded, the streets busy and the ferries packed with daytrippers. Nevertheless the sands, sea and sporting facilities provide a welcome break from city culture. The backwaters pro-vide a green respite from the heat of Venice.

Exploring the island

The Lido can be covered by bus but a popular form of transport is the bicycle. Visitors can hire one from the shop almost opposite the *vaporetto* stop at Santa Maria Elisabetta.

The east side of the island is fringed by sandy beaches. For passengers arriving by ferry at the main landing stage, these beaches are reached by bus, taxi or on foot along the Gran Viale Santa Maria Elisabetta. This is the main shopping street of the Lido. At the end of the Gran Viale turn left for the beaches of San Nicolò or right along the Lungomare G Marconi, which boasts the grandest hotels and the best beaches. The hotels control the beaches in this area, and levy exorbitant charges (except to hotel residents) for the use of their beach facilities.

The long straight road parallel to the beach leads southwest to the village of

Cabanas on the Lido beaches, hired out to holidaying Venetians

Malamocco. There are some pleasant fish restaurants, but there is little evidence that this was once the 8th-century seat of the lagoon's government.

Alberoni, at the southern end of the Lido, is the site of a golf course, a public beach and the landing stage for the ferry across to Pellestrina.

San Nicolò

The Lido's only quarter of cultural interest is San Nicolò in the north.

Across the Porto di Lido, it is possible to see the fortress of Sant'Andrea on the island of Le Vignole, built by Michele Sanmicheli between 1435 and 1449 to guard the main entrance of the lagoon.

It was to the Porto di Lido that the doge was rowed annually to cast a ring into the sea in symbolic marriage each spring *(see p33)*. After the cer-emony he would visit the nearby church and monastery of San Nicolò, which was founded in 1044 and rebuilt in the 16th century.

The nearby Jewish ceme-tery, open to the public, dates from 1386. The rest of this northern area is given over to an airfield. The aeroclub located there can organize private flying lessons.

Jewish Cemetery
Tel 041 71 53 59.
call in advance for a guided visit.

San Clemente ⓫

San Clemente Palace Hotel
Tel 041 244 50 01.
www.sanclemente.thi.it

From a refuge for pilgrims en route to the Holy Land, the island of San Clemente became the site of a monastery. During the Republic, doges frequently met distinguished visitors here, but from 1630, when it was hit by the plague, it served as a military depot. In the 19th century the island was turned into a lunatic asy-lum; most of the buildings date from that time. The beau-tifully restored San Clemente Palace Hotel can be reached by launch from Piazza San Marco.

INTERNATIONAL FILM FESTIVAL

Film fans flock to the Lido every year in late summer for the International Film Festival. The event was inaugurated in 1932 under the auspices of the Biennale *(see p256)* and was so successful that the Palazzo del Cinema was built four years later. During its history the festival has attracted big names in the film world; it has also been plagued by bureaucracy and political in-fighting. There are signs however that the event is making a comeback and the famous names are now returning to the Lido.

The event takes place over two weeks in late August/early September. Films are shown day and night in numerous venues including the Palazzo del Cinema (tickets are sold outside). You can normally spot the stars (along with the paparazzi) for the price of a drink on the terrace of the Excelsior Hotel. See also page 259.

Poster advertising the first Lido International Film Festival, 1932

Lazzaretto Nuovo ⓬

Tel 041 244 40 11. No. 13. Apr–Oct: 9:45am & 4pm Sat & Sun. donation.

A mere stone's throw from Sant'Erasmo, in the northern lagoon, Lazzaretto Nuovo is one of the few uninhabited visitable islands. Archaeologists continue to unearth medieval structures dating back to the late 1400s, when the island was used as a quarantine station for crews of ships hailing from distant lands where the plague was rife. Cargoes would be fumigated with rosemary and juniper. During the terrible pestilence that afflicted Venice in 1576, the island housed 10,000 victims.

Poveglia ⓭

No public access.

Formerly called Popilia on account of all its poplar trees, the island was once a thriving community with its own government. After the 1380 war with Genoa, it fell into decline, and over the centuries became a refuge for plague victims, an isolation hospital and a home for the aged. Today the land is used for growing crops and vines.

San Clemente in the southern lagoon, seen through the evening mist

The picturesque lakeside setting of Alleghe in the Dolomites ▷

THE VENETO
AREA BY AREA

The Veneto at a Glance

The Veneto's sheer variety makes it one of
Italy's most fascinating regions to explore. The
cities of Verona, Padua and Vicenza are all
noted for outstanding architecture, churches
and museums. Villas in the rural hinterland are
gorgeously frescoed with scenes from ancient
mythology. The lagoon has busy fishing ports
and beach resorts, while Lake Garda, with its
glorious mountain scenery, historic castles and
water sports, makes a perfect holiday playground. Northwards lie the majestic Dolomites,
Italy's premier region for skiing, which attract
visitors in the summer, too, with their alpine
beauty and excellent hiking facilities.

Monti Lessini
*Scores of scenic villages, such as
Giazza (see p191), nestle in the
vineyard-clad valleys of the
Lessini mountains.*

Verona
*An ancient Roman stronghold,
famous as the home of the lovers
Romeo and Juliet, Verona today
is a city of opera, theatre and
art (see pp192–203).*

VERONA AND LAKE GARDA
Pages 186–209

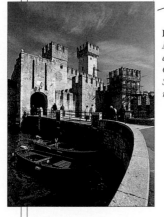

Lake Garda
*Most beautiful of
all the Italian lakes,
Garda is surrounded by
Scaligeri castles such as the
magnificent Sirmione (see p204).*

Vicenza
*Dominated by the architecture of
Palladio, Vicenza (see pp168–73) is
the model Renaissance city.*

Dolomites
Erosion has sculpted the limestone peaks of the Dolomites into bizarre columns and spires, with alpine villages hidden in steep valleys (see p216).

THE DOLOMITES
Pages 210–219

Villa Barbaro
Veronese's lavish frescoes are the perfect complement to one of Palladio's grandest rural villas, surrounded by statue-filled formal gardens, grottoes and pools (see p24).

0 kilometres   30

0 miles   15

THE VENETO PLAIN
Pages 162–185

Portogruaro
Roman and early Christian finds fill the museums of this ancient town (see p175).

Padua
The domes and minaret-like spires of St Anthony's basilica (see p182) lend an Eastern air to this historic university town.

Chioggia
Flocks of wading birds frequent the wild marshland around Chioggia (see p185), the Venetian lagoon's principal fishing port.

THE VENETO PLAIN

he great arc of land that forms the Veneto Plain is one of tremendous contrast, and has much to offer the visitor. Its ancient cities are rich in history and their magnificent architecture is world-renowned. The source of the region's wealth is manifest in the industrial landscapes around the towns, but these are never far from beautiful countryside, which includes the green Euganean Hills, calm lagoons and the undulating foothills of the Dolomites.

The area known as the Veneto Plain sweeps round from the Po river delta in the southwest to the mountains that form the border between Italy and Slovenia. The whole region is crossed by a series of rivers, canals and waterways, all of which converge in the Adriatic sea.

The river-borne silt deposits that created the Venetian Lagoon cover the region, making the land fertile. The Romans established their frontier posts here, and these survive today as the great cities of Vicenza, Padua and Treviso. Their strategic position at the hub of the empire's road network enabled them to prosper under Roman rule, as they continued to do under the benign rule of the Venetian empire more than 1,000 years later.

Wealth from agriculture, commerce and the spoils of war paid for the beautification of these cities through the construction of Renaissance palaces and public buildings, many of them designed by the region's great architect, Andrea Palladio. His villas can be seen all over the Veneto, symbols of the idyllic and leisured existence once enjoyed by the region's aristocrats.

The symbols of modern prosperity – factories and scarred landscapes – are encountered frequently, especially around the town of Mestre. Yet there are areas of extraordinary beauty as well. Petrarch *(see p184)*, the great medieval romantic poet, so loved the area that he made his home among the gently wooded Euganean Hills.

Fishing from a breakwater in the lagoon at Chioggia

◁ Classical figure in the nymphaeum of the Villa Barbaro near Asolo

Exploring the Veneto Plain

The landscape of the Veneto Plain is as flat as a board, but it is far from dull. Villagers in the small communities dotted throughout the region used to compete to build the tallest church tower, and these seemingly needle-thin landmarks soaring skywards draw the traveller on. Great stone castles, dating from the 14th century, rise on almost every promontory, each with a backdrop on clear days of the distant Alps.

SEE ALSO

• *Where to Stay* pp233–4

• *Where to Eat* pp247–8

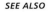

The castellated walls of Montagnana, dating from medieval times

GETTING AROUND

An extensive rail network and good bus services make this region easy to explore by public transport. Roads are heavily used, so avoid cities and *autostrade* during rush hours.

Palladio's Villa Rotonda near the town of Vicenza

The colourful quayside market in the town of Chioggia, the lagoon's principal fishing port

0 kilometres 20

0 miles 10

KEY

══ Motorway

= = Motorway under construction

── Major road

── Secondary road

── Minor road

── Scenic route

── Main railway

── Minor railway

══ Regional border

Vicenza **1**

See pp168–73.

Thiene **2**

🏠 20,000. 🚌 ℹ️ *Piazza Ferrarin 20. (0445 36 95 44).* 🖊️ *Mon am.*

Thiene is one of the area's many textile towns, manufacturing jeans and sweatshirts for sale all over Europe. Two villas nearby are worth a visit. The heavily fortified towers and battlemented walls of the **Castello Porto-Colleoni** are offset by pretty Gothic windows. At the time it was built, it stood in open countryside, and the defences were a precaution against bandits and raiders. Inside, 16th-century frescoes by Giambattista Zelotti add a lighter note and many portraits of horses remind the visitor that the villa's owners, the Colleoni family, were employed by the Venetian cavalry.

Zelotti also frescoed the **Villa Godi Malinverni**, the first villa designed by Palladio *(see pp24–5).* The garden is charming, and the frescoes are magnificent. Inside are works by Italian Impressionists and a lovely portrait by Pietro Annigoni (1910–88) called *La Strega* (the Sorceress).

♦ **Castello Porto-Colleoni**
Corso Garibaldi 12. **Tel** *0445 36 60 15.* 🕐 *mid-Mar–mid-Nov: Sun pm & public hols; Groups by appt.* 🅿️ 🔲

🏛️ **Villa Godi Malinverni**
Via Palladio 44. **Tel** *0445 86 05 61.* 🕐 *Mar–Nov: Tue, Sat & Sun afternoons; other times, phone ahead.* 🅿️

The human chess game in the town square of Maròstica

Maròstica **3**

🏠 12,500. 🚌 ℹ️ *Piazza Castello 1. (0424 721 27).* 🖊️ *Tue.*

Marostica is an almost perfect medieval fortified town, with town walls built in 1370 by the Scaligeri *(see p207).* The rampart walk from the **Castello Inferiore** (lower castle) to the **Castello Superiore** (upper castle) has fine views.

The lower castle exhibits costumes worn by participants in the town's human chess tournament, the *Partita a Scacchi*, held every other September *(see p35).* Up to 650 people participate in this colourful re-enactment of a game first played here in 1454.

♦ **Castello Inferiore**
Piazza Castello 1. **Tel** *0424 47 09 95.* 🕐 *9am–12:30pm, 3–6:30pm daily.* 🅿️

Bassano del Grappa **4**

🏠 38,770. 🚉 🚌 ℹ️ *Largo Corona d'Italia 35. (0424 52 43 51).* 🖊️ *Thu & Sat am.*

This peaceful town is synonymous with Italy's favourite after-dinner drink. Although grappa is produced here, it is not named after the town, but after the Italian term for the lees *(graspa)* used to distil the liquor. Information on this and on the role played by Bassano during both world wars is given at the **Museo degli Alpini**, across the Ponte degli Alpini bridge. Designed in 1569 by Palladio, the current bridge dates from 1948: its timber allows it to flex when hit by spring meltwaters.

Bassano is also famous for the majolica wares *(see p256)* at **Palazzo Sturm**. The locally born artist Jacopo Bassano (1510–92) and sculptor Canova (175–1822) are celebrated in the **Museo Civico**.

🏛️ **Museo degli Alpini**
Via Angarano 2. **Tel** *0424 50 36 62.* 🕐 *9am–8pm Tue–Sun.* 🔲 *10 days in Jan.*

🏛️ **Palazzo Sturm**
Via Schiavonetti 40. **Tel** *0424 52 49 33.* 🕐 *9am–1pm, 3–6pm Tue–Sun.* 🅿️

🏛️ **Museo Civico**
Piazza Garibaldi. **Tel** *0424 52 33 36.* 🕐 *9am–6:30pm Tue–Sat, 3:30–6:30pm Sun.* 🔲 *public hols.* 🅿️

The Ponte degli Alpini at Bassano del Grappa

Cittadella ❺

🏠 18,000. 🚉 🚌 ℹ️ Porte
Bassanesi 2 (0499 40 44 85). 🛒
Mon am.

This attractive town is the
twin of Castelfranco. Each
was fortified and Cittadella
still preserves its 13th-century
moated walls. These are
interrupted by four gates and
by 16 towers. The Torre di
Malta near the southern gate
was used as a torture chamber
by Ezzelino de Romano, who
ruled in the mid-13th century.
Far more pleasant to
contemplate is the *Supper
at Emmaus* in the **Duomo**,
a masterpiece by local Renaissance artist,
Bassano.

**Fresco from the Villa Emo at
Fanzolo, near Castelfranco**

Castelfranco ❻

🏠 30,000. 🚉 🚌 ℹ️ Via
Francesco Maria Preti 66 (0423
49 14 16). 🛒 Tue & Fri am.

Fortified in 1199 by rulers of
Treviso, the historic core of
this town lies within the well-
preserved walls. **Casa di
Giorgione**, claimed to be the
birthplace of artist Giorgione
(1478–1511), houses a museum
devoted to his life. He created
such moody and mysterious
works as *The Tempest (see
p131)*. His *Virgin and Child
with Saints Liberal and Francis*
(1504) is displayed in the
Duomo. It was commissioned
Tuzio Costanza to stand above
the tomb of his son, Matteo,
killed in battle in 1504.

At Fanzolo, 8 km (5 miles)
northeast of Castelfranco, is
the **Villa Emo**, designed in
1564 by Palladio. Here,

The pretty town of Asolo in the foothills of the Dolomites

Zelotti's sumptuous frescoes
reveal the love lives of the
Greek deities.

🏛 Casa di Giorgione
Piazzetta del Duomo. **Tel** 0423 72
50 22. ⭕ 9am–noon, 3–6pm Tue–
Sun. ⬤ public hols. 🖼

🏛 Villa Emo
Fanzolo di Vedelago. **Tel** 0423 47
63 34. 🚉 Fanzolo. 🚌 5. ⭕ Apr–
Oct: 3–6:30pm Mon–Sat; 10:30am–
12:30pm, 3–6:30pm Sun & public
hols; Nov–Mar: 2–4pm daily
(4:30pm Sat, Sun & public hols). ⬤
25 & 26 Dec. 🖼 📷

Asolo ❼

🏠 2,000. 🚌 ℹ️ Piazza Garibaldi 73
(0423 52 90 46). 🛒 Sat.

Asolo is beautifully sited
among the cypress-clad
foothills of the Dolomites.
Queen Caterina Cornaro
(1454–1510) once ruled this
tiny walled town *(see p43)*,
and the poet Cardinal Pietro
Bembo coined the verb
asolare to describe the
bittersweet life of enforced
idleness she endured. Others
who have fallen in love with
these narrow streets include
poet Robert Browning, who
named a volume of poems
Asolando (1889) after the
town, and travel writer Freya
Stark, who lived here until
her death in 1993.

Just 10 km (6 miles) east
of Asolo is the **Villa Barbaro**
at Masèr *(see pp24–5)*, while
10 km (6 miles) north is the
village of Passagno, birthplace
of Antonio Canova. Canova's
remains lie inside the huge
temple-like church which he
designed himself. Nearby is
the family home, the **Casa di
Canova**. The Gypsoteca here
houses the plaster casts and
clay models for many of
Canova's sculptures.

🏛 Villa Barbaro
Masèr. **Tel** 0423 92 30 04. ⭕
Mar–Oct: 3–6pm Tue, Sat, Sun &
public hols; Nov–Feb: 2:30–5pm Sat,
Sun & public hols. ⬤ 24 Dec–6 Jan,
Easter. 🖼

🏛 Casa di Canova
Piazza Canova. **Tel** 0423 54 43 23.
⭕ Tue–Sun. ⬤ 1 Jan, Easter, 25
Dec. 🖼

Valdobbiadene ❽

🏠 10,700. 🚌 ℹ️ Via Piva 53 (0423
97 69 75). 🛒 Mon.

Valdobbiadene, surrounded
by vine-covered hills, is a
centre for the sparkling
white wine called Cartizze,
a type of Prosecco. To the
east, the Strada del Vino
Bianco (white wine route)
stretches 34 km (21 miles)
to the town of Conegliano
(see p175), passing vineyards
offering wine to try and
to buy.

Environs
About 10 km (8 miles)
northeast of Valdobbiadene
is the small town of Follina,
which is renowned for its
wonderfully well-preserved
Romanesque abbey.

Vines near Valdobbiadene

Street-by-Street: Vicenza ①

Detail on
No. 21
Contrà Porti

Vicenza is known as the city of Andrea Palladio (1508–80), arguably the most influential architect of his time. Although Palladio was born in Padua, Vicenza was his adoptive home and, walking around the city, one can see the evolution of his distinctive style. In the centre is the monumental basilica he adapted to serve as the town hall, while all around are the palaces he built for Vicenza's wealthy citizens.

Contrà Porti
has some of the
most elegant
palazzi in Vicenza

Loggia del Capitaniato
This covered arcade was designed by Palladio in 1571.

Palazzo Valmarana
Palladio's impressive building of 1566 was originally intended to be three times larger. It was not completed until 1680, 100 years after the architect's death.

Duomo
Vicenza's cathedral was rebuilt after bomb damage during World War II left only the façade and choir intact.

KEY

━ ━ ━ Suggested route

STAR SIGHTS

★ Piazza dei Signori

★ Casa Pigafetta

0 metres   150

0 yards   150

VISITORS' CHECKLIST

116,000. FS ⊞ *Piazza Stazione.* ℹ *Piazza Matteotti 12 (0444 32 08 54).* Ⓐ *Tue & Thu.* ⚑ *Concert season (May–Jun); Classical music in villas (end Jun–early Jul); Theatre season (Sep–Oct).*

★ Piazza dei Signori
Encircled by grand 15th-century buildings including the city's green-roofed basilica and slender brick tower, the piazza is a lively spot, with a colourful market and cafés.

The Torre di Piazza is 82 m (269 ft) high. Begun in the 12th century, its height was increased in 1311 and 1444.

The 15th-century basilica has a magnificent loggia built by Palladio in 1549.

Andrea Palladio
This memorial to Vicenza's most famous citizen is often surrounded by market stalls.

The Quartiere delle Barche contains numerous attractive palaces built in the 14th-century Venetian Gothic style.

Piazza delle Erbe, the city's market square, is overlooked by a 13th-century torture chamber, the Torre del Tormento.

★ Casa Pigafetta
This striking house was the birthplace of Antonio Pigafetta, who in 1519 set sail round the world with Magellan.

Ponte San Michele
This elegant stone bridge, built in 1620, provides lovely views of the surrounding town.

Exploring Vicenza

Vicenza, the great palladian city, is celebrated all over the world for its architecture. It is also one of the wealthiest cities in the Veneto, with much to offer, from Roman and Renaissance art (a combined museum ticket is available) to elegant shops selling fine goods.

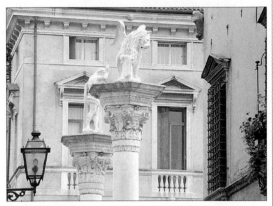

Statues gazing down from their pillars in the Piazza dei Signori

⛪ Piazza dei Signori

At the heart of Vicenza, this square is dominated by the startling bulk of the Palazzo della Ragione, often referred to as the "basilica". Open to the public, its green, copper-clad roof is shaped like an upturned boat with a balustrade bristling with the statues of Greek and Roman gods. The colonnades were designed by Palladio in 1549 to support the city's 15th-century town hall, which had begun to subside. This was his first public commission, and his solution ensured the survival of the building.

The astonishingly slender Torre di Piazza alongside has stood since the 12th century. Opposite is the elegant café Gran Caffè Garibaldi, which is next to Palladio's Loggia del Capitaniato (1571). The Loggia's upper rooms contain the city's council chamber.

⛪ Contrà Porti

Contrà (an abbreviation of *contrada*, or district) is the local dialect word for street. On the western side is a series of pretty Gothic buildings with painted windows and ornate balconies, including Palazzo Porto-Colleoni (No. 19). These houses reflect the architecture of Venice, a reminder that

Vicenza was part of the Venetian empire.

Several fine Palladian *palazzi* stand on this street. The Palazzo Thiene (No. 12) of 1545–50, the Palazzo Porto Barbarano (No. 11) of 1570, and the Palazzo Iseppo da Porto (No. 21) of 1552 all illustrate the sheer variety of Palladio's style – Classical elements are common to all three, but each is unique. The Palazzo Thiene reveals some intriguing details of Palladio's methods: though the building appears to be of stone, close inspection reveals that it is built of cheap lightweight brick, cleverly rendered to look like masonry.

⛪ Casa Pigafetta

Contrà Pigafetta. *No public access.*
This highly decorated Spanish Gothic building of 1481 has clover-leaf balconies, gryphon brackets and Moorish windows. The owner, Antonio Pigafetta, sailed round the world with Magellan in 1519–22, being one of only 20 men who survived the voyage.

🏛 Museo Civico

Piazza Matteotti 37–9. **Tel** 0444 32 13 48. ◯ 9am–5pm Tue–Sun.
● 25 Dec, 1 Jan. 🈂 ♿
The excellent Museo Civico is housed in Palladio's Palazzo Chiericati, built in 1550. Inside is a fresco by Domenico Brusa-zorzi of a naked charioteer, representing the Sun, who appears to fly over the ceiling of the entrance hall. In the upstairs rooms are many great pictures. Among the Gothic altarpieces from local church-es is Hans Memling's *Crucifix-ion* (1468–70), the central panel of a triptych whose side panels are now in New York.

In the later rooms are newly cleaned works by the local artist Bartolomeo Montagna (c.1450–1523), including his remarkable *Virgin Enthroned with Child, St John the Baptist and Saints Bartholomew, Augustine and Sebastian.*

⛪ Santa Corona

This impressive Gothic church was built in 1261 to house a thorn from Christ's Crown of Thorns, donated by Louis IX of France. In the Porto Chapel is the tomb of Luigi da Porto (died 1529), author of the novel *Giulietta e Romeo*, upon which Shakespeare based his

Brusazorzi's ceiling fresco in the large entrance hall of the Museo Civico

famous play. Notable paintings include Giovanni Bellini's *Baptism of Christ* (c.1500–5) and Paolo Veronese's *Adoration of the Magi* (1573). In the cloister the Museo Naturalistico-Archeologico exhibits natural history and archaeology.

San Lorenzo

The portal of this church is a magnificent example of Gothic stone carving, decorated with figures of the Virgin and Child, and St Francis and St Clare. The frescoes inside are damaged, but there are fine tombs. The cloister, north of the church, is a flower-filled haven of calm.

The elegant Villa Rotonda, most famous of all Palladio's works

The beautiful cloister of the church of San Lorenzo

Palazzo Leoni Montanari

Contra' Santa Corona 25. *800 57 88 75.* ☐ *10am–6pm Tue–Sun.*
This Baroque building was completed around 1720, commissioned by Giovanni Leoni Montanari, who had made his fortune producing and selling cloth. Today the Palazzo houses an art gallery renowned for its collections of Venetian paintings and Russian icons.

Monte Berico

Basilica di Monte Berico. ☐ *daily.*
Monte Berico is the green, cypress-clad hill to the south of the city to which wealthy Vicenzans once escaped in the heat of summer to enjoy cooler air and bucolic charms. The wide avenue linking the city to the basilica on top of the hill features shady colonnades with many shrines along the route. The Baroque basilica was built in the 15th century and is

dedicated to the Virgin who appeared during the 1426–8 plague to declare that Vicenza would be spared.

Many pilgrims still travel to the lovely church, where Bartolomeo Montagna's moving *Pietà* fresco (1572) makes an impact within the ornate interior. Other attractions include a fossil collection in the cloister, and Veronese's fine painting *The Supper of St Gregory the Great* (1572) in the refectory. The large canvas was cut to ribbons by bayonet-wielding soldiers during the revolutionary outbursts of 1848 and painstakingly restored.

Villa Valmarana

Via dei Nani 12. *Tel 0444 54 39 76.* ☐ *mid-Mar–5 Nov: 10am–noon, 3–6pm Tue–Sun; Nov–mid-Mar: 10am–noon, 2–4pm Sat & Sun.*
www.villavalmarana.com
The wall alongside the Villa Valmarana (which was built in 1688 by Antonio Muttoni) is topped by the figures of dwarfs, which

The Baroque hilltop church, the Basilica di Monte Berico

give this building its alternative name – *ai Nani* (at the Dwarfs). Inside the villa, the walls are covered with frescoes by Tiepolo, in which pagan gods float on clouds watching scenes from the epics of Homer and Virgil. In the separate Foresteria (guest house), the frescoes with themes of peasant life and the seasons, painted by Tiepolo's son, Giandomenico, are equally decorative but more earthily realistic.

The villa can be reached by a 10-minute walk from the basilica on Monte Berico. Head downhill along Via M d'Azeglio to the high-walled convent on the right where the road ends, then take the Via San Bastiano. There is also a bus service from town.

Villa Rotonda

Via della Rotonda 45. *Tel 0444 32 17 93.* **Villa** ☐ *mid-Mar–4 Nov: Wed.* **Garden** ☐ *mid-Mar–4 Nov: 10am–noon, 3–6pm Tue–Sun; 5 Nov–mid-Mar: 10am–noon, 2:30–5pm Tue–Sun.*
With its regular, symmetrical forms, this is the epitome of Palladio's architecture, and the most famous of all his villas. The design is simple yet satisfying, as is the contrast between the green lawns, white walls and terracotta roof tiles. Built between 1550 and 1552, it has inspired lookalikes in cities as far away as Delhi and St Petersburg. Fans of *Don Giovanni* will recognize locations used in Joseph Losey's 1979 film. The villa can be reached by bus from town, or on foot, following the path that passes the Villa Valmarana.

Vicenza: Teatro Olimpico

Europe's oldest surviving indoor theatre, the Teatro Olimpico is an elegant and remarkable structure, largely made of wood and plaster and painted to look like marble. Fashionable architect Andrea Palladio *(see pp24–5)* began work on the design in 1579, but he died the following year without finishing it. His pupil, Vincenzo Scamozzi, took over the project and completed the theatre in time for its ambitious opening performance of Sophocles' tragic drama, *Oedipus Rex*, on 3 March 1585.

Bacchantes
Euripides' Greek tragedy is still performed using Scamozzi's versatile scenery.

Main ticket office

★ **Odeon Frescoes**
The gods of Mount Olympus, after which the theatre is named, decorate the Odeon, a room used for music recitals.

Anteodeon
Oil lamps from the original stage set are now displayed in the theatre's Anteodeon, whose frescoes (1595) depict the theatre's opening performance.

★ **Stage Set**
Scamozzi's scenery represents the Greek city of Thebes. The streets are cleverly painted in perspective and rise at a steep angle to give the illusion of great length.

STAR SIGHTS

★ Stage Set by Vincenzo Scamozzi

★ Odeon Frescoes

Courtyard Sculptures

The courtyard of the former castle is decorated with sculpture donated by members of the Olympic Academy, the learned body that built the theatre.

VISITORS' CHECKLIST

Piazza Matteotti.
Tel 0444 22 28 00.
to Piazza Matteotti.
9am–4:30pm Tue–Sun
(sometimes closes later in Jul
& Aug). 1 Jan, 25 Dec.
Regular theatre performances.

Armoury Gateway

This stone gateway, with its military-style carvings, leads from Piazza Matteotti into the picturesque theatre courtyard.

The auditorium was designed by Palladio to resemble the outdoor theatres of ancient Greece and Rome, such as the arena at Verona *(see p195),* with a semi-circle of "stone" benches (actually made of wood) and a ceiling painted to portray the sky.

Costume Designs for Sofonisba

Ancient Greek vases inspired the costumes for this tragedy (1562) by Palladio's patron, GG Trissino.

Façade Statues

The toga-clad figures are portraits of sponsors who paid for the theatre's construction.

The medieval town of Treviso, built around ancient canals

Treviso **9**

🏛 *81,700.* 🚌 **FS** 🛈 *Piazzetta Monte di Pietà 8. (0422 54 76 32).* 🛒 *Tue & Sat am.*

Full of attractive balconied houses overlooking willow-fringed canals, Treviso is a rewarding city for visitors. Comparisons are often made with Venice, but Treviso has its own distinctive character. A good place to explore the architecture is the main street, Calmaggiore, which links the cathedral with the rebuilt 13th-century town hall, the **Palazzo dei Trecento**. The tradition of painting the exterior of the houses dates back to the medieval period, and this form

of decoration, applied to brick and timber, compensated for the lack of suitable building stone. The bustling **fish market** also dates back to medieval times. It is held on an island in the middle of Treviso's river Sile so that the remains of the day's trading can be flushed away instantly.

🏛 Duomo

Treviso's cathedral, founded in the 12th century, was reconstructed in the 15th, 16th and 18th centuries. Inside is Titian's *Annunciation* (1570), but it is upstaged by the striking *Adoration of the Magi* fresco (1520) of Titian's arch rival, Il Pordenone. Other memorable works are *The Adoration of*

the Shepherds fresco by Paris Bordone, and the monument to Bishop Zanetti (1501) by Pietro Lombardo and his sons

🏛 Museo Civico

Via Santa Caterina. **Tel** *0422 54 48 64.* 🕘 *9am–12:30pm, 2:30–6pm Tue–Sun.* 🔴 *public hols.* 🔳 🔳
The Museo Civico houses an archaeology collection and a picture gallery in the restored convent of Santa Caterina dei Servi. The best works are Lorenzo Lotto's *Portrait of a Dominican* (1526), Titian's *Portrait of Sperone Speroni* (1544) and Bassano's *Crucifixion* as well as Tomaso da Modena's 14th-century frescoes of the life of St Ursula.

🏛 San Nicolò

Nestling near the 16th-century town wall is the bulky Dominican church of San Nicolò, full of tombs and frescoes, including some by Lorenzo Lotto. There is a gigantic painting of St Christopher by Antonio da Treviso and the piers of the nave bear vivid portraits of saints by Tomaso da Modena. The latter also painted the humorous pictures of monks (1352) on the walls of the chapter house (*Sala del Capitolo*), which has a separate entrance through the Seminario Vescovile.

TREVISO TOWN CENTRE

Duomo and Battistero di San Giovanni ①
Museo Civico ⑤
Palazzo dei Trecento ③

Pescheria (fish market) ④
San Nicolò ②

0 metres 200
0 yards 200

Key to Symbols *see back flap*

Conegliano ⑩

🚶 35,300. 🚃 FS ℹ️ *Via XX
Settembre 61. (0438 21 230).* 🗓️ *Fri.*
***Shops closed** Mon am.*

Conegliano lies between the
Prosecco-producing vineyards
and those that produce fine
red wine *(see pp240–41)*.
Wine makers from both areas
learn their craft at Conegliano's
renowned wine school. The
town's winding and arcaded
main street, Via XX Settembre,
is lined by 15th- to 18th-cen-
tury *palazzi*, some decorated
with external frescoes, some
in Venetian Gothic style. The
Duomo contains a gorgeous
altarpiece by Cima da Conegliano (1460–1518) showing
the *Virgin and Child with
Saints* (1493). This was commissioned by the religious
brotherhood whose headquarters, the Scuola di Santa Maria
dei Battuti *(flagellants)*, stands
beside the Duomo.

Reproductions of Cima's
paintings are displayed in the
Casa di Cima, the artist's birthplace. His detailed landscapes
were based on the hills around
the town; they can still be seen
from the gardens surrounding
the **Castelvecchio** (old castle).
A small museum of local history is housed in the castle.

🏛️ Casa di Cima
Via Cima. **Tel** *0438 21 660.* ⬜ *3–
6pm Sat & Sun (4–7pm Apr–Sep).* 🎫

🏛️ Castelvecchio
Piazzale Castelvecchio 8. **Tel** *0438
228 71.* ⬜ *Museum: Tue–Sun (Nov:
Sat & Sun only); gardens: daily
(except Nov).* 🎫

The foundations of Roman buildings in Concordia, near Portogruaro

Portogruaro ⑪

🚶 26,000. 🚃 FS ℹ️ *Via Cimetta 1
(0421 735 58).* 🗓️ *Thu am.* ***Shops
closed** Mon.*

Situated on the main road
linking Venice to Trieste,
Portogruaro is the medieval
successor to the Roman town
of Concordia Sagittaria. Finds
from Concordia, including
statues, tomb inscriptions
and mosaics, are displayed
in the town's **Museo Concordiese**. These objects were
unearthed in the modern
village of Concordia, 2 km
(1 mile) south of Portogruaro,
where the footings of
ruined Roman buildings can
be seen all around the church
and baptistry.

🏛️ Museo Concordiese
Via Seminario 26. **Tel** *0421 726 74.*
⬜ *daily.* ⬛ *1 Jan, 25 Dec.* 🎫

Caorle ⑫

🚶 11,700. 🚃 ℹ️ *Calle delle
Liburniche 18. (0421 810 85).*
🗓️ *Sat am.*

Like Venice, Caorle was built
among the swamps of the
Venetian lagoon by refugees
fleeing the Goths in the 5th
century. Today it is a fishing
village and a busy beach
resort perched

on the edge of a huge
expanse of purpose-built
lagoons, carefully managed to
encourage fish to enter and
spawn. The young are then
fed and farmed.

The area is also of great
interest to naturalists for the
abundant bird life of the reed-
fringed waters. The town's
11th-century **Duomo** is worth
a visit for its Pala d'Oro, a
gilded altarpiece made up of
12th- and 13th-century Byzantine panel reliefs.

Local fishermen at work in the
village of Caorle

Mestre ⑬

🚶 179,000. 🚃 🗓️ *Wed & Fri am.*

Mestre, the industrial off-
spring of Venice, is often
favoured by visitors as a
relatively less expensive
base for exploring the
region than Venice or other
towns. Flying into Venice's
Marco Polo airport *(see
pp278–9)*, you cannot miss
the factories and oil
terminals that surround
Mestre and its neighbour,
Marghera, vital to the
region's economy.

A mythical statue outside the theatre in Conegliano's Via XX Settembre

For hotels and restaurants in this region see pp223–4 and pp247–8

Street-by-Street: Padua ⑭

The city centre of Padua (Padova) is one of the liveliest in northern Italy, thanks to a large student population and to the two street markets, one specializing in fruit and the other in vegetables. These take place every day except Sunday around the vast Palazzo della Ragione, the town's medieval law court and council chamber. The colonnades round the exterior of the *palazzo* shelter numerous bars, restaurants and shops selling meat, game, cheeses and wine.

Palazzo del Capitanio
Built between 1599 and 1605 for the head of the city's militia, the tower incorporates an astronomical clock made in 1344.

Piazza dei Signori is bordered by attractive arcades which house small speciality shops, interesting cafés and old-fashioned wine bars.

Corte Capitaniato, a 14th-century arts faculty (open for concerts), contains frescoes which include a rare portrait of Petrarch.

Loggia della Gran Guardia
Now used as a conference centre, this fine Renaissance building, dating from 1523, once housed the Council of Nobles.

PIAZZA CAPITANIATO

VIA SAN CLEMENTE

PIAZZA DEI SIGNORI

VIA MONTE DI PIETA

VIA MANIN

VIA SONCIN

PIAZZA DEL DUOMO

VIA SONCIN

VIA VANDELLI

The **Palazzo del Monte di Pietà** has 16th-century arcades and statues enclosing a medieval building.

★ **Duomo and Baptistry**
The 12th-century baptistry of the Duomo contains one of the most complete medieval fresco cycles to survive in Italy, painted by Giusto de' Menabuoi in 1378 and now restored.

KEY

— — — Suggested route

0 metres	75
0 yards	75

★ **Caffè Pedrocchi**
Built like a Classical temple, the Caffè Pedrocchi has been a famous meeting place for students and intellectuals since it opened in 1831.

VISITORS' CHECKLIST

220,000. **FS** Piazza Boschetti. Piazzale della Stazione 13a. Tel 049 875 20 77. Mon–Sat at Prato della Valle. **Shops closed** Mon am (clothes), Wed pm (food). concert season (Oct–Apr).

Palazzi Communali
This complex, which houses the city's council offices, has a 13th-century defensive tower.

The Palazzo della Ragione, the "Palace of Reason" was, in medieval times, the city court of justice. Its interior is covered with magnificent astrological frescoes.

Padua University
Founded in 1222, this is the second oldest university in Italy. The main building dates back to the 16th century.

★ **Piazza delle Erbe**
There are good views on to the market place from Palladio's 16th-century loggia, which runs alongside the Palazzo della Ragione.

STAR SIGHTS

★ Duomo and Baptistry

★ Caffè Pedrocchi

★ Piazza delle Erbe

Exploring Padua

Padua is an old university town with an illustrious academic history. Rich in art and architecture, it has two particularly outstanding sights. The first is the Scrovegni Chapel *(see pp180–81)*, in the north of the city, which is renowned for Giotto's lyrical frescoes. Close to the railway station, it forms part of the Eremitani museums complex. The second is the Basilica di Sant'Antonio, one of Italy's most popular pilgrim shrines, which forms the focal point for a number of sights in the south of the city *(see p182)*. A combined museum ticket is available.

Sundial on the façade of the Palazzo della Ragione

Detail from the Egyptian room, upper floor of the Caffè Pedrocchi

🏛 Caffè Pedrocchi
Via VIII Febbraio 15. **Tel** 049 878 12 31. ☐ daily (Jun–Oct: Tue–Sun).
Museo del Risorgimento e dell'Età Contemporanea Tel 049 820 50 07. ☐ 9.30am–12.30pm 3.30–6pm Tue–Sun. ● Aug. 🖾

Grand cafés have long played an important role in the intellectual life of northern Italy, and many philosophical issues have been thrashed out at the Caffè Pedrocchi since it first opened in 1831. Politics superseded philosophy when it became a centre of the Risorgimento movement, dedicated to liberating Italy from Austrian rule; it was the scene of uprisings in 1848, for which several student leaders were executed. Later it became famous as the café that never closed its doors. Recently restored, these days people come to talk, read, play cards or watch the world go by as they eat and drink.

The upstairs rooms, decorated in Moorish, Egyptian and Greek styles, are now the premises of a museum.

🏛 Palazzo del Bo (University)
Via VIII Febbraio 2. **Tel** 049 820 97 11. ☐ Tue, Thu & Sat am, Mon, Wed & Fri pm (may vary, phone to check). 🖾 🎫
Named after a tavern called *Il Bo* (the ox), the historic main university building is mostly

used today for graduation ceremonies. Originally it housed the medical faculty, renowned throughout Europe. Among its famous teachers and students was Gabriele Fallopio (1523–62), after whom the Fallopian tubes are named.

Elena Lucrezia Corner Piscopia was the first female graduate in 1678 – long before women could study at many of Europe's other universities. Her statue is on the staircase leading to the upper gallery of the 16th-century courtyard.

Visitors on the tour are shown the pulpit Galileo used when he taught here from 1592 until 1610. They also see the world's oldest surviving anatomy theatre (1594), viewing the room from the centre looking up.

🏛 Palazzo della Ragione
Piazza delle Erbe. **Tel** 049 820 50 06. ☐ Tue–Sun. ● 1 Jan, 1 May, 25 Dec. 🖾 🖶 🛦
The "Palace of Reason", also known as the "Salone" by locals, was built to serve as Padua's law court and council chamber in 1218. The vast main hall was originally frescoed by the celebrated artist Giotto, but fire destroyed his work in 1420. The frescoes that survive today are by the relatively unknown Nicola Miretto, though their astrological theme is fascinating.

The Salone is breathtaking in its sheer size. It is Europe's biggest undivided medieval hall, 80 m (260 ft) long, 27 m (90 ft) wide and 27 m (90 ft) high. The scale is reinforced by the wooden horse displayed at one end – a massive beast, copied from Donatello's Gattamelata statue *(see p183)* in 1466 and originally made to be pulled in procession during Paduan festivities.

The walls are covered in Miretto's frescoes (1420–25), a total of 333 panels depicting the months of the year with appropriate gods, zodiacal signs and seasonal activities.

Also within the *palazzo* is the Stone of Shame, on which bankrupts were exposed to ridicule before they were sent into exile.

The 16th-century galleried anatomy theatre in the Palazzo del Bo

Eremitani Museums

This major museum complex occupies a group of 14th-century monastic buildings attached to the church of the Eremitani, a reclusive Augustinian order. The admission ticket includes entry to the Scrovegni Chapel (see pp180–81), which stands on the same site, overlooking the city's Roman amphitheatre, and to the Archaeology Museum, the Bottacin Museum of coins and medals, and the Medieval and Modern Art Museum, all of which are housed around the cloisters.

The tomb of the Volumni family in the archaeological collection

EREMITANI CHURCH

Alongside the museum complex is the Eremitani church (1276–1306), with its magnificent roof and wall tombs. Interred here is Marco Benavides (1489–1582), a professor of law at the city university, whose mausoleum was designed by Ammannati, a Renaissance architect from Florence. Sadly missing from the church are Andrea Mantegna's celebrated frescoes of the lives of St James and St Christopher (1454–7), which were destroyed during a bombing raid in 1944. Two scenes from this magnificent work survive in the Ovetari Chapel, south of the sanctuary. *The Martyrdom of St James* was reconstructed from salvaged fragments, and *The Martyrdom of St Christopher* was removed carefully and stored elsewhere before the bombing. Otherwise only photographs on the walls remain to hint at the quality of the lost works.

THE MUSEUMS

The highlight of the rich archaeological collection is the temple-like tomb of the Volumni family, dating from the 1st century AD. Among several other Roman tombstones from the Veneto region is one to the young dancer, Claudia Toreuma – sadly, a fairly dull inscribed column rather than a portrait. The collection also includes some fine mosaics, along with several impressive life-size statues depicting muscular Roman deities and toga-clad dignitaries. For most visitors the Renaissance bronzes are likely to be

Angels in Armour (15th century) by Guariento in the Art Museum

the most appealing feature of the museum, especially the comical *Drinking Satyr* by Il Riccio (1470–1532).

Coin collectors should make a point of visiting the Bottacin Museum. Among the exhibits there is an almost complete set of Venetian coinage and some very rare examples of Roman medallions.

The Modern Art Museum is currently closed to the public. However, the massive Medieval Museum is well worth a visit. It covers the history of Venetian art, with paintings from Giotto to the 1700s. Another museum looks at Giotto and his influence on local art, using the Crucifix from the Scrovegni Chapel as its centrepiece. The Crucifix is flanked by an army of angels (late 15th century) painted in gorgeous colours by the artist Guariento. Another 15th-century painting worth a look is *Portrait of a Young Senator* by Giovanni Bellini.

Early 14th-century crucifix on loan from the Scrovegni Chapel

VISITORS' CHECKLIST

Piazza Eremitani.
Tel 049 820 45 51.
⬜ 9am–7pm Tue–Sun.
Only chapel open Mon.
🔴 1 Jan, 1 May, 25 & 26 Dec.

Padua: Scrovegni Chapel

Enrico Scrovegni built this chapel in 1303, hoping thereby to spare his dead father, a usurer, from the eternal damnation wished upon him by the poet Dante in his *Inferno*. The chapel is filled with harmonious frescoes of scenes from the life of Christ, painted by Giotto between 1303 and 1305. As works of great narrative force, they exerted a powerful influence on the development of European art.

The Nativity
The naturalism of the Virgin's pose marks a departure from Byzantine stylization, as does the use of natural blue for the sky, in place of celestial gold

Expulsion of the Merchants
Christ's physical rage, the cowering merchant and the child hiding his face are all typical of Giotto's style.

The Coretti
Giotto painted the two panels known as the Coretti as an exercise in perspective, creating the illusion of an arch with a room beyond.

View towards altar

| West entrance | North side | Altar | South side | West entrance |

GALLERY GUIDE

It is compulsory to book your visit to the Scrovegni Chapel in advance, since there are strict limits on the number of visitors allowed in the chapel at any one time. Prior to entry, all visitors must spend 15 minutes in a "decontamination chamber", and the duration of the visit to the chapel is also limited to 15 minutes. An explanatory film is shown while you wait in the chamber. The rest of the Eremitani complex is also worth a visit.

KEY

- ☐ Episodes of Joachim and Anna
- ☐ Episodes from the Life of Mary
- ☐ Episodes from the Life and Death of Christ
- ☐ The Virtues and Vices
- ☐ The Last Judgment

For hotels and restaurants in this region see pp233–4 and pp247–8

The Last Judgment
This scene fills the entire west wall of the chapel. Its formal composition is closer to the Byzantine tradition than some of the other frescoes, with parts probably painted by assistants. A model of the chapel is shown, being offered to the Virgin by Scrovegni.

View towards entrance

Mary is Presented at the Temple
Giotto sets many scenes against an architectural background, using the laws of perspective to give a sense of three dimensions.

Injustice
The Virtues and Vices are painted in monochrome. Here Injustice is symbolized by scenes of war, murder and robbery.

Lament over the Dead Christ
Giotto's figures express their grief in different ways, some huddled, some gesturing wildly.

GIOTTO

The great Florentine artist Giotto (1266–1337) is regarded as the father of Western art. His work, with its sense of pictorial space, naturalism and narrative drama, marks a decisive break with the Byzantine tradition of the preceding 1,000 years. He is the first Italian master whose name has passed into posterity, and although he was regarded in his lifetime as a great artist, few of the works attributed to him are fully documented. Some may have been painted by others, but his authorship of the frescoes in the Scrovegni Chapel need not be doubted.

The lofty interior of Padua's 16th-century duomo

🔒 Duomo and Baptistry

Baptistry *Tel* 049 65 69 14.
⬜ 10am–6pm daily. ● Easter, 25 Dec. 🎫 ⬜

Padua's duomo was commissioned from Michelangelo in 1552, but his designs were altered during the construction. Of the 4th-century cathedral which stood on the site, the domed Romanesque baptistry still survives, with its frescoes by Giusto de' Menabuoi (c.1376). The frescoes cover biblical stories, such as the Creation, Christ's Passion, Crucifixion and Resurrection and the Last Judgment.

🔒 Basilica di Sant'Antonio

This exotic church, with its minaret-like spires and Byzantine domes, is also known as Il Santo. It was begun in 1232 to house the remains of St Anthony of Padua, a preacher who modelled himself on St Francis of Assisi. Although he was a simple man who rejected worldly wealth, the citizens of Padua built one of the most lavish churches in Christendom to serve as his shrine.

The outline reflects the influence of Byzantine architecture; a cone-shaped central dome is surrounded by a further seven domes, rising above a façade that combines Gothic with Romanesque elements. The interior is more conventional, however. Visitors are kept away from the high altar, which features Donatello's magnificent reliefs (1444–5) on the miracles of St Anthony, and his statues of the Virgin, the Crucifixion and several Paduan saints. There is access to the tomb of St Anthony in the north transept, which is hung with offerings and photographs of people who have survived serious illness or car crashes with the saint's help. The walls around the

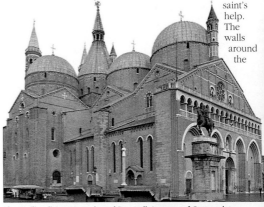

The Basilica di Sant'Antonio and Donatello's statue of Gattamelata

The Brenta Canal

The River Brenta, between Padua and the Venetian Lagoon, was canalized in the 16th century. Flowing for a total of 36 km (22 miles), its potential as a transport route was quickly realized, and fine villas were built along its length. Today, these elegant buildings can still be admired. Three open their doors to the public: the Villa Foscari at Malcontenta, the Villa Widmann-Foscari at Mira, and the Villa Pisani at Stra. They can be visited either on an 8 to 9-hour guided tour from Padua to Venice (or viceversa) along the river on a motor launch, or by bus, a cheaper and faster alternative.

The picturesque town of Mira on the Brenta Canal

Fiessa d'Artico •

S11

← *PADOVA*

KEY

▬▬	Tour route
═══	Roads
⛴	Boat stops

Villa Pisani ①
This 18th-century villa features an extravagant frescoed ceiling by Tiepolo.

shrine are decorated with large marble reliefs depicting St Anthony's life, carved in 1505–77 by various artists, including Jacopo Sansovino and Tullio Lombardo. These are rather cold by comparison with the *Crucifixion* fresco (1380s) by Altichiero da Zevio in the opposite transept. This pageant-like painting of everyday scenes from medieval life shows depictions of people, animals and plants.

Statue of Gattamelata
Near the entrance to the basilica stands one of the great Renaissance works. This gritty portrait of the mercenary soldier Gattamelata (whose name means "Honey Cat") was created in 1443–52, honouring a man who in his life did great service to the Venetian Republic. Donatello won fame for the monument, the first equestrian statue made of this size since Roman times.

Scuola del Santo and Oratorio di San Giorgio
Piazza del Santo. **Tel** 049 878 97 22. 9am–12:30pm, 2.30–7pm daily (to 5pm in winter). 1 Jan, 25 Dec. (combined ticket).
These two linked buildings contain excellent frescoes, including the earliest documented paintings by Titian. These comprise two scenes from the life of St Anthony in the Scuola del Santo, executed in 1511. The delightful saints' lives and scenes from the life of Christ in the San Giorgio oratory are the work of two artists, Altichiero da Zevio and Jacopo Avenzo, who painted them in 1378–84.

Orto Botanico
Via Orto Botanico 15. **Tel** 0498 27 21 19. Apr–Oct: 9am–1pm, 3–7pm daily; Nov–Mar: 9am–1pm Mon–Sat.
Founded in 1545, Padua's botanical garden is the oldest in Europe, and it retains much of its original appearance; one of the palm trees dates to 1585. Originally intended for the cultivation of medicinal plants, the pathways now spill over with exotic foliage, shaded by ancient trees. The gardens were used to cultivate the first lilacs (1565), sunflowers (1568) and potatoes (1590) grown in Italy.

Prato della Valle
The Prato (field) claims to be the largest public square in Italy, and its elliptical shape reflects the form of the Roman theatre that stood on the site.

St Anthony of Padua used to preach sermons to huge crowds here, but subsequent neglect saw the area turn into a malaria-ridden swamp. The land was drained in 1767 to create the canal that now encircles the Prato. Four stone bridges cross the picturesque channel, which is lined on both sides by statues of 78 eminent citizens of Padua. On Saturdays there is a market.

One of four stone bridges spanning the canal around Prato della Valle

Villa Foscari ③ Also known as the Malcontenta, this villa was built by Palladio in 1560 and is decorated with magnificent frescoes by Zelotti.

Oriago

S11

LAGUNA VENETA

• *Fusina*

VENEZIA

Canale Nuovissimo

S309

la Widmann-Foscari ② uilt in 1719, but altered in e 19th century, the erior is decorated in a ench Rococo style.

0 kilometres   4

0 miles   2

TIPS FOR PASSENGERS

Padua to Venice.
Wed, Fri and Sun, Mar–Oct. Dep bus station, Piazza Boschetti, 8:15am. **Arr** Piazza San Marco 6:30pm.
Venice to Padua.
Tue, Thu and Sat, Mar–Oct. **Dep** Piazza San Marco 9am. **Arr** bus station, Piazza Boschetti 6:30pm.

Booking necessary through a local travel agent or www.ilburchiello.it **Ticket includes** bus between Padua and Stra, boat tour and guide, entrance to two villas (ticket for Villa Pisani not included). Return trip (not included in cost) by train or bus (approx. 45 mins).

The Euganean Hills, formed by ancient volcanic activity

Euganean Hills ⓯

🏠 10,000. 🛈 Viale Stazione 60, Montegrotto Terme. (049 892 83 11).

The Euganean Hills, remnants of long-extinct volcanoes, rise abruptly out of the Veneto plain and offer plenty of walking opportunities. Hot springs bubble up out of the ground at Abano Terme and Montegrotto Terme where scores of establishments offer thermal treatments, ranging from mud baths to immersion in the hot sulphurated waters. Spa cures such as these date back to Roman times, and visitors can see extensive remains of the Roman baths and theatre at Montegrotto.

🏠 Abbazia di Praglia

Via Abbazia di Praglia, Bresseo di Teòlo. **Tel** 049 999 93 00. ⬜ Mar–Oct: 3:30–5:30pm Tue–Sun; Nov–Feb: 2:30–4:30pm Tue–Sun. 💳 Donations welcome.

The Benedictine monastery at Praglia, 6 km (4 miles) west of Abano Terme, is a peaceful haven in the tree-clad hills. The monks have long been growing herbs commercially and there is a shop selling aromatic wares. They also lead guided tours of parts of the abbey and the Renaissance church (1490–1548), with its beautiful cloister.

🏛 Casa di Petrarca

Via Valleselle 4, Arquà Petrarca. **Tel** 0429 71 82 94. ⬜ Tue–Sun. ⬤ most public hols. 💳 🖼

The picturesque town of Arquà Petrarca, on the southern edge of the Euganean hills, was once simply Arquà. Its name changed in 1868 to honour the medieval poet Francesco Petrarca, or Petrarch (1303–74), who lived here in his old age. He had often sung the praises of the well-tended landscape of olive groves and vineyards, and spent his last few years in a house frescoed with scenes from his poems. The house still contains the poet's desk and chair, his bookshelves and his mummified cat. Petrarch is buried in a sarcophagus in the piazza in front of the church.

🏛 Villa Barbarigo

Valsanzibio. **Tel** 049 805 92 24. ⬜ Mar–Nov: 10am–1pm, 2pm–sunset. 💳 🖼 🚻 ♿

To the north of Arquà is the Villa Barbarigo at Valsanzibio, the only one of scores of villas, built by wealthy Paduans, regularly open to the public. The villa itself is of a simple design compared with the Baroque garden. Planted from 1669, it is full of variety, with fountains, statues and lakes.

The house of the poet Petrarch in the town of Arquà Petrarca

Montagnana ⓰

🏠 12,000. 🚆 🚌 🛈 Piazza Trieste 15. (0429 813 20). ⬤ Thu am. **Shops closed** Mon am & Wed pm.

Medieval brick walls encircle this town, extending for 2 km (1 mile), pierced by four gateways and defended by 24 towers. Just inside the castellated Padua Gate is the town's archaeological museum. The Gothic-Renaissance **Duomo** contains Paolo Veronese's *Transfiguration* (1555). Outside the city walls is Palladio's **Villa Pisani** (c.1560). Now rather neglected, its façade features the original owner's name (Francesco Pisani) in bold letters below the pediment.

Antique market in Montagnana

Este ⓱

🏠 17,600. 🚆 🚌 🛈 Via Guido Negri 9. (0429 600 462). ⬤ Wed & Sat am. **Shops closed** Mon am (clothes) & Wed pm (food).

Excavations at Este have uncovered impressive remains of the ancient Ateste people, who flourished from the 9th century BC until they were conquered by the Romans in the 3rd century BC. The archaeological finds, including funerary urns, figurines, bronze vases and jewellery, are on display in the excellent **Museo Nazionale Atestino**, set within the walls of the town's 14th-century castle. The museum also displays examples of Roman and medieval art, and pieces of local pottery, famous since the Renaissance period, and still produced.

⌂ Museo Atestino
Palazzo Mocenigo. *Tel 0429 20 85.* ◯ *Tue–Sun.* ◉ *1 Jan, 1 May, 25 Dec.*

Monsélice ⑱

🏠 *17,000.* **FS** 🚌 **ℹ** *Via del Santuario 6. (0429 78 30 26).* ⊛ *Mon & Fri.* **Shops closed** *Tue am (clothes), Wed pm (food).*

The town of Monsélice stands at the foot of two hills, one of which has been quarried extensively for rich deposits of crystalline minerals. The other is topped by ruined **Castle Rocca**, now a nature reserve. It is worth walking up the cobbled Via del Santuario as far as **San Giorgio**, to see its exquisite inlaid marble work.

Other features on the way up are the 13th-century cathedral and the statue-filled Baroque gardens of the Villa Nani that can be glimpsed through the villa gates. Nearby is **Ca' Marcello**, a 14th-century castle featuring period furnishings, suits of armour, frescoes and tapestries.

Marble inlay detail from San Giorgio

⌂ Ca' Marcello
Via del Santuario. *Tel 0429 729 31.* ◯ *Apr–Nov: Tue–Sun; Dec–Mar: groups only; book in advance.*

The sanctuary of San Giorgio on the hill top at Monsélice

Polésine and Rovigo ⑲

FS 🚌 **ℹ** *Piazza Matteotti 1, Porto Viro. (0426 63 30 12).*

Polesine is the flat expanse of fertile agricultural land, crisscrossed by canals and subject to flooding, between the river Adige and the Po. The Po Delta is now a national park and has a wealth of fascinating birdlife, including egrets, herons, and bitterns.

The most scenic areas are around Scardovari and Porto Tolle, on the south side of the Po. Companies in Porto Tolle offer canoe and bicycle hire and half-day boat cruises.

The modern city of Rovigo has one outstanding monument, the splendid octagonal church called **La Rotonda** (1594–1602), decorated with paintings and statues in niches.

Environs
Adria, 22 km (14 miles) east of Rovigo, gave its name to the Adriatic Sea and was once a Greek and later an Etruscan port. A programme of silt deposition, undertaken to increase Adria's agricultural potential, left the city dry, apart from a 24-km (15-mile) canal. Among the exhibits on display in the **Museo Archeologico** is a complete iron chariot dating from the 4th century BC.

⌂ Museo Archeologico
Via Badini 59, Adria. *Tel 0426 216 12.* ◯ *daily.* ◉ *25 Dec, 1 Jan, 1 May.*

Chioggia ⑳

🏠 *56,000.* 🚌 **FS** ⛴ **ℹ** *Lungomare Adriatico 52. (041 40 10 68).* ⊛ *Thu.*

Chioggia is the principal fishing port on the lagoon and the bustling, colourful **fish market** is a good reason to come here early in the day (open every morning except Monday). Many visitors enjoy the gritty character of the port area, with its smells, its vibrantly coloured boats and the tangle of nets and tackle. The town also has numerous inexpensive restaurants which serve fresh fish in almost every variety. Eel, crab and cuttlefish are the local specialities. There is a beach area at Sottomarina, on the western part of the island. Worth seeking out for a special visit is Carpaccio's *St Paul* (1520), the artist's last known work, which is permanently housed in the church of **San Domenico**.

Net mending in the traditional way, Chioggia

VERONA AND LAKE GARDA

erona is one of northern Italy's most alluring cities, its noble palaces, quiet cloisters and ancient streets every bit as romantic as you would expect of Romeo and Juliet's city. On its doorstep are the well-known vineyards of Soave, Bardolino and Valpolicella, set against the rugged slopes of the Little Dolomites. To the west lie the beautiful shores of Lake Garda, a mere 30 minutes' drive from Verona by car, but a world away in atmosphere.

Set within the curves of the river Adige, Verona has been a prosperous and cosmopolitan city since the Romans colonized it in 89 BC. It stands astride two important trade routes – the Serenissima, connecting the great port cities of Venice and Genoa, and the Brenner Pass, used by commercial travellers crossing the Alps from northern Europe. This helps to explain the Germanic influence in Verona's magnificent San Zeno church, or the realism of the paintings in the Castelvecchio museum, owing more to Dürer than to Raphael.

Verona's passion and panache, however, are purely Italian. Stylish shops and cafés sit amid the impressive remains of Roman monuments. The massive Arena amphitheatre fills with crowds of 20,000 or more, who thrill to opera beneath the stars. All over the city, art galleries and theatres testify to a crowded calendar of cultural activities.

Italy's largest lake, Lake Garda, is renowned for its beautiful scenery. The broad southern end of the lake, with its waterfront promenades, is very popular with Italian and German visitors. Those in search of peace can escape to the heights of the Monte Baldo mountain range, rising above the eastern shore. The ridge marks the western edge of the mountainous region north of Verona. Here is the great plateau of Monti Lessini, with its little river valleys that fan out southwards to join the river Adige.

o Giusti in Verona, one of Italy's finest Renaissance gardens

oats outside Rocca Scaligera castle, Sirmione

Exploring Verona and Lake Garda

Verona makes an excellent touring base, with lofty mountains, castles and vineyards all within easy reach of the city. Lake Garda, whose western shore is actually over the border in Lombardy, is a popular destination for excursions from Verona. The many resort towns have excellent hotels, harbourside fish restaurants and lakeside gardens, and the lake is perfect for watersports such as windsurfing or dinghy racing. Less exhausting are the steamer excursions, offering mid-lake views of entrancing beauty.

SIGHTS AT A GLANCE

Bolca **6**
Bosco Chiesanuova **8**
Garda **10**
Gardone Riviera **15**
Giazza **7**
Grezzana **2**
Malcésine **17**
Montecchio Maggiore **4**
Peschiera **11**
Riva del Garda **16**
Salò **14**
Sant'Anna d'Alfaedo **9**
Sirmione Peninsula pp206–7 **13**
Soave **3**

Solferino **12**
Valdagno **5**
Verona pp192–203 **1**

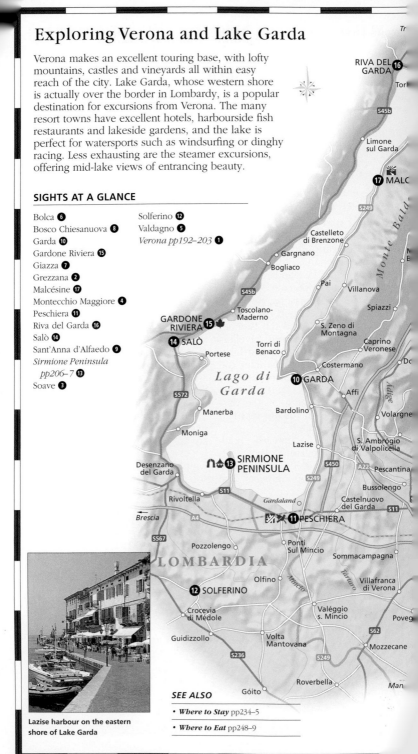

Lazise harbour on the eastern shore of Lake Garda

SEE ALSO

GETTING AROUND

The roads around Verona are heavily used by commercial vehicles and commuter traffic, so expect delays, especially during morning and evening rush hours. Motorways are faster, even though those in this region are among the oldest in Italy. There are good rail services linking Verona with Lake Garda to the west and with Bolzano to the north. The Brenner pass also runs northwards from Verona. For information on ferries across Lake Garda, see p204.

The green pastures of Bolca, an area rich in fossil remains

A vineyard in spring on the hillsides around Verona

KEY

═══	Motorway
═══	Major road
──	Secondary road
═══	Minor road
──	Scenic route
──	Main railway
──	Minor railway
═══	Regional border
△	Summit

0 kilometres   10

0 miles   5

The 14th-century Castello Romeo, on a hill overlooking Montecchio

Verona ❶

See pp192–203.

Grezzana ❷

🏠 9,680. 🚌 🔄 1st Wed and 3rd Fri each month.

In Grezzana itself, seek out the 13th-century church of Santa Maria which, though frequently rebuilt, retains its robustly carved Romanesque font and its beautiful campanile of gold, white and pink limestone.

Environs:
Grezzana is in the foothills of the scenic Piccole Dolomiti or Little Dolomites. Close to the town, at nearby Cuzzano, is the 17th-century Baroque **Villa Allegri-Arvedi**. To the south, in Santa Maria in Stelle, is a Roman nymphaeum (a shrine to the nymphs who guard the fresh-water spring) next to the church (known as the Pantheon).

🏛 Villa Allegri-Arvedin
Cuzzano di Grezzana.
Tel 045 90 70 45. ⬜ for groups only (book by phone). 📷 ♿

Soave ❸

🏠 6,200. 🚌 🚻 Foro Boario 1 (045 619 07 73). 🔄 Tue am.

Soave is a heavily fortified town ringed by 14th-century walls. Its name is familiar all over Europe because of the light and dry white wine that is produced and exported from here in great quantity. Visitors will see few vineyards around the town, since they are mainly located in the hills to the north, but evidence of the industry can be seen in the gleaming factories on the outskirts, where the Garganega grapes are crushed and the fermented wine bottled. Cafés and wine cellars in the town centre provide plenty of opportunity for sampling the excellent local wine.

The city walls rise up the hill to the dramatically sited **Rocca Scaligera**, an ancient castle enlarged in the 14th century by the Scaligeri rulers of Verona. It has been furnished in period style.

♠ Rocca Scaligera
Via Castello Scaligero. **Tel** 045 768 00 36. ⬜ Tue–Sun. 📷

Rocca Scaligera, the ancient castle in Soave

Montecchio Maggiore ❹

🏠 20,000. 🚌 🚻 Via Pietro Ceccato 88, Alta di Montecchio (0444 69 65 46). 🔄 Fri am.

Visitors to industrialized Montecchio Maggiore come principally to see the two 14th-century castles on the hill above the town. Although these are known as the **Castello di Romeo** and the **Castello di Giulietta** (which includes a restaurant), there is no evidence that they belonged to Verona's rival Capulet and Montague families (*see p199*), but they look romantic, and provide lovely views over the vineyard-clad hills to the north.

♠ Castello di Romeo
Via Castelli 4. ⬜ Sun. 📷

♠ Castello di Giulietta
Via Castelli 4. **Tel** 0444 69 61 72. ⬜ Thu–Tue.

The dramatic gorge of Montagna Spaccata, north of Valdagno

Valdagno ❺

🏠 28,000. 🚌 🚻 Viale Trento 4–6 (0445 40 11 90). 🔄 Tue am, Fri am.

A scenic drive of 20 km (12 miles) from Montecchio Maggiore leads to Valdagno, a town of woollen mills and 18th-century houses. Just northwest is the Montagna Spaccata, its rocky bulk split by a dramatic 100-m (330-ft) deep gorge and waterfall.

Fossilized plant remains found in the rocks near Bolca

Bolca ⑥

🏠 500. 🚌 **Shops closed** Mon am (clothes), Wed pm (food).

Pretty Bolca sits at the centre of the Monti Lessini plateau, looking down the valley of the river Alpone and encircled by fossil-bearing hills. The most spectacular finds have been transferred to Verona's Museo Civico di Scienze Naturali (*see p203*), but the local **Museo di Fossili** still has an impressive collection of fish, plants and reptiles preserved in the local basalt stone. A circular walk of 3 km (2 miles) from the town (details available from the museum) takes in the quarries where the fossils were found.

🏛 **Museo di Fossili**
Via San Giovanni Battista. **Tel** 045 656 50 88. ⬜ Mar–Oct: 9am–noon, 2–6:30pm Tue–Sun; Nov–Feb: 10am–noon, 2–5pm Tue–Sun. 🖼

Giazza ⑦

🏠 150. 🚌 **Shops closed** Wed pm (food).

The small town of Giazza has an almost Alpine appearance. Its **Museo dei Cimbri** covers the history of the Tredici Comuni (the Thirteen Communes). In reality there are far more than 13 little hamlets dotted about the plateau, many of them settled by Bavarian farmers who migrated from the German side of the Alps in the 13th century. Cimbro, their German-influenced dialect, has now almost

completely disappeared, but other traditions survive. For example, their huge mountain horns, *tromboni*, are still part of local festivities.

🏛 **Museo dei Cimbri**
Via dei Boschi, 62.
📞 045 784 70 50. ⬜ Wed pm, Sat & Sun. 🖼 ✔ 📷

Bosco Chiesanuova ⑧

🏠 3,000. 🚌 ℹ️ Piazza della Chiesa 34 (045 705 00 88). 🛒 Sat am.

One of the principal ski resorts of the region, Bosco Chiesanuova is well supplied with hotels, ski lifts and cross-country routes. To the east, near Camposilvano, is the picturesque **Valle delle Sfingi** (valley of the sphinxes), so called because of its landscape of large and impressive rock formations.

Sant'Anna d'Alfaedo ⑨

🏠 2,500. 🚌 ℹ️ in Bosco Chiesanuova. 🛒 Wed am.

Distinctively alpine in character, Sant'Anna d'Alfaedo is noted for the stone tiles used to roof local houses. The hamlet of Fosse, immediately to the north, is a popular base for walking excursions up the **Corno d'Aquilio** (1,546 m/5,070 ft), a mountain which boasts one of the world's deepest pot-holes, the **Spluga della Preta**, 850 m (2,790 ft) deep.

More accessible is another natural wonder, the **Ponte di Veia**, just south of Sant'Anna, a great stone arch bridging the valley. Prehistoric finds have been excavated from the caves at either end. This spectacular natural bridge is one of the largest of its kind in the world.

The town of Giazza, spectacularly situated on the Monti Lessini plateau

Verona ❶

Dragon carving on Duomo façade

Verona is a vibrant and self-confident city, the second biggest in the Veneto region (after Venice) and one of the most prosperous in northern Italy. Its ancient centre boasts many magnificent Roman remains, second only to those of Rome itself, and *palazzi* built of *rosso di Verona*, the local pink-tinged limestone, by the city's medieval rulers. Verona has two main focal points, the massive 1st-century AD Arena and the Piazza Erbe with its colourful market, separated by a maze of narrow lanes lined with some of Italy's most elegant boutiques.

Verona as seen from the Museo Archeologico

Verona's rulers

In 1263 the Scaligeri began their successful 127-year rule of Verona. They used ruthless tactics in their rise to power, earning nicknames like Mastino (Mastiff) and Cangrande (Big Dog), but once in power the Scaligeri family brought peace to a city racked by civil strife and inter-family rivalry. They proved to be relatively just and cultured rulers – the poet Dante was welcomed to their court in 1301–4 and dedicated his *Paradise*, the final part of the epic *Divine Comedy*, to Cangrande I.

Verona fell to the Visconti of Milan in 1387, and a succession of outsiders – Venice, France and Austria – followed before the Veneto was united with the rest of Italy in 1866.

Key to Symbols *see back flap*

| 0 metres | 500 |
| 0 yards | 500 |

Fruit and vegetable stall in a side street of old Verona

For hotels and restaurants in this region see pp234–5 and pp248–9

⚜ Castelvecchio

Corso Castelvecchio 2. **Tel** 045 806 26 11. ☐ 8:30am–7:30pm daily (from 1:30pm Mon); 9am–7pm public hols. ☐ 1 Jan, 25–26 Dec. 🖼 🅿 🛈

This spectacular castle, built by Cangrande II between 1355 and 1375, has been transformed into one of the Veneto's finest art galleries. Various parts of the medieval structure have been linked together using aerial walkways and corridors, designed by Carlo Scarpa to give striking views of the building itself, as well as the exhibits within, which are excellent and varied.

The first section contains a wealth of late Roman and early Christian material, including a 7th-century silver plate that shows armoured knights in combat, 5th-century brooches and glass painted with a portrait of Christ the Shepherd in gold. The martyrdom scenes depicted on the carved marble sarcophagus of Saints Sergius and Bacchus (1179) are gruesomely realistic.

The following section, which is devoted to medieval and early Renaissance art, vividly demonstrates the influence of northern art on local painters, suggesting strong links with Verona's neighbours across the Alps. Here, instead of the serene saints and virgins of Tuscan art, the emphasis is on brutal realism. This is summed up in the 14th-century *Crucifixion with Saints*, which depicts the torture musculature of Christ and the racked faces of the mourners in painful detail. Far more lyrical is a beautiful 15th-century painting by Stefano da Verona called *The Madonna of the Rose Garden*. This contains many allusions to popular medieval fables, including the figure of Fortune with her wheel. In the painting the Virgin sits in a pretty garden alive with decorative birds and angels gathering rosebuds.

Cangrande I's horse in ceremonial garb

Other Madonnas from the 15th century, attributed to Giovanni Bellini, are displayed among the late Renaissance works upstairs. Jewellery, suits of armour, swords and shield bosses feature next, some dating back to the 6th and 7th centuries when

VISITORS' CHECKLIST

🏠 261,000. ✈ Villafranca 14 km (9 miles). 🚉 🛈 Piazzale 25 Aprile (045 800 08 61). 🚌 Piazza Cittadella. 🛈 Via Degli Alpini 9 (045 806 86 80). 🚌 daily. **Shops closed** Wed pm (food), Mon am (department & clothing stores). 🍷 Vinitaly – Italy's largest wine fair (Apr);Festival della Lirica (opera festival) (end Jun–Aug), Estate Teatrale Veronese, including Shakespeare Festival (end Jun–Aug).

Verona was under attack from Teutonic invaders from beyond the Alpine range.

After the armour room, take the walkway that leads out along the river flank of the castle, with its dizzying views of the swirling waters of the river Adige and the Ponte Scaligero *(see p194)*. Next, turning a corner, one finds Cangrande I, his equestrian statue dramatically displayed out of doors on a plinth. This 14th-century statue once graced Cangrande's tomb *(see p198)*, and is remounted here. It is possible to study every detail of the horse and rider draped in their ceremonial garb. Despite Cangrande's cherubic cheeks and inane grin, his face is compelling.

Beyond lie some of the museum's celebrated paintings, notably Paolo Veronese's *Deposition* (1565) and a portrait attributed by some to Titian, by others to Lorenzo Lotto.

SIGHTS AT A GLANCE

Courtyard of Castelvecchio

Around the Arena

Most visitors to Verona first arrive at Piazza Brà, a large, irregularly shaped square with a public garden. On the north side is an archway known as the Portoni della Brà. Dominating the eastern side of the piazza is the Roman Arena, Verona's most important monument, still in use today for operatic performances. The piazza is ringed with 19th-century buildings resembling ancient temples and historical landmarks.

Ponte Scaligero, part of the old defence system of Castelvecchio

🏛 Ponte Scaligero

This medieval bridge was built by Cangrande II between 1354 and 1376. The people of Verona love to stroll across it to ponder the river Adige in all its moods, or to admire summer sunsets and distant views of the Alps. Such is their affection for the bridge that it was rebuilt after the retreating Germans blew it up in 1945, an operation that involved dredging the river to salvage the medieval masonry. The bridge leads from Castel-vecchio *(see p193)* to the Arsenal on the north bank of the Adige, built by the Austrians between 1840 and 1861 and now fronted by public gardens. Looking back from the gardens it is possible to see how the river was used as a natural moat to defend the castle, with the bridge providing the inhabitants with an escape route.

🏛 Arco dei Gavi and Corso Cavour

Dwarfed by the massive brick walls of Castelvecchio, the monumental scale of this Roman triumphal arch is now hard to appreciate. Originally the arch straddled the main Roman road into the city, today's Corso Cavour. But French troops who were occupying Castelvecchio in 1805 damaged the monument so much that a decision was made to move it to its present, less conspicuous position just off the Corso in 1933.

Continuing up Corso Cavour, there are some fine medieval and Renaissance palaces to see (especially Nos. 10, 11 and 19) before the Roman town gate, the **Porta dei Borsari**, is reached. The gate dates from the 1st century BC, but looking at the pedimented windows and niches it is easy to see what influenced the city's Renaissance architects.

The Roman Arco dei Gavi, 1st century AD

🏛 Museo Lapidario Maffeiano

Piazza Brà 8. *Tel 045 590 087.* ☐ 8:30am–7:30pm daily (from 1:30pm Mon). ● 1 Jan, 25–26 Dec. 🖾 This "museum of stone" displays all kinds of architectural fragments hinting at the last splendour of the Roman city. There are numerous carved funerary monuments, and a large part of the collection consists of Greek inscriptions collected by the museum's 18th-century founder, Scipione Maffei.

🏛 San Fermo Maggiore

Stradone San Fermo. *Tel 045 59 28 13.* ☐ Mar–Oct: 10am–6pm; Nov–Feb: 10am–4pm. ● Mon. 🖾 🚫 San Fermo Maggiore consists of not one but two churches. This can best be appreciated from the outside, where the eastern end is a jumble of rounded Romanesque arches below with pointed Gothic arches rising above. The lower church, now rather dank due to frequent flooding, dates from 1065, but the upper church (1313) is more impressive. It has a splendid ship's keel roof and lots of medieval fresco work. Frescoes from the 14th century, just inside the main door, are by Stefano de Zevico. They show the fate meted out to four Franciscan missionaries who journeyed to India in the mid-14th century. Nearby is the Brenzoni mausoleum (1439) by Giovanni di Bartolo with Pisanello's *Annunciation* fresco (1426) above. In the south aisle is an unusually ornate pulpit of 1396 with saints in canopied niches above, surrounded by frescoes of the Evangelists and Doctors of the Church.

The apse of the lower church of San Fermo Maggiore

The Arena

Verona's amphitheatre, completed around AD 30, is the third largest in the world, after Rome's Colosseum and the amphitheatre at Capua, near Naples. Originally, the Arena could hold almost the entire population of Roman Verona, and visitors came from across the Veneto to watch mock battles and gladiatorial combats. Since then, the Arena has been used for public executions, fairs, theatre performances, bullfighting and opera.

VISITORS' CHECKLIST

Piazza Brà, Verona. *Tel 045 800 32 04.* 8:30am–7:30pm daily (from 1:30pm Mon; last admission 6:30pm). Closes mid-afternoon on performance days. 1 Jan, 25 Dec. partial. Operas & classical concerts (see pp256–7).

Interior
The interior has survived virtually intact, maintained by the Arena Conservators since 1580.

The façade of the Arena seen from Piazza Brà

The elliptical amphitheatre is 139 m (456 ft) long and 110 m (361 ft) wide.

Gladiators and wild beasts entered the arena from both sides.

Stone seats in 44 tiers

Below ground were cages for lions, tigers and other wild beasts, and a maze of passages.

Blood Sports
Prisoners of war, criminals and Christians died in their thousands in the name of entertainment.

Opera in the Arena
Today, performances of Verdi's Aida *and other popular operas can attract a capacity crowd of 25,000.*

Street-by-Street: Verona

Since the days of the Roman empire, the Piazza Erbe has been the centre of Verona's commercial and administrative life. Built on the site of the ancient Roman forum, it is an enjoyably chaotic square, bustling with life. Shoppers browse in the colourful market at stalls sheltered from the sun by wide-brimmed umbrellas. The massive towers and *palazzi* of the Scaligeri rulers of Verona have retained their medieval feel, even though they have been altered and adapted many times.

★ **Piazza dei Signori**
This square is bordered by individual Scaligeri palazzi linked by Renaissance arcades and carved stone archways.

Statue of Dante
Dante, the medieval poet, stayed in Verona as a guest of the Scaligeri during his period in exile from his native Florence. His statue (1865) looks down on Piazza dei Signori.

The 17th-century Palazzo **Maffei** is surmounted by a balustrade supporting statues of gods and goddesses.

CORSO SANT' ANASTAS

Colonna di San Marco (1528) is surmounted by St Mark's Lion, the symbol of Venetian rule.

PIAZZA ERBE

Piazza Erbe
Verona's medieval herb market is now lined with art galleries, up-market boutiques and inviting pavement cafés.

The fountain of 1368 is topped by a figure known as the Madonna of Verona; in fact, the statue is Roman and probably symbolizes Commerce.

Torre dei Lamberti, 84 m (275 ft) high

VIA CAP

Palazzo della Ragione
The medieval Palace of Reason features an elegant Renaissance staircase. It leads from the exterior courtyard into the magistrates' rooms on the upper floor.

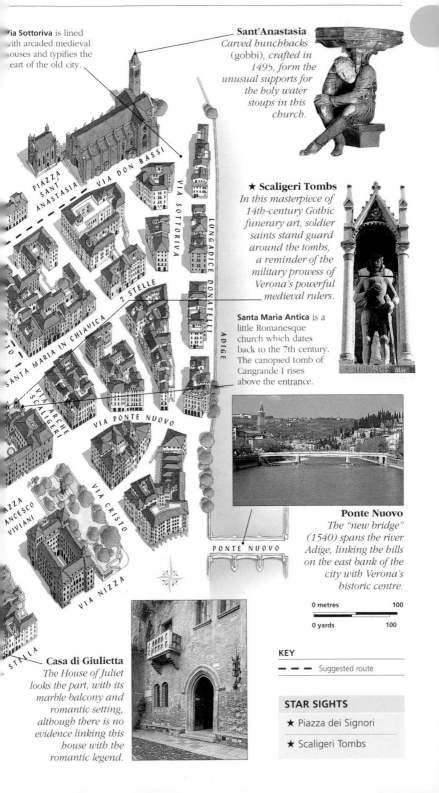

Via Sottoriva is lined with arcaded medieval houses and typifies the heart of the old city.

Sant'Anastasia
Carved hunchbacks (gobbi), crafted in 1495, form the unusual supports for the holy water stoups in this church.

★ Scaligeri Tombs
In this masterpiece of 14th-century Gothic funerary art, soldier saints stand guard around the tombs, a reminder of the military prowess of Verona's powerful medieval rulers.

Santa Maria Antica is a little Romanesque church which dates back to the 7th century. The canopied tomb of Cangrande I rises above the entrance.

Ponte Nuovo
The "new bridge" (1540) spans the river Adige, linking the hills on the east bank of the city with Verona's historic centre.

PIAZZA SANT' ANASTASIA
VIA DON BASSI
VIA SOTTORIVA
LUNGADICE DONATELLI
ADIGE
2 STELLE
SANTA MARIA IN CHIAVICA
VIA ARCHE SCALIGERI
VIA PONTE NUOVO
PIAZZA FRANCESCO VIVIANI
VIA CRISTO
VIA NIZZA
STELLA
PONTE NUOVO

| 0 metres | 100 |
| 0 yards | 100 |

Casa di Giulietta
The House of Juliet looks the part, with its marble balcony and romantic setting, although there is no evidence linking this house with the romantic legend.

KEY

- - - Suggested route

STAR SIGHTS

★ Piazza dei Signori

★ Scaligeri Tombs

Central Verona

The streets of this ancient city centre owe their grid-like layout to the order and precision of the Romans. At the heart is the lively Piazza Erbe, where crowds shop in the ancient market place. The fine *palazzi*, churches and monuments date mostly from the medieval period.

An elegant café in the spacious Piazza dei Signori

🏛 Piazza Erbe

Piazza Erbe is named after the city's old herb market. Today's stalls, shaded by huge umbrellas, sell everything from lunchtime snacks of herb-flavoured roast suckling pig in bread rolls to fresh-picked fruit or delicious wild mushrooms.

The **Venetian lion** that stands on top of a column to the north of the square marks Verona's absorption in 1405 into the Venetian empire. The statue-topped building that completes the north end of Piazza Erbe is the baroque **Palazzo Maffei** (1668), now converted to shops and luxury apartments. An assortment of boutiques and cafés lines the edge of the square.

The **fountain** that splashes away quietly in the middle of the piazza is often overlooked amid the competing attractions of the market's colourful stalls. Yet the statue at the fountain's centre dates from Roman times, a reminder that this long piazza has been in almost continuous use as a market place for 2,000 years.

🏛 Piazza dei Signori

Torre dei Lamberti **Tel** 045 927 30 27. ◯ 8:30am–7:15pm daily (later in summer).

In the centre of Piazza dei Signori is a 19th-century **statue of Dante**, who surveys the surrounding buildings with an appraising eye. His gaze is fixed on the grim **Palazzo del Capitano**, home of Verona's military commander, and the equally intimidating **Palazzo della Ragione**, the palace of Reason, or law court, both built in the 14th century. The Palazzo della Ragione is not quite so grim within. The courtyard has a handsome external stone staircase, added in 1446–50. Fine views of the Alps can be had by climbing

Stonework detail, Piazza dei Signori

the 84-m (275-ft) **Torre dei Lamberti**, which rises from the western side of the courtyard.

Behind the statue of Dante is the pretty Renaissance **Loggia del Consiglio**, or council chamber, with its frescoed upper façade (1493) and statues of Roman worthies born in Verona. These include Catullus the poet, Pliny the natural historian and Vitruvius the architectural theorist.

The piazza is linked to Piazza Erbe by the Arco della Costa or the arch of the rib, whose name refers to the whale rib hung beneath it, put up here as a curiosity in the distant past.

🏛 Santa Maria Antica

This tiny Romanesque church is almost swamped by the bizarre Scaligeri tombs built up against its entrance wall. Because Santa Maria Antica was their parish church, the Scaligeri rulers of Verona chose to be buried here, and their tombs speak of their military prowess *(see p207)*.

Over the entrance to the church is the impressive tomb of Cangrande I, or Big Dog (died 1329), topped by his equestrian statue. This statue is a copy; the original is now in the Castelvecchio *(see p193)*. The other Scaligeri tombs are next to the church, surrounded by an intricate wrought-iron fence featuring the ladder motif of the family's original name (*della Scala*, meaning "of the steps"). Towering above the fence are the spire-topped tombs of Mastino II, or Mastiff (died 1351)

The fountain in Piazza Erbe, erected in the 14th century

...nd Cansignorio, meaning ...oble Dog (died 1375). These ...wo tombs are splendidly dec-...rated with Gothic pinnacles. ...n their craftsmanship and ...esign there is nothing else in ...uropean funerary architec-...ure quite like these spiky, ...nrusting monuments.

Plainer tombs nearer the ...hurch wall mark the resting ...lace of other members of the ...caligeri family – Mastino ...died 1277) who founded the ...caligeri dynasty, having been ...lected mayor of Verona in ...260, and two who did not ...ave dog-based names: ...3artolomeo (died 1304) and ...3iovanni (died 1359).

🏛 Sant'Anastasia

Tel 045 592 813. ☐ Mar–Oct: 9am–
5pm Tue–Sat, 1–6pm Sun; Nov–Feb:
1–5pm Tue–Sun. 📷 ♿ 🚫
A huge church, Sant'Anastasia
was begun in 1290 and built to
hold the massive congregations
who came to listen to the
rousing sermons preached by
members of the fundamentalist
Dominican order. The most
interesting aspect of the church

The lofty, Romanesque interior of
Sant'Anastasia

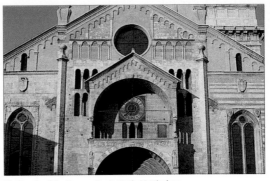

The façade of the Duomo, Santa Maria Matricolare

is its Gothic portal, with its
faded 15th-century frescoes
and carved scenes from the
life of St Peter Martyr. Inside,
the two holy water stoups are
supported on realistic figures
of beggars, known as *i gobbi*,
the hunchbacks (the one on
the left carved in 1495, the
other a century later).

Off the north aisle is the
sacristy, home to Antonio
Pisanello's fresco, *St George
and the Princess* (1433–38).
Despite being badly damaged,
the fresco still conveys something of the aristocratic grace
of the Princess of Trebizond,
with her noble brow and her
ermine-fringed cloak, as St
George prepares to mount his
horse in pursuit of the dragon.

🏛 Duomo

Tel 045 592 813. ☐ Nov–Feb: 10am–
1pm, 1:30–4pm Tue–Fri, 1–5pm Sat &
Sun; Mar–Oct: 10am–5:30pm Mon–Fri,
1:30–5:30pm Sat & Sun. ♿ 📷 🚫
Visitors to Verona's cathedral
pass through a magnificent

Romanesque portal carved
by Nicolò, one of the master
masons who carved the façade
of San Zeno *(see pp200–201)*.
Here he sculpted the sword-
bearing figures of Oliver and
Roland, knights whose exploits
in the service of Charlemagne
were celebrated in medieval
poetry. Nearby, stand saints
and evangelists with bold star
ing eyes and flowing beards.
To the south there is a second
Romanesque portal carved
with Jonah and the Whale
(removed for restoration) and
comically grotesque caryatids
(load-bearing figures).

The highlight is Titian's
Assumption (1535–40) in the
first chapel on the left. Further
down is the entrance to the
Romanesque cloister with
excavated remains of earlier
churches on the site. It leads
to the baptistry, known as San
Giovanni in Fonte (St John of
the Spring). This 8th-century
church features a huge
marble font carved in 1200.

ROMEO AND JULIET

The tragic story of Romeo and Juliet, written by Luigi
da Porto of Vicenza in the 1520s, inspired countless
poems, films, ballets and dramas. At the **Casa di
Giulietta** (Juliet's house), No. 27 Via Cappello (tel:
045 803 43 03), Romeo is said to have climbed to
Juliet's balcony. In reality this is a restored 13th-
century inn. The run-down **Casa di Romeo** is in
Via delle Arche Scaligere, while the so-called
Tomba di Giulietta (tel: 045 800 03 61) is in a
crypt below the cloister of San Francesco al
Corso on Via del Pontiere. The stone sarcophagus
is empty and rather plain, but the setting is
atmospheric. Juliet's house is open 8:30am–7:30pm
daily (from 1:30pm Mon), her tomb 9am–7pm.

The lovers *Romeo and Juliet* from a 19th-century illustration

Verona: San Zeno Maggiore

Stone façade detail

Built between 1120 and 1138 to house the shrine of Verona's patron saint, San Zeno is northern Italy's most ornate Romanesque church. The façade is embellished with marble reliefs of biblical scenes, matched in vitality by bronze door panels showing the miracles of San Zeno. Beneath an impressive rose window, a graceful porch canopy rests on two slim columns. A brick campanile soars to the south, while a squat tower to the north is said to cover the tomb of King Pepin of Italy (777–810).

Nave Ceiling
The nave has a magnificent example of a ship's keel ceiling, so called because it resembles the inside of an upturned boat. This ceiling was constructed in 1386 when the apse was rebuilt.

Striped brickwork is typical of Romanesque buildings in Verona. Courses of local pink brick are alternated with ivory-coloured tufa.

Altarpiece
Andrea Mantegna's three-part altarpiece (1457–59) depicts the Virgin and Child with various saints. The painting served as an inspiration to local artists.

★ Cloister
North of the church the fine, airy cloister (1293–1313) has rounded Romanesque arches on one side and pointed Gothic arches on the other.

STAR FEATURES
★ Cloister
★ West Doors
★ Crypt

BRONZE DOOR PANELS

The 48 bronze panels of the west doors are primitive but forceful in their depiction of biblical stories and scenes from the life of San Zeno. Those on the left date from 1030 and survive from an earlier church on the site; those on the right were made 100 years later. Huge staring eyes and Ottoman-style hats, armour and architecture feature prominently, and the meaning of some scenes is not known – the woman suckling two crocodiles, for example.

Descent into limbo   **Christ in Glory**   **Human head**

VISITORS' CHECKLIST

Piazza San Zeno. **Tel** 045 59 28 13.
31, 32, 33 from Castelvecchio.
Mar–Oct: 8:30am–6pm daily (from 1pm Sun); Nov–Feb: 10am–1pm, 1:30–4pm Tue–Sat, 1–5pm Sun & public hols. times vary. during mass.

Nave and Main Altar
The nave of the church is modelled on an ancient Roman basilica, the Hall of Justice. The main altar is situated in the raised sanctuary where the judge's throne would have stood.

The campanile, started in 1045, reached its present height of 72 m (236 ft) in 1173.

Rood Screen
Marble statues of Christ and the Apostles, dating from 1250, are ranged along the sanctuary rood screen.

The rose window symbolizes the Wheel of Fortune: figures around the rim show the rise and fall of human fortunes.

Marble side panels, carved in 1140, depict events from the life of Christ to the left of the doors, and scenes from the Book of Genesis to the right.

★ West Doors
Each of the wooden doors has 24 bronze plates joined by bronze masks, nailed on to the wood to look like solid metal. A bas relief above the doors depicts San Zeno vanquishing the devil.

★ Crypt
The vaulted crypt contains the tomb of San Zeno, appointed eighth bishop of Verona in AD 362, who died in AD 380.

Across the Ponte Romano

The Ponte Romano, or Roman Bridge, links Verona's city centre to the eastern bank of the river Adige. This up-market residential district is dotted with fine palaces, gardens and churches, and offers good views back on to the towers and domes of the medieval city.

View from the Teatro Romano across the river Adige

⋔ Teatro Romano

Rigaste Redentore 2. **Tel** 045 800 03 60. ⏲ 8:30am–7:30pm daily (from 1:30pm Mon; also open Mon am on public hols). 🖼 ♿

When this theatre was built, in the 1st century BC, the plays performed would have included satirical dramas by such writers as Terence and Plautus. The tradition continues with open-air performances at the annual Shakespeare festival.

The theatre is built into a bank above the river Adige. The views over the city must have been as entrancing to Roman theatregoers as the events on stage. Certainly it is for the views that the theatre is best visited today, since little is left of the original stage area, though the semi-circular seating area remains largely intact.

In the foreground of the view is one of three Roman bridges that brought traffic into the city. The only one to have survived, this had to be painstakingly reconstructed after being blown up in 1945 by retreating German soldiers who were attempting to delay the advance of Allied troops. Of the five arches, the two nearest to the theatre are least altered.

Augustus Caesar, Museo Archeologico

🏛 Museo Archeologico

Rigaste Redentore 2. **Tel** 045 800 03 60. ⏲ 8:30am–7:30pm daily (from 1:30pm Mon; also open Mon am on public hols). 🖼

A lift carries visitors from the Teatro Romano up through the cliffs to the monastery above. This is now converted into an archaeological museum in which panoramic city views vie for attention with the range of exhibits. The first part of the museum displays well-restored mosaics, one of which depicts the kind of gory gladiatorial combat that once went on in Verona's amphitheatre (see p195). Such barbaric performances, seen as a legitimate way of disposing of criminals and prisoners of war, finally came to an end in the early 5th century following a decree from the Christian Emperor Honorius.

In the little monastic cells to the side of this room, visitors can see a bronze bust of the first Roman emperor, the young Augustus Caesar (63 BC–AD 14), who succeeded in outmanoeuvring his opponents, including Mark Antony and Cleopatra, to become the sole ruler of the Roman world in 31 BC. The subject of the female bust in the adjoining cell is unknown. Next comes the tiny cloister, littered with mosaics and ancient masonry fragments, and a warren of ancient rooms used to display pottery, glass, inscriptions and tombstones. Labelling stops after a while, leaving visitors to puzzle out the nature and age of exhibits for themselves.

🔒 Santo Stefano

This is one of the city's oldest churches; the original, long-demolished building was constructed in the 6th century. It served as Verona's cathedral until the 12th century when the new Duomo was built (see p199) on the opposite bank of the Adige. Visitors to Santo Stefano are afforded a striking view of the Duomo across the river, taking in the Romanesque apse and the bishop's palace alongside. Santo Stefano itself was rebuilt at the same time by Lombard architects and given its octagonal red brick campanile, but the original apse survives.

Inside the church there is a Byzantine-influenced arrangement of a stone bishop's seat and bench, and a gallery with 8th-century carved capitals. The apse (which is often locked) is even older, dating back to the original 6th-century building. In the crypt there are fragments of 13th-century frescoes and a 14th-century statue of St Peter.

Figure of St Peter, Santo Stefano

Towering above the church to the east is Castel San Pietro, strikingly fronted by flame-shaped cypress trees. The present castle was built in 1854 under Austrian rule, but it stands on the ruins of an earlier castle which was built by the Visconti of Milan when the Milanese captured Verona in 1387.

🔒 San Giorgio in Braida

San Giorgio is a rare example in Verona of a domed Renaissance church. It was begun in 1477 by Michele Sanmicheli, an architect best known for his military works. Sanmicheli also designed the classically inspired altar, which is topped by Paolo Veronese's *Martyrdom of St George* (1566). This celebrated painting is outshone by the calm and serene *Virgin Enthroned between St Zeno and St Lawrence* (1526) by Girolamo dai Libri. This work has a beautifully detailed background landscape and a lemon tree growing behind the Virgin's throne.

Marquetry cockerel in Santa Maria in Organo

🔒 Santa Maria in Organo

Some of the finest inlaid woodwork to be seen in Italy is in this church. The artist was Fra Giovanni da Verona, an architect and craftsman who worked for nearly 25 years, from 1477 to 1501, on these stunning examples of illusionistic marquetry. The seat backs in the choir and cupboard fronts in the sacristy are full of entertaining detail. By clever interpretation of perspective, Fra Giovanni gave depth to flat landscapes, depicted city views glimpsed through an open window, and created "cupboard interiors" stacked with books, musical instruments or bowls of fruit. Most charming of all are the little animal pictures – look out for the rabbit on the lectern and the owl and the cockerel in the sacristy.

Fossilized fish from Verona's natural history museum

🏛 Museo Civico di Scienze Naturali

Lungadige Porta Vittoria 9. **Tel** 045 807 94 00. ◐ 9am–5pm Mon–Thu, 9am–1pm Sat, 2–6pm Sun and public hols. ● 1 Jan, Easter, 1 May, 25 Dec. 📷 🚫

Verona's natural history museum contains an outstanding collection of fossils, which can be enjoyed by experts and newcomers alike. Whole fish, trees, fern leaves and dragonflies are captured in extraordinary detail. The fossils were found in rock in the foothills of the Little Dolomites north of the city during quarrying for building stone (*see* Bolca, *p191*).

Human prehistory is represented by finds from ancient settlements round Lake Garda, and there are reconstructions of original lake villages. On the upper floor, cases full of stuffed birds, animals and fish provide an extensive account of today's living world, making this a good museum for visiting with children.

🍀 Giardino Giusti

Via Giardino Giusti 2. **Tel** 045 803 40 29. ◐ summer: 9am–8pm; winter: 9am–sunset. ● 25 Dec. 📷 ♿

Hidden among the dusty façades of the Via Giardino Giusti is the entrance to one of Italy's finest Renaissance gardens. They were laid out in 1580 and, as with other gardens of the period, artifice and nature are deliberately juxtaposed. The lower garden of clipped box hedges, gravel walks and potted plants is contrasted with an upper area of wilder woodland, the two parts linked by stone terracing.

Past visitors have included the English traveller Thomas Coryate who, writing in 1611, called this garden "a second paradise". The diarist John Evelyn, visiting 50 years later, thought it the finest garden in Europe. Today the garden makes an excellent, picturesque spot for a quiet picnic.

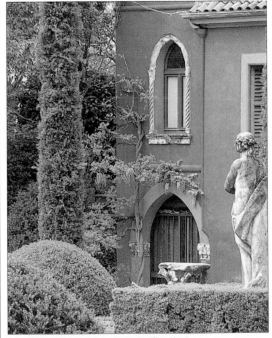

Italianate topiary and statuary in the Giardino Giusti

Around Lake Garda

Garda, the largest and easternmost of the Italian Lakes, is a favourite summer playground for sports lovers. Strong winds make ideal conditions for wind-surfing and sailing, there are numerous yacht harbours and artificial beaches, and luxury hotels offer tennis and horse-riding facilities. The less energetic can explore the lake and shore by steamer, while the magnificent scenery of snow-capped peaks and spectacular sunsets will appeal to every visitor.

Malcésine
The streets of this town are full of character, clustering beneath an imposing medieval castle.

RIVA DEL GARDA

TORBOLE

LIMONE SUL GARDA

MALCESINE

ASSENZA

BRENZONE

CASTELLETTO

GARGNANO

BOGLIACO

La Gardesana

TOSCOLANO MADERNO

GARDONE RIVIERA

SALÒ

PORTESE

TORRI DEL BENACO

GARDA

MANERBA

MONIGA

BARDOLINO

LAZISE

SIRMIONE

DESENZANO

PESCHIERA DEL GARDA

The Sirmione peninsula is best seen from the lake.

Desenzano
With its lively harbour and palm-fringed promenades, Desenzano is the main terminus for steamer excursions.

Bardolino gave its name to the well-known red wine.

Torri del Benaco
Built by the Republic of Venice in 1452, the Hotel Gardesana was originally used to host the meetings of the Council.

KEY

···· Steamer routes

···· Car ferry

0 kilometres   10

0 miles   5

LA GARDESANA

This is the name given to the 143-km (89-mile) perimeter road that hugs the lake shore. For much of its route the road is cut through solid rock, sometimes following a narrow ledge in the cliff face, sometimes passing through tunnels (around 80 in total). The switchback route offers spectacular views at every turn, particularly at Gargnano, and there are numerous viewing points. Places of interest along La Gardesana include the splendid 18th-century gardens of Palazzo Bettoni at Bogliaco and the castle at Riva del Garda.

The scenic road to Limone

LAKE TRIPS

Lake Garda's ferries are still called steamers, even though they are diesel-powered today. The major towns around the southern rim of the lake all have jetties where visitors can buy a ticket and board the boat for a leisurely cruise. Gardens and villas that are otherwise hidden from view can be seen from the water. A trip from one end of the lake to the other takes approximately two hours 20 minutes by hydrofoil, and four hours by steamer. Catamarans also operate around the southern end of the lake.

The hydrofoil operating out of Desenzano harbour

Lake Garda steamer at dusk near Peschiera

Garda ❿

🏠 3,400. 🚌 🛈 Piazzetta Donatori di Sangue 1 (045 627 03 84). 🔼 Fri am. **Shops closed** Wed pm (food).

Numerous pavement cafés brighten the streets around the central Palazzo dei Capitani, built in the 15th century for the use of the Venetian militia. In a different vein, a series of prehistoric rock engravings features along the Strada dei Castei, an old route above the town.

Peschiera ⓫

🏠 8,900. 🚌 FS 🛈 Piazzale Bettelone 15. (045 755 16 73). 🔼 Mon am. **Shops closed** Wed in winter.

At Peschiera the River Mincio flows out of Lake Garda to join the River Po. The main site of interest is a fortress built in the 19th century. Named Fortezza del Quadrilatero because of its square shape, it replaced a 15th century stronghold.

Environs

Just outside town are **Gardaland**, a theme park with a replica of the ancient Egyptian Valley of the Kings (free bus from Peschiera station), and **Parco Natura Viva**, a zoo with a safari park and models of dinosaurs.

🎢 Gardaland
Loc. Ronchi, 37014 Castelnuovo del Garda. **Tel** 045 644 97 77. 🕐 end Mar–Sep: daily; Oct & Christmas period: Sat & Sun. 🅿 ⛔

🐾 Parco Natura Viva
Nr. Bussolengo. **Tel** 045 717 01 13. 🕐 mid-Mar–Nov: daily. ⛔ Wed in Nov. 🅿 ⛔

Solferino ⓬

🏠 2,118. 🚌 🔼 Sat pm. **Shops closed** Mon pm.

The battle of Solferino (1859) left 40,000 Italian and Austrian troops dead and injured, abandoned without medical care or burial. Shocked by such neglect, a Swiss man named Henri Dunant began a campaign for better treatment. The result was the first Geneva Convention, signed in 1863, and the establishment of the International Red Cross. In the town of Solferino there is a war museum and an ossuary chapel, lined with bones from the battlefield. There is also a memorial to Dunant built by the Red Cross with donations from member nations.

The ossuary chapel at Solferino, lined with skulls

For hotels and restaurants in this region see pp234–5 and pp248–9

Sirmione Peninsula ⑬

Charming Sirmione is a finger of land extending into the southern end of Lake Garda, connected to the mainland by a bridge. The Roman poet Catullus (born in 84 BC) owned a villa here: the ruins of the Grotte di Catullo lie among ancient olive trees at the northern tip. The Rocca Scaligera castle stands guard at the base of the peninsula, and beyond, the narrow streets of the village give way to peaceful lakeside walks and elegant spa hotels.

View Towards the Grotto
The high central tower commands views over the castle and the whole of the Sirmione peninsula.

★ Rocca Scaligera
The castle was built in the 13th century by the Scaligeri of Verona. It is cleverly designed to trap shipborne invaders, leaving them vulnerable to missiles dropped from the castle walls.

The main keep tower was used for bombarding attackers trapped below.

The moat, originally a complex defence system, is today home to carp.

Piazza Castello

Sirmione Old Town
Narrow stone-paved streets are packed with shops selling crafts and souvenirs.

Visiting the Peninsula
Cars must be parked before entering Sirmione, leaving the medieval streets for pedestrians.

STAR FEATURES

- ★ Rocca Scaligera
- ★ Grotte di Catullo

Lakeside Walk
Following the eastern shores of the peninsula, this pretty walk links the village to the Grotte di Catullo.

VISITORS' CHECKLIST

🚌 🚢 ℹ️ *Viale Marconi 8.
(030 91 61 14).*
Rocca Scaligera *Tel 030 91 64
68.* ⬜ *8:30am–7pm Tue–Sun.*
⬤ *1 Jan, 1 May, 25 Dec.* 📷
Grotte di Catullo *Tel 030 91
61 57.* ⬜ *8:30am–7pm Tue–Sun
(Nov–Feb: to 5pm).*
⬤ *1 Jan, 1 May, 25 Dec.* 📷 ♿
📷 *Sat, Sun.*

San Pietro
Founded in AD 765, on Sirmione's highest point, this church contains a 12th-century fresco of Christ in Majesty.

★ Grotte di Catullo
This complex of villas, baths and shops, built as a resort for wealthy Romans from the 1st century BC, lies ruined here. Finds are displayed in the Antiquarium building.

The inner harbour provided a haven for fishermen during lake storms and an anchorage for the castle fleet.

The drawbridge is heavily fortified, linking the castle to the mainland and offering an escape route to its inhabitants.

THE SCALIGERI

The Rocca Scaligera is one of many castles built throughout the Verona and Lake Garda region by the Scaligeri family *(see p192)*. During the turbulent 13th and 14th centuries, powerful military rulers fought each other incessantly in pursuit of riches and power. Despite the autocratic nature of their rule, the Scaligeri brought a period of peace and prosperity to the region, fending off attacks by the predatory Visconti family who ruled neighbouring Lombardy.

The Scaligeri ruler, Cangrande I

Salò ⑭

🏛 10,000. 🚌 ⛴ *Sat am.*

Locals prefer to associate this elegant town with Gaspare da Salò (1540–1609), the inventor of the violin, rather than with Mussolini, the World War II dictator. Mussolini set up the so-called Salò Republic in 1943 and ruled northern Italy from here until 1945, when he was shot by the Italian resistance.

Happier memories are evoked by Salò's buildings, including the cathedral with its unusual wooden altarpiece (1510) by Paolo Veneziano. The main appeal of the town derives from its pastel-coloured waterfront buildings, picturesque squares and alleyways, and the lake views. Salò marks the beginning of the Riviera Bresciana, where the shore is lined with villas and grand hotels set in semi-tropical gardens.

Gardone Riviera ⑮

🏛 2,500. 🚌 ℹ *Via Repubblica 8. (0365 203 47).*

Gardone's most appealing feature is the terraced public park that cascades down the hillside, planted with noble and exotic trees. Equally exotic are the Mediterranean and African plants in the **Hruska Botanical**

The Art Deco Grand Hotel in Gardone Riviera

Gardens, founded in 1910, which benefit from the town's mild winters. Gardone has long been a popular resort – the magnificent 19th-century **Villa Alba** (now a congress centre) was built for the Austrian emperor to escape the bitter winters of his own country. The Art Deco **Grand Hotel** on the waterfront was built for lesser beings.

High above the town is the **Villa il Vittoriale**, built for the poet Gabriele d'Annunzio. His Art Deco villa has blacked-out windows (he professed to loathe the world) and is full of curiosities, including a coffin-shaped bed. The garden has a landlocked warship, the prow raised high over Lake Garda.

🌺 **Hruska Botanical Gardens**
Via Roma. **Tel** 336 41 08 77.
⏰ Mar–Oct: 9am–7pm daily. 🏛

🏛 **Villa il Vittoriale**
Via Vittoriale 12. **Tel** 0365 29 65 23. ⏰ Tue–Sun (garden daily). ●
1 Jan, 24 & 25 Dec. 🏛 🏛 🏛 🏛

Valpolicella Wine Tour

This circular tour takes in the beautiful, remarkably varied scenery of the wine district that lies between Verona and Lake Garda. On the shores of Lake Garda itself, deep and fertile glacial soils provide sustenance for the grapes that are used to make Bardolino, a wine that is meant to be drunk young *(see pp238–9)*. Inland, the rolling foothills of the Lessini mountains shelter hamlets where lives and working rhythms are tuned to the needs of the vines. These particular vines are grown to produce the equally famed Valpolicella, a red wine that varies from light and fruity to full-bodied.

TIPS FOR DRIVERS

Starting point: *Verona.*
Length: *45 km (28 miles).*
Approximate driving time: *3 hours.*
Stopping-off points: *The main village of the Valpolicella region, San Pietro in Cariano, has cafés and restaurants.*

Bardolino ③
Famous for its light red wine, Bardolino hosts a grape festival in September and has numerous cellars offering tastings.

KEY

━━━ Tour route

═══ Other roads

Affi ④
This wine-producing village is surrounded by vineyards planted in the sheltered basin of the Adige Valley.

LAGO DI GARDA

SS249

PESCHIERA DI GARDA

Lazise ②
Lazise has long been the chief port of Garda's eastern shore, its picturesque harbour and medieval church guarded by a 14th-century castle.

Looking across Lake Garda from Riva del Garda

Riva del Garda 16

🏠 13,600. 🚌 ℹ️ Largo Medaglie d'Oro. (0464 55 44 44). 🔼 2nd Wed (& 4th Wed in summer). **Shops closed** Mon (non-food); Mon pm (food) & Sat pm in winter.

Riva's waterfront is over-looked by the moated **Rocca di Riva**, a former Scaligeri fortress. Inside is a museum with exhibits from the region's pre-historic lake villages, built by driving huge piles into the lake bed to support platforms. The lake is popular with windsurfers.

🏛️ **Rocca di Riva**
Piazza Cesare Battisti 3. **Tel** 0464 57 38 69. ◻ mid-Mar–Oct: Tue–Sun (Mon also in Jul–Sep). 📷 ♿ ⓘ

Malcésine 17

🏠 3,500. 🚌 🚢 Sat.

German visitors who come to Malcésine trace the journey taken by the poet Goethe in 1788. His travels were full of mishaps, and at Malcésine he was accused of spying and locked up.

From Malcésine, visitors can take the rotating **cable car** up to the broad ridge of Monte Baldo (1,745 m/5,725 ft). The journey takes 15 minutes, and on a clear day it is possible to see the distant peaks of the Dolomites, including the Brenta range. Footpaths for walkers are signposted at the top. The lower slopes are designated nature reserves; a good place to see the local flora is the **Riserva Naturale Gardesana Orientale**, just to the north of Malcésine, on the western side of Monte Baldo.

Sant'Ambrogio di Valpolicella ⑤
Apart from red wine, this village is a source of the pink stone used for Verona's palaces.

Gargagnago ⑥
The Alighieri wine estate is owned by a direct descendant of the medieval poet Dante, and set around a 14th-century villa built by Dante's son.

Cloisters of San Giorgio in Valpolicella

Pedemonte ⑦
The Villa Santa Sofia wine estate operates out of a theatrical villa designed by Palladio, but never completed.

San Giorgio

San Floriano

San Pietro in Cariano

ENTO

S12

Pescantina

Adige

Biffi

PADOVA

Verona ①
The city has numerous old-fashioned bars, called *osterie*, where visitors can go to sample local wine.

0 kilometres   3
0 miles   2

THE DOLOMITES

*T*he name of the Dolomites conjures up a vision of spectacular mountains, as noble and awe-inspiring as the Alps. To the south of the region lie the cities of Feltre, Belluno and Vittorio Veneto. To the north is the renowned ski resort of Cortina d'Ampezzo. In between, travellers will encounter no more cities – just ravishing views, unfolding endlessly, and pretty hamlets tucked into remarkably lush and sunny south-facing valleys.

The Dolomites cover a substantial portion of the Veneto's land mass, and it is easy to forget, when visiting the cities of the flat Veneto plain, that behind them lies this range of mountains rising to heights of 2,000 m (6,500 ft) and more. Catering for an urban population hungry for fresh air and freedom, the towns and villages of the Dolomites have striven to balance the needs of tourism and nature.

Italian is the region's principal language, but in the northwest a German influence can sometimes be heard, reflecting the region's strong historic links with the Austrian Tyrol. Once ruled by the Hapsburgs, certain areas of the region only became part of Italy in 1918, after the break up of the Austro-Hungarian empire at the end of World War I. Some of that war's fiercest fighting took place in the Dolomites, as both sides tried to wrest control of the strategic valley passes linking Italy and Austria-Hungary. Striking war memorials in many villages and towns provide a sad reminder of that time.

Today the region is renowned for its winter sports facilities. International cross-country ski competitions were held in Cortina d'Ampezzo as early as 1902, and in 1956 the town hosted the Winter Olympics. Today, Cortina is considered to be Italy's most exclusive resort, the winter playground of film stars and royalty.

Outdoor café in the old town of Feltre

◁ Pleasure boats on Lake Misurina, looking towards the peaks of the Sorapiss

Exploring the Dolomites

Titian's statue, Pieve di Cadore

The environment of the Dolomites is completely different from the industrialized Veneto plain. Huge areas are designated nature reserves, while others, accessible by chair lifts, allow visitors to enjoy the views and appetite-sharpening treks in the mountain meadows. Refuges, dotted along the high trails, offer dormitory accommodation and refreshments, while hamlets have comfortable hotels. Snow covers the peaks from October to May, and it is possible to ski all year round on Marmolada, at 3,343 m (10,970 ft) the highest peak in the Dolomites.

Mountain chalet near the stadium at Cortina d'Ampezzo

SIGHTS AT A GLANCE

Belluno **5**
Cortina d'Ampezzo **1**
The Dolomites (Dolomiti) pp216–17 **4**
Feltre **7**
Misurina **2**
Pieve di Cadore **3**
Valzoldana **6**
Vittorio Veneto **8**

0 kilometres   10

0 miles   5

Dobbiaco

Tre Cime di Lavaredo
2999m

2 MISURINA   Giralba

Stabiziane

S48

Anster

C a d o r e

San Pietro
di Cadore

Santo Stéfano
di Cadore   S355   Sappada

Auronzo
di Cadore

Lago di
S. Caterina   S52   Monte Terza Grande
2585m

ppo delle Marmarole

to
ore   Domegge
di Cadore

Lorenzo di
Cadore

S52

PIEVE DI
CADORE **3**

Lago di Pieve
di Cadore

Ampezzo   Valle di Cadore

Cibiana
S347 di Cadore

sighe

di Zoldo

Piave

Monte Pera
2333m

e Belvedere
ni   S51

S1

Longarone

Igne

Schiara

S50   A27

BELLUNO

Monte Cavallo
2251m

Lago di
San Croce

Fadalto

Bosco del Cansiglio

S51   S422

evine

VITTORIO
VENETO **8**

Tarzo   A27

Cordignano

Bagnolo   S13

↓ Treviso

Monte Pelmo from Zoppe di Cadore

GETTING AROUND

The S50 and S51 are kept clear of snow all year. There
are steep gradients on the S48 and minor roads, so use
snow chains in winter. Roadside notices warn when
the high passes are closed. There is only one railway
line (up the Piave valley), but the region is well served
by comfortable express buses.

Piaggio Vespa truck, a common sight in the Dolomites

KEY

▬▬	Motorway
▬	Major road
▬	Minor road
▬	Scenic route
⊷	Main railway
▬	Minor railway
▬▬	International border
▬	Regional border
△	Summit

Cortina d'Ampezzo ❶

🏛 *6,800.* 🚌 🛈 *Piazzetta San Francesco 8. (0436 3231).* 🛒 *Tue am, Fri am.*

Italy's top ski resort, much favoured by the smart set from Turin and Milan, is well supplied with restaurants and bars. The reason for its popularity is the dramatic scenery, which adds an extra dimension to the pleasure of speeding down the slopes. Guests are surrounded by crags

Strolling along the Corso Italia in Cortina d'Ampezzo

Skiers at Cortina

and spires, which rise skyward, thrusting their weather-sculpted shapes above the trees.

As a consequence of hosting the 1956 Winter Olympics, Cortina has better-than-normal sports facilities. There is a ski jump and a bobsleigh run, the Olympic ice stadium holds skating discotheques, and there are several swimming pools as well as tennis courts and riding facilities.

During the summer months, Cortina becomes an excellent base for walkers. Information on the many trails and guided walks is available from the tourist office or, during the summer, from the Guides' office opposite.

Visitors can also take the cable car *Freccia nel Cielo* (Arrow in the Sky), which goes to a height of 3,243 m (10,639 ft) above sea level.

The Dolomite Road

The Strada Delle Dolomiti, or Dolomite Road, is one of the most beautiful routes anywhere in the Alps, and is a magnificent feat of highway construction. It starts in the Trentino-Alto Adige region at Bolzano and enters the Veneto region at Passo Pordoi, at 2,239 m (7,346 ft) the most scenic of all the Dolomite passes. From here the route follows the winding S48 for another 35 km (22 miles) east to the resort of Cortina d'Ampezzo.

There are plenty of stopping places along the route where it is possible to stop and enjoy the spectacular views. In many of the ski resorts, cable cars will carry visitors up to alpine refuges (some with cafés attached) that are open from mid-June to mid-September. These refuges mark the start of a series of signposted walks.

TIPS FOR WALKERS

Starting point: Passo Pordoi.
Length (within the Veneto): 35 km (22 miles).
Approximate driving time: Two hours, but allow a full day to include the return journey and time to stop and enjoy the stunning scenery.
Stopping-off points: The small towns of Pieve di Livinallongo and Andraz have good cafés and restaurants.

Passo Pordoi ①
To the north of Passo Pordoi, the Gruppo di Sella rises to 3,152 m (10,340 ft).

← *BOLZANO*

KEY

🚍 Tour route

═ Other roads

🔆 View point

0 kilometres   5

0 miles   2

Arabba ②
Arabba is a pleasant resort with a cable car to Porta Vescovo (2,478 m/8,129 ft) to the south.

Misurina ❷

82. 🚌 **ℹ** *Via Misurina.* (0435 90 16). ☐ *Jul–Aug; late Dec–arly Jan.*

Smaller and quieter than Cortina, Misurina nestles by the exquisite Lake Misurina. The lake's mirror-like surface reflects the peaks of Monte Sorapiss and the Cadini group. Take the toll road that climbs northeast for 8 km (5 miles) to the Auronzo mountain refuge and to the base of the Tre Cime di Lavaredo peaks (2,999 m/9,840 ft).

One of the creeks flowing into Lake Misurina

Titian's house at Pieve di Cadore

Pieve di Cadore ❸

🏘 4,000. 🚌 **ℹ** *Piazza Municipio 13.* (0435 316 44). ☐ *Wed am (at Tai).*

For centuries the Cadore forests supplied Venice with its timber. The main town of this vast mountainous region is Pieve di Cadore, primarily known as the birthplace of Titian. The humble **Casa di Tiziano** can be visited, and the nearby **Museo Archeologico** has exhibits of finds from the pre-Roman era.

Principally, though, this is a base for touring the scenic delights of the region. North of Pieve the valley narrows to a dramatic ravine, and the road north to Comelica and Sesto is noted for its alpine scenery and its traditional balconied houses. Continuing northeast, the Piave river can be followed to its source, 8 km (5 miles) north of Sappada.

🏛 Casa di Tiziano
Via Arsenale 4. **Tel** 0435 322 62.
☐ *Jun–Sep: Tue–Sun (Aug: daily); Oct–May: by appointment.* 🅿

🏛 Museo Archeologico Romano e Preromano
Palazzo della Magnifica Comunità Cadorina, Piazza Tiziano 2. **Tel** 0435 322 62. ☐ *Jun–Sep: Tue–Sun (Aug: daily); Oct–May: by appointment.* 🅿

Falzarego ⑤
War memorials record the fighting that took place here in 1914–18 on the frontier between Austria and Italy.

Cortina d'Ampezzo ⑥
Descending to Cortina, the view is dominated by the irregularly shaped Cinque Torri (Five Towers).

Andraz ④
The partially restored Castello di Andraz, sitting on a rocky outcrop, was built in the 1300s to prevent banditry and to control the approach to the Passo Falzarego.

Pieve di Livinallongo ③
The chief town of the scenic Cordevole valley, Pieve offers spectacular views of dolomitic peaks and cliffs.

Visitors at Passo Falzarego, by the war memorials

The Dolomites ❹

The Dolomites are the most distinctive and beautiful mountains in Italy. They were formed of mineralized coral which was laid down beneath the sea during the Triassic era, and uplifted when the European and African continental plates dramatically collided 60 million years ago. Unlike the glacier-eroded saddles and ridges of the main body of the Alps, the pale rocks here have been carved by the corrosive effects of ice, sun and rain, sculpting the cliffs, spires and "organ pipes" that we see today. The eastern and western ranges of the Dolomites have slightly different characteristics; the eastern section is the more awe-inspiring, especially the Catinaccio (or Rosengarten) range which is particularly beautiful, turning rose pink at sunset.

Onion dome, a comm
local feature

STRADA DELLE DOLOMITI

One of the most spectacular routes through the Dolomites links Bolzano with Cortina d'Ampezzo *(see p214)*. It follows the lie of the land, passing some of the greatest peaks, and the most majestic landscape.

Dobbiaco

TRE CIME DI LAVAREDO

Lago di Misurina

Cortina d'Ampezzo

SASSO LUNGO

TORRI DEL VAIOLET

Bolzano

Canazei

CINQUE TORRI

MARMOLADA

Pieve di Cadore

0 kilometres 10

0 miles 5

DISTINCTIVE PEAKS OF THE DOLOMITES

The peaks of the Dolomites include several with distinctive shapes and some of the highest mountains in the range. Many are easily identifiable and have been individually named.

Marmolada
3,343 m
(10,968 ft)

Sasso Lungo
3,179 m
(10,430 ft)

Cinque Torri
2,366 m
(7,762 ft)

4,000 m
(13,123 ft)

3,000 m
(9,842 ft)

2,000 m
(6,562 ft)

1,000 m
(3,281 ft)

Approximate heights

The Cinque Torri *or Five Towers rise from one base between Passo Falzarego and Cortina d'Ampezzo.*

Sasso Lungo *is a tall peak easily recognized by its distinctive scar. It is joined to the Sasso Piatto.*

Marmolada *is the highest peak in the Dolomite chain. A cable-car ascends to 3,000 m above the glacier.*

Lago di Misurina *is a large and beautiful lake lying beside the resort of Misurina. The crystal clear waters reflect the surrounding mountains, mirroring various peaks such as the distinctive and dramatic Sorapiss, in shimmering colours.*

Outdoor activities *in this area of dramatic landscapes include skiing in winter, and walking and rambling along the footpaths, and to picnic sites, in summer. Chair-lifts from the main resorts provide easy access up into the mountains themselves, transporting you into some breathtaking scenery.*

Torri del Vaiolet
2,243 m
(7,375 ft)

Tre Cime di Lavaredo
2,999 m
(9,839 ft)

The Torri del Vaiolet *is part of the beautiful Catinaccio range, known for its colour.*

Tre Cime di Lavaredo *or Drei Zinnen dominate the valleys north of the Lago di Misurina.*

NATURE IN THE DOLOMITES

Forests and meadows support a breathtaking richness of wildlife in the region. Alpine plants, which flower between June and September, have evolved their miniature form to survive the harsh winds.

THE FLORA

Gentian roots *are used to make a bitter local liqueur.*

The orange mountain lily *thrives on sun-baked slopes.*

The pretty *burser's saxifrage grows in clusters on rocks.*

Devil's claw *has distinctive pink flower heads.*

THE FAUNA

The ptarmigan *changes its plumage from mottled brown in summer to snow white in winter for effective camouflage. It feeds on mountain berries and young plant shoots.*

The chamois, *a shy mountain antelope prized for its soft skin, is protected in the national parks, where hunting is forbidden.*

Roe deer *are very common as their natural predators – wolves and lynx – have now died out. Their keen appetite for tree saplings causes problems for foresters.*

Belluno ❺

🏠 *35,800.* FS 🚌 ℹ️ *Piazza Duomo 2. (0437 94 00 83).* 🅰️ *Sat am.* **Shops closed** *Mon am (clothes) & Wed pm (food).*

Picturesque Belluno, capital of Belluno province, serves as a bridge between the two very different parts of the Veneto, with the flat plains to the south and the Dolomite peaks to the north. Both are encapsulated in the picture-postcard views to be seen from the 12th-century **Porta Rugo** at the southern end of Via Mezzaterra, the main street of the old town. Even more spectacular are the views from the campanile of the 16th-century **Duomo** which was designed by Tullio Lombardo, but rebuilt twice after damage by earthquakes.

The nearby baptistry contains a font cover with the figure of John the Baptist carved by Andrea Brustolon (1662– 1732), whose elaborate furnishings decorate Ca' Rezzonico in Venice *(see p126)*. Brustolon's works also grace the churches of **San Pietro** (two altarpieces) and **Santo Stefano** (crucifix and angels).

Façade and entrance to Palazzo dei Rettori in Belluno

Exterior fresco, Zoppe di Cadore

On the same square is the 12th-century **Torre Civica**, all that survives of the Bishop's Palace, and the city's most elegant building, the Renaissance **Palazzo dei Rettori** (1491), once home to Belluno's Venetian rulers.

The **Museo Civico** is worth visiting for the archaeological exhibits, and the paintings by Bartolomeo Montagna (1450–1523) and Sebastiano Ricci (1659– 1734). Just to the right of the museum is the town's finest square, the **Piazza del Mercato**, which features arcaded Renaissance palaces and a fountain built in 1410.

South of the town are the ski resorts of the Alpe del Nevegal. It is worth taking the chair lift in the summer to the Rifugio Brigata Alpina Cadore (1,600 m/5,250 ft) which has superb views and a botanical garden specializing in alpine plants.

🏛 **Museo Civico**
Piazza Duomo 16. **Tel** *0437 94 48 36.* 🕐 *May–Sep: Tue–Sun; Oct–Apr: daily.* 🈳 ✔️ 📷

Valzoldana ❻

🚌 *from Longarone.* ℹ️ *Via Roma 10, Forno di Zoldo. (0437 78 73 49).*

The wooded Zoldo valley is a popular destination for walking holidays. Its main resort town is Forno di Zoldo and the surrounding villages are noted for their Tyrolean-style alpine chalets and hay-lofts. Examples built in wood on stone foundations can be

BELLUNO

Duomo ②
Museo Civico ④
Palazzo dei Rettori ③
Piazza del Mercato ⑦
Porta Rugo ①
San Pietro ⑥
Santo Stefano ⑧
Torre Civica ⑤

0 metres   500
0 yards   500

Key to Symbols
see back flap

seen at Fornesighe, 2 km (1 mile) northeast of Forno di Zoldo, and on the slopes of Monte Penna at Zoppe di Cadore, 8 km (5 miles) north.

If there is time, a circular tour is a good way to explore the area. Drive north on the S251, via Zoldo Alto to Selva di Cadore, then west via Colle di Santa Lucia (a favourite viewpoint for photographers). From here take the S203 south through the lakeside resort of Alleghe. The route passes through wonderful scenery with woodland, flower-filled meadows and pretty mountain hamlets which complement the splendour of the rocky crags.

The southernmost town of the area is Agordo, nestling in the Cordevole Valley. From here, a spectacularly scenic route follows the S34 north-east to the Passo Duran (1,605 m/5,270 ft), descending to Dont, close to the starting point of the tour. Wayside shrines mark the route and it is worth stopping on the way down to visit village shops selling local woodcarving. Take care when driving along this narrow and winding road.

Palazzo Guarnieri, one of the Renaissance palaces in Feltre

Feltre ❼

🚶 19,600. ⟒⟒ 🚌 ℹ️ Piazzetta Trento e Trieste 9. (0439 2540). 🛍️ Tue & Fri am. **Shops closed** Mon am (clothes), Wed pm (food).

Feltre owes its venerable good looks to the vengeful Holy Roman Emperor, Maximilian I. He sacked the town twice, in 1509 and in 1510, at the outbreak of the war against Venice waged by the League of Cambrai (see p44). Despite the destruction of its buildings and the murder of most of its citizens, Feltre remained

Selva di Cadore from Colle di Santa Lucia, northwest of Valzoldana

stoutly loyal to Venice, and Venice repaid the debt by rebuilding the town after the war. Thus the main street of the old town, Via Mezzaterra, is lined with arcaded early 16th-century houses, most with steeply pitched roofs to keep snow from settling.

Follow the steep main street to the striking Piazza Maggiore, where it is possible to see the remains of Feltre's medieval castle, the church of **San Rocco** and a fountain by Tullio Lombardo (1520).

On the eastern side of the square is Via L Luzzo, a beautiful street lined with Renaissance palaces, one of which houses the **Museo Civico**. The museum displays a fresco by the local artist Lorenzo Luzzo, who was known as Il Morto da Feltre (The Dead Man of Feltre), a nickname given to him by his contemporaries because of the deathly pallor of his skin.

🏛️ **Museo Civico**
Palazzo Villabruna, Via L Luzzo 23. **Tel** 0439 88 52 41. ⏱️ Tue–Sun. ⬤ public hols. 🎫

Vittorio Veneto ❽

🚶 30,000. ⟒⟒ 🚌 ℹ️ Viale della Vittoria 110. (0438 572 43). **Shops closed** Tue (clothes), Wed pm (food). 🛍️ Mon.

Two separate towns, Ceneda and Serravalle, were merged and renamed Vittorio Veneto in 1866 to honour the unification of Italy under King Vittorio Emanuele II. The town later gave its name to the last decisive battle fought in Italy in World War I. The **Museo della Battaglia** in the Ceneda quarter, the commercial heart of the town, commemorates this. Serravalle is more picturesque, with many fine 15th-century *palazzi*, and pretty arcaded streets. Franco Zeffirelli shot scenes for his film *Romeo and Juliet* in this town that sits at the base of the rocky Meschio gorge. To the east, via Anzano, the S422 climbs up to the Bosco del Cansiglio, a wooded plateau.

🏛️ **Museo della Battaglia**
Piazza Giovanni Paolo I. **Tel** 0438 576 95. ⏱️ Tue–Sun. 🎫

Vittorio Veneto old town and river

TRAVELLERS' NEEDS

WHERE TO STAY

Venice's perennial attraction to romantics and art lovers means it has an astonishing number of hotels for its size, many of them in former *palazzi*. On the mainland, ancient cities abound with hotels and *pensioni*, often housed in magnificent old buildings and extravagantly decorated. Those in the smaller towns are often run by families who take pride in their reputation.

Lake Garda is a long-established resort area with many hotels to choose from, and the mountainous north of the

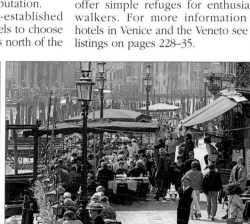

Sign for a small hotel

region is an all-year-round holiday area with accommodation of all types. Here you can find self-catering in a small farmhouse at very reasonable cost, and there are also numerous idyllically situated and well-equipped campsites. Budget options in the cities include self-catering flats, hostels and dormitory accommodation, and the mountains offer simple refuges for enthusiastic walkers. For more information on hotels in Venice and the Veneto see the listings on pages 228–35.

WHERE TO LOOK

Unlike most other cities, Venice has hardly any "undesirable" addresses. You will pay considerably more for a hotel in the immediate vicinity of the Piazza San Marco, but in such a compact city even apparently outlying areas such as Cannaregio or Santa Croce *(see pp14–15)* are never far from places of interest. Addresses in Venice are immensely confusing *(see p285)* but a map reference for each hotel on the main islands is given in the listings. The maps referred to are to be found on pages 290–301.

Most visitors feel it is worth splashing out for a few nights' stay in Venice itself, despite the high cost, though an increasing number are choosing to stay in Verona or Padua instead and

Hotel Europa e Regina *(see p229)* overlooking the Grand Canal

◁ Pavement cafés line the Riva del Vin by the Grand Canal

Outside the Hotel Marconi *(see p230)* on the busy Riva del Vin

"commute" into Venice by train. Do not be tempted by the relatively low prices of the Mestre hotels, unless you are prepared to stay in a sprawling industrial town. Remember, too, that if you are travelling by car you will have to pay stiff parking charges at the Piazzale Roma car park or one of its satellites for the duration of your stay in Venice *(see pp286–7)*.

Many of the hotels in minor inland towns of the Veneto cater primarily for business travellers, but if you plan to explore the region you will find some lovely villa hotels in the countryside. Padua and Verona have a number of hotels, but those in Verona are fully booked for months ahead in the summer opera season, so forward planning is essential. Further north there is more choice. The

hotels are geared to holiday-makers, with lovely gardens, swimming pools and sports facilities. But bear in mind that Italians as well as foreign tourists flock to the lakes and mountains, so it is always advisable to plan your trip and book in advance.

HOTEL PRICES

Hotel charges were de-regulated in 1994, so that hotels are free to charge what they feel the market will bear rather than being tied to the tariffs determined by their star rating. Venice is an expensive place to stay and nowadays can hardly be said to have a "low season" with the benefits of lower or negotiable prices. It is difficult but not impossible to find a basic double room for less than €50. Occasionally you can find some cheaper rooms from November to February, when the weather is often superb. But remember that many hotels close out of season. Some re-open for Carnival – and raise their prices accordingly.

July and August are the most expensive months at the resorts along Lake Garda. In the Dolomites winter is the high season, when skiers flock to the area, and the hotels may close during the summer.

Single room rates are higher than individual rates for two people sharing a double room. Prices include tax.

HIDDEN EXTRAS

If you are travelling on a budget, try to avoid hotels with inclusive breakfast as this is rarely good value for money. You are expected to tip at least €1 for room service and bellboys, even if service is included in the price of the room. Laundry services are usually expensive, as are drinks from the minibar and telephone calls from hotel rooms. Check all the rates when you make the booking. Some small hotels in Venice, and most in holiday areas like Lake Garda, may expect you to take full- or half-board during the high season.

HOTEL GRADINGS AND FACILITIES

Italian hotels are classified by a rating system from one to five stars. However, each province sets its own

level for grading, so standards for each category may vary from one area to another. Some hotels may not have a restaurant, but those which do sometimes welcome non-residents who wish to eat.

Air-conditioning is rare in old buildings. Although the thick stone walls provide good insulation against the summer's heat, if you cannot tolerate high temperatures it is well worth choosing air-conditioned accommodation in Venice during the hottest months. Under Italian law, central heating remains off, whatever the temperature outside, until 1 November. This is something that is worth remembering if you plan a late-October trip.

Children are welcome everywhere but smaller hotels have limited facilities. Although Venice is not thought to be child-friendly, it can be an excellent holiday for families. The Lido is a good base as children will have access to the beach and probably a garden.

WHAT TO EXPECT

Hotels are obliged by law to register you with the police, so they will ask for your passport when you arrive. They may need to keep it for a few hours, but make sure you take it back, because you will need identification to change money or travellers' cheques. Italian

Terrace, Hotel Bauer *(see p229)*

Excelsior Palace
(see p233)

hotel rooms are not "cosy": carpets are rare, the storage space is usually very limited and luxuries such as tea-making facilities are unknown, even in four- and five- star establishments. The decor may be simple and Italian taste can be rather different from what you are used to. However, hotel staff will be friendly and charming, and the standard of cleanliness is high. The bathrooms are, almost without exception, spotlessly clean, even when they are shared. Less expensive hotels are unlikely to have bathtubs; showers are considered more hygienic and more economical on water. Rooms without a bathroom usually have a washbasin and towels are provided.

Breakfast is very light – a cup of coffee and a brioche (a plain or cream- or jam-filled pastry), though hotels generally include fruit juice, bread rolls and jam as well. It is always cheaper to have breakfast in a bar.

With the exception of Venice, where the only sounds are water-borne or human, Italian towns can be very noisy. If you are a light sleeper, ask for a room that is away from the street, or come equipped with earplugs to deaden traffic sounds and church bells.

Check-out time is usually noon in four- and five-star hotels and between ten and noon in small establishments. If you stay longer you will be asked to pay for an extra day.

The Palazzo Abadessa is set in beautiful gardens *(see p232)*

BOOKING AND PAYING

Book at least two months in advance if you want to stay in a particular hotel in the high season; some people book as far as six months or a year ahead in Venice itself. The local tourist office will have listings of all the hotels in the area, and they will be able to advise you on the best hotels in each star category. Hotels above the €50 price bracket usually take credit cards, but check which cards are accepted when you make your reservation. You can generally pay the deposit by credit card, or by sending an international money order.

Under Italian law, a booking is valid as soon as the deposit is paid and confirmation is received. As in restaurants, you are required by law to keep your hotel receipts until you leave the country.

DISABLED TRAVELLERS

Facilities for the disabled are limited throughout Italy, and Venice poses its own particular problems. Recently several strategic bridges have been fitted with mechanized

The conveniently located Hotel La Fenice *(see p228)*

lifts for wheelchairs. The key must be requested in advance from the town hall. A list of tour operators that specialize in holidays for the disabled can be obtained from the **Italian State Tourist Office**. For further advice, see p269.

HOTELS IN HISTORIC BUILDINGS

Many of Venice's hotels are housed in buildings of historical or artistic interest, for example in Gothic *palazzi*. Some of the best are included

in the listings below. In the Veneto there are also some attractive villa hotels – see the **Relais and Châteaux** guide for more details.

SELF-CATERING

Self-catering flats in Venice proper are fairly easy to find. **International Chapters** handle some holiday lets within the city, as do **Tailor Made Tours** and **Vacanze in Italia**. Alternatively you could try one of the Venetian agents, such as **Sant'Angelo**

DIRECTORY

TOURIST OFFICE

Italian State Tourist Office (ENIT)
1 Princes Street,
London W1R 8AY.
Tel 020 7408 1254.

HISTORIC HOTELS

Relais & Châteaux
35–37 Grosvenor Gardens,
London SW1W 0BS.
Tel 0800 960 239.

SELF-CATERING

Centro Immobiliare NG
Rio Terra Canal, Dorsoduro
3066. **Map** 6 D2.
Tel 041 522 09 32.

International Chapters
47–51 St John's Wood
High Street, London NW8
7NJ. **Tel** 020 7722 9560.

Sant'Angelo
Campo Sant'Angelo, San
Marco 3818. **Map** 6 F2.
Tel 041 522 15 05.

Tailor Made Tours
22 Church Rise,
London SE23 2UD.
Tel 020 8291 9736.

Vacanze in Italia
www.homeabroad.com

Venice Rentals
90 Sea Street, Suite 121,
N. Weymouth, MA
02191 USA. **Tel** 617 472
5392. **www**.
venicerentals.com

BUDGET ACCOMMODATION

Associazione Italiana Alberghi per la Gioventù
Via Cavour 44, 00184
Rome. **Tel** 06 487 11 52.

Foresteria Venezia
Campo Santa Maria
Formosa, Castello 5170.
Map 7 C1.
Tel 041 528 67 97.
www.foresteriavenezia.it

Ostello Venezia
Fondamenta delle Zitelle,
Giudecca 86.
Map 7 B5.
Tel 041 523 82 11.

Santa Fosca
Fmta Diedo, Cannaregio
2372.
Map 2 F3.
Tel 041 71 57 75.

CAMPSITES AND MOUNTAIN REFUGES

Club Alpino Italiano
Via Petrella 19,
20124 Milan.
Tel 02 205 72 31.

Marina di Venezia
Via Montello 6,
Punta Sabbioni.
Tel 041 530 09 55.

San Nicolò
Riviera San Nicolò 65, Lido.
Tel 041 526 74 15.

Touring Club Italiano
Corso Italia 10, 20122
Milan.
Tel 02 852 61.

WATERBORNE ACCOMMODATION

Boat and Breakfast
Giudecca 212A, 30133.
Tel 335 666 6241.

Navigador
Tel 348 814 6123.
www.navigador.com

or **Centro Immobiliare NG**, although they may prefer to deal with longer rentals.

Venice Rentals offers a variety of accommodation, from small apartments on the Lido to a palatial home on the Grand Canal. Other options might be a simple conversion or a luxurious and spacious villa with a swimming pool. Prices reflect these variations, and they also fluctuate according to the time of year. Low-season prices for four people start at about €500 per week.

BUDGET ACCOMMODATION

One- or two-star budget hotels charging from €20 to €40 per person per night are generally small, family-run places. These used to be known as *pensioni*, but the term is no longer used very much officially. However, many places retain the name and the personal character that has made them so popular. They rarely offer breakfast and have very few rooms with private bathrooms. You should not expect particularly high standards of service. A variation on these *pensioni* are *affittacamere*, or rented rooms. These are even smaller establishments, and they also offer excellent value for money.

Accommodation in hostels and dormitories is sometimes available at convents and religious institutions, and it is often possible to arrange it through the local tourist offices. The **Associazione Italiana Alberghi per la Gioventù** (Italian Youth Hostel Association) in Rome has lists of youth hostels throughout the whole of Italy. The main youth hostel in Venice is the beautifully situated **Ostello Venezia** on the Giudecca. It is essential to book well ahead if you want to stay in July or August.

Detail on the Hotel Danieli

Lists and booking forms for youth hostels are available through the Italian Tourist Board worldwide, or from local offices. The Venice office also produces a simple typed list of all kinds of hostel accommodation in Venice itself.

CAMPSITES AND MOUNTAIN REFUGES

There are good campsites throughout the region, concentrated mainly on the mainland to the north of Venice, on the shores of Lake Garda and in the northern mountains. A list of campsites and mountain refuges can be obtained from **ENIT** or local tourist offices. Most huts in the mountain districts are owned by the **Club Alpino Italiano**, based in Milan, who

can provide full information. Some huts offer just a bed for the night, whereas others may have staff who prepare meals and drinks. The **Touring Club Italiano** publishes annually a list of campsites: *Campeggi e Villaggi Turistici in Italia.*

A suitcase boat transporting visitors' luggage to a hotel

WATERBORNE ACCOMMODATION

Venice and the Veneto offer a vast selection of accommodation ranging from basic to luxurious. However, there are options for guests who are looking for something a little different.

For a city that is based on water there is surprisingly little in the way of floating lodgings. The options that are available often represent good value for money and are a more exciting alternative to a standard hotel room.

Roberto Terzi operates a Turkish schooner, **Navigador**, as a sumptuous bed and breakfast. The boat sleeps between six and eight people, although there is a larger schooner, Udachi, which sleeps 20. Both boats are capable of making trips around the lagoon.

Another company catering to the nautically minded is **Boat & Breakfast**. Guest stay in a 1930s yawl moored on the tranquil southern side of the Giudecca. There are seven beds in three cabins, which have all been beautifully decorated. At the front of the ship is an authentic 60s kitchen and on deck there is a hammock, which is perfect for lazing in on sunny days.

Garden terrace of the Hôtel des Bains on the Lido (see p233)

Venice's Best Hotels

Hotels in Venice range from the luxurious and renowned, which are mainly clustered along the Grand Canal, to simple, family-run places in the quieter parts of the city. Wherever you stay, you will be within easy reach of the main attractions, with restaurants and shops close at hand. All the hotels shown on this map have something special to recommend them, whether it is the waterside position, a garden or a quiet location away from the crowds. Always book well in advance, and remember that many Venetian hotels are shut at some stage in winter. The hotels shown here are the best in their particular style or price range.

Zecchini
One of the most attractive hotels on the busy Lista di Spagna, the Zecchini is good value. (See p232.)

Cannaregio

Al Sole
Situated beside a tranquil canal, this Gothic palazzo is away from the main tourist haunts, but within easy reach by foot or water of all the sights. (See p230.)

San Polo and Santa Croce

Dorsoduro

0 metres	500
0 yards	500

Agli Alboretti
This charming hotel in a central location has attractive rooms and a garden courtyard. (See p231.)

Gritti Palace
One of Venice's most famous hotels, the Gritti offers rooms and service of impeccable standard in an historic palazzo on the Grand Canal. (See p228.)

Giorgione
This high-class, spacious hotel, with its excellent facilities, offers every modern comfort at lower prices than others of similar calibre. (See p232.)

Marconi
This efficiently run hotel, housed in an old palazzo, has views of the Grand Canal and the Rialto Bridge. (See p230.)

La Residenza
This family-run hotel offers good value for money and is away from the crowds. It has frescoed public rooms and antiques, but the bedrooms are more simple. (See p230.)

Flora
A flower-filled garden is just one of the attractions of this delightful hotel. (See p228.)

Londra Palace
Tchaikovsky once stayed in this grand palazzo with its views to San Giorgio Maggiore. Today's guests appreciate the welcoming bar and restaurant. (See p231.)

Choosing a Hotel

The hotels listed here have been selected across a wide price range for facilities, good value, and location. All rooms have private bath, TV, and are accessible by wheelchair unless otherwise indicated. Most have Internet access. The hotels are listed by area. For information on other types of accommodation, *see pp222–25.*

PRICE CATEGORIES
The following price ranges are for a double room per night, including breakfast, tax and service.

€ Under 100 euros
€€ 100–200 euros
€€€ 200–300 euros
€€€€ 300–400 euros
€€€€€ Over 400 euros

VENICE

SAN MARCO Al Gazzettino   €€
Calle di Mezzo 4971, 30124 **Tel** *041 528 65 23* **Fax** *041 522 343 14* **Rooms** *10*   **Map** *7 A3*

This long-standing hotel was named after the adjacent premises of the popular local newspaper, *Al Gazzettino,* which has since moved to the mainland. The walls of the ground-floor *trattoria* are covered with pages from the paper. The location is excellent, close to both Rialto and St. Mark's, and the atmosphere is friendly. **www.algazzettino.com**

SAN MARCO Locanda ai Bareteri   €€
Calle di Mezzo 4966, 30124 **Tel** *041 523 22 33* **Fax** *041 244 34 50* **Rooms** *12*   **Map** *7 B1*

Located in a quiet back alley, only a few minutes walk from the Mercerie shopping district and St. Mark's Square, this comfortable bed and breakfast recently installed air conditioning and internet facilities for its guests. It is also close to the *vaporetto* landing stage at Rialto. **www.bareteri.com**

SAN MARCO Locanda Fiorita   €€
Campiello Novo e dei Morti 3457/A, 30124 **Tel** *041 523 47 54* **Fax** *041 522 80 43* **Rooms** *15*   **Map** *6 F2*

This welcoming hotel offers lovely spacious rooms decorated with 18th-century style furniture and fitted out with all mod cons. It is located just off the delightful Campo S. Stefano, and is in an ideal position for visiting the major art collections such as the Accademia gallery and privately-run Palazzo Grassi. **www.locandafiorita.com**

SAN MARCO Al Gambero   €€€
Calle dei Fabbri 4687, 30124 **Tel** *041 522 43 84* **Fax** *041 520 04 31* **Rooms** *30*   **Map** *7 B2*

Gondolas glide beneath the windows of this recently renovated guesthouse, conveniently set halfway between Rialto and Piazza San Marco. The rooms have been decorated in an old-fashioned style, and offer a full range of services. Good restaurants and shops abound in the neighbouring alleys. **www.locandaalgambero.com**

SAN MARCO Antico Panada   €€€
Calle Specchieri 646, 30124 **Tel** *041 520 90 88* **Fax** *041 520 96 19* **Rooms** *48*   **Map** *7 A2*

Located in a quiet street, very close to the main sights, the Panada occupies a converted 17th-century mansion. The cosy bar is decorated with historic mirrors, possibly made by the craftsmen who once had their workshops in this district. The continental breakfast buffet features delicious pastries. **www.hotelpanada.com**

SAN MARCO Flora   €€€
Via XXII Marzo 2283a, 30124 **Tel** *041 520 58 44* **Fax** *041 522 82 17* **Rooms** *43*   **Map** *7 A3*

This tiny hotel is squeezed in a narrow alley just off one of the major fashion-shopping streets, close to Piazza San Marco and the *vaporetto* landing stages. The rooms are a little cramped, but well equipped. A small but pleasant garden can be enjoyed when the weather is fine. It is advisable to reserve in advance. **www.hotelflora.it**

SAN MARCO La Fenice & des Artistes   €€€
Campiello Fenice 1936, 30124 **Tel** *041 523 23 33* **Fax** *041 520 37 21* **Rooms** *70*   **Map** *7 A2*

In a quiet square alongside the renowned opera house La Fenice, this pretty hotel is furnished with antiques and period-style fittings. The staff are very helpful. The premises consist of two buildings joined by a patio, and there is an atmospheric bar for a relaxing aperitif as the day draws to a close. **www.fenicehotels.com**

SAN MARCO Concordia   €€€€
Calle Larga San Marco 367, 30124 **Tel** *041 520 68 66* **Fax** *041 520 67 75* **Rooms** *53*   **Map** *7 B2*

Crammed in between the souvenir shops and near to the Piazza, this excellent family-managed hotel has many rooms with good views. It is furnished with impeccable period pieces. The top-notch restaurant specializes in seasonal produce. It is best to book well in advance. **www.hotelconcordia.it**

SAN MARCO Gritti Palace   €€€€
Santa Maria del Giglio 2467, 30124 **Tel** *041 79 46 11* **Fax** *041 520 09 42* **Rooms** *91*   **Map** *7 A3*

Ernest Hemingway described this sumptuous 15th-century palace as "the best hotel in a city of great hotels". It combines deluxe standards with a superb setting on the magnificent Grand Canal. Service is meticulous and a meal at the waterside restaurant is highly recommended. **www.luxurycollection.com/grittipalace**

Key to Symbols *see back cover flap*

SAN MARCO Monaco and Grand Canal

Calle Vallaresso 1332, 30124 **Tel** *041 520 02 11* **Fax** *041 520 05 01* **Rooms** *99*

Map *7 B3*

Incorporating the carefully restored Ridotto theatre, this elegant hotel also has a renowned restaurant on the Grand Canal. The rooms are a little small and not all have canal views, however, each is beautifully furnished and has all modern facilities. A modern annexe nearby has larger rooms. **www.hotelmonaco.it**

SAN MARCO Rialto

Riva di Ferro 5149, 30124 **Tel** *041 520 91 66* **Fax** *041 523 89 58* **Rooms** *79*

Map *7 A1*

This rambling establishment has good family rooms, excellent facilities and a canalside restaurant in the summer months. Its marvellous position at the foot of the Rialto bridge ensures spectacular views from many of its rooms, and the *vaporetto* is very convenient. **www.rialtohotel.com**

SAN MARCO Santo Stefano

Campo Santo Stefano 2957, 30124 **Tel** *041 520 01 66* **Fax** *041 522 44 60* **Rooms** *11*

Map *6 F3*

A charming hotel that occupies a tall narrow building overlooking Campo Santo Stefano – popular with children in the afternoon. The rooms have been renovated and are fully equipped, though several are quite small. It is only a ten-minute walk to Piazza San Marco or the Rialto district. **www.hotelsantostefanovenezia.com**

SAN MARCO Bauer

Campo San Moisè 1459, 30124 **Tel** *041 520 70 22* **Fax** *041 520 75 57* **Rooms** *109*

Map *7 A3*

This deluxe hotel is right in the heart of Venice amidst top-name boutiques. The Bauer also boasts wonderful Grand Canal views from many of its rooms, extending across to the Salute church, and gondolas can be hired outside the front door. The waterfront restaurant does a gourmet buffet. **www.bauerhotels.com**

SAN MARCO Europa & Regina

Calle Larga XXII Marzo 2159, 30124 **Tel** *041 240 00 01* **Fax** *041 523 15 33* **Rooms** *185*

Map *7 A3*

This splendid establishment was the home of the 18th-century artist Tiepolo. Occupying an inspiring position on the Grand Canal, close to Piazza San Marco, it has beautifully decorated spacious rooms and sumptuous public areas. The excellent al fresco waterside restaurant is recommended. **www.westin.com**

SAN MARCO Luna Hotel Baglioni

Calle Larga dell'Ascension 1243, 30124 **Tel** *041 528 98 40* **Fax** *041 528 71 60* **Rooms** *104*

Map *7 B3*

A recent addition to the Baglioni Hotels group, this sophisticated and surprisingly spacious hotel once hosted knights en route to the Holy Land. The breakfast room is particularly sumptuous with chandeliers and frescoes by pupils of Tiepolo. Close to San Marco this is an excellent base for sightseeing. **www.baglionihotels.com**

SAN MARCO San Clemente Palace

Isola di San Clemente 1, 30124 **Tel** *041 244 50 01* **Fax** *041 244 58 00* **Rooms** *200*

A special haven well away from the bustle of Venice, the luxury San Clemente has its own island, complete with vast gardens, swimming pool and conference and fitness centre. The superb rooms are wonderfully spacious and light-filled. A private launch ferries guests back and forth to San Marco. **www.sanclemente.thi.it**

SAN POLO Alex

Rio Terrà Frari 2606, 301 25 **Tel** *041 523 13 41* **Fax** *041 523 13 41* **Rooms** *11*

Map *6 E1*

Not all the rooms have private bathroom facilities and there is no air conditioning, however, this friendly and simple family-run hotel is great value for money. Situated in the vicinity of the Frari church, it is also handy for the Rialto markets. The closest *vaporetto* stop is Piazzale Roma or San Tomà. **www.hotelalexinvenice.com**

SAN POLO Al Campaniel

Calle del Campaniel 2889, 30125 **Tel** *041 275 07 49* **Fax** *041 275 07 49* **Rooms** *4*

Map *6 E2*

Right next to the San Tomà *vaporetto* stop, this cosy and spotless guesthouse in a quiet street is run by a Spanish-Venetian couple. Guests have tea- and coffee-making facilities in their rooms, otherwise a handy self-contained apartment is available for families who would prefer self-catering. Closed Aug. **www.alcampaniel.com**

SAN POLO Hotel Marconi

Riva del Vin 729, 30125 **Tel** *041 522 20 68* **Fax** *041 522 97 00* **Rooms** *26*

Map *7 A1*

A popular hotel with English-speaking tourists, the Marconi has a wonderful street café on the lively Grand Canal next to the Rialto bridge. A refurbished 16th-century palace with an opulent reception area, its rooms are a little disappointing and cramped. It is essential to reserve in advance. **www.hotelmarconi.it**

SAN POLO Pensione Guerrato

Calle drio la Scimia 240/A, 30125 **Tel** *041 522 71 31* **Fax** *041 241 14 08* **Rooms** *19*

Map *3 A5*

This old-fashioned, former *osteria* (tavern) claims it was established in 1288. The rooms are charming and comfortable, although some share bath facilities. There is a lovely breakfast, and the location is excellent, virtually in the middle of the Rialto fresh produce market. Discounted rates can sometimes be negotiated. **www.pensioneguerrato.it**

SANTA CROCE B&B Al Gallion

Calle Gallion 1126, 30135 **Tel** *041 524 47 43* **Fax** *041 275 81 26* **Rooms** *3*

Map *2 D5*

Perfect for visitors arriving by either road or rail, B&B Al Gallion is only five minutes walk from Piazzale Roma and the railway station. Its spotless, great value rooms were recently refurbished and are located in a 16th-century palace in a quiet neighbourhood. The staff often have great tips on visiting the city. **www.algallion.com**

SANTA CROCE Hotel Falier
€€   Map 5 C1

Salizzada San Pantalon 130, 30135 **Tel** *041 71 08 82* **Fax** *041 520 65 54* **Rooms** *19*

This friendly hotel boasts a wisteria-filled garden that will delight summer visitors. The pleasant rooms are well equipped. A brief walk from the transport hub of Piazzale Roma, the Falier is close to San Rocco and other attractions. The staff are extremely friendly and helpful. Breakfast is included. **www.hotelfalier.com**

SANTA CROCE Al Sole
€€   Map 5 C1

Fondamenta Minotto 136, 30135 **Tel** *041 244 03 28* **Fax** *041 72 22 87* **Rooms** *51*

Book well in advance to stay in this lovely 14th-century palace, with a marble-floored reception area and photogenic façade. The courtyard is a blaze of scented blooms in summer. The inviting rooms have views over the canal or a private garden. Close to Piazzale Roma for buses and *vaporetti*. **www.alsolehotels.com**

SANTA CROCE Locanda Sturion
€€   Map 7 A1

Calle del Sturion 679, 30125 **Tel** *041 523 6243* **Fax** *041 522 8378* **Rooms** *11*

Situated very close to the Grand Canal, the Sturion's central location, beautiful views and a history going back to the 1200s, all add to its appeal. This friendly hotel is very good value for money. Breakfast is served in a stylish room dominated by a Murano glass chandelier. **www.locandasturion.com**

SANTA CROCE San Simeon Ai Due Fanali
€€   Map 2 D5

Campo San Simeon Grande 946, 30135 **Tel** *041 718 490* **Fax** *041 244 87 21* **Rooms** *16*

Formerly a monastery, this pleasant building stands close to the church of the same name, and on the outside wall is a huge bas relief of St. Simeon. Several rooms have retained their timber rafters and there is a roof terrace with panoramic views. Conveniently placed for both Piazzale Roma and the railway station. **www.aiduefanali.com**

SANTA CROCE San Cassiano - Ca' Favretto
€€€   Map 2 F4

Calle della Rosa 2232, 30135 **Tel** *041 524 17 68* **Fax** *041 72 10 33* **Rooms** *35*

One of the city's favourite upmarket hotels, Ca' Favretto opens directly onto the Grand Canal, and guests can disembark at the private landing stage. In fact this is easier than arriving by land due to the labyrinth of alleys that need to be navigated to reach it! Elegance and attention to service are trademarks. **www.sancassiano.it**

CASTELLO Casa per Ferie 'S. Maria della Pietà'
€   Map 8 D2

Calle della Pietà 3701, 30122 **Tel** *041 244 36 39* **Fax** *041 241 15 61* **Rooms** *15*

Founded by the Franciscans in 1346 as a home for abandoned children and single mothers, this is now a friendly hotel behind Vivaldi's church. The peaceful rooms are spotless, although the bathrooms are shared. There is a superb panoramic terrace, which is lovely in summer. Book ahead in peak periods. **www.pietavenezia.org**

CASTELLO Corte Campana
€   Map 7 C1

Calle del Rimedio 4410, 30122 **Tel** *041 523 36 03* **Fax** *041 523 36 03* **Rooms** *3*

Corte Campana offers friendly lodgings close to Campo S. Maria Formosa and San Marco. The rooms are spacious, light-filled and overlook a pretty courtyard. They also have a TV and free Internet access. Two self-catering flats in the same building are also available. Closed 10–31 Jan, 5–25 Aug. **www.cortecampana.com**

CASTELLO Foresteria Valdese
€   Map 7 C1

Calle Lunga S. Maria Formosa 5170, 30122 **Tel** *041 528 67 97* **Fax** *041 241 62 38* **Rooms** *21*

Remember to book well ahead to get a room in the welcoming Foresteria Valdese. Run by the Waldensian and Methodist community, it offers dormitory accommodation as well as cosy private guest rooms, several of which are en suite. Breakfast is served at a long table in a refectory atmosphere. **www.foresteriavenezia.it**

CASTELLO La Residenza
€€   Map 8 E2

Campo Bandiera e Moro 3608, 30122 **Tel** *041 528 53 15* **Fax** *041 523 88 59* **Rooms** *15*

La Residenza started life as a 14th-century *palazzo* built in the Venetian Gothic style. Restored in 2001, the bedrooms are now elegant and comfortable with period furnishings. The common areas boast frescoed ceilings and antique furniture. A few minutes walk from the bustling Riva Schiavoni waterfront. **www.venicelaresidenza.com**

CASTELLO Locanda La Corte
€€   Map 3 C5

Calle Bressana 6317, 30121 **Tel** *041 241 13 00* **Fax** *041 241 59 82* **Rooms** *16*

The inviting rooms in this converted 16th-century palace, the former residence of an ambassador, are tastefully furnished. In the summer, guests can enjoy breakfast in a charming courtyard. Water taxis can pull up at the entrance, otherwise public transport is close by at the Fondamente Nuove. **www.locandalacorte.it**

CASTELLO Pensione Wildner
€€   Map 8 D2

Riva degli Schiavoni 4161, 30122 **Tel** *041 522 74 63* **Fax** *041 241 46 40* **Rooms** *16*

This small family-run hotel with immaculate rooms has a lovely roof terrace where guests can enjoy a leisurely buffet-style breakfast, along with wonderful views over St. Mark's Basin to the island of San Giorgio. The novelist Henry James stayed here in 1881 while working on *Portrait of a Lady*. **www.veneziahotels.com**

CASTELLO Liassidi Palace Hotel
€€€   Map 8 D1

Ponte dei Greci 3405, 30122 **Tel** *041 520 56 58* **Fax** *041 522 18 20* **Rooms** *26*

This ultra-modern establishment near the Greek church St George successfully blends an old palace with new stylish facilities. There's a lovely entrance courtyard, pleasant bars with canal views and attractively decorated bedrooms. The staff can be a little abrupt at times. **www.liassidipalacehotel.com**

Key to Price Guide *see p.228* **Key to Symbols** *see back cover flap*

CASTELLO Paganelli

€€€

Riva degli Schiavoni 4182, 30122 **Tel** *041 522 43 24* **Fax** *041 523 92 67* **Rooms** *22*

Map *8 D2*

This hotel has an excellent location on the San Marco waterfront, close to ferry services. There are wonderful views from the front rooms, which are furnished in a formal style but are cosy all the same. The accommodation in the annexe (*dipendenza*) is quieter but less attractive. Babysitting can be arranged. **www.hotelpaganelli.com**

CASTELLO Londra Palace

€€€€

Riva degli Schiavoni 4171, 30122 **Tel** *041 520 05 33* **Fax** *041 522 50 32* **Rooms** *53*

Map *8 D2*

Elegance, excellent service and spacious rooms characterize this luxury hotel. Located close to the monument to King Vittorio Emanuele on the broad bustling Riva a short stroll from the Piazza, it has splendid views over the water. It was here that Tchaikovsky composed his Fourth Symphony. **www.hotellondra.it**

CASTELLO Hotel Danieli

€€€€€

Riva degli Schiavoni 4196, 30122 **Tel** *041 522 64 80* **Fax** *041 520 0208* **Rooms** *225*

Map *7 C2*

The Danieli is the epitome of luxury. It was the palace of the Dandolo family and has strong literary and musical connections. The reception rooms are lit by resplendent Venetian glass chandeliers. There are two wings, one built in the 1940s and an older section (the first choice for guests). **www.luxurycollection.com/danieli**

DORSODURO Agli Alboretti

€€

Rio Terrà Foscarini 884, 30123 **Tel** *041 523 00 58* **Fax** *041 521 01 58* **Rooms** *23*

Map *6 E4*

Set in a peaceful spot close to the Accademia and Zattere for *vaporetto* transport, this cosy hotel is popular with English-speaking guests. The bedrooms are very attractive if a little small. A garden is available in the summer, and there's a good restaurant. Closed 7 Jan–7 Feb. **www.aglialboretti.com**

DORSODURO Istituto Artigianelli

€€

Rio Terrà Foscarini 909/A, 30123 **Tel** *041 522 40 77* **Fax** *041 528 62 14* **Rooms** *62*

Map *6 E4*

This religious institution has bright rooms with en suite bathrooms, which were recently restored. It is close to the sunny Zattere as well as the Accademia gallery. Winter guests share the premises with students, so reserving well in advance is essential. **www.donorione-venezia.it**

DORSODURO Istituto Canossiano

€€

Fondamenta delle Romite 1323, 30123 **Tel** *041 240 97 11* **Fax** *041 240 97 12* **Rooms** *60*

Map *6 D3*

This vast modernised convent hosts both university students and tourists in its simple but adequate rooms. There's a midnight curfew and breakfast is available from a vending machine. The Istituto is located a short distance from the Zattere waterfront. Closed 10 days in Aug, one week at Christmas. **www.fdcc.org/province/sanmarco/santrovaso**

DORSODURO Locanda Ca' Zose

€€

Calle del Bastion 193/B, 30123 **Tel** *041 522 66 35* **Fax** *041 522 66 24* **Rooms** *12*

Map *6 F4*

This guesthouse is run by two local sisters, and is just around the corner from the Guggenheim collection and La Salute *vaporetto* stop. The comfortable, well-equipped rooms are tastefully furnished and several have enchanting canal views. **www.hotelcazose.com**

DORSODURO Locanda San Barnaba

€€

Calle del Traghetto 2785-2786, 30123 **Tel** *041 241 12 33* **Fax** *041 241 38 12* **Rooms** *13*

Map *6 D3*

A wonderful place to come back to after a hard day's sightseeing, this converted palace has a roomy foyer and a pretty garden for summer guests. Only metres from the Ca' Rezzonico ferry stop. The spotless rooms are named after the plays of Venice's own Carlo Goldoni. **www.locanda-sanbarnaba.com**

DORSODURO Montin

€€

Fondamenta Eremite 1147, 30123 **Tel** *041 522 71 51* **Fax** *041 520 02 55* **Rooms** *11*

Map *6 D3*

Well off the beaten track, but only a matter of minutes from the lovely Zattere. The simply furnished rooms, most with en suite bathrooms, are in a Venetian apartment block situated above a renowned restaurant, overlooking a lovely canal. Montin offers a pleasant stay, but breakfast is extra. **www.locandamontin.com**

DORSODURO Pausania

€€

Fondamenta Gherardini 2824, 30123 **Tel** *041 522 20 83* **Fax** *041 522 29 89* **Rooms** *24*

Map *6 D3*

This hotel has elegant light-filled rooms with modern facilities, and a common Internet point is available. There is a delightful veranda for breakfast, flanked by a spacious garden. Located on the Rio San Barnaba canal, Pausania is handy for Campo S. Margherita where nightlife is guaranteed. **www.hotelpausania.it**

DORSODURO Pensione La Calcina

€€

Zattere ai Gesuati 780, 30123 **Tel** *041 520 64 66* **Fax** *041 522 70 45* **Rooms** *27*

Map *6 E4*

Book well in advance for this marvellous guesthouse as it is very popular. Everything is perfect here, starting from the waterside terrace, the pleasant breakfast room, the pretty rooms and the exquisite service. Sunsets over the the Lagoon Islands are memorable. Five apartments are also available nearby. **www.lacalcina.com**

DORSODURO Ca' Pisani

€€€

Rio Terrà Foscarini 979a, 30123 **Tel** *041 240 14 11* **Fax** *041 277 10 61* **Rooms** *29*

Map *6 E4*

This converted 15th-century palace is well located for the Accademia galleries and the Peggy Guggenheim Collection. The historic atmosphere is complemented by stunning modern design, a roof terrace and a relaxing Turkish bath. **www.capisanihotel.it**

DORSODURO Pensione Accademia Villa Maravegie

€€€

Fondamenta Bollani 1058, 30123 **Tel** *041 521 01 88* **Fax** *041 523 91 52* **Rooms** *27* **Map** *6 E3*

After traversing the pretty garden, where an excellent buffet breakfast can be enjoyed, it's the courtesy of the staff that is memorable. This beautiful 17th-century villa was once the Russian embassy and provides a tranquil haven from the hustle and bustle of the city's main sights. **www.pensioneaccademia.it**

CANNAREGIO Al Gobbo

€

Campo S. Geremia 312, 30121 **Tel** *041 71 50 01* **Fax** *041 71 47 65* **Rooms** *12* **Map** *2 D4*

This modest but reliable hotel has some rooms overlooking the bustling thoroughfare of Campo San Geremia. It is located a short walk from the railway station. The immaculately kept premises are comfortable and cool (some rooms have air conditioning), and continental breakfast is served in the rooms. Closed Nov–Dec. **www.albergoalgobbo.it**

CANNAREGIO Al Saor

€

Calle Zotti 3904/A, 30125 **Tel** *041 296 06 54* **Fax** *041 713 287* **Rooms** *3* **Map** *3 A4*

This friendly brand-new guesthouse close to the Ca' D'Oro, is run by a local family who serve homemade cookies for breakfast. All guests have access to kitchen facilities, and there is a fully equipped apartment available for self-catering families. Trips in the owners' rowing boat are also on offer. **www.alsaor.com**

CANNAREGIO Hotel Zecchini

€

Lista di Spagna 152, 30121 **Tel** *041 71 50 66* **Fax** *041 71 56 11* **Rooms** *27* **Map** *2 D4*

The Zecchini occupies two floors of an attractive building and is reached via a flight of stairs. The rooms overlook one of Venice's busiest streets, so it can be a bit noisy. One great advantage is the location, only a short walk from the railway station. **www.hotelzecchini.com**

CANNAREGIO Abbazia

€€

Calle Priuli di Cavalletti, 66-68, 30121 **Tel** *041 71 73 33* **Fax** *041 71 79 49* **Rooms** *50* **Map** *1 C4*

Near the railway station and just off busy Lista di Spagna, with its host of shops, the Abbazia is an oasis of peace. It has a lovely garden where drinks are served in summer. The rooms are comfortable if not huge, a reflection of the building's original purpose as a monastery. **www.abbaziahotel.com**

CANNAREGIO Ai Mori d'Oriente

€€€

Fondamenta della Sensa 3319, 30121 **Tel** *041 71 10 01* **Fax** *041 71 42 09* **Rooms** *22* **Map** *2 F3*

This attractive new hotel overlooks a peaceful canal in the Cannaregio neighbourhood and guests arriving by water can disembark directly at the front door, which is lit by candles in the evening. Behind the lovely Byzantine-style façade are stylish if somewhat small rooms, but the bathrooms are divine. **www.hotelaimoridoriente.it**

CANNAREGIO Continental

€€€

Lista di Spagna 166, 30121 **Tel** *041 71 51 22* **Fax** *041 524 24 32* **Rooms** *93* **Map** *2 D4*

This sizeable modern hotel caters mainly to large groups. It boasts a restaurant with panoramic views of the Grand Canal. Many rooms also have views of the canals, while others overlook a shady square. The hotel's location is especially good for one of the city's main tourist shopping districts. **www.hotelcontinentalvenice.com**

CANNAREGIO Giorgione

€€€

Calle dei Proverbi 4587, 30125 **Tel** *041 522 58 10* **Fax** *041 523 90 92* **Rooms** *76* **Map** *3 B5*

This highly recommended hotel has been completely refurbished. The Giorgione is extremely comfortable and well situated – only a ten-minute walk from Piazza San Marco, and five minutes from the lively Rialto market. Several suites have terraces with wonderful views looking over the city's rooftops. **www.hotelgiorgione.com**

CANNAREGIO Palazzo Abadessa

€€€

Calle Priuli 4011, 30131 **Tel** *041 241 37 84* **Fax** *041 521 22 36* **Rooms** *12* **Map** *3 A4*

The garden is the first thing that strikes you on arriving at this beautifully restored *palazzo*. From the atmospheric entrance hall, with thick carpets and chandeliers, elegant staircases lead to spacious and well-equiped rooms furnished with antiques. It really is like spending time in a private palace. **www.abadessa.com**

THE LAGOON ISLANDS Monastero di San Giorgio

€

Isola di San Giorgio, 30124 **Tel** *041 241 47 17* **Fax** *041 520 65 79* **Rooms** *5* **Map** *8 D4*

Visitors who desire peace and quiet should head to the island of San Giorgio. This heaven of shade and greenery is just across St Mark's Basin and is well served by *vaporetto*. A simple breakfast is shared with the hospitable monks, although there are also self-catering apartments.

THE LAGOON ISLANDS Residenza Junghans

€

Ramo Terzo della Palada 394, Giudecca, 30133 **Tel** *041 521 08 01* **Fax** *041 521 09 72* **Rooms** *59*

Modern architecture is a rare thing in Venice, however this former industrial island has been transformed into a showcase of bright sleek structures such as this hotel. Rooms are simply but adequately furnished. Frequent ferries to the railway and bus stations are nearby. Breakfast for groups only. Closed Christmas. **www.residenzajunghans.com**

THE LAGOON ISLANDS Ca' del Borgo and Ca' Alberti

€€

Piazza delle Erbe 8, Malamocco, 30126 **Tel** *041 77 07 49* **Fax** *041 77 07 44* **Rooms** *20*

Well off the beaten track, this charming 15th-century villa with a private garden is in the fishing village of Malamocco on the Venice Lido. It is a 30-minute trip to Venice but only minutes to the sea wall and a bicycle ride to the beaches. An open fireplace ensures a cosy ambience in the winter months. **www.cadelborgo.com**

Key to Price Guide *see p.228* **Key to Symbols** *see back cover flap*

THE LAGOON ISLANDS Hotel des Bains

€€€

Lungomare Marconi 17, Lido di Venezia, 30126 **Tel** *041 526 59 21* **Fax** *041 526 01 13* **Rooms** *192*

Here you will find wonderful Art Deco ambience, cool arcades with plush armchairs and top-level service. The superb rooms have everything a guest could desire. Hotel des Bains is open for guests from mid-Mar to Nov. Thomas Mann set his famous novel *Death in Venice* here. **www.ho10.net**

THE LAGOON ISLANDS Locanda Cipriani

€€€

Piazza Santa Fosca 29, Torcello, 30012 **Tel** *041 73 01 50* **Fax** *041 73 54 33* **Rooms** *6*

Illustrious guests at this comfortable old-style *locanda* on the island of Torcello have included Hemingway and the British royal family. The rooms are comfortably furnished and a range of reading matter is on hand. It is advisable to book well in advance. Closed Jan. **www.locandacipriani.com**

THE LAGOON ISLANDS Villa Mabapa

€€€

Riviera San Nicolò 16, Lido di Venezia, 30126 **Tel** *041 526 05 90* **Fax** *041 526 94 41* **Rooms** *67*

This 1930s villa, originally built as a private residence, has been converted into a comfortable guesthouse. An attractive shady garden welcomes guests back from sightseeing expeditions. Close to the *vaporetto* landing stages, it is situated on a promenade overlooking the lagoon. **www.villamabapa.com**

THE LAGOON ISLANDS Excelsior Palace

€€€€

Lungomare Marconi 41, Lido di Venezia, 30126 **Tel** *041 526 02 01* **Fax** *041 526 72 76* **Rooms** *197*

Luxury and flamboyance are combined at this superb historic beachfront hotel, where the *cabanas* are styled like Arab tents. The service and facilities are all excellent. This hotel is packed with VIPs and *paparazzi* during the Film Festival in late summer. Closed Nov–mid-Mar and due to close for renovation in 2010, call ahead. **www.ho10.net**

THE LAGOON ISLANDS Hotel Cipriani

€€€€€

Giudecca 10, 30133 **Tel** *041 520 77 44* **Fax** *041 520 39 30* **Rooms** *95*   **Map** *7 C5*

Set in luxurious gardens occupying the eastern tip of one of the the Lagoon Islands, the Cipriani has been one of the world's great hotels since it opened in 1963. The bedrooms and suites are furnished with tasteful opulence. The terrace restaurant is renowned and the outdoor pool a bonus. Closed Nov–mid-Mar. **www.hotelcipriani.com**

THE VENETO PLAIN

ASOLO Hotel Duse

€€

Via R. Browning 190, 31011 **Tel** *0423 552 41* **Fax** *0423 95 04 04* **Rooms** *14*

Located right in the centre of Asolo, this charming small hotel represents good value for money. The rooms are attractively decorated, although some of them are rather cramped as is the entrance hall. Most have views over the main square or over the rooftops. The staff are helpful and friendly. **www.hotelduse.com**

ASOLO Al Sole

€€€

Via Collegio 33, 31011 **Tel** *0423 95 13 32* **Fax** *0423 95 10 07* **Rooms** *23*

The orange façade of this hotel is decorated with green shutters. Many of the rooms overlook the main square and the old town walls. The public rooms are slightly impersonal, but the bedrooms and suites are spacious and well furnished. It has a lovely terrace, which is ideal for breakfast or a pre-dinner drink. **www.albergoalsole.com**

ASOLO Villa Cipriani

€€€€

Via Canova 298, 31011 **Tel** *0423 52 34 11* **Fax** *0423 95 20 95* **Rooms** *31*

This exceptionally comfortable hotel is in a 16th-century villa in which Robert Browning once lived. A popular feature is its beautiful garden, which has a lovely view over the countryside. It also has a fine restaurant serving Venetian specialities and a good wine list. A great base for exploring the area. **www.villaciprianiasolo.com**

BASSANO DEL GRAPPA Victoria

€

Viale Diaz 33, 36061 **Tel** *0424 50 36 20* **Fax** *0424 50 31 30* **Rooms** *21*

Just outside the city walls, the pleasant Victoria has comfortable, simply-furnished rooms with private bathrooms featuring hydromassage baths. It is a busy hotel that can occasionally be noisy. However, it is ideally placed for sight-seeing, being a short walk from Palladio's bridge and the historic town centre. **www.hotelvictoria-bassano.com**

BASSANO DEL GRAPPA Bonotto Hotel Belvedere

€€

Piazzale G Giardino 14, 36061 **Tel** *0424 52 98 45* **Fax** *0424 52 98 49* **Rooms** *83*

Standing in one of Bassano's main squares, this busy hotel is the best equipped in the area, and the location is good for exploring the city. Rooms are comfortable and pretty, and the service is excellent. The hotel has a modern restaurant and spacious reception rooms and bar. **www.bonotto.it**

BASSANO DEL GRAPPA Ca' Sette

€€

Via Cunizza da Romano 4, 36061 **Tel** *0424 38 33 50* **Fax** *0424 39 32 87* **Rooms** *19*

This Venetian villa has been attractively converted into a stylish hotel. Ca' Sette is on the outskirts of the city in a formal garden and surrounded by olive groves. Rooms are all individually decorated, some with original frescoes. The restaurant offers creative cuisine, including a vegetarian menu. **www.ca-sette.it**

CHIOGGIA Grande Italia

Rione S. Andrea 597, 30015 **Tel** *041 40 05 15* **Fax** *041 40 01 85* **Rooms** *56*

This unpretentious old-fashioned hotel at the head of the main street has a Liberty-style façade, and has recently been refurbished. It has elegant, comfortable rooms and an up-to-date wellbeing centre. Grande Italia is conveniently situated for boats running to Venice. **www.hotelgrandeitalia.com**

CONEGLIANO Il Faè

Via Faè1, San Pietro di Feletto, 31020 **Tel** *0438 78 71 17* **Fax** *0438 78 78 17* **Rooms** *8*

This comfortable guesthouse is in a converted farmhouse amongst hills and vineyards. It has good views over the foothills of the Alps and is a ten-minute drive from Conegliano. The hosts also offer activities for their guests including cookery classes. **www.ilfae.com**

PADUA Augustus Terme

Viale Stazione 150, Montegrotto Terme, 35036 **Tel** *049 79 32 00* **Fax** *049 79 35 18* **Rooms** *120*

A big, comfortable hotel with opulent rooms and a vast restaurant. It has spacious, welcoming public areas, as well as tennis courts.The wellbeing and beauty centre, along with the hot thermal springs, are the real focal point of this pleasant complex. **www.hotelaugustus.com**

PADUA Plaza

Corso Milano 40, 35139 **Tel** *049 65 68 22* **Fax** *049 66 11 17* **Rooms** *139*

An established and efficiently run hotel with a deservedly good reputation. Though its 1970s exterior appears somewhat unattractive, inside it offers up-to-date technology and all modern comforts. The Plaza provides a full range of services and a thoroughly warm welcome. **www.plazapadova.it**

PORDENONE Palace Hotel Moderno

Viale Martelli 1, 33170 **Tel** *0434 282 15* **Fax** *0434 52 03 15* **Rooms** *96*

A comfortable, refurbished traditional hotel with a good range of facilities in all its bedrooms. It is centrally located close to the station. The restaurant (which is under separate management) specializes in traditional cuisine, particularly fish dishes. Amenities include a fitness room and sauna. **www.palacehotelmoderno.it**

SARCEDO Casa Belmonte

Via Belmonte 2, 36030 **Tel** *0445 88 48 33* **Fax** *0445 88 41 34* **Rooms** *6*

A small hotel set on the top of a hill surrounded by vineyards and olive groves. The rooms are luxuriously decorated with antiques and rich drapes. Breakfast is served outside in the summer or in the conservatory. There is a large pool for the guests. A good base from which to explore the Palladian villas. **www.casabelmonte.com**

TREVISO Ca' del Galletto

Via Santa Bona Vecchia 30, 31100 **Tel** *0422 43 25 50* **Fax** *0422 43 25 10* **Rooms** *67*

Set in its own grounds and only a ten-minute walk from the city walls, Ca' del Galletto's bedrooms are spacious and modern, though slightly lacking in charm. However, the friendly staff and excellent sports facilities, as well as the peaceful surroundings, make for a pleasant stay. **www.hotelcadelgalletto.it**

TREVISO Il Focolare

Piazza Ancillotto 4, 31100 **Tel** *0422 566 01* **Fax** *0422 566 01* **Rooms** *14*

One of Treviso's best budget hotels, Il Focolare is clean, welcoming and situated in the heart of the historic centre. The rooms are rather small, as are the bathrooms, but the location makes up for it. There is an excellent restaurant opposite which serves traditional Treviso dishes. **www.albergoilfocolare.net**

VICENZA Casa San Raffaele

Viale X Giugno 10, 36100 **Tel** *0444 54 57 67* **Fax** *0444 54 22 59* **Rooms** *29*

This tranquil hotel is set in charming surroundings with excellent views of the slopes of Monte Berico. The comfortable rooms are all en suite. Friendly staff and simple style can be found at this centrally located establishment. No high season means that this is one of the best budget choices in the area.

VICENZA Campo Marzio

Via Roma 27, 36100 **Tel** *0444 54 57 00* **Fax** *0444 32 04 95* **Rooms** *35*

A stylish boutique hotel with good facilities, just a short stroll from the city centre and the principal Palladian sites. The bedrooms are large and beautifully furnished – each one with its own individual decor and wireless Internet connection. Campo Marzio is situated in a peaceful location. **www.hotelcampomarzio.com**

VERONA AND LAKE GARDA

GARDA Locanda San Vigilio

San Vigilio, 37016 **Tel** *045 725 66 88* **Fax** *045 627 81 82* **Rooms** *14*

One of the loveliest, most exclusive hotels on Lake Garda, the San Vigilio exudes Old World charm and is set in peaceful grounds with a small church dedicated to the saint of the same name. Comfort and service live up to expectations and there is a private beach and free mooring for boats. Closed Dec–Feb. **www.punta-sanvigilio.it**

Key to Price Guide *see p.228* **Key to Symbols** *see back cover flap*

MALCESINE Sailing Center Hotel

€€

Via Gardesana 187, 37018 **Tel** *045 740 00 55* **Fax** *045 740 03 92* **Rooms** *32*

A modern hotel just outside town, away from the crowds. Rooms are cool and pleasant, and there is a tennis court and private beach. The hotel offers low-key service and immaculate grounds. Its lakeside setting makes it an ideal base for guests keen on watersports. Closed mid-Oct–Mar. **www.hotelsailing.com**

PESCHIERA DEL GARDA Peschiera

€

Via Parini 4, 37010 **Tel** *045 755 05 26* **Fax** *045 755 04 44* **Rooms** *30*

The hotel is set in its own verdant grounds and has lofty, cool bedrooms. There are fine lake views, though some of the rooms look out onto the equally pretty hills. There is a sun terrace and a private swimming pool. The hotel can arrange riding in the hills or golf at the course nearby. **www.hotel-peschiera.com**

TORRI DEL BENACO Hotel Gardesana

€€

Piazza Calderini 20, 37010 **Tel** *045 722 54 11* **Fax** *045 722 57 71* **Rooms** *34*

The 15th-century harbour master's house overlooking Lake Garda has been converted into a friendly, comfortable hotel. Its spectacular location means that there are views of the castle from the restaurant terrace, while rooms on the third floor have wonderful views of the lake. **www.hotel-gardesana.com**

VERONA Il Torcolo

€€

Vicolo Listone 3, 37121 **Tel** *045 800 75 12* **Fax** *045 800 40 58* **Rooms** *19*

This small, family-run hotel is a few minutes walk from the Arena, making it a popular destination during the opera season. Though some of the reception areas are rather cramped, the guest rooms are pretty and traditional. Il Torcolo has its own breakfast terrace. Closed 5 days Christmas, 2 weeks end Jan. **www.hoteltorcolo.it**

VERONA Due Torri Hotel Baglioni

€€€

Piazza Sant'Anastasia 4, 37121 **Tel** *045 59 50 44* **Fax** *045 800 41 30* **Rooms** *90*

Standing alongside a beautiful church in the heart of medieval Verona, this sumptuous 14th-century building is one of Italy's most eccentric hotels. Each bedroom is decorated and furnished in the style of a different era. The public areas are equally opulent in this unique establishment. **www.baglionihotels.com**

THE DOLOMITES

BELLUNO Albergo Cappello e Cadore

€

Via Ricci 8, 32100 **Tel** *0437 94 02 46* **Fax** *0437 29 23 19* **Rooms** *31*

Centrally situated, Cappello e Cadore is popular with skiers in winter and walkers in summer. The rooms are comfortable, with independent heating and air conditioning. Most overlook the square, but a few have panoramic views of the mountains. **www.albergocappello.com**

CORTINA D'AMPEZZO Menardi

€€

Via Majon 110, 32043 **Tel** *0436 24 00* **Fax** *0436 86 21 83* **Rooms** *49*

This rather old-fashioned hotel on the outskirts of Cortina has been in the same family since 1900. It is tastefully furnished with antiques and has a welcoming atmosphere. Service is attentive and excellent. There is also a comfortable annexe behind the main building. Closed 10 Apr–10 Jun, 10 Sep–1 Dec. **www.hotelmenardi.it**

CORTINA D'AMPEZZO Montana

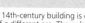

€€

Corso Italia 94, 32043 **Tel** *0436 86 04 98* **Fax** *0436 86 82 11* **Rooms** *31*

Montana is conveniently situated in the town centre, close to the main shops. The area is pedestrianized, making the hotel quiet and a popular choice. Some of the rooms are rather small, although all are attractively decorated and bathrooms have hydromassage baths. Good value for money. **www.cortina-hotel.com**

FOLLINA Villa Abbazia

€€€

Via Martiri della Liberta, 31051 **Tel** *0438 971277* **Fax** *0438 970001* **Rooms** *18*

This delightful 17th-century villa has been tastefully restored by the Zanon family. The spacious rooms are all individually decorated in an English country house style. A small garden makes a wonderful place to relax or enjoy a drink in the early evening. A good base from which to explore the area. **www.villaabbazia.it**

PIEVE D'ALPAGO Albergo Dolada

€€

Via Dolada 21, 32010 **Tel** *0437 479 141* **Fax** *0437 478 068* **Rooms** *7*

A small, stylish hotel with an excellent restaurant much patronized by Venetians. The bedrooms are modern and bright, each decorated in a colour of the rainbow. Most have good views over the surrounding countryside. In the restaurant creative dishes are prepared following a seasonal menu. **www.dolada.it**

SAPPADA Haus Michaela

€

Borgata Fontana 40, 32047 **Tel** *0435 46 93 77* **Fax** *0435 66131* **Rooms** *18*

Located in a small ski resort at the foothills of the Dolomites, Haus Michaela's rooms are simply decorated, spacious and comfortable. Facilities include a pool, a fitness centre and a sauna. A good spot for a family holiday in summer and winter. The restaurant serves up hearty mountain dishes. Closed Apr–mid-May, Oct–Nov. **www.hotelmichaela.com**

RESTAURANTS, CAFES AND BARS

Restaurants in Venice and the Veneto serve predominantly Italian food from the region, with the emphasis in Venice very much on fish. Wherever you go, you will find the cooking simple, with dishes that make full use of the traditional local ingredients.

Most Venetians eat lunch *(pranzo)* around 12:30pm and dinner *(cena)* from 8pm, though restaurants start serving dinner earlier to cater for the many foreign visitors.

Egyptian detail, Caffè Pedrocchi

Restaurants may be closed for several weeks during the winter and also for two to three weeks during the staff summer holidays. Closing dates are included in the listings, but avoid disappointment by asking your hotel to phone first to confirm that the restaurant is open. Finding restaurants can be confusing in Venice, so use the map references provided. The restaurants listed on pages 242–49 are some of the best across all price ranges.

El Gato restaurant, Chioggia, famous for its fish *(see p247)*

TYPES OF RESTAURANTS

Italian eating places have a bewildering variety of names, and the differences between them can be considerable. A *ristorante* is smarter than a *trattoria* or an *osteria*, for example, and is likely to be more expensive. Nowadays, there is also a growing number of fast-food joints and *tavola calda* establishments, which have no cover or service charge. A *birreria* and a *spaghetteria* are more down-market eating places that sell beer, pasta dishes and snacks; you will mainly find these outside Venice itself. A good *pizzeria* will use wood-fired ovens efor the pizza; if this is the case it will normally be open only in the evenings.

If you do not want to eat a full meal at lunchtime you can always stop in a bar or café for a snack. For further information on light meals see page 250.

OPENING TIMES AND CLOSING DAYS

Opening times are virtually the same throughout Venice and the Veneto: from noon to 2:30pm for lunch, and from 7:30pm to 10:30pm for dinner. Under Italian law all restaurants close one day a week and some close for an additional evening as well; closing days are staggered so there is always somewhere open in the area. Individual restaurants' closing days are given in the listings.

The main bar of the historic Caffè Pedrocchi *(see p178)*

VEGETARIAN FOOD

Italians find it difficult to understand vegetarianism, but if you eat fish you should have no difficulty eating well. If not, there is still a variety of meatless dishes since many starters *(antipasti)*, soups and pasta sauces are vegetable-based. Salads and vegetables are always good, and most places will be happy to serve an omelette *(frittata)* or a selection of cheese.

FIXED-PRICE MENUS

In the days when Italy was building its tourist industry all restaurants had to supply a fixed-price menu. This has largely fallen into abeyance, particularly outside the main tourist centres. Restaurants may often have the so-called *menu turistico* pinned up in the street, but not on offer inside. Such menus, if you do find them, are usually boring and offer no opportunity to sample the wonderful variety of the local cuisine. If money is tight it is far better to have a good pasta dish and some salad, which is acceptable in all but the grandest places.

The *menu gastronomico* is a fixed-price menu consisting of six or seven courses, which allows you to sample the full range of a chef's specialities.

HOW MUCH TO PAY

Transport charges can add as much as 30 per cent to the price of basic commodities coming into Venice, which partly explains the high cost of eating. In cheaper eating places and *pizzerie* you can have a two-course meal with half a litre of wine for around €10–15. Three-course meals average about €18–25, and in up-market restaurants you can easily pay €50–70. In the Veneto, prices are lower, except for stylish restaurants in Verona and along Lake Garda during the summer.

Nearly all restaurants have a cover charge *(pane e coperto)*, usually €1–3. Many also add a 10 per cent service charge *(servizio)* to the bill *(il conto)*, so always establish whether or not this is the case. Where leaving a tip is a matter of your own discretion, 12–15 per cent is acceptable.

Restaurants are obliged by law to give you a receipt *(una ricevuta fiscale)*. Scraps of paper with an illegible scrawl are illegal, and you are within your rights to ask for a proper bill. The preferred form of payment is cash, but many restaurants will accept payment by major credit cards. Check which cards are accepted when booking.

MAKING RESERVATIONS

Whatever the price range, Venice's best restaurants are always busy, so it is best to reserve a table, especially if you are making a long boat trip to get there. If restaurants do not accept bookings, try to arrive early to avoid queuing.

DRESS CODE

Italians like to dress up in general, and dining out is no exception. However, this does not mean that women have to wear evening attire at a restaurant, or that men have to wear a tie, and you will rarely feel under-dressed without a jacket. Smart casual clothes are the general rule for both men and women.

Eating under the loggia of Treviso's Palazzo dei Trecento *(see p174)*

READING THE MENU

Both lunch and dinner in a restaurant follow the same pattern and usually start with an *antipasto*, or hors d'oeuvres (seafood, olives, beef carpaccio, ham, salami), followed by the *primo* (soup, rice or pasta). The main course, or *secondo*, will be fish or meat, either served alone or accompanied by vegetables *(contorni)* or a salad *(insalata)*. These are never included in the price of the main course.

To finish, there will probably be a choice of fruit *(frutta)*, a pudding *(dolce)* or cheese *(formaggio)*, or a combination of all three. Coffee – Italians always have an *espresso*, never a *cappuccino* – is ordered and served right at the end of the meal, often with a *digestivo*. In cheaper restaurants, the menu *(il menu)* may be chalked up or the waiter may simply recite the day's special dishes at your table.

A short break at Carnival

CHOICE OF WINE

House wines are usually local *(see pp240–41)*. Cheaper restaurants will have a limited wine list, but at the top of the scale there should be a wide range of Italian wines and a selection of foreign vintages.

CHILDREN

Children are welcome in restaurants, particularly in simple, family-run ones. Smart places may be less welcoming, particularly in the evenings. Special facilities such as high chairs are not commonly provided. Most restaurants will prepare a half-portion *(mezza porzione)* if requested, and some charge less for these smaller helpings.

SMOKING

Smoking in enclosed public spaces, including restaurants, is now banned in Italy. The ban does not extend to tables on outside terraces.

WHEELCHAIR ACCESS

Very few restaurants make special provision for wheelchairs, though a word when booking should ensure a conveniently situated table and assistance on arrival.

EATING ON A BUDGET

Eating out all the time can become very expensive, especially in Venice, a cheaper option is to make your own picnic. Most supermarkets stock a range of fresh washed salads, local cheeses and tasty cold cuts. The Coop chain has several outlets in Venice, including a flagship store at Piazzale Roma. Otherwise try Billa, which has store throughout the Veneto. Alternatively support the local shops, many of which will make large rolls from your choice of fillings.

There are plenty of lovely places to stop and enjoy an al fresco meal. In Venice the Park at Saint Elena is a shady spot even in summer. Verona has many picturesque squares and most towns will have a quiet park to stop and take a break.

The Flavours of Venice and the Veneto

The cuisine of Venice and the Veneto reflects the region's varied landscape, from cattle-grazing and agricultural land to mountains and coastline. The most important sources of ingredients, however, are the waters – both inland and coastal – that yield a constant supply of fish and seafood. In general, the cooking is light, fresh and delicately flavoured, without heavy sauces. Fish may be simply grilled or poached with herbs, while *carpaccio* of raw beef is sliced to transparent thinness. The vibrant colours of dishes recall canvases by Tintoretto or Titian: bright yellow saffron or polenta, emerald green fresh peas, dark red radicchio and the blue-black stain of cuttlefish ink in *riso nero* risotto.

Saffron

Produce from the Veneto is loaded onto the Venetian canalside

VENETIAN FOOD

Food in Venice is almost always Italian, and many restaurants serve local specialities. There are very few ethnic eating places despite the city's long history as a trading port and home to foreign settlers. Foodstuffs have always been traded, starting with the local salt and fish. In the 15th and

16th centuries, when Venice was the prosperous gateway to the East, imported spices, pepper, raisins, pine nuts and sugar made their way into the diet. Recipes from the period cite ingredients such as ginger, nutmeg, saffron, cloves, cinnamon and coriander. The city's noble families liked their food to be appealing to the eye as well as the palate, and so they introduced fine, locally-made glassware to enhance the table. They served extravagant fare such as peacock, roasted whole with

spices and then garnished with gold leaf. A few traces of these exotic influences still appear in classic Venetian cooking, such as Asian-style sweet and sour combinations and the use of spices as well as herbs. *Baccalà* (dried salted cod) originally brought from the Baltic area, is still very popular, often cooked with milk or wine and garlic or onion. Superb vegetables are grown in market gardens on the islands of the lagoon, not least the delicious purple artichokes *(castraure)* from Sant' Erasmo.

Caper berries   **Marinated white anchovies**   **Olives wrapped in anchovies**

Seafood cocktail

Selection of Venetian *antipasti*, the perfect appetizer

REGIONAL DISHES AND SPECIALITIES

Antipasto di frutti di mare (a mixed seafood appetizer) is a special favourite in Venice, where the ingredients come fresh from the Adriatic. From lovely Lake Garda, *anguilla del pescatore* (stewed eel), *lavarelli al vino bianco* (lake fish in white wine) and *carpione* (a type of lake trout) are all fishy delights. Another fish speciality of the region is *baccalà alla veneziana*, made with dried salt cod. Pork and salamis feature throughout the area but in Friuli goose is often used as an alternative to pork, with succulent cured meat offerings such as *salame d'oca* (goose salami). Game is also found on the menu, together with sauerkraut and filling goulash, while desserts often have an Austrian flavour, too, such as *apfel strudel*. But the region is also proud of claiming as its own the voluptuous, classic Italian dessert *tiramisù*.

Asparagus

Sarde in Saor *is a Venetian speciality of fried sardines in a sweet and sour onion marinade, with pine nuts.*

Enjoying an aperitif in the sunshine of St Mark's Square in Venice

thick brown soup of highly-prized borlotti beans from Lamon, near Belluno. Fish comes from the inland rivers and Lake Garda, while farms produce chicken, duck, turkey and goose. Towards the mountains there are pigs for cured hams, salami and sausages like the pork *sopressa*, as well as veal, beef and dairy cattle, and wild game in season. An Austrian legacy is tasted in the dumplings and apple strudels of the Dolomites.

FOOD OF THE VENETO

The region's staples have long been polenta and rice, although pasta is also popular. Polenta, made from ground maize (corn) that was originally imported from America in the 16th century,

Fishing on the tranquil waters of Lake Garda

was always a peasant food. Today, it often accompanies a main course and can appear as a thick purée or be allowed to set into in a more solid form, when it can be cut into slices and grilled. The Veneto is one of Italy's main rice-growing regions. Rice was introduced from Spain by the Arabs, and the *vialone nano* variety grown around Verona is the favourite for risotto, giving a superbly creamy finish when cooked in stock with meat, fish or vegetables in season. A huge range of vegetables is grown in the Veneto. Bassano di Grappa is noted for its asparagus, and Treviso for a long variety of radicchio that is eaten raw, baked (*radicchio in forno*), grilled or in risotto. Soups are made from vegetables and beans, notably *pasta e fagiola* – a

VENETIAN FISH DISHES

The catch from the region's waters includes sardines, mussels, clams, sea snails, squid, cuttlefish, eel, prawns, crab and lobster. These are served as *antipasti*, made into soups (*brodo di pesce*), and cooked in risottos or with pasta, such as the popular *spaghetti alle vongole* (with clams). Regional specialities include:

Bisato su l'aro Eel baked with bayleaf is a dish from Murano, where it was cooked in the glass furnaces.

Sarde in Saor Sardines in a sweet and sour sauce.

Moleche frite Soft-shelled crabs from the lagoon, coated with beaten egg and fried.

Seppie alla Veneziana Cuttle-fish cooked in their own ink.

Zuppa di Cozze Mussels steamed with white wine, garlic and parsley.

Risi e bisi *mixes rice with fresh peas in a soft, moist risotto, sometimes with ham and Parmesan cheese.*

Fegato alla Venezia *is calf's liver served on a bed of sautéed onions. Grilled polenta is a good side dish.*

Tiramisù *(the name means "pick me up") is rich pudding of mascarpone, sponge fingers, coffee and marsala.*

What to Drink in Venice and the Veneto

Italy has been making wine for over 3,000 years, and production in the Veneto reflects this, with the largest output in Italy of superior DOC wines. The area produces an abundance of different wines, which include not only well-known names such as Soave, Valpolicella and Bardolino, but many others which are also excellent value for money. Although Italians tend to drink lighter wines with their food, the area is also noted for some excellent strong wines. Italy's famous *digestivo*, grappa, originated in this corner of the country, and meals are often preceded by an *aperitivo* or a glass of sparkling local Prosecco.

Grapes drying in Valpolicella

RED WINE

Red wines in the veneto are produced mainly near Bardolino and Valpolicella between Verona and Lake Garda (*see pp208–9*). Made predominantly from the Corvina grape, they are usually light and fruity, but quality can vary so it is worth looking for reliable names.

Valpolicella comes in several forms. In addition to the normal easy-drinking wine, it is available as a *ripasso*, boosted in colour and strength by macerating the skins of the grapes before pressing. Recioto della Valpolicella is very different, a rich, sweet wine made from selected air-dried grapes. Some Reciotos undergo further fermentation to remove the sweetness, producing the strong, dry Recioto Amarone. These are some of the strongest naturally alcoholic wines in the world and are delicious but expensive.

Excellent red wines are also made by producers such as Venegazzù and Maculan from the Cabernet Sauvignon and Merlot grapes.

Red Venegazzù   Masi's ripasso

Bardolino wine is light, fruity and garnet-red in colour.

Amarone is full-bodied, rich, full of fruit and very alcoholic.

READING WINE LABELS

Italian wines are classified by four quality levels. Starting at the top, DOCG status (*Denominazione di Origine Controllata e Garantita*) has been awarded to a small number of Italian growing areas, none of which are in the Veneto. Most quality wines – more than 250 in the whole of Italy – are in the DOC category (as above but without the "guarantee") and these can be relied on as good value, quality wines. IGT (*Indicazione Geografica Tipica*) is a category new to Italy, corresponding to the popular French Vin de Pays. The final classification is *vino da tavola*, or table wine, but due to the inflexible Italian wine laws many superb wines appear in this category.

No vintage recommendations are given in the chart because almost all Veneto wines are made for young drinking.

WINE TYPE	RECOMMENDED PRODUCERS
White Wine	
Soave	Anselmi, Bertani, Col Baraca (Masi), Boscaini, CS di Soave, Masi, Pieropan, Scamperle, Tedeschi, Zenato, Zonin
Bianco di Custoza	Cavalchina, Le Tende, Le Vigne di San Pietro, Pezzini, San Leone, Tedeschi, Zenato
Breganze di Breganze	Maculan
Gambellara	CS di Gambellara, Zonin
Red Wine	
Bardolino	Alighieri, Bertani, Bolla, Boscaini, Guerrieri-Rizzardi, Masi, Tedeschi
Valpolicella	Alighieri, Allegrini, Bertani, Bolla, Boscaini, Guerrieri-Rizzardi, Masi, Tedeschi, Zenato
Ripasso Valpolicella (non-DOC)	Serègo Alighieri, Jago (Bolla), Le Cane (Boscaini), Le Sassine (Le Ragose), Campo Fiorin (Masi), Capitel San Rocco (Tedeschi)
Recioto and Recioto Amarone della Valpolicella	Serègo Alighieri, Allegrini, Masi, Quintarelli, Le Ragose, Tedeschi

WHITE WINE

The Veneto produces more white wine than red, and most of the region's whites are from vineyards around the hilltop town of Soave *(see p190)*. These wines can be dull, but increasing numbers of producers are trying to raise Soave's image. Bianco di Custoza, a creamy, richer tasting "super Soave" from the eastern shores of Lake Garda, is well worth trying. Breganze is a name to look out for, with Maculan a leader in making fresh, clean, inexpensive wines and world-class dessert wines. Gambellara is made mainly from Soave's Garganega grape and is seldom of poor quality. Venegazzù is another producer you can trust for good quality white wines.

Bianco di Custoza

White Recioto

Pieropan is a top quality producer of Soave. The single-vineyard wines from here are superb.

White vino da tavola wines range from pale and dry to sweet and golden coloured.

Venegazzù's Pinot Grigio wine is dry and goes well with Venetian seafood.

Puiatti's white Ribolla wine is fruity but dry. It is made in neighbouring Friuli.

APERITIFS AND OTHER DRINKS

Italian aperitifs tend to be wine-based, bitter, herb-flavoured drinks such as Martini and Campari. Less familiar are the herbal Punt e Mes, Cynar (made from artichokes), and the vivid orange Aperol, which is good mixed with white wine and soda. Crodino is a popular non-alcoholic choice. For settling the stomach after a good meal there are *amari* (bitters) and *digestivi*. Montenegro and Ramazzotti are well worth trying, and grappa, distilled from wine lees *(see Bassano del Grappa p166)*, is another favourite. A local speciality, Trevisana, is mixed with an extract of the long red radicchio from Treviso. Italian brandy can be rather oily, but Vecchia Romagna is a reliable name.

Grappa

Crodino

PROSECCO

The Veneto's own sparkling wine, Prosecco is perfect as either a refreshing light *aperitivo* or with a meal. It originates in Conegliano *(see p175)*, the home of Italy's greatest wine school, and comes in both *secco* (dry) or *amabile* (medium-sweet) forms, and as *frizzante* or *spumante* (semi and fully sparkling). An excellent accompaniment to both fruit and seafood, it is also the traditional base for Bellini, a delicious *aperitivo* of wine mixed with fresh white peach juice *(see p92)*. This drink has bred several variants, such as Mimosa (with orange) and Tiziano (with red grape juice).

Prosecco   **Bellini cocktail**

SOFT DRINKS

Italian bottled fruit juices come in delicious flavours such as pear, apricot and peach. Many bars will squeeze you a *spremuta* of fresh orange *(arancia)* or grapefruit *(pompelmo)* juice on the spot. A *frullato* is an ice-cold mix of milk and fresh fruit.

Spremuta di arancia

COFFEE

Coffee is an essential part of Italian life. Milky *cappuccino* with chocolate powder is drunk at breakfast time, and tiny cups of strong black *espresso* throughout the day. If you like your coffee with milk, choose a *caffè con latte*, or with just a dash of milk, *caffè macchiato*. Black coffee that is not too strong is *caffè lungo*; a *doppio* has an extra kick and a *corretto* has a good measure of alcohol.

Espresso   **Cappuccino**

Choosing a Restaurant

The restaurants listed below have been selected across a wide price range for their fine food, good value and interesting location. They are listed alphabetically according to area, starting with San Marco in the centre of Venice. For more details on regional food and alternative places to eat, *see pp236–241*.

VENICE

SAN MARCO Cavatappi   €
Campo della Guerra 525/526, 30124 **Tel** *041 296 02 52*   **Map** *7 B1*

An inviting, modern wine bar that serves mouth-watering pasta dishes on elegant plates. Artichokes and smoked ricotta cheese are also on offer, as well as tender roast meats and regional cheeses. Make sure you leave space for a dessert. Closed 9pm and all day Mon; 1 month in winter.

SAN MARCO Devil's Forest Pub   €
Calle dei Stagneri 5185, 30124 **Tel** *041 520 06 23*   **Map** *7 B1*

Always buzzing with life, this Venetian pub serves excellent dishes, such as pasta with prawn, pumpkin and radicchio sauce, that are good value for money. The kitchen closes at midnight but the dart games go on until much later. It is in the vicinity of the central square Campo San Bartolomeo.

SAN MARCO Moscacieka   €
Calle dei Fabbri 4717, 30124 **Tel** *041 520 80 85*   **Map** *7 B2*

Halfway between Rialto and Piazza San Marco, this fun restaurant with young staff offers reasonably priced light meals such as grilled sandwiches, lasagne and salads at lunchtime. It also features knock-you-off-your-feet Spritz aperitifs. Closed public holidays.

SAN MARCO Rosticceria San Bartolomeo   €
Calle della Bissa 5424, 30124 **Tel** *041 522 35 69*   **Map** *7 B1*

Popular with the locals, who pop in for the delicious deep-fried snack *mozzarella in carrozza*, Rosticceria San Bartolomeo also prepares a vast range of pasta, risottos and soups including *pasta e fagioli* (with beans). It is cheaper to order your food at the counter and find yourself a seat, otherwise restaurant-style seating is upstairs.

SAN MARCO Ai Assassini   €€
Rio Terà dei Assassini 3695, 30124 **Tel** *041 528 79 86*   **Map** *7 A2*

Tucked away off the main thoroughfare, this friendly *osteria* attracts both locals and tourists alike. The menu changes on a daily basis and follows the seasons closely. It includes game and fish dishes and a great array of vegetables, such as *Treviso radicchio* in winter. Closed Sun.

SAN MARCO Al Bacareto   €€
Calle delle Botteghe 3447, 30124 **Tel** *041 528 93 36*   **Map** *6 F2*

A cheerful family-run *osteria* that prides itself on serving traditional dishes such as *baccalà* (creamed salt cod) and *bigoli in salsa* (wholemeal spaghetti with onion and anchovies) along with delicious seafood. Outside tables let you enjoy good food while watching the world pass by on its way to nearby Palazzo Grassi. Closed Sat pm & Sun.

SAN MARCO Osteria da Carla   €€
Corte Contarina 1535, 30124 **Tel** *041 523 78 55*   **Map** *7 A2*

A tiny but very popular *osteria* squeezed in a back alley close to Piazza San Marco, da Carla is run by a young crew. Try the tasty *guazzeto di calamari*, a stew with tomato and chili served with polenta. A quick bite at the bar of *tramezzini panini* (sandwiches) or a typical Venetian *cicheto* snack is also recommended. Closed Sun.

SAN MARCO Acqua Pazza   €€€
Campo Sant'Angelo 3808/10, 30124 **Tel** *041 277 06 88*   **Map** *6 F2*

A winning blend of Mediterranean cuisine from Amalfi and Campania is on the menu at this bright restaurant that spreads into Campo Sant'Angelo during the summer. The crusty pizzas are hard to resist though other offerings featuring capers, fresh tomato, aubergine (eggplant) and anchovies are memorable too. Closed Mon, 7 Jan–7 Feb.

SAN MARCO Da Raffaelle   €€€
Ponte delle Ostreghe 2347, 30124 **Tel** *041 523 23 17*   **Map** *7 A3*

This well-established lively restaurant offers a vast range of regional dishes in an especially romantic setting. Dishes worth trying include *granseola* (spider crab) as an antipasto, and risotto with scampi and turbot as a main course. Closed Thu; Dec–late Jan.

Key to Symbols *see back cover flap*

SAN MARCO Le Bistrot de Venise

Calle dei Fabbri 4685, 30124 **Tel** *041 523 66 51*

€€€
Map 7 B2

This welcoming restaurant serves traditional Venetian cuisine as well as special dishes based on historic recipes. The desserts are definitely worth saving space for, and the wine list is truly international. A meeting place for local artists and poets, the Bistrot regularly holds cultural events in the afternoons and evenings. Closed Christmas week.

SAN MARCO Ristorante alla Borsa

Calle delle Veste 2018, 30124 **Tel** *041 523 54 34*

€€€
Map 7 A2

Alla Borsa was named after the stock exchange formerly in the vicinity. The Stanziani family from Abruzzo have been serving Mediterranean food here since the 1700s. The best dish is fish baked with a flavoursome sauce of clams, capers and tomato. The extensive wine list is mainly Italian. Closed Wed.

SAN MARCO Ristorante all'Angelo

Calle Larga S. Marco 403, 30124 **Tel** *041 520 92 99*

€€€
Map 7 C2

This wonderful bustling restaurant, situated below the hotel of the same name, is just off Piazza San Marco. It used to be a meeting point for great artists and scholars, and specialises in seafood such as Chioggia-style soup and grilled fish. For dessert, try the luscious *zuppa inglese* (trifle).

SAN MARCO Centrale

Piscina Frezzaria 1659, 30124 **Tel** *041 296 06 64*

€€€€
Map 7 A2

A unique relaxing lounge-bar-restaurant close to the Fenice opera house, the Centrale serves innovative Mediterranean cuisine with an Asian flair. It is open until 2am every day with soft music, avant-garde art and romantic candle-lit tables. The impressive wine list has 800 labels, both Italian and foreign.

SAN MARCO Antico Martini

Campo San Fantin 1983, 30124 **Tel** *041 522 41 21*

€€€€€
Map 7 A2

Alongside the Fenice theatre, this smart restaurant boasts high-quality cuisine, a vast choice of wines and impeccable service. The lamb with balsamic sauce is just one of the many recommended dishes. An excellent choice for dinner. Closed lunch in winter (excluding holidays).

SAN MARCO Do Forni

Calle Specchieri 468, 30124 **Tel** *041 523 21 48*

€€€€€
Map 7 B2

This is a large "show business" establishment where the guest book includes politicians and heads of state. The Do Forni has two dining rooms furnished in contrasting styles, one rustic but smart and the other more elegant. The mixed grilled fish is a house speciality that should not be missed. Book ahead.

SAN MARCO Grand Canal

Calle Vallaresso 1332, 30124 **Tel** *041 520 02 11*

€€€€€
Map 7 B3

Perfect for stylish dining all year round, the Grand Canal has a winter dining room and a summer terrace with views of the island of San Giorgio Maggiore. The menu features traditional Venetian cuisine, including pasta made freshly every day, and wonderful fish and meat dishes. It is advisable to book in advance.

SAN MARCO Harry's Bar

Calle Vallaresso 1323, 30124 **Tel** *041 528 57 77*

€€€€€
Map 7 B3

Known the world over as Ernest Hemingway's favourite watering hole in Venice, Harry's Bar is a hallowed institution as well as a cosy café. Coffee and toasted sandwiches can be ordered, or a Bellini cocktail. The renowned food on the menu includes *carpaccio* (raw marinated beef), a dish invented by the owner.

SAN POLO Osteria alla Patatina

Ponte San Polo 2741A, 30123 **Tel** *041 523 72 38*

€
Map 6 E1

Delicious battered vegetables, creamy *baccalà* (cod) and tender octopus are on display at the counter at this typically Venetian *osteria*. Locals drop in for a quick glass of wine accompanied by hot chips (*patatina*, hence the name of the place), though sit-down meals are also served. Closed Sun; one week mid-Aug.

SAN POLO Al Nono Risorto

Sottoportego di Sior Bettina 2337, 30135 **Tel** *041 524 11 69*

€€
Map 2 F5

Going strong until late into the night, this busy pizzeria and modest restaurant has a pretty shady courtyard for summer dining. Located near the Rialto market area, it is popular with the locals, and booking is advisable at weekends. Closed Wed, Thu lunch; three weeks Jan, one week mid-Aug.

SAN POLO Trattoria alla Madonna

Calle della Madonna 594, 30123 **Tel** *041 522 38 24*

€€
Map 7 A1

In this well-known fish restaurant in the Rialto area, waiters dash around loaded with platters of traditional seafood, such as delicate *granceola* (spider crab) and *seppie in nero* (squid in black-ink sauce). Arrive early to avoid having to wait for a table. Closed Wed; Jan, 5–20 Aug, Christmas.

SAN POLO Poste Vecie

Rialto Pescheria 1608, 30125 **Tel** *041 72 18 22*

€€€
Map 3 A5

Poste Vecie claims to be the oldest restaurant in the city, and traces its history back to the 1500s. The entrance is from the fish market at Rialto, and the baked turbot is excellent, as are the homemade ravioli and *tagliolini* (ribbon pasta). The wine list and the dessert trolley cannot fail to impress. Closed Tue.

SAN POLO Da Fiore

Calle del Scaleter 2202, 30125 **Tel** *041 72 13 08* **Map** 2 E5

An exclusive establishment hidden behind Campo San Polo, Da Fiore is probably the city's best restaurant. Seasonal produce is the rule. Gourmet diners appreciate the sea bass with balsamic vinegar, tuna with rosemary, and *molecche* (soft-shelled crabs). Leave room for a delicate fruit sorbet. Closed Sun, Mon; three weeks Aug, Christmas–mid-Jan.

SANTA CROCE Il Réfolo

Campo del Piovan 1459, 30135 **Tel** *041 524 00 16* **Map** 2 E5

Set in a picturesque square on a canalside near San Giacomo dell'Orio, this modern establishment serves innovative gourmet pizzas and simple pasta meals. Il Réfolo belongs to the family who run the nearby Osteria da Fiore. Closed Mon, Tue lunch; Dec–Jan.

SANTA CROCE La Zucca

Calle del Megio 1762, 30135 **Tel** *041 524 15 70* **Map** 2 E5

This pretty canalside restaurant is beloved of locals and tourists alike. Serving tasty meat dishes, plus vegetarian options, the menu focuses on traditional Veneto cuisine with some international variations. The pumpkin flan is famous and the puddings are exquisite. Booking is advisable. Closed Sun.

SANTA CROCE Antica Bessetta

Salizzada Ca' Zusto 1395, 30135 **Tel** *041 72 16 87* **Map** 2 D5

This tiny, long-established restaurant is flanked by a famous narrow alley close to San Giacomo dell'Orio. It prides itself on Venetian cuisine such as *tagliolini con granseola* (thin ribbon pasta with spider crab). The selection of delicious desserts include lemon mousse with strawberry puree. Closed Tue & Wed lunch.

CASTELLO Aciugheta

Campo SS Filippo e Giacomo 4357, 30122 **Tel** *041 522 42 92* **Map** 7 C2

Popular with the young local crowd for apéritifs, this place remains busy until the early hours of the morning. Sleek and modern, it serves light salads and snacks for lunch, as well as excellent pasta dishes. The outdoor seating is the perfect way to watch the world go by. Only minutes from Piazza San Marco.

CASTELLO L'Olandese Volante

Campo San Lio 5658, 30122 **Tel** *041 528 93 49* **Map** 7 B1

An extended stop for a cold beer and light meal at this laid-back pub known as the 'Flying Dutchman' is always rewarding. The tasty salads have names of ships such as the *Galeone*, which is a concoction of prawn and egg, while the rolls are named after pirates! Extensive outdoor seating. Closed Sun am.

CASTELLO Trattoria Giorgione

Via Garibaldi 1533, 30122 **Tel** *041 522 87 27* **Map** 8 F3

A great neighbourhood *trattoria* serving flavoursome traditional-style fish meals (such as fish lasagne) and delicious risotto. The jovial owner entertains diners with Venetian folk songs and guitar music. Set on an animated avenue beyond the Arsenale. Closed Wed; two weeks Nov.

CASTELLO Alla Rivetta

Ponte San Provolo 4625, 30122 **Tel** *041 528 73 02* **Map** 7 C2

This tiny place with a mouth-watering window display of glistening fish is squeezed in at the foot of a busy bridge only minutes from St. Mark's Square. Popular with gondoliers as well as tourists, it has been serving delicious fresh seafood and pasta for years. Closed Mon; mid-Jul–mid-Aug.

CASTELLO Osteria Ae Due Porte

Corte delle Due Porte 6492, 30122 **Tel** *041 520 88 42* **Map** 4 D5

The fragrance of the fish cooking on the huge grill at this quiet family-managed restaurant in the back streets of Castello often wafts out over the adjoining square. Ae Due Porte has an attractive timber-panelled interior. Only open for lunch. Closed Sat, Sun; one week mid-Aug, one week Christmas.

CASTELLO Al Mascaron

Calle Lunga S. Maria Formosa 5225, 30122 **Tel** *041 522 59 95* **Map** 7 C1

Advance booking is essential here as this restaurant has become very popular. Both cramped and chaotic at times, this old style *osteria* does memorable fish and pasta meals, washed down by house wine served in short glasses as dictated by tradition. Closed Sun, 20 Dec–mid-Jan.

CASTELLO Da Remigio

Salizzada dei Greci 3416, 30122 **Tel** *041 523 00 89* **Map** 8 D2

Since this is a favourite with Venetians and seating is limited, you should book ahead. A memorable seafood meal is guaranteed, and should include the creamy *risotto ai frutti di mare* (seafood risotto). Conclude with a *sgroppino*, a lemon sorbet and prosecco delight. Closed Mon dinner, Tue; Christmas–20 Jan, two weeks Jul–Aug.

CASTELLO Al Covo

Campiello della Pescaria 3968, 30122 **Tel** *041 522 38 12* **Map** 8 E2

This hidden gem tucked away behind the Arsenale boat stop is run by husband and wife team Cesare and Diane Benelli. Cesare is the chef and the focus is on fish dishes of the highest quality. Save room for one of Diane's desserts. Closed Wed, Thu; 2 weeks Jan, 1 week Aug.

Key to Price Guide *see p242* **Key to Symbols** *see back cover flap*

DORSODURO Improntacafé

Crosera San Pantalon 3815, 30123 **Tel** *041 275 03 86*   **Map** *6 D2*

A new trendy wine bar in the city's university district, Improntacafé is a good place to hang out. You can spend hours watching passers-by thanks to the vast windows. As well as decent wines, you will also find plates of pasta and salads at very reasonable prices. Closed Sun; 10–25 Aug, Christmas, first week Jan.

DORSODURO Pizzeria ai Sportivi

Campo S. Margherita 3052, 30123 **Tel** *041 521 15 98*   **Map** *6 D2*

Summertime diners at this busy pizzeria can enjoy outdoor seating in one of the city's most delightful squares, Campo S. Margherita. The long menu includes specialties such as pizza with Treviso red chicory, radicchio and mouthwatering buffalo mozzarella cheese. Booking is advisable.

DORSODURO Pizzeria Ae Oche

Fondamenta Zattere 1414, 30123 **Tel** *041 520 66 01*   **Map** *6 E4*

This lively pizzeria (part of a small Venetian chain) attracts young and old locals, as well as tourists, with its great selection of pizzas. Ae Oche also offers a decent restaurant menu in a wonderful waterside setting overlooking the Giudecca canal. Closed Christmas.

DORSODURO Taverna San Trovaso

Fondamenta Priuli 1016, 30123 **Tel** *041 520 37 03*   **Map** *6 E3*

This bustling restaurant just around the corner from the Accademia gallery is extremely popular with English-speaking tourists, so book a table in advance or be prepared to queue. Pizzas are a staple, along with simple but flavoursome pasta, fish and meat dishes. There is also a good range of desserts. Closed Mon.

DORSODURO Cantinone Storico
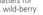

Fondamenta Bragadin 660, 30123 **Tel** *041 523 95 77*   **Map** *6 E4*

Situated near the Peggy Guggenheim Collection and Accademia, this pleasant trattoria serves a wonderful *risotto terra mare* (a blend of seafood, vegetables and porcini mushrooms), complemented by a good selection of wines from their cavernous cellar. Book ahead for a table outside. Closed Sun; Nov, first week Dec.

DORSODURO La Rivista

Rio Terrà Foscarini 979/A, 30123 **Tel** *041 240 14 25*   **Map** *6 E4*

A modern, welcoming establishment close to the Accademia, La Rivista also does light salads and cold platters for lunch. Imaginative meat, pasta and vegetable dishes are also on the menu, as are divine desserts such as wild-berry cream. The menu changes on a monthly basis. Closed Mon.

DORSODURO Agli Alboretti

Rio Terrà Antonio Foscarini 884, 30123 **Tel** *041 523 00 58*   **Map** *6 E4*

Agli Alboretti is welcoming during the winter and refreshing in summer, when you can eat outside under the pergola. The cooking has innovative touches and the menu changes monthly to follow the seasons. Try one of their speciality *risotti* such as beer and beetroot. Closed Wed & Thu lunch.

DORSODURO L'Avogaria

Calle dell'Avogaria 1629, 30123 **Tel** *041 296 04 91*   **Map** *5 C3*

This modern stylish restaurant close to the Zattere is run by a young, creative team. They specialize in food from Puglia, such as delectable stuffed calamari and tasty *tiedda*, a summer dish made with rice, mussels and potatoes. Wines are from all over Italy. Closed Tue; one week Jan, two weeks Jul–Aug.

DORSODURO Ai Gondolieri

San Vio 366, 30123 **Tel** *041 528 63 96*   **Map** *6 F4*

Close to the Guggenheim Collection, this restaurant is located in elegant wood-panelled premises where regional meat and vegetable specialities are served with flair. The stewed chicken with polenta and white truffles from Piedmont is especially recommended. Book ahead. Closed Tue; lunchtime Jul–Aug.

CANNAREGIO Brek

Lista di Spagna 124, 30121 **Tel** *041 244 01 58*   **Map** *2 D4*

This vibrant self-service restaurant close to the railway station serves freshly prepared food all day long. It is handy for a quick sandwich or pastry with a coffee or a longer sit-down meal, and the reasonable prices make it accessible to all pockets. Tasty pasta and meat dishes are prepared while you wait.

CANNAREGIO Pizzeria Al Faro

Ghetto Vecio 1181A, 30121 **Tel** *041 275 07 94*   **Map** *2 D3*

A pleasant neighbourhood pizzeria run by international staff who prepare crunchy pizzas heaped with delicious toppings. Pasta and meat dishes are also on the menu. Tables are set out under the shady trees in the square for most of the year. Closed Tue; two weeks Nov.

CANNAREGIO La Cantina

Strada Nuova 3689, 30121 **Tel** *041 522 82 58*   **Map** *2 F4*

This jovial wine bar opens on to the bustling thoroughfare Strada Nuova. Mouthwatering snacks and substantial dishes are prepared on the spot with fresh seafood, roast meats, cheeses and cold cuts to accompany the excellent range of wines. Closed Sun; two weeks Jan, two weeks Aug.

CANNAREGIO Osteria Da Rioba
€€

Fondamenta della Misericordia 2553, 30121 **Tel** *041 524 43 79* **Map** *2 F3*

This pleasant restaurant is set on a lively canalside in the Cannaregio neighbourhood. Specialities include *baccalà alla vicentina* (stewed cod), and tasty seafood risotto along with a variety of meat dishes. The wine list is short but very well rounded. Closed Mon.

CANNAREGIO Trattoria da Gigio
€€

Rio Terrà San Leonardo 1594, 30121 **Tel** *041 71 75 74* **Map** *2 D3*

During the week this busy *trattoria* is filled with stallholders from the nearby produce market, which adds to the lively atmosphere. On the menu you will find fresh seafood dishes and huge fillet steaks. The friendly service is another pleasant plus. Closed Sun, Mon dinner.

CANNAREGIO Osteria Giorgione
€€€

Calle Larga dei Proverbi 4582A, 30121 **Tel** *041 522 17 25* **Map** *3 B4*

A cosy, sophisticated establishment with a good wine list. Giorgione serves seasonal fish specialities such as *carpaccio alle tonno*, while meat eaters will enjoy the *fegato alla veneziana* (Venetian-style liver with onions). Temptation comes in the form of scrumptious desserts, such as hot chocolate flan with ice cream. Closed Mon.

CANNAREGIO Vini Da Gigio
€€€

Fondamenta San Felice 3628A, 30121 **Tel** *041 528 51 40* **Map** *3 A4*

Here you will find an elegant atmosphere and refined dishes based on seasonal produce. Risotto with prawns or grilled cuttlefish often feature on the menu, along with delicious duck and local artichokes. There is also a vast wine list to choose from. Advance booking is advisable. Closed Mon, Tue; mid-Jan–5 Feb, three weeks Aug.

CANNAREGIO Fiaschetteria Toscana
€€€€

Salizzada San Giovanni Grisostomo 5719, 30131 **Tel** *041 528 52 81* **Map** *3 B5*

Along with a superb wine list, the Busatto family serve fresh seafood such as a delicious warm octopus salad, followed by turbot in caper sauce. Do book ahead – this is one of Venice's leading stylish restaurants. Closed Tue & Wed lunch; late Jul–Aug.

THE LAGOON ISLANDS Food & Art
€

Campazzo di Dentro 554, Giudecca, 30133 **Tel** *041 241 14 13*

Something of a workers' canteen in the midst of the boatbuilding yards on the Giudecca, this place guarantees the cheapest meal in Venice. Diners help themselves to a good selection of salads and vegetables, and there's always a mountain of pasta with meat or tomato sauces. Open lunch only, Mon–Fri.

THE LAGOON ISLANDS Ai Cacciatori
€€

Mazzorbo 23, 30012 **Tel** *041 73 01 18*

A reasonably priced traditional *trattoria* on the island adjoining Burano, this establishment serves tasty dishes with fresh fish, such as *gnocchi* with crab. In the autumn months, duck and game also feature prominently on the menu. Only minutes from the ferry stop on Mazzorbo. Closed Mon; Dec–first week Feb.

THE LAGOON ISLANDS Da Romano
€€

Via Galuppi 221, Burano, 30012 **Tel** *041 73 00 30*

It is advisable to book ahead to avoid disappointment since this is the leading restaurant on the island of Burano. A wide range of fish is served in traditional Venetian fashion, under the watchful eye of a descendant of the original 19th-century owner. Closed Sun dinner, Tue; mid-Dec–Jan.

THE LAGOON ISLANDS Ai Pescatori
€€€

Via Galuppi 371, Burano, 30012 **Tel** *041 73 06 50*

The menu at this welcoming establishment focuses on ancient Burano recipes, such as *broeddo* (fish soup), and fresh seafood such as crayfish or cuttlefish served in black sauce with *tagliolini* (ribbon pasta), and accompanied by tiny, tasty local artichokes. Winter diners can also enjoy game dishes. Extensive wine list. Closed Tue; 10 Jan–10 Feb.

THE LAGOON ISLANDS Trattoria Busa alla Torre Da Lele
€€€

Campo S. Stefano 3, Murano, 30141 **Tel** *041 73 96 62* **Map** *4 E2*

Tables from this superb restaurant occupy a good part of the charming square, which is a marvellous setting. Come hungry as there's a lot to taste. Start with fragrant *granseola* (spider crab) and proceed with fish-stuffed ravioli and *fritto misto* (mixed fried seafood). Desserts include nougat delights and *tiramisu*. Open for lunch only.

THE LAGOON ISLANDS Locanda Cipriani
€€€€

Piazza Santa Fosca 29, Torcello, 30012 **Tel** *041 73 01 50*

A fisherman's inn in the 1930s, this charming exclusive island restaurant has a lovely shady courtyard where guests can enjoy dishes made with fresh produce from the kitchen garden. The risotto and seafood *fritto misto* (fried fish platter) are both excellent. Closed Tue; Jan.

THE LAGOON ISLANDS Cipriani
€€€€€

Giudecca 10, 30122 **Tel** *041 520 77 44*

A courtesy launch ferries guests from the San Marco waterfront to this exclusive island hotel with two restaurants for a unique meal. The food and service at both the formal Fortuny and the more relaxed Cip are impeccable and the views stunning. Children under eight are not admitted and there is a strict dress code. Closed Nov–March.

Key to Price Guide *see p242* **Key to Symbols** *see back cover flap*

THE LAGOON ISLANDS Harry's Dolci

Fondamenta San Biagio 773, Giudecca, 30133 **Tel** *041 522 48 44*   **Map** 5 C5

A divine veranda on the Giudecca waterfront, far from the bustle of San Marco, gives diners a leisurely view of the craft plying the broad canal. Famous for its pastries and *gelati* (ice creams), this elegant restaurant also serves superb meals. Booking recommended. Closed Mon dinner, Tue; Nov–Apr.

THE VENETO PLAIN

ASOLO Villa Cipriani
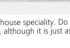

Via Canova 298, 31011 **Tel** *042 352 34 11*

Set in one of the grand hotels of the Veneto, this restaurant leads out on to the hotel gardens with breathtaking views of the verdant hills below. Local and seasonal ingredients are used in the creative cuisine, with dishes such as ricotta gnocchi with rosemary sauce.

BASSANO DEL GRAPPA Alla Riviera

Via San Giorgio 17, 36061 **Tel** *0424 50 37 00*

A traditional *osteria* serving Venetian dishes such as *pasta e fagioli* (a bean and pasta soup served tepid). *Baccalà* (cod) is served as an antipasto in the form of pâté and eaten with bread. Homemade desserts and a good selection of wine, including good local choices sold as *vino sfuso* (by the glass). Closed Sun dinner, Mon; two weeks mid-Aug.

CAORLE Duilio

Via Strada Nuova 19, 30021 **Tel** *0421 810 87*

A spacious restaurant with a nautically inspired decor, where fish-based regional cuisine is the house speciality. Do not miss the *broeto alla Duilio*, a wine-drenched mixed fish soup. Less boozy is the grilled sole, although it is just as delicious. Closed Mon in winter; early Jan–early Feb.

CASTELFRANCO Barbesin

Via Circonvallazione Est 41, 31033 **Tel** *0423 49 04 46*

A restaurant serving regional dishes, including risotto with asparagus or porcini mushrooms. However, it is the local radicchio that predominates. Other dishes include a generous mixed grill and *baccalà alla vicentina* (cod prepared according to a local recipe). Closed Wed dinner, Thu; 1–15 Jan, three weeks Aug.

CHIOGGIA El Gato

Campo Sant'Andrea 653, 30015 **Tel** *041 40 18 06*

Classic cooking based on seafood in an elegant setting. El Gato, one of the oldest restaurants in town, is located next to a 14th-century bell tower, and the outdoor tables look out on to Chioggia's main square. Inside there are three dining rooms. Closed Wed, Sun dinner (Nov–Mar).

CONEGLIANO Al Salisa

Via XX Settembre 24, 31015 **Tel** *0438 242 88*

An elegant restaurant set in a medieval house with a pretty veranda for al fresco dining. The traditional menu includes snails and homemade pasta served with a range of vegetarian sauces. The *guanciale di vitello* (veal) and the exemplary wine list guarantee a feast. Closed Tue dinner, Wed.

DOLO Alla Posta

Via Ca' Tron 33, 30031 **Tel** *041 41 07 40*

This outstanding fish restaurant, in an old Venetian posthouse overlooking the town's main canal, prepares regional specialities with fresh ingredients and well-blended flavours. On the menu you will find dishes such as lobster served with steamed vegetables. Closed Mon; Sun dinner.

GRANCONA Isetta

Via Pederiva 96, 36040 **Tel** *0444 88 99 92*

This pretty little restaurant, just 15 minutes from Vicenza, serves regional food, with the emphasis on grilled meats and good puddings, based on recipes handed down by the owner's grandmother, Isetta. Set in the Berici Hills, the restaurant also offers accommodation in ten rooms. Closed Tue dinner, Wed.

MIANE Da Gigetto

Via De Gaspari 5, 31050 **Tel** *043 896 00 20*

Traditional Venetian cuisine served with flair awaits at this restaurant. The menu is seasonal, and in the autumn the pumpkin and mushroom dishes are particularly good. Game dishes such as hare and deer are also served in the winter. The wine cellar is enormous. Closed Mon dinner, Tue; two weeks Jan, three weeks Aug.

NOVENTA PADOVANA Boccadoro

Via della Resistenza 49, 35027 **Tel** *049 62 50 29*

A family-run restaurant offering good Paduan food in surroundings that have an air of relaxed elegance. The *bigoli* pasta with goose sauce is well worth sampling, as is the guinea fowl with *radicchio au gratin*. The service is exemplary. Closed Tue dinner, Wed; three weeks Aug, 27 Dec–6 Jan.

ODERZO Dussin €€

*Via Maggiore 60, Località Piavon, 31046 **Tel** 0422 75 21 30*

Good-value traditional cuisine is served in Dussin. Fish is a speciality, with such dishes as seafood risotto and grilled tuna. However, the homemade desserts are something special. The setting is tranquil, the restaurant being situated just outside the town centre. Closed Mon dinner, Tue; two weeks Aug.

PADUA La Braseria €

*Via Tommaseo 48, 35121 **Tel** 049 876 09 07*

A friendly restaurant with good cooking. Typical Veneto dishes include penne with porcini and smoked bacon, but the chef (from Basilicata) also offers southern specialities. The *battuta siciliana* is a non-fried variation of the beef cutlet. The *crème brulée* is also excellent. Closed Sat lunch, Sun; one week Aug.

PADUA Antico Brolo €€

*Corso Milano 22, 35100 **Tel** 049 66 45 55*

This quietly chic restaurant delivers appropriately elegant food, for example ravioli stuffed with courgette flowers. Veal's head cooked in vinegar and onion is the house's speciality. The menu includes a well-rounded wine list. Good for families and groups. Closed Mon lunch.

ROVIGO Trattoria Al Sole €

*Via Bedendo Nino 6, 45100 **Tel** 0425 229 17*

An old-fashioned *trattoria* serving unpretentious, traditional local cuisine. The tripe broth and the *baccalà alla vicentina* (salt cod) are two favourites. Homemade traditional cakes are served for pudding. The service is friendly and prompt. Closed Sun.

TREVISO Toni del Spin €€

*Via Inferiore 7, 31100 **Tel** 0422 54 38 29*

A homely restaurant serving regional fare. Though busy serving office workers at lunchtime, this *trattoria* slows down in the evenings, offering a more intimate experience. House specialities include pasta and *fagioli* (beans), the ubiquitous *risotto al radicchio*, tripe and *tiramisu*. Closed Sun and Mon lunch; last week Jul–Aug.

TREVISO Osteria all'Antica Torre €€€

*Via Inferiore 55, 31100 **Tel** 0422 58 36 94*

Here, outstanding wines accompany superb local cuisine. In season, radicchio is used in many ways, including in the making of the grappa. However, fish is the main contender on the menu, with imaginative dishes such as cuttlefish risotto. Art exhibitions are also held here. Closed Sun and Mon dinner; three weeks Aug.

VICENZA Taverna Aeolia €€

*Piazza Conte da Schio 1, Costozza di Longare, 36023 **Tel** 0444 55 50 36*

This restaurant is housed in an elegant villa with a beautiful frescoed ceiling. The menu is especially strong in creative meat dishes, with kangaroo, bison and frog all available to choose from. Vegetarians can enjoy the lemon risotto, and a children's menu is also available. Closed Tue; 1–15 Jan.

VICENZA Rosso Aragosta €€€

*Piazzetta Porta Padova 65–67, 36100 **Tel** 0444 50 61 23*

A stylish restaurant within the city walls serving nothing but fish. Dishes include a mixed plate of scampi and squid, or roast turbot on a bed of potatoes and olives. The mint and liquorice *semifreddo* (ice-cream dessert) will help you to digest the generous portions. Closed Sat lunch, Sun, Mon lunch; Aug.

VERONA AND LAKE GARDA

BREGANZE Al Toresan €€

*Via Zabarella 1, 36042 **Tel** 0445 87 32 60*

In the autumn the locals flock here for the delicious wild-mushroom dishes. Mushrooms come in every shape and form: stuffed, as filling for ravioli, and grilled. The cooking is hearty and complemented by the local wines, of which the reds are particularly good. Closed Thu; three weeks Aug.

LAKE GARDA Antica Locanda Mincio €€

*Via Michelangelo Buonarroti 12, Valeggio sul Mincio, 37067 **Tel** 045 795 00 59*

Once a staging post, this is now a delightful restaurant, with frescoed walls and open fireplaces serving good regional food. The shaded seating outside overlooks the river. Specialities include trout and eels caught in the nearby Lake Garda. Closed Wed, Thu; two weeks Feb, two weeks Nov.

LAKE GARDA Locanda San Vigilio €€€€€

*Localita San Vigilio, Garda, 37016 **Tel** 045 725 66 88*

This excellent restaurant overlooking Lake Garda has been welcoming guests with a good selection of wines and food for five centuries. Nowadays, it has an astounding range of freshwater fish and seafood dishes. The spacious garden has shady olive trees. Closed mid-Nov–mid-Mar.

MONTECCHIO DI CROSARA Alpone

Via Pergola 17, 37030 **Tel** *045 617 53 87*

A refined restaurant offering a seasonal-inspired menu. In the spring, try dishes based on mushrooms or cherries. Also on offer is an *à la carte* menu with *gnocchi*, *crespelle* (pancakes) and grilled vegetables. End your meal with a plate of local cheeses served with a variety of chutneys and jams. Closed Sun dinner, Tue; two weeks Jan, two weeks Aug.

MONTECCHIO DI CROSARA Baba Jaga

Via Cabalao 12, 37030 **Tel** *045 745 02 22*

Black-truffle risotto is a good choice in this restaurant situated in the heart of the Soave wine-producing region. Other dishes worth trying in this friendly, informal setting include stuffed duck thigh in an Amarone wine sauce or tagliatelle with quail sauce. Closed Sun dinner, Mon; three weeks Jan, three weeks Aug.

VERONA Al Bersagliere

Via Dietro Pallone 1, 37121 **Tel** *045 800 48 24*

Traditional Veronese food served in a friendly atmosphere is available at the centrally located Al Bersagliere. A superb wine cellar hosts wine-tasting evenings, while the garden offers respite for those dining with children. Dishes include *pastisada* (meat stew) and *bigoli con l'anatra* (pasta with duck). Closed Sun; two weeks Jan, 10 days mid-Aug.

VERONA Ristorante Greppia

Vicolo Samaritana 3, 37121 **Tel** *045 800 45 77*

Run by the Guizzardi family since 1975, this restaurant, named after the local word for a feeding trough, offers superb food. As well as delicious, freshly made pasta, there is a memorable *bollito misto* (boiled-meats platter): diners choose their meat from a trolley. Booking recommended. Closed Mon; two weeks Jun.

VERONA Arche

Via Arche Scaligere 6, 37121 **Tel** *045 800 74 15*

This long-established fish restaurant opened for business in 1879. It is perfectly situated next to Romeo's house, a location that only adds to its charm. On the menu: smoked oysters with horseradish and caviar, and marinated rock lobster. Closed Sun, Mon lunch; three weeks Jan.

VERONA Il Desco

Via Dietro San Sebastiano 5–7, 37121 **Tel** *045 59 53 58*

One of Italy's finest restaurants, set in a 16th-century *palazzo*, Il Desco truly deserves its two Michelin stars. It is both romantic and understated. Dishes include pumpkin and Amarone wine risotto and the famous aubergine ravioli. The gourmet menu offers a staggering seven courses. Closed Sun, Mon; two weeks Jun, two weeks Christmas.

THE DOLOMITES

BELLUNO Ristorante Taverna

Via Cipro 7, 32100 **Tel** *0437 25 192*

Centrally placed and popular with the locals, the Taverna specialises in grilled meat, game and traditional dishes. Try *schiz*, a type of fresh cheese that has been oven-baked, and *pastin*, a tasty blend of minced meats flavoured with juniper berries. Closed Sun.

BELLUNO Terracotta

Via Garibaldi 61, 32100 **Tel** *0437 94 26 44*

Regional specialities in this friendly restaurant include pork wrapped in Parma ham with a grain mustard sauce. The menu changes each month. Views from the restaurant are limited, but there is a pretty wisteria-covered pergola. An extensive wine list suits all budgets. Closed Tue.

CORTINA D'AMPEZZO Baita Fraina

Località Fraina 1, 32043 **Tel** *0436 36 34*

This lovely wood-panelled mountain restaurant features a terrace with panoramic views and a large play area for children. The pasta dishes are good, as are the game dishes, which include *tagliata di cervo* (venison). There is an excellent wine list and a choice of over 100 types of grappa. Closed Mon low season; May–Jun, Oct–Nov.

CORTINA D'AMPEZZO Ristorante Pizzeria Croda Cafè

Corso Italia 163, 32043 **Tel** *0436 86 65 89*

In the traffic-free centre of Cortina d'Ampezzo, this conveniently placed establishment serves up affordable meals. These range from traditional dishes such as *polenta con funghi* to good pizzas. When it's time for dessert *frutti di bosco* (summer berries) is a good bet, accompanied by a scoop of ice cream. Closed Tue.

PASSO FALZAREGO Rifugio Col Gallina

Passo Falzarego 2, 32043 **Tel** *0436 29 39*

A cosy chalet with lodgings high above Cortina d'Ampezzo and snowbound in winter, this *rifugio* serves hearty alpine fare in a wonderful Dolomite setting. Try the delicious polenta with melted cheese or the homemade *casunziei* (ravioli stuffed with beetroot and covered with poppy seeds). Closed mid-Apr–mid-Jun, mid-Sep–mid-Dec.

Bars and Cafés in Venice

Many bars in Venice draw their trade from tourists and are busy throughout the day, as visitors ease their aching feet and consult their guide-books. Custom is swelled mid-morning and around lunchtime as the Venetians drop in for a drink or snack. Cafés range from basic one-room bars patronized by local workmen, to opulent coffee houses in old-world style, such as **Caffè Quadri** and **Caffè Florian**. Even the humblest establishment provides a continuous range of refreshments and you can enjoy anything from a morning coffee or lunchtime beer, to an aperitif or a final brandy before bed. Bars also serve snacks throughout their opening hours: freshly baked morning pastries and lunchtime sandwiches, rolls, cakes, biscuits and sometimes home-made ice cream. Wine bars often have a wide range of traditional Venetian snacks, and so make good places to stop for lunch.

BARS

Italians will often stop for breakfast in a bar on their way to work.This normally consists of a *cappuccino* (milky coffee) and a *brioche* (a plain, jam- or cream-filled pastry). **Pasticceria Dal Mas**, on the main route from the station to the Rialto, is much favoured by early morning commuters.

A wide range of alcoholic drinks is on offer, and you can ask for a glass of wine or beer on tap. Beer from the keg is called *birra alla spina* and comes in three different sizes: *piccola, media* and *grande*. Italian and imported bottled beers are also available, though the latter can be expensive. All bars serve glasses of mineral water and it is acceptable to request a glass of tap water *(acqua del rubinetto)*, which will be free. Most bars also serve delicious freshly squeezed fruit juices *(una spremuta)* and milk-shakes made with fruit *(un frullato)*. Italian bottled juices are good and are available in unusual flavours such as apricot and pear.

All bars serve a range of sandwiches *(tramezzini)* and filled rolls *(panini)*, and often have toasted sandwiches and pizzas as well. Some double as cake-shops *(pasticceria)*, and these have a tempting range of calorie-filled delights on display to eat in or take away. If you are near the Accademia, seek out the tiny **Pasticceria Vio** for wonderful cakes, or for an expensive treat, go to **Harry's Dolci** on the Giudecca *(see p246)*.

Bear in mind that sitting down to drink in a bar or café can cost a lot more than standing at the bar, as there is a table charge, which can be high. This rises proportionally as you draw nearer San Marco. Some bars, particularly in the less tourist-frequented areas, have a stand-up counter only. All have a lavatory *(il bagno* or *il gabinetto)*, though you may have to ask at the desk for the key. It is also worth noting that bars and cafés tend to shut earlier here than in other parts of Italy, particularly in winter.

The normal procedure is to choose what you want to eat or drink, then ask for it and pay at the cashdesk. You will be given a receipt *(lo scontrino)* which you present at the bar. If they are busy, a small tip will usually speed things up. If you decide to sit down, either inside or at an outside table, your order will be taken by a waiter who will bring the bill when he delivers the drinks. You should expect to pay double or more for this, but you can stretch your drink out for as long as you like.

WINE BARS

There is an old tradition in Venice called *cichetti e l'ombra*, meaning "a little bite and the shade". The little bite ranges from a slice of bread and *prosciutto crudo* (raw cured ham), meatballs or fried vegetables, to sardines and *baccalà* (salt cod). The shade is a glass of wine, so called because the gondoliers used to snatch a glass in the shade away from the glare of the sun on the water. Wine bars serving these snacks and a range of wines are numerous and heavily populated by locals. Many, such as **Do Mori**, are in the crowded alleys off the Rialto, but one of the nicest is the **Cantina del Vino già Schiavi** near the Ponte San Trovaso.

CAFES AND ICE CREAM PARLOURS

Coffee houses have played their part in the history of the Veneto – notably Padua's **Caffè Pedrocchi** *(see p178)* – and a visit to Venice would not be complete without a drink at the historic **Caffè Florian** or **Caffè Quadri**. It is a hard decision whether to take a table outside and watch the crowds or to experience the elegant charm of the interior rooms, with their atmosphere of past eras. The prices are sky-high, but you can take your time and be entertained by the resident orchestras.

Harry's Bar *(see p92)*, is another world-famous bar and café. In summer it is crammed with foreigners and the prices are always high, but for a treat, sip a Bellini, a mixture of Prosecco and fresh white peach juice, in the place where it was invented.

The cafés along the Zattere, with their lovely views across the Giudecca Canal, make good places to pause, and the prices are much lower. Many Venetian squares have cafés with tables outside. There are several in the Campo Santo Stefano, or try **Bar Colleoni** in Campo Santi Giovanni e Paolo (San Zanipolo). **Il Caffè** is the nicest in Campo Santa Margherita.

Venetian ice cream is definitely among the best in Italy, with ice cream shops *(gelaterie)* serving a wide selection of seasonal flavours, some unique to Venice. The Venetians eat ice cream all year round, often instead of pudding or as the finale to the evening stroll, or *passeggiata*. It comes as either a cone *(un cono)* or a cup *(una coppa)* and it is normal to have at least three flavours. **Paolin** on Campo Santo Stefano is one of the best ice cream shops. You could also try **Il Doge**, which is in Campo Santa Margherita, and **Nico** on the Zattere, where you will find *gianduiotto*, a rich chocolate-based Venetian speciality. Make certain you buy ice cream made on the premises, *artigianato* or *produzione propria*, and experiment with what is clearly seasonal; the high-summer fruit ices such as melon, peach and apricot are delightfully refreshing.

DIRECTORY

SAN MARCO

Bar Gelateria Paolin
Campo Santo Stefano,
San Marco 2962A.
Map 6 F3.

Caffè Florian
Piazza San Marco,
San Marco 56/59.
Map 7 B2.

Caffè Quadri
Piazza San Marco,
San Marco 120–24.
Map 7 B2.

Harry's Bar
Calle Vallaresso,
San Marco 1323.
Map 7 B3.

Hostaria ai Rusteghi
Campiello del Tentor,
San Marco 5513.
Map 7 B1.

Osteria Terrà Assassini
Rio Terrà degli Assassini,
San Marco 3695.
Map 7 A2.

Rosa Salva
Calle Fiubera, San Marco 951. **Map** 7 B1.

Vino Vino
Ponte delle Veste,
San Marco 2007.
Map 7 A3.

SAN POLO AND SANTA CROCE

Al Prosecco
C. San Giacomo dell'Orio,
S. Croce 1503. **Map** 2 E5.

Bar Dogale
Campo dei Frari, San Polo 3012. **Map** 6 E1.

Do Mori
Calle Do Mori,
San Polo 429.
Map 3 A5.

CASTELLO

Bar Colleoni
Campo Santi Giovanni
e Paolo, Castello 6811.
Map 3 C5.

Bar Gelateria Riviera
Ponte de la Pietà,
Riva degli Schiavoni 4153.
Map 8 D2.

Bar Mio
Via Garibaldi,
Castello 1820.
Map 8 F3.
Bar Orologio
Campo Santa Maria
Formosa, Castello 6130.
Map 7 C1.

Caffè al Cavallo
Campo Santi Giovanni
e Paolo, Castello 6823.
Map 3 C5.

La Boutique del Gelato
Campo San Lio,
Castello 5727.
Map 7 B1.

Snack & Sweet
Salizzada San Lio,
Castello 5689.
Map 7 B1.

DORSODURO

Accademia Foscarini
Rio Terra A Foscarini,
Dorsoduro 878/C. 0
Map 6 E4.

Ai do Draghi
Calle della Chiesa,
Dorsoduro 3665.
Map 6 F4.

Al Chioschetto Zattere
Dorsoduro 1406A.
Map 6 D4.

Bar Gelateria Causin
Campo Santa Margherita,
Dorsoduro 2995.
Map 6 D2.

Bar Gelateria Il Doge
Campo Santa Margherita,
Dorsoduro 3058A.
Map 6 D2.

Bar Gelateria Nico
Zattere ai Gesuati,
Dorsoduro 922.
Map 6 D4.

Bar Pasticceria Vio
Rio Terrà della Toletta,
Dorsoduro 1192.
Map 6 D3.

Cantina del Vino già Schiavi
Ponte San Trovaso,
Dorsoduro 992.
Map 6 E4.

Il Caffè
Campo Santa Margherita,
Dorsoduro 2963.
Map 6 D3.

Soto Sopra
Calle San Pantalon,
Dorsoduro 3740.
Map 6 D2.

CANNAREGIO

Alla Bomba
Calle dell'Oca,
Cannaregio 4297.
Map 3 A5.

Bar Algiubagio
Fondamente Nuove,
Cannaregio 5039.
Map 3 C4.

Bar Gelateria Solda
Campo Santi Apostoli,
Cannaregio 4440.
Map 3 B5.

Caffè Pasqualigo
Salizzada Santa Fosca,
Cannaregio 2288.
Map 2 F4.

Enoteca Boldrin
San Canciano,
Cannaregio 5550.
Map 3 B5.

Il Gelatone
Rio Terrà Maddalena,
Cannaregio 2063.
Map 2 F3.

Osteria da Alberto
Calle Larga
Giacinto Gallina,
Cannaregio 5401.
Map 3 C5.

Pasticceria Dal Mas
Lista di Spagna,
Cannaregio 150/A.
Map 2 D4.

THE LAGOON ISLANDS

Bar della Maddalena
Mazzorbo.

Bar Ice
Campo San Donato,
Murano.
Map 4 F2.

Bar La Palanca
Fondamenta Santa
Eufemia, Giudecca 448.
Map 6 D5.

Bar Palmisano
Via Baldassare Galuppi,
Burano.

Bar Trono di Attila
Torcello.

Harry's Dolci
Fondamenta San Biagio,
Giudecca 773.
Map 6 D5.

Lo Spuntino
Via Baldassare
Galuppi, Burano.

SHOPS AND MARKETS

The narrow streets of Venice are lined with beautifully arranged windows that cannot fail to tempt shoppers, and the city has the additional bonus of being truly pedestrianized. Few cities of similar size have such a wide variety of goods to browse through as you explore the fascinating and diverse neighbourhoods. There is still a strong

Piece of traditional Murano glass

artisan tradition in Venice, and alongside glass and lace you will find high-quality fashion and leather goods, antiques and jewellery. In the Veneto, which is one of Italy's most prosperous regions, every town boasts a wide range of shops, and many have seasonal speciality markets. In country areas you can buy wine and olive oil direct from the producers.

Display of jewellery in a shop window in the Frezzeria

WHEN TO SHOP

Generally, shops open around 9 or 9:30am and close for lunch at 12:30 or 1pm, with the exception of food shops and markets, which are in business from 8am. In the afternoon stores are open from 3:30pm to 7:30pm in winter, and 4pm to 8pm in summer. In Venice, many stores aimed directly at tourists are open all day and even on Sundays, as are big out-of-town supermarkets and hypermarkets – useful if you are self-catering in the region.

Monday is usually the traditional closing day in northern Italy though, again, this does not apply to all shops in Venice itself. The smaller towns in the Veneto often have very variable opening hours, with perhaps food shops closing on Mondays but ironmongers and clothes shops closing on Wednesdays. Shops and markets in the Veneto are

often closed for two or three weeks during the national holiday time in August.

The best time for finding bargains is during the January and July sales: look out for window signs with the words *saldi* or *sconti*.

WHERE TO SHOP IN VENICE

The glittering Mercerie *(see p95)*, which runs from Piazza San Marco to the Rialto, has been the main shopping street since the Middle Ages and, together with the parallel Calle dei Fabbri, is still a honey pot for the crowds. West of San Marco, the zigzagging Frezzeria is full of interesting and unusual shops. The main route from the Piazza to the Accademia Bridge is lined with up-market speciality stores, while the streets north of Campo Santo Stefano *(see p93)* are another excellent trawling ground for quality souvenirs and gifts.

Across the Grand Canal, the narrow streets from the Rialto southwest towards Campo San Polo *(see p101)* are lined with a wide variety of less

A colourful display of T-shirts with the "Venezia" logo

expensive stores, while near the station the bustling Lista di Spagna and the route along the Strada Nova towards the Rialto cater for the everyday needs of ordinary Venetians.

The islands of Murano and Burano *(see pp150–51)* are *the* places to buy traditional glass and lace.

HOW TO PAY

Major credit cards are usually accepted in the main stores for larger purchases, but cash is preferred for small items, and smaller shops will want cash. Travellers' cheques are also accepted, though the rate that you will get is less favourable than at a bank.

By law, shopkeepers should give you a receipt *(ricevuta fiscale)*, which you should keep until you are some distance away from the store (legally this is 600 m). If a purchased item is defective, most shops will change the article or give you a credit note, as long as you show the till receipt. Cash refunds are not usually given.

VAT EXEMPTION

Visitors from non-European Union countries can reclaim the 19 per cent sales tax (IVA) on goods exceeding €160 from the same shop. Ask for an invoice when you buy the goods and inform the shop that you intend to reclaim the tax. The invoice must be stamped at customs as you leave Italy. The shop will reimburse the tax in euros once they have received the stamped invoice.

Designer clothes shop in Treviso

FASHION AND ACCESSORIES

In Venice, the big names in fashion are all found near San Marco. **Armani, Gucci, Missoni and Roberto Cavalli** all have stylish shops just off the Piazza. For really innovative and outrageous designs visit **Fiorella** in Campo Santo Stefano. The stalls at the foot of the Ponte delle Guglie on Suada Nuova sell a range of good value leather shoes and a wide variety of traditional Venetian slippers in a stunning range of colourful velours. For a genuine gondolier's shirt, take a look in **Emilio Ceccato**.

FABRICS AND INTERIOR DESIGN

Venice has long been famed for sumptuous brocades, fine silks and figured velvets. **Trois** sells silks by the metre, including the gossamer-fine pleated silks invented by Fortuny for his Delphos dresses *(see p94)*, and **Il Canapè** has wonderful designer silks and other fabrics in its shop near Campo San Pantalon. The famous house of **Rubelli** has its headquarters at Palazzo Corner Spinelli near Campo Sant'Angelo. Here you will find a variety of rich brocades and velvets. **Color Casa**, in San Polo, has equally lovely textiles at slightly lower prices. **Luigi Bevilacqua**, at Ponte della Canonica, sells beautiful brocades, velvets, damasks and other luxury fabrics, all woven on 17th-century hand-operated looms.

MASKS AND COSTUMES

You can buy cheap, mass-produced masks all over the city, but a genuine one is a good souvenir, and you will be spoilt for choice. **Papier Maché** in Castello specializes in traditional mask-making and their designs are absolutely stunning. Near Campo San Polo **Tragicomica** sells costumes and masks, as well as Commedia dell'Arte figures. You will find these at **Leon d'Oro** on the Frezzeria too, where they also make string puppets. Dorsoduro has several workshops; **Mondonovo**, just off Campo Santa Margherita, has a marvellous selection of masks and costumes. In the weeks leading up to Carnival, maskmakers are, of course,

A typical Venetian mask

extremely busy, but at other times of the year many workshops welcome visitors and are pleased to show you their craft *(see p31)*.

GLASS

The best place to buy glass is on the island of Murano, where it has been made since the 13th century *(see p151)*. All the main manufacturers have their furnaces and showrooms here, catering to mainstream taste. Some manufacturers also have showrooms in Venice itself.

On Murano, **Seguso** and **Barovier e Toso** make glass to traditional designs with good simple lines. Another option is **Totem-il Canale**, which has an excellent selection of both traditional and contemporary designs. **Venini** has shops near San Marco; it represents the top end of the market and some of its designs are very pleasing. For other important glass designware, go to **Ma.Re** in Frezzeria.

JEWELLERY

Venice's smartest jewellers are **Missiaglia** and **Nardi**, both in the arcades of Piazza San Marco. Shops on the Rialto Bridge sell cheaper designs, and this is a good place to find bracelets and chains, whose price is determined by the weight of the gold. For inexpensive, pretty Venetian glass earrings, necklaces and bracelets try **FGB** in Campo Santa Maria Zobenigo.

Wide range of fruit and vegetables for sale in the Rialto market

A typical general food store in the San Marco area

DEPARTMENT STORES

Department stores are not as common in Italy as in many other countries. The main chain store in Venice is Coin, which sells everything from umbrellas to tableware. Oviesse and Upim are cheaper supermarket-style options. You will find branches of these in other towns in the Veneto.

Treasure trove in one of the art shops on Murano

BOOKS AND GIFTS

The best general bookshop in Venice is **Goldoni**, which also sells maps. **Filippi Editori Venezia** stocks facsimile editions of old books and books about Venice. **Fantoni** is a specialist art

bookshop, and English books are sold at **Cafoscarina 2, Libreria Mondadori and Libreria Emiliana**.

Hand-made marbled and dragged paper are typically Venetian, and used as book covers and made up into writing desk equipment. **Linda Gonzalez** sells marbled paper and handcrafted leather masks. **Paolo Olbi** has a wide range of papers, while **Alberto Valese-Ebru** uses a distinctive marbling technique on fabrics as well as paper. For watercolour views of Venice, try the stalls in Campo dei Santi Apostoli.

The San Barnaba area has several art and craft shops where you can buy unusual gifts and souvenirs. **Signor Blum** on the Campo San Barnaba has charming carved and painted wooden objects and toys. Another carver, **Livio de Marchi**, makes large whimsical wooden ornaments. **L'Arte di Alesia** sells interesting paper objects and masks. For unusual soaps and other toiletries browse in **Il Melograno**, a herbalist in Campo Santa Margherita.

MARKETS AND FOOD SHOPS

One of the delights of Venice is a morning spent exploring the food markets and shops around the Rialto. Fruit and vegetable stalls

sprawl to the west of the bridge and the Pescheria, or fish market, lies right beside the Grand Canal (see p100). The neighbouring streets are full of unusual and excellent food shops. Olive oil, vinegar and dried pasta, which comes in many colours, shapes and flavours, are all good choices if you are looking for food to take home. **Aliani (Casa del Parmigiano)** is a superlative cheese shop right by the vegetable market, where you can also buy a selection of fresh pasta, salamis and ready-made dishes for a picnic.

On Ruga Rialto, the **Drogheria Mascari** has a fine range of coffees, teas, dried fruits, and nuts. **Pasticceria Tonolo** is one of Venice's best pasticcerie, selling traditional sweetmeats as well as cakes and biscuits.

Viale Santa Maria Elisabetta, the main shopping street of the Lido

DIRECTORY

FASHION AND ACCESSORIES

Armani
Calle Goldoni, San Marco 4412. **Map** 7 A2.
Tel 041 523 47 58.

Emilio Ceccato
Sottoportico di Rialto, San Polo 16/17.
Map 7 A1.
Tel 041 522 27 00.

Fiorella Gallery
Campo Santo Stefano, San Marco 2806.
Map 6 F3.
Tel 041 520 92 28.

Gucci
Calle Larga XXII Marzo, San Marco 2102.
Map 7 A3.
Tel 041 277 73 01.

Missoni
Calle Vallaresso, San Marco 1312. **Map** 7 B3.
Tel 041 520 57 33.

Roberto Cavalli
Calle Vallaresso, San Marco 1314. **Map** 7 B3.
Tel 041 520 57 33.

Stalls at the foot of Ponte delle Guglie
Strada Nuova, Cannaregio. **Map** 2 D3.

FABRICS AND INTERIOR DESIGN

Annelie
Calle Lunga San Barnaba, Dorsoduro 2748.
Map 6 D3.
Tel 041 520 32 77.

Color Casa
Calle della Madonneta, San Polo 1990.
Map 6 F1.
Tel 041 523 60 71.

Il Canapè
Calle San Pantalon, Dorsoduro 3736.
Map 6 D2.
Tel 041 714 264.

Luigi Bevilacqua
Ponte della Canonica, San Marco 337B.
Map 7 C2.
Tel 041 528 75 81.

Rubelli
Palazzo Corner Spinelli, San Marco 3877.
Map 7 B2.
Tel 041 523 61 10.

Trois
Campo San Maurizio, San Marco 2666.
Map 6 F3.
Tel 041 522 29 05.

MASKS AND COSTUMES

Atelier Pietro Longhi
Rio Terrà Frari, San Polo 26046.
Map 6 E1.
Tel 041 714 478.

Leon d'Oro
Frezzeria, San Marco 1770. **Map** 7 A2.
Tel 041 520 33 75.

Mondonovo
Rio Terrà Canal, Dorsoduro 3063.
Map 6 D3.
Tel 041 528 73 44.

Papier Maché
Calle Lunga Santa Maria Formosa, Castello 5175.
Map 7 C1.
Tel 041 522 99 95.

Tragicomica
Calle dei Nomboli, San Polo 2800.
Map 6 F1.
Tel 041 72 11 02.

GLASS

Barovier e Toso
Fondamenta Vetrai 28, Murano. **Map** 4 E3.
Tel 041 73 90 49.

Ma.Re
Frezzeria, San Marco 1586–8. **Map** 7 B3.
Tel 041 241 26 87.

Seguso
Fondamenta Vetrai 143, Murano.
Map 4 E2.
Tel 041 73 94 23.

Totem-il Canale
Campo Carità, Dorsoduro 8786.
Map 6 E3.
Tel 041 522 36 41.

Venini
Piazzetta dei Leoncini, San Marco 314. **Map** 7 B2.
Tel 041 522 40 45.

JEWELLERY

FGB
Campo Santa Maria Zobenigo, San Marco 2514. **Map** 7 C1.
Tel 041 523 65 56.

Missiaglia
Procuratie Vecchie, San Marco 125. **Map** 7 B2.
Tel 041 522 44 64.

Nardi
Procuratie Nuove, Piazza San Marco, San Marco 69/71. **Map** 7 B2.
Tel 041 522 57 33.

BOOKS AND GIFTS

Alberto Valese-Ebru
Campiello Santo Stefano, San Marco 3471. **Map** 6 F3. *Tel 041 523 88 30.*

Cafoscarina 2
Calle Foscari, Dorsoduro 3259. **Map** 6 D2
Tel 041 522 18 65

Cartoleria Accademia
Rio Terrà Carità, Dorsoduro 1044. **Map** 6 E3.
Tel 041 520 70 86.

Cartoleria Testolini
Calle dei Fabbri, San Marco 4745. **Map** 7 A1.
Tel 041 522 30 85.

Daniela Porto
Rio Terrà dei Nomboli, San Polo 2753. **Map** 6 E1.
Tel 041 523 13 68.

Erborista Il Melograno
Campo Santa Margherita, Dorsoduro 2999. **Map** 6 D2. *Tel 041 528 51 17.*

Fantoni
Salizzada San Luca, San Marco 4119. **Map** 7 A2.
Tel 041 522 07 00.

Filippi Editori Venezia
Calle Casselleria, Castello 5284. **Map** 7 C1.
Tel 041 523 69 16.

Goldoni
Calle dei Fabbri, San Marco 4742. **Map** 7 A1.
Tel 041 522 23 84.

L'Arte di Alesia
Ponte San Barnaba, Dorsoduro 2806.
Map 6 D3.
Tel 041 523 08 25.

Libreria Emiliana
Calle Goldoni, San Marco 4487. **Map** 7 A2.
Tel 041 522 07 93.

Libreria Mondadori
Salizzada San Moisè, San Marco 1345. **Map** 7 A3. *Tel 041 522 21 93.*

Libreria della Toletta
Sacca della Toletta, Dorsoduro 1214. **Map** 6 D3. *Tel 041 523 20 34.*

Linda Gonzalez
Campo San Fantin, San Marco 1854. **Map** 7 A2.
Tel 041 528 55 63.

Livio de Marchi
Salizzada San Samuele, San Marco 3157/A. **Map** 6 E2. *Tel 041 528 56 94.*

Paolo Olbi
Calle della Mandola, San Marco 3653. **Map** 6 F2.
Tel 041 528 50 25.

Signor Blum
Campo San Barnaba, Dorsoduro 2840.
Map 6 D3.
Tel 041 522 63 67.

FOOD SHOPS

Aliani (Casa del Parmigiano)
Erberia Rialto, San Polo 214/5. **Map** 3 A5.
Tel 041 520 65 25.

Drogheria Mascari
Ruga Rialto, Calle dei Spezieri San Polo 381. **Map** 3 A5. *Tel 041 522 97 62.*

Pasticceria Tonolo
Calle San Pantalon, Dorsoduro 3764.
Map 6 D2.
Tel 041 523 72 09.

What to Buy in the Veneto

Glass is the most popular Venetian souvenir, but there are many other possibilities, ranging from Carnival masks and ceramics to fabrics and lace. For food lovers there is a wide selection of local olive oils, honey, wines and preserves. In the Veneto many food producers sell direct to the public, while different craft and food specialities are found in individual towns and islands.

Modern vase of
opaque glass

Traditional glass with gold overlay

Two-coloured
goblet

Venetian Glass
In traditional rich colours of blue and claret, or in striking modern designs, you will find anything from scent bottles to chandeliers.

Gift box covered in
marbled paper

Address book

Venetian Marbled Paper
Marbled paper is a Venetian speciality. The sheets of paper are dipped into liquid gum before adding the paint. You can buy a large range of stationery items covered in the paper, as well as paper by the individual sheet. Each sheet of marbled paper is unique.

Pretty trinket box

Sheets of marbled paper

Delicate lace collar from Burano

Crafts from the Veneto
The ancient patterns of Burano lace are used to great advantage on table linen and to trim exquisite lingerie. Handpainted vases, plates and bowls are produced in the picturesque old town of Bassano del Grappa.

Decorated ceramic
vase from Bassano

Silver spoon with Venetian lion finial

Red and gold mask

Masks *(see pp30–31)*
Mask designs range from Commedia dell'Arte motifs to modern abstracts from young designers, and many are intricate and colourful. They are available all year, but at Carnival time you can buy them from street stalls.

Carnival mask

Colourful child's sweater

Clothing
As everywhere in Italy, stylish designer shops abound. Clothes for children are particularly bright and inventive. Velvet slippers, which are made in rich jewel-like colours, are worn at home as well as to dress up in at Carnival time.

Velvet slippers

Pasta
Attractively packaged dried pasta comes in many colours, shapes and flavours. Tomato, herb and spinach are the most popular varieties, but beetroot, garlic, artichoke, salmon, squid, and even chocolate can also be found in many shops.

Artichoke

Beetroot

Squid

Pasta shapes

Balsamic vinegar and extra virgin olive oil

Panettone

Amaretto biscuits

Orange liqueur   **Lime liqueur**   **Pear liqueur**

Delicacies from the Veneto
Panettone is the light yeast cake, flavoured with vanilla and studded with currants and candied peel, that is traditionally eaten at Christmas. Other local delicacies include olive oil from the shores of Lake Garda, vinegars, mountain honey from Belluno, fruit-flavoured liqueurs, grappa from Bassano (see p166), and after-dinner Amaretto biscuits.

ENTERTAINMENT IN THE VENETO

Venice was once one of Europe's liveliest night-time cities, and today it still has an impressive range of special events throughout the year. At every season there are some splendid festivals unique to Venice, and in late summer the normal city diet of opera, theatre and concerts is augmented by the International Film Festival and the Biennale, which rank among the best world-class cultural events. The day-to-day evening entertainment in Venice itself now tends to be far less frenetic than in the heyday of the Republic (see pp46–7), but there

Poster advertising the Film Festival

are a few clubs and discos, and many more across the causeway in Mestre. Or you could have a little flutter at the casino.

Whatever you choose, your enjoyment will be enhanced by the idyllic backdrop of Venice itself. The ultimate and quintessential Venetian romantic experience is, of course, a gondola ride by moonlight (see p284). However, an evening's entertainment could more usually comprise the traditional stroll, or *passeggiata*, followed by a drink at a bar or café in one of the squares or amid the floodlit splendours of the Piazza San Marco.

PRACTICAL INFORMATION

Information about what's on in Venice can be found in *Leo Bussola*, a free bilingual Italian and English booklet published quarterly by the Tourist Board. Another publication, *Un Ospite di Venezia* (A Guest in Venice), is produced by the Hotels' Association. This comes out fortnightly during the summer and monthly in the winter, and is available from most hotels. The Venetian newspaper *Il Gazzettino* also lists cinema performances, rock concerts and discos under *Spettacoli*. Look out for posters advertising forthcoming cultural events, which are displayed all over town.

For details of events and festivities in the other towns and cities in the Veneto, ask at the local tourist offices. Regional newspapers also often have listings of what is on in their area.

Music and coffee at Caffè Florian, Piazza San Marco (see p251)

BOOKING TICKETS

Booking in advance is not part of the Italian lifestyle, where decisions are made on the spur of the moment. If you want to be certain of a seat you will have to visit the box office in person, as they usually do not take bookings over the telephone. You may

also have to pay an advance booking supplement, or *prevendita,* which is usually about 10 per cent of the price of the seat.

The price of a theatre ticket starts at about €16, though prices are likely to be five times as much for star-name performances. Tickets for popular music concerts are normally sold through record and music shops whose names are displayed on the publicity posters.

Whereas tickets for classical concerts are sold on the spot for that day's performance, opera tickets are booked months ahead. There are very few ticket touts, so it is almost impossible to obtain tickets when the box office has sold out. The **Goldoni** box office is open 10am–1pm and 3–7pm.

La Fenice opera house before the 1996 fire (see p93)

CINEMA AND THE FILM FESTIVAL

There are four cinemas in Venice, mainly showing dubbed versions of international films. These are known as *prima visione* (first run). The **Giorgione Movie d'Essai** shows "art-house" films as well as the usual commercial fare. You will find these listed in *Il Gazzettino*.

The annual Film Festival, which takes place in August and September, is one of the major world cinema showcases and has been running since 1932. Screenings are held in the **Palazzo del Cinema** on the Lido, and in several cinemas in Venice itself. Tickets are sold to the public direct from the cinema on the day of performance. Programmes can be obtained in advance from the tourist office, and you will see posters for the festival displayed all over the city.

Outdoor entertainment in the courtyard of the Doge's Palace

Gondolier serenading on the Grand Canal

MUSIC AND THEATRE

Like many Italian cities, Venice makes good use of the most magnificent churches as concert halls. La Pietà *(see p112)* was Vivaldi's own church and is still used for concerts, as are the churches of the Frari *(see pp102–3)* and Santo Stefano *(see p93)*. Other concerts are held from time to time in Scuola di San Giovanni Evangelista *(see p104)* and the Palazzo Prigioni Vecchie, the old prison attached to the Doge's Palace *(see pp84–9)*. In the summer, the garden

of Ca' Rezzonico *(see p126)* is also used as an outdoor concert hall, as is the Doge's Palace's courtyard, albeit occasionally.

La Fenice *(see p93)*, one of Italy's most charming opera houses and the main local venue for major operas, suffered a disastrous fire in early 1996. It re-opened in November 2004 and now shares the opera, classical music and ballet programme with **Teatro Malibran**.

Venice's principal theatre is **Teatro Goldoni** where, not surprisingly, the repertoire is mainly drawn from the 250 or more comic works written by the Venetian dramatist Carlo Goldoni (1707–93). Most performances are staged in Italian and run from November to June.

At Carnival time in February *(see pp30–31)*, the whole city takes on a party atmosphere as it is invaded by merry-makers in fancy dress. Many theatrical and musical events take place, both in theatres and in the streets and *campi*.

FACILITIES FOR THE DISABLED

Access for disabled people is difficult everywhere in Venice, and theatres are no exception, although concerts are often held in easily accessible churches. PalaFenice and Teatro Malibran guarantee obstacle-free entrance for the disabled if contacted one week in advance (fax: 041 786 50). For more advice, see page 269.

Masked reveller at Carnival time *(see pp30–31)*

THE BIENNALE AND OTHER EXHIBITIONS

Venice is without doubt one of the leading art exhibition centres in Europe, offering shows on themes ranging from art history to photography, and frequently playing host to the world's major travelling exhibitions. There are excellent facilities for such exhibitions, and these include the Doge's Palace, the Museo Correr, the Palazzo Grassi, the Querini-Stampalia, the Peggy Guggenheim and the Fondazione Cini. *Un Ospite di Venezia* will give details, as will the tourist office and posters around the city.

One of the best and largest exhibitions is the Biennale, an international display of contemporary and avant-garde art which was first begun in 1895. It is held from June to September in odd-numbered years. The main site is the Giardini Pubblici *(see p121)*, where the specially built pavilions represent about 40 different countries. Another branch of the exhibition showing the work of less established artists, takes place around the city in venues such as the old rope factory in the Arsenale *(see p119)*. The Biennale also organizes architecture, theatre, dance and music festivals.

Exhibit by Larry Rivers at the 1992 Biennale exhibition

CASINOS, CLUBS AND DISCOS

If you want to gamble or play roulette during your visit to Venice, there is a magnificent casino housed in the **Palazzo Vendramin-Calergi** on the Grand Canal *(see p61)* and you can sweep up to the stately entrance by gondola.

The **Antico Martini** is the best-known late-night club. Open until 2am, it has live music in smart surroundings. A few other bars also feature live bands, including the **Paradiso Perduto** in Cannaregio. Discos are few and far between in Venice. You could try **Piccolo Mondo**, near the Accademia, **Café Blue**, near Piazzale Roma, or alternatively go to the mainland, where Mestre has many discos to choose from. You will find these clubs advertised in the *Spettacoli* listings in *Il Gazzettino*.

SPORT AND CHILDREN

Venetians are very keen on rowing and sailing. There are several clubs in the city, and the tourist office will be able to give you information. Most of the other sporting facilities are on the Lido, where you can ride, swim, cycle, and play golf or tennis.

In the city itself, there are few attractions for young children, but the mainland is more promising. Around Lake Garda there are plenty of watersports and a theme park, Gardaland *(see p205)*.

MUSIC AND THEATRE IN VERONA

Verona has two exceptional venues for theatre and music: the superb Arena *(see p195)*, and the 1st-century Teatro Romano *(see p202)* on the far side of the River Adige. Both stage open-air performances during the summer months.

The Arena is a popular site for rock concerts, and is internationally renowned for its summer opera season. The Teatro Romano stages a succession of ballets and drama, including a Shakespeare Festival, in Italian translation. Tickets for the Teatro can be ordered by post; they are also sold at the box office at the Arena. Tickets to some events are free. Information about all the entertainment is given in the Verona newspaper, *L'Arena*.

Placido Domingo singing at the Verona Festival

OPERA AT THE ARENA

Almost everyone will enjoy the experience of hearing opera in the magnificent open-air setting of the Arena. Real opera buffs should be aware, however, that Verona performances are very much "opera for all". You should be prepared for less-than-perfect acoustics, noisy audiences, and even small children running about. The opera season runs from the first week in July until the beginning of September, and every year features a lavish production of Verdi's *Aida*. Performances start at 9pm, as dusk is falling, and it is customary to buy one of the little candles that are on sale. Ten minutes before the "curtain

Giant dragon at the Gardaland theme park, Lake Garda *(see p205)*

◁ Venice's colourful Marriage with the Sea festival

Aida, performed annually in Verona's Roman Arena

goes up", the whole Arena becomes a breathtaking sight, with a sea of flickering lights.

During the intervals, most people eat the picnics they have brought with them, or buy *panini* and ice creams. Glass bottles are not allowed in the Arena, so if you are taking a drink make sure it is in a plastic bottle. Be warned that toilets are few and far between and are most likely to have lengthy queues during the intervals.

Ticket prices are high, though there are some concessions. An unreserved, un-numbered, backless seat in the *gradinata*, or tiers, is €21, while the *poltrone*, literally "armchairs", either on the steps or in the stalls, range from €85 to €160. If you decide to get a cheap seat, arrive at least two hours before the performance and sit halfway down the tiers, where the acoustics are better. You can hire an air cushion for about €3. Numbered seats

are more comfortable, but seats lower in the Arena can be very hot and airless and the view of the stage can be restricted. You may well prefer to sacrifice comfort for fresh air and a bird's-eye view. Unless you have a seat in the best stalls with the glitterati, there is no need to dress up.

Visitors flock to Verona to attend the opera season, so you need to book accommodation well in advance.

DIRECTORY

MUSIC AND THEATRE

Teatro La Fenice
Campo San Fantin,
San Marco 1965.
Tel 041 24 24.
www.teatro
lafenice.it

Teatro Goldoni
Calle Goldoni,
San Marco 4650/B.
Map 7 A2.
Tel 041 240 20 11.
www.teatrostabile
veneto.it

Teatro Malibran
Corte del Milion,
Cannaregio 5873.
Map 7 B1.
Tel 041 24 24.
www.teatro
lafenice.it

CINEMAS

Giorgione Movie d'Essai
Rio Terra dei Franceschi,
Cannaregio 4612. **Map** 7
A2. *Tel 041 522 62 98.*

Multisala Astra
Via Corfù 9, Lido.
Tel 041 526 57 36.

Palazzo del Cinema
Lungomare G Marconi,
Lido. *Tel 041 272 65 01.*

CASINOS, CLUBS AND DISCOS

Antico Martini
Campo San Fantin, San
Marco 1980. **Map** 7 A2.
Tel 041 522 41 21.

Café Blue
Calle della Scuola,
Dorsoduro 3778.
Map 5 C1.
Tel 041 522 76 13.

Palazzo Vendramin-Calergi
Strada Nuova,
Cannaregio 2040.
Tel 041 529 71 11.

Paradiso Perduto
Fondamenta della Miseri-
cordia, Cannaregio 2540.
Map 1 C4.
Tel 041 72 05 81.

Piccolo Mondo
Calle Corfù, Dorsoduro
1056/A. **Map** 6 E3.
Tel 041 520 03 71.

SPORTS

Cycling
Bruno Lazzari
21/B Gran Viale, Lido.
Tel 041 526 80 19.

Golf
Alberoni
Lido. *Tel 041 73 13 33.*
www.circologolf
venezia.it

Rowing
Canottieri Bucintoro
Punta Dogana,
Dorsoduro 15. **Map** 7 B4.
Tel 041 520 56 30.
www.bucintoro.org

Tennis
Tennis Club Venezia
Lungomare G Marconi
41/d, Lido. *Tel 041 526
03 35.*

VERONA OPERA

Main box office
ENTE Arena
Piazza Brà 28, 37121
Verona. *Tel 045 800 51 51.*
Fax 045 801 32 87.
www.arena.it

Ticket agent
Vertours
Galleria Pelliciai 13,
37121 Verona.
Tel 045 929 82 00.
Fax 045 595 748.
www.vertours.com

SPECIALIST HOLIDAYS AND OUTDOOR ACTIVITIES

The Veneto's rich cultural heritage and wide range of natural landscapes makes it a perfect location for numerous specialist holidays and outdoor excursions. The city of Venice hosts a dazzling array of study courses and craft workshops, including traditional mask-making and glass-blowing. It is also an unforgettable location in which to learn Italian. Outside of the city, the region's coastal and inland waterways provide space for many types of boating as well as more active watersports and bird-watching. The towering mountains in the alpine hinterland are challenging walking and climbing country, while in the winter there is skiing, facilitated by an excellent network of cable cars and lifts. Between mountain and sea are gentle hills, perfect for horse-riding enthusiasts and home to various relaxing local spas.

Skiing in the mountains

Cookery courses at Tasting Places

COOKERY COURSES AND WINE TASTING

Visitors wishing to discover the secrets of the local cusine should try one of the cookery courses on offer in Venice. Most include a shopping visit to the fish and fresh produce market at Rialto followed by the preparation of a meal using seasonal ingredients. The enthusiastic young chefs at **Venice & Veneto Gourmet** cater to groups. Alternatively, longer intensive classes are held, often by Michelin-starred chefs, at the exclusive Hotel Cipriani *(see p233)*. In the hills outside Verona a magnificent country estate hosts tempting cooking classes run by **Tasting Places**. The Rome-based organisation **Delicious Italy** can arrange for residential cooking lessons around the Veneto that focus specifically on regional specialities.

Lessons on wine appreciation are organised by **Millevini**, a well-stocked winery at the foot of the Rialto bridge.

ARTS AND CRAFTS

Each summer the **Venice in Peril Fund** organises a series of lectures on the precious heritage of the city, aimed at history of art enthusiasts.

More practical courses are given by expert local craftspeople to anyone wishing to discover the intricacies of a range of crafts. Following a centuries-old tradition of glass-making, the **Scuola del Vetro Abate Zanetti** prides itself on teaching traditional and contemporary methods and styles at its brand-new premises on the island of Murano, the heart of the city's glass trade. Glass-making is also on offer through the craft organisation Confartigianato, as are lessons in furniture restoration. Techniques for repairing stucco and marble work can be learned at the well-established **European School for the Trades and Professions** set in the grounds of Villa Fabris near Vicenza.

Visitors interested in ceramics can join hands-on sessions at the cosy **Laboratorio Fustat** in Campo S. Margherita, where oriental raku and Italian styles are practised. Lessons in crafting papier-mâché carnival masks are given at the dynamic **Ca' Macana** workshop and can be followed in several different European languages.

Year-round courses in oil and watercolour painting, as well as printmaking, are run by the friendly atelier **Bottega del Tintoretto**. A larger institution, with a vast range of open-air painting and graphics classes, is the **Scuola Internazionale di Grafica.** Courses on old textiles are occasionally held at **Palazzo Mocenigo**, home to the Centro Studi di Storia del Tessuto e del Costume. Even the ancient intricate art of lace-making is still demonstrated, by its few remaining expert practitioners, at the **Museo del Merletto** on the distant and colourful island of Burano.

Students gaining practical experience in restoration techniques

Climbing in the spectacular Dolomites

WALKING AND CLIMBING

During the summer and autumn months keen walkers and trekkers should head straight up to the imposing Dolomites, where hundreds of kilometres of clearly marked pathways wind their way through brightly flowered meadows and spectacular rocky landscapes. Easy access combined with a net work of high-altitude refuge huts make this a very accessible activity. For walkers who require extra assistance, **Cortina Guides** can provide specialist help with their team of friendly experts. **Club Alpino Italiano** offers qualified alpine guides for such climbs as the *via ferrata* routes, as well as for more general walking tours. The club has branches in all major towns, so it is not difficult to find help when needed. UK-based **Colletts Mountain Holidays** also offers a good range of walking and climbing trips.

WATER SPORTS

A quick glance at a map reveals the many coastal and inland waterways along the Veneto's Adriatic coast. With so much water around it is unsurprising that water sports are a speciality here. It is possible to explore the region at your own pace by hiring a motor boat from **Brussa is Boat**. (Customers will need to demonstrate some experience in handling craft.) Another truly unique holiday can be experienced on a houseboat in the lagoon, exploring its myriad islands and waterways. **Italiabella** have a fleet anchored at Chioggia, while **Houseboat Holidays Italia** are based at Porto Levante in the Po Delta. For those who have never sailed before, or would like a more relaxed trip, **Il Bragozzo** arrange day trips on the Venice Lagoon, with an experienced sailor at the helm.

In Venice there are many opportunities to take advantage of the waterways. A good sense of balance and plenty of energy are required for rowing in the traditional standing-up style. Clubs such as the **Bucintoro** on the Zattere, active since 1882, welcome visitors and provide lessons for novices. Sailing enthusiasts, on the other hand, can contact one of the city's clubs: those keen on old-style wooden craft with colourful sails should contact the **Associazione Vela al Terzo**, or for sleek modern yachts there is the prestigious **Compagnia della Vela**, which is based on the island of San Giorgio.

Further afield Lake Garda is the place for windsurfers. Schools such as **Surfsegnana**, at Torbole in the northern reaches of the lake, offer a good range of courses and holidays. The lake also guarantees superb swimming, especially off Sirmione in the south, where the bleached rocks and crystal clear water are reminiscent of the Caribbean. A string of yellow-sand beaches line the Adriatic coast of the Veneto. Well frequented in summer by the locals, the Veneto seaside resorts also cater to the needs of overseas visitors. Caorle and Jesolo, close to Venice, are very popular as is Rosolina Mare and Albarella, which is near the Po Delta. The Venice Lido is also a very pleasant place to swim, although a fee is charged to use the beach huts. For a free public beach head along to the Alberoni.

Lastly, for those in search of a more challenging experience, there is white-water rafting and canoeing at Valstagna on the Brenta River. The experienced crew at **Ivan Team** can arrange a craft, with all the necessary equipment, and transport.

Windsurfing near Torbole Lago di Garda Veneto

LANGUAGE COURSES

One of the best and most beautiful places to learn the Italian language is in Venice. Visitors who are keen to take part in a course should enrol in Italian for Foreigners at the **Centro Linguistico Interfacoltà** of the Ca' Foscari University. Classes are in an atmospheric modernised palazzo and are supplemented by access to well-stocked multimedia labs with all manner of support material. Another centrally located school is the **Istituto Venezia**, which offers a good range of lessons, as well as arranging for concerts, cultural initiatives and excursions. Accommodation is either homestays or self-catering flats.

WINTER SPORTS

A winter holiday in the breath-taking Dolomite mountains can include an extraordinary range of activities. Wrapped up warm and plastered with high-factor sun protection cream, visitors in need of relaxation can laze on the sun decks in the ski resorts. Those in search of exciting downhill skiing can head for Arabba, which has a superb series of cable cars to whisk skiers up to the snow fields, including the Marmolada glacier. Val Zoldana, dominated by the magnificent Civetta and Pelmo mountains, is another excellent location. If a chic ambience is important, you must stay at Cortina d'Ampezzo, which hosted the Winter Olympics in 1956 and now boasts excellent modern ski facilities and lifts, including the Tofana cable car. All the resorts are managed by **Dolomiti Superski**, which includes 12 ski areas and an amazing 1,200 km (750 miles) of pistes all covered by a single pass. Slopes for intrepid snow-boarders are also included.

Toddlers to adults, beginners to more advanced skiers, and anyone in between can attend the ski school run by the qualified ski instructors of the **Scuola Sci** which is found at all the main centres.

Cortina d'Ampezzo, Alleghe and Val Zoldana also have indoor ice rinks, which make a refreshing change to the high energy of the slopes.

Experienced skiers wishing to get away from the pistes can join a group accompanied by a local alpine guide to explore the more secluded slopes. Snow-shoeing is also undergoing a revival. Guides and modern equipment can be found at all the major resorts. There is superb cross-country skiing in the Veneto. The vast undulating Asiago plateau north of Vicenza has hundreds of kilometres of prepared tracks for both classical and skating techniques. Contact the **Consorzio Turistico** for information about the main centres, such as Campolongo and Enego, which all have top-level facilities. Further west is the Monti Lessini above Verona, where pistes fan out from Bosco Chiesanuova; the best source of information is the **Lessinia Turistsport**.

SPA HOLIDAYS

As the ancient Romans discovered to their delight, naturally occurring spas are dotted across the Veneto, and visitors can pamper body and mind with a soak in a thermal pool or with a relaxing massage. Abano-Montegrotto Terme in the Euganean Hills has numerous hotels with steaming outdoor and indoor pools, catering to both long-term and day visitors. The **Consorzio Terme Euganee** can help organise your holiday.

Further afield, on the southern shore of Lake Garda, is the state-of-the-art spa facilities at **Terme di Sirmione**, which continue a tradition going back to the 1500s.

BIRDWATCHING

Pink flamingoes flock in spectacular numbers to the sprawling **Po Delta Park** in the winter months, though the local waterfowl are worth visiting at any time of year. Also, on the western edge of the Venice Lagoon, located on the Romea road that links Mestre with Chioggia, is the wetland reserve **Oasi Valle Averto**, run by the World Wide Fund for Nature. This reserve is accessible by bus.

Horse riding at Salten Jenesien

HORSERIDING AND GOLF

The rolling Euganean Hills east of Venice together with the foothills of the Dolomites have plenty of quiet roads and lanes suitable for horse riding. Several agriturismo establishments, such as **Il Faè** near Conegliano and **Le Frassanelle** beyond Padua, keep stables and all the facilities needed for riding holidays. Le Frassanelle also has access to a golf course.

Many of the other notable golfing facilities in the Veneto are to be found in the hinterland. These include a course in the lovely garden premises of **Golf Club Villa Condulmer** at Mogliano. However, for a game with a difference, visitors can play a few rounds at the **Circolo Golf Venezia** at Alberoni, situated on the Venice Lido.

Cable car and downhill slopes in the Dolomite mountains

DIRECTORY

COOKERY COURSES AND WINE TASTING

Delicious Italy
Via Angelo Piliziano 58,
Rome. *Tel 064 547 61 23.*
www.deliciousitaly.com

Millevini
San Marco 5362, Venice.
Map 7 B1.
Tel 041 520 60 90.

Tasting Places London
Tel +44 (0)2089 645 333.
www.tastingplaces.com

Venice & Veneto Gourmet
www.veneceveneto
gourmet.com

ARTS AND CRAFTS

Bottega del Tintoretto
Fondamenta dei Mori
Cannaregio 3400, Venice.
Map 2 F3.
Tel 041 722 081.
www.tintorettovenezia.it

Ca' Macana
Calle delle Botteghe,
Dorsoduro 3172, Venice.
Map 6 D3.
Tel 041 277 61 42.
www.camacana.com

European School for the Trades and Professions
Villa Fabris, Via Trieste 43,
Thiene.
Tel 0445 372 329.
www.artigiani.vi.it

Laboratorio Fustat
Campo S. Margherita,
Dorsoduro 2904, Venice.
Map 6 D2.
Tel 041 523 85 04.

Museo del Merletto
Piazza Galuppi 187,
Burano, Venice.
Tel 041 73 00 34.
www.museicivici
veneziani.it

Palazzo Mocenigo
Santa Croce 1992, Venice.
Map 2 F5.
Tel 041 72 17 98.
www.museicivici
veneziani.it

Scuola del Vetro Abate Zanetti
Calle Briati 8/b, Murano,
Venice. **Map** 4 F2.
Tel 041 273 77 11.
www.abatezanetti.it

Scuola Internazionale di Grafica
Calle del Cristo, Cannaregio
1798, Venice. **Map** 2 E4.
Tel 041 721 950.
www.scuolagrafica.it

Venice in Peril Fund
Unit 4, Hurlingham
Studios, Ranelagh
Gardens, London, UK.
Tel (44) 02077 366 891.
www.veniceinperil.org

WALKING AND CLIMBING

Cortina Guides Office
Corso Italia 69/a, Cortina
d'Ampezzo.
Tel 043 686 85 05.
www.guidecortina.com

Club Alpino Italiano
www.cai.it

Colletts Mountain Holidays
Harvest Mead, Great
Hormead, Buntingford,
Herts. UK.
Tel (44) 01763 289 660.
www.colletts.co.uk

WATER SPORTS

Associazione Vela al Terzo
www.velaalterzo.it

Brussa is Boat
Ponte delle Guglie,
Cannaregio 331, Venice.
Map 2 D3.
Tel 041 715 787.
www.brussaisboat.it

Bucintoro Rowing Club
Zattere, Dorsoduro 15,
Venice. **Map** 7 A4.
Tel 041 520 56 30.
www.bucintoro.org

Compagnia della Vela
S. Marco 2, Venice.
Map 7 A3.
Tel 041 520 08 84.
www.compvela.com

Houseboat Holidays Italia
Via C. Colombo 36/A,
Porto Levante,
Porto Viro.
Tel 042 666 60 25.
www.houseboat.it

Il Bragozzo
Tel 388 182 60 10
www.ilbragozzo.it

Italiabella
Viale delle Terme 163,
Abano Terme.
Tel 049 667 201.

Ivan Team
Via Oliero di Sotto 85,
Valstagna.
Tel 042 455 82 50.
www.ivanteam.com

Surfsegnana
Foci del Sarca, Torbole.
Tel 046 450 59 63.
www.surfsegnana.it

LANGUAGE COURSES

Centro Linguistico Interfacoltà
Campiello San Sebastiano,
Dorsoduro 1686, Venice.
Map 5 C3.
Tel 041 234 97 13.
www.unive.it/cli

Isituto Venezia
Campo S. Margherita,
Dorsoduro 3116a, Venice.
Map 6 D2.
Tel 041 522 43 31.
www.istitutovenezia.com

WINTER SPORTS

Consorzio Turistico
Asiago 7 Comuni Viale,
Trento Trieste 19, Asiago.
Tel 0424 464137.
www.asiago7comuni.to

Dolomiti Superski
www.dolomitisuperski.
com

Lessinia Turistsport
www.leturispo.it

Scuola Sci Alleghe Civetta
Corso Italia 20, Alleghe.
Tel 043 772 37 16.
www.scuolascialleghe
civetta.it

Scuola Sci Arabba
Passo Pordoi, Arabba.
Tel 043 679 160.
www.scuolasciarabba.com

Scuola Sci Cortina d'Ampezzo
Corso Italia 67, Cortina
d'Ampezzo.
Tel 043 629 11.
www.scuolascicortina.com

SPA HOLIDAYS

Consorzio Terme Euganee
Largo Marconi 8, Abano
Terme.
Tel 049 866 66 62.
www.abanomontegrotto.it

Terme di Sirmione
Piazza Virgillo 1, Sirmione.
Tel 030 916 81.
www.termedisirmione.com

BIRDWATCHING

Oasi Valle Averto
Lugo di Campagnalupia.
Tel 041 518 50 68.
www.wwf.it/oasi

Po Delta Park
Visitors Centre Ca'
Vendramin, Taglio di Po.
Tel 042 638 09 04.
www.parcodeltapo.org

HORSERIDING AND GOLF

Circolo Golf Venezia
Strada Vecchia 1, Alberoni,
Lido di Venezia.
Tel 041 731 333.
www.circologolfvenezia.it

Il Faè
Via Fae, S. Pietro di Feletto.
Tel 043 878 71 17.
www.ilfae.com

Le Frassanelle
35030 Rovolon.
Tel 049 875 12 34.
www.frassanelle.it

Golf Club Villa Condulmer
Via della Croce 3, Zerman
di Mogliano, Veneto.
Tel 041 457 062.
www.golfvillacondulmer.
com

SURVIVAL GUIDE

PRACTICAL INFORMATION

The enormous wealth of art and architecture found in Venice and the historic cities of Padua, Verona and Vicenza can dazzle and overwhelm. The best way to avoid cultural overload is to concentrate on sights in the morning, when they are most likely to be open, relax over your lunch as the Italians do, and leave any shopping or sightseeing of churches until the late afternoon or early evening. The inconsistency of museum opening hours and the fact

ENTE NAZIONALE ITALIANO PER IL TURISMO
Tourist Board logo

that some sights or large sections of them are closed for years for restoration can be frustrating. This is particularly true of Venice, where you may often see scaffolding and the signs *chiuso per restauro* (closed for restoration), so it is best to check opening hours with individual museums in advance. However, on the plus side, the principal sights are all within easy walking distance of one another, and exploring by boat and on foot is an exciting experience.

Tourists crossing the white stone Ponte della Paglia

TOURIST INFORMATION

Most towns in the Veneto have tourist offices, and in season Verona and Padua each have two. The offices in smaller towns may be of limited help. In contrast, the Verona offices publish a useful free booklet, *Agenda di Verona*, with information on what to see and do. Travel agents can supply information on city and other tours on offer. Tourist offices in Venice provide city maps, lists of accommodation, *vaporetto* maps and other literature. Tourist offices and hotels also have leaflets on local entertainment and events *(see pp32–5)*. To obtain information prior to travel, contact **ENIT** (Italian State Tourist Board) in your home country, or write to the **Azienda di Promozione Turistica di Venezia**.

The **Forum per la Laguna**, a cultural association promoting the lagoon area, also has an information service on Venice and the surrounding area.

GUIDED TOURS

City tours in Venice with English-speaking guides (by foot or motorboat) can be booked through many agencies, including **American Express, Venice-scapes** and **Bucintoro**. In Verona and Padua half-day tours are organized in the tourist season by each town's tourist office. Boat trips along the Brenta Canal *(see pp182–3)* between Venice and Padua are available from March to late October. **Venice Events'** tours of the hills of the Veneto depart from Venice daily. They also offer walking holidays in the Dolomites.

i

AZIENDA
PROMOZIONE
TURISTICA

A Tourist Information sign

MUSEUMS AND MONUMENTS

The opening hours of museums, galleries and palaces change frequently. Ask at the local tourist office for a list of opening times or, if in Venice, consult the free booklets *Leo Bussola* or *Un Ospite di Venezia*. Civic museums are often shut on Mondays, otherwise there is no pattern to opening times. Many places shut at 1pm or 2pm and do not re-open in the afternoon. Most museums charge an admission fee, but there may be concessions for children, students and, in a few cases, senior citizens. In Venice, a "Museum Card" is available, givng one year's entrance to many museums. Churches are often open in the mornings from around 9am until noon, then again from mid-afternoon until 6 or 7pm.

A selection of local tourist information publications

A mechanically operated
wheelchair ramp across a bridge

VENICE FOR THE DISABLED

The stepped bridges of Venice make it almost impossible for the disabled to get around the city. A further problem are the *vaporetti*, particularly the *motoscafi*, which are hazardous for those confined to wheelchairs *(see pp282–3)*.

One of the few aids for the disabled is the plan of the city prepared by the Tourist Board. This shows places of interest which can be visited by the disabled, and how to reach them by *vaporetto* or by streets avoiding any bridges. Few of the sights have special facilities for the disabled, but a few important bridges have now been fitted with mechanically operated ramps. The key is always available from the tourist office.

The Venice tourist office brochure that lists available accommodation also indicates which hotels are suitable for disabled guests.

ETIQUETTE

Any attempt by visitors to speak Italian is always appreciated by the local people. Few people speak English in the Veneto, but hotel receptionists are usually helpful and will readily offer to make any enquiries and reservations on your behalf.

To avoid offence always dress decently, particularly if visiting churches, and make sure that you are never drunk in a public place. Smoking is banned in all public buildings, including restaurants and bars, as well as on the *vaporetti*.

Feeding the pigeons in Piazza San Marco is illegal and if caught you may be fined.

VISITING CHURCHES

Bare shoulders and shorts are frowned upon in Italian churches and those unsuitably dressed may well be refused entry. Church interiors tend to be very dark but there are usually coin-operated light meters to illuminate works of art. Make sure you take plenty of coins. Machines that provide recorded information on the church and its artifacts are available to hire, but the commentaries are sometimes inaudible. The majority of churches charge an entrance fee or encourage contributions. Photography is forbidden in most churches.

Pedestrians shopping in Verona

TIPPING

Always keep a few euros close to hand for porters, chambermaids, restaurant staff and custodians of churches. Italian taxi drivers do not expect a tip and there is no need to tip a gondolier.

WCS (RESTROOMS)

There are few public toilets in the Veneto, although Venice is better served. Those in Venice are usually signposted and cost about 50 cents. You can also use those at the station, or toilets in cafés, bars, or museums. Ask for *il bagno* or *il gabinetto*. The toilets are always short of paper, so it is a good idea to carry tissues with you.

Students relaxing in the sun in Verona

IMMIGRATION AND CUSTOMS

European Union (EU) residents and visitors from the United States, Canada, Australia and New Zealand do not need visas for stays of up to three months. However, all visitors need to bring a full passport. A visa is needed for stays longer than three months. It is advisable for all visitors to check their requirements before travelling.

All visitors to Italy should, by law, register with the police within three days of arrival. Most hotels will register visitors when they check in. If in doubt, contact a local police department or phone the **Questura**.

In 1999, the intra-EU Duty and Tax Free Allowances, better known as Duty-free, were abolished. However, for EU residents the amount of these goods that can be imported for personal use has increased. Consulates can provide information on customs regulations. To find

out what you can take back from Italy to non-EU countries, contact that particular country's customs office.

The refund system for Value Added Tax (IVA in Italy) for non-EU residents is complicated and is worth reclaiming only if you have spent at least €160 in one single establishment.

STUDENT INFORMATION

An International Student Identity Card (ISIC) or a Youth International Educational Exchange Card (YIEE) will usually get reductions on museum admissions and other charges. Venice Municipality's Rolling Venice card for 14- to 29-year-olds offers, for a small fee, a package of useful information on the city. It includes alternative itineraries, fashionable haunts, and lists of shops, hotels, theatres and restaurants offering card-holder discounts.

Discount rail tickets are sold at CTS, near the university, and at the train station, from the front desk situated to the right of the entrance.

EDUCATIONAL COURSES

In Venice, the **Società Dante Alighieri**, the **Istituto Venezia** and the **Venice University Centro Linguistico** organize Italian courses for foreigners. In Padua the **Istituto Linguistico Bertrand Russell** organizes Italian language courses that run throughout the year.

The **Istituto Europeo di Design**, situated on the island of Certosa, offers summer courses. Three- and four-week courses in English are available in the fields of fashion, design and the visual arts. The **Scuola Internazionale di Gràfica** in Venice specializes in short summer courses in painting, printing and sketching.

NEWSPAPERS, RADIO AND TV

The local newspapers are the *Gazzettino* and the *Nuova Venezia*. European and American newspapers and magazines are available at the main news kiosks, normally a day or two after publication. The state TV channels are RAI Uno, RAI Due and RAI Tre. Satellite and cable TV transmit European channels in many languages, as well as CNN news in English. BBC World Service is broadcast on radio on 15.070 MHz (short wave) in the mornings and 648 KHz (medium wave) at night.

Newspaper stall selling a variety of national publications

Standard Italian plug

EMBASSIES AND CONSULATES

If you lose your passport or need other help, contact your national embassy or consulate as listed in the directory below.

ELECTRICAL ADAPTORS

Electrical current in Italy is 220V AC, with either two- or three-pin, round-pronged plugs. It is probably better to purchase an adaptor before leaving for Italy. Most hotels graded above three star have electrical points for shavers and hairdryers in all bedrooms.

ITALIAN TIME

Italy is one hour ahead of Greenwich Mean Time (GMT). The time difference between Venice and other

The clock of San Giacomo di Rialto in San Polo, Venice

cities is: London: –1 hour; New York: –6 hours; Perth: +7 hours; Auckland: +11 hours; Tokyo: +8 hours. Daylight saving time is between April and October. For all official purposes the Italians use the 24-hour clock.

CONVERSION TABLE

Imperial to Metric
1 inch = 2.54 centimetres
1 foot = 30 centimetres
1 mile = 1.6 kilometres
1 ounce = 28 grams
1 pound = 454 grams
1 pint = 0.6 litres
1 gallon = 4.6 litres

Metric to Imperial
1 centimetre = 0.4 inches
1 metre = 3 feet, 3 inches
1 kilometre = 0.6 miles
1 gram = 0.04 ounces
1 kilogram = 2.2 pounds
1 litre = 1.8 pints

DIRECTORY

POLICE (QUESTURA)

Venice
Santa Croce 500.
Tel 041 271 55 11.

Vicenza
Viale Mazzini 213.
Tel 0444 33 75 11.

Padua
Piazza G. Polatucci 5.
Tel 049 83 31 11.

Verona
Lungadige Galtarossa 11.
Tel 045 809 04 11.

STUDENT INFORMATION

Comune di Venezia
(Informagiovani), Viale Garibaldi 155, Mestre.
Tel 041 534 62 68.
www.veneziagiovane.net

CTS
Calle Foscari,
Dorsoduro 3252, Venice.
Map 6 D2.
Tel 041 520 56 60.

Ferrovia dello Stato
Fondamenta Santa Lucia,
Cannaregio, Venice.
Tel 041 89 20 21.
www.trenitalia.com

Hellovenezia
Piazzale Roma, Santa Croce, Venice.
Tel 041 24 24.
www.hellovenezia.it

EDUCATIONAL COURSES

Istituto Europeo di Design
Isola della Certosa 51,
30126 Venice.
Tel 041 277 11 64.
www.ied.it

Istituto Linguistico Bertrand Russell
Via Filiberto 6, 35122
Padua. *Tel 049 65 40 51.*

Istituto Venezia
Campo Santa Margherita,
Dorsoduro 3116/a, Venice.
Map 6 D2.
Tel 041 522 43 31.

Società Dante Alighieri
Sant'Elena 3, Venice.
Tel 041 523 45 90.
www.venicedante alighieri.it

Scuola Internazionale di Gràfica
Calle del Cristo, Cannaregio 1798, Venice. **Map** 2 E4. *Tel 041 72 19 50.*
www.scuolagrafica.it

Venice University Centro Linguistico
Campiello San Sebastiano,
Dorsoduro 1686.
Tel 041 234 97 13.

EMBASSIES AND CONSULATES

Australia
Via Antonio Bosio 5,
Rome. *Tel 06 85 27 21.*

Canada
Riviera Ruzzante 25,
Padua. *Tel 049 876 48 33.*

New Zealand
Via Clitunno 44, Rome.
Tel 06 853 75 01.

United Kingdom
Via XX Settembre 804,
Rome. *Tel 064 220 00 01.*

US
Via Principe Amedeo 2/10,
Milan. *Tel 02 29 03 51.*

RELIGIOUS SERVICES

Anglican
St George's Anglican Church, Campo San Vio,
Dorsoduro, Venice.
Map 6 F4.
Tel 041 520 05 71.

Greek Orthodox
Greek Orthodox Church
Ponte dei Greci,
Castello 3412,
Venice. **Map** 8 D2.
Tel 041 523 95 69.

Jewish
Sinagoga, Ghetto Vecchio,
Cannaregio,
Venice. **Map** 2 D3.
Tel 041 71 53 59.

Lutheran
Chiesa Evangelica
Luterana,
Campo Santi Apostoli,
Cannaregio 4448,
Venice. **Map** 3 B5.
Tel 041 522 71 49.

Methodist
Chiesa Evangelica Valdese
e Metodista, Campo Santa
Maria Formosa, Castello
5170, Venice. **Map** 7 C1.
Tel 041 522 75 49.

Personal Security and Health

Venice is one of the safest cities in Europe. Violent crime is very rare and petty crime minimal in comparison with other main cities. Nevertheless, it is wise to take a few simple precautions, particularly against pickpockets, both in Venice and elsewhere in the Veneto. Leave valuables and any important documents in the hotel safe and carry only the minimum amount of money necessary for the day.

Make sure you take out adequate travel insurance before leaving for Italy, as it is very difficult to obtain once you are in the country.

Venice by night, not always well-lit but safe

LOOKING AFTER YOUR PROPERTY

Travellers' cheques are the safest way to carry large sums of money. Always keep your cheques and your cheque receipts separately to be on the safe side, and keep a photocopy of all vital documents such as your passport.

Safeguard against attracting the attention of pickpockets and bagsnatchers, particularly at railway stations, markets and on the buses. In Venice take extra care while waiting at the *vaporetto* landing stages; be especially vigilant when crowds are jostling to get on to the boats.

If you drive while in the Veneto, always remember to lock the car before you leave it and never leave valuables on display inside. Hired cars or those with foreign number plates are favourite targets of car thieves.

PERSONAL SAFETY

Venice is uneventful by night and you can stroll through the streets without any threat. There is no red light quarter or any area that could be described as unsavoury. Women alone in Venice are unlikely to encounter anything more troublesome than the usual Latin roving eye. Elsewhere in the Veneto, in the less touristy towns particularly, unescorted females are likely to attract more attention.

Avoid unauthorized taxi drivers, who may not be insured and almost invariably overcharge. Airports are their favourite haunts. Make sure you take only official taxis which have the licence number clearly displayed *(see p278)*.

POLICE

The *vigili urbani*, or municipal police, are most often seen in the streets regulating traffic and enforcing local laws. They wear blue uniforms in winter and white during the summer. The *carabinieri*, with red striped trousers, are the armed military police, responsible for public law and order. *La polizia*, or state police, wear blue uniforms with white belts and berets. They specialize in serious crimes. Any of these should be able to help you.

In the event of theft go straight to the nearest police station *(polizia or carabinieri)* to make a statement. If there is a language problem, you should consult your nearest consulate *(see p271)*, which you should also do in the case of a lost passport.

EMERGENCY NUMBERS

Ambulance
Venice
Tel 118.
Verona
Tel 118.
Padua
Tel 118.
Vicenza
Tel 118.

Automobile Club d'Italia
Tel 803 116.
Car accident and breakdown.

Fire
Tel 115.

General SOS
Tel 113.

Medical Emergencies
Tel 118.

Police (Carabinieri)
Tel 112.

Traffic Police
Venice
Tel 041 274 70 70.
Verona
Tel 045 807 84 11.
Padua
Tel 049 820 51 00.
Vicenza
Tel 0444 54 53 11.

MEDICAL PRECAUTIONS

Visitors from the European Union (EU) are entitled to reciprocal state medical care in Italy. Before you travel, obtain a European Health

A group of Venetian Carabinieri on the Riva degli Schiavoni

Insurance Card (EHIC) from the post office or online, which covers you for emergency medical treatment. You may wish to take out additional medical insurance, as an EHIC does not cover repatriation costs. Australia has a reciprocal medical agreement with Italy, but other visitors from outside the EU should take out a comprehensive medical insurance policy. If you are taking prescribed medication, take supplies or prescriptions with you.

Inoculations are not needed for the Veneto, but take sunscreen and mosquito repellent in the summer. Because of the canals, mosquitoes can be irksome in Venice. An electric gadget, from pharmacies or department stores, will repel insects in your room for up to 12 hours. Tap water is safe, but locals often prefer mineral water, either fizzy *(con gas)* or still *(naturale)*.

Electric mosquito deterrent

MEDICAL TREATMENT

If you are in need of urgent medical attention, go to the *Pronto Soccorso* (First Aid) department of the nearest main hospital. Standards of health care are generally better than those in the south of Italy, although not as high as in Britain or the US. There are usually queues at the emergency departments and many hospitals expect the patient's family or friends to help with his or her nursing.

Should you require a consultation with a doctor, ask the advice of your hotel or look in the yellow pages of the telephone directory, under *medici*. (A *dottore* is not necessarily a doctor of medicine.) If you have a serious medical complaint or allergy you should bring a letter, preferably translated, from your doctor at home.

Pharmacy sign

Many doctors in the region speak at least a little English. There are first aid facilities with the services of a doctor at airports and at most railway stations.

Dentists are expensive in Italy. You can find the nearest one in the yellow pages of the telephone directory, listed under *dentisti medici chirurghi*, or ask your hotel receptionist for his or her recommendation.

For insurance claims, make sure you keep all receipts for medical treatment and any medicines prescribed.

Pharmacies are open during the summer months from 8:30am to 12:30pm and 4pm to 8pm Monday to Friday, and from 9am to noon on Saturday. Winter hours are slightly shorter. All towns offer a 24-hour pharmacy service, with a night-time and Sunday rota. You will find the rota posted on the doors of pharmacies. Opening times can also be found in the local newspapers or, if you are in Venice, the booklet *Un Ospite di Venezia*.

Italian pharmacists are well-trained to deal with minor ailments and can prescribe many drugs without needing a doctor's prescription. The majority of pharmacies do not stock quantities of foreign medicines but can usually supply the local equivalent. Many of the words for minor complaints and remedies are similar in Italian, for example *lassativo* (laxative), *aspirina* (aspirin) and *tranquillante* (tranquillizer).

USEFUL INFORMATION

Venice Hospital
Ospedale Civile,
Campo Santi Giovanni e Paolo.
Map 3 C5.
Tel 041 529 41 11.

Verona Hospital
Ospedale Borgo Trento
Piazzale Stefani 1.
Tel 045 812 11 11.

Padua Hospital
Ospedale Civile
Via Giustiniani 2.
Tel 049 821 11 11.

Vicenza Hospital
Ospedale di Vicenza
Via Rodolfi 37.
Tel 044 475 31 11.

Lost Property Offices
Ferrovia Santa Lucia,
Venice. **Map** 1 B4.
Tel 041 78 52 38.
Railway Station, Verona.
Tel 045 802 38 27.
Railway Station, Padua.
Tel 049 822 44 56.

Missing Credit Cards
American Express
Tel 06 72 90 03 47.
Diners Club
Tel 800 86 40 64 (freephone).
Eurocard
Tel 800 87 08 66 (freephone).
MasterCard (Access)
Tel 800 87 08 66 (freephone).
VISA
Tel 800 87 72 32 (freephone).

Missing Travellers' Cheques
American Express
Tel 800 87 20 00 (freephone).
Thomas Cook
Tel 800 87 20 50 (freephone).
VISA
Tel 800 87 41 55 (freephone).

An ambulance boat on the Grand Canal

Banking and Local Currency

Visitors to the Veneto have a number of options available to them for changing money. Banks tend to give more favourable rates than bureaux de change, hotels and travel agents, but the paperwork is usually more time consuming. Alternatively, credit cards can be used for purchasing goods. When changing travellers' cheques you will need to show some form of identification.

Cash dispenser which also accepts VISA and MasterCard (Access)

CHANGING MONEY

Banking hours can be erratic, especially the day before a public holiday, so it is safest to acquire some local currency before you arrive in Italy. Exchange rates will vary from place to place. For the best rates, try a bank (look for the sign *cambio*) or the American Express office *(see p269)*. Hotels tend to give poor rates, even if they charge modest commissions.

A more convenient way to change money is to use the electronic exchange machines. These are found at Marco Polo airport, Venice railway station and at several banks in the city. All major towns in the Veneto have foreign exchange machines. These machines have multilingual instructions and the exchange rate is displayed on screen. You simply feed in notes of the same foreign currency, and you will get euros in return.

TRAVELLERS' CHEQUES

Travellers' cheques are probably the safest way to carry large sums of money.

Choose a name that is well known, such as American Express, or cheques issued through a major bank. Always record the travellers' cheques numbers and keep this information separate from the cheques themselves, in case they are stolen.

There is usually a minimum commission charge, which may make changing small sums of money uneconomical. Some establishments will charge you for each cheque.

Check the exchange rates before you travel and decide whether sterling, dollar or euro travellers' cheques are more appropriate for your trip. Bear in mind that it may be more difficult to cash euro travellers' cheques, especially in hotels, because they are not very profitable for the exchanger.

CREDIT CARDS

Credit cards are widely accepted throughout Italy and it is worth bringing one with you, particularly for hotel and restaurant bills, shopping, car hire and booking tickets by telephone. VISA and Access (MasterCard) are the most popular, with American Express and Diners Club trailing well behind. Some banks and cash dispensers accept VISA or Access for cash advances, although interest is payable once the money is withdrawn. In Venice, cash dispensers accepting credit cards can be found throughout the city, although they may not be so evident in the quieter areas.

Some establishments require a minimum expenditure to accept credit card payment. Always make sure that you have enough cash in case your card is not accepted.

BANKING HOURS

Banks are usually open from 8:30am to 1:30pm, Monday to Friday. Most also open for an hour in the afternoon from about 2:35pm until 3:35pm. They close at weekends and for public holidays, and they also close early the day before a major holiday. Exchange offices stay open longer, but the rates are less favourable. The exchange offices at Venice airport and railway station stay open until the evening and at weekends.

USING BANKS

Changing money at a bank can at times be a frustrating process, as it involves endless form-filling and queuing.

Plaque of the Cassa di Risparmio in Campo Manin

You must apply first at the window displaying the *cambio* sign, then move to the *cassa* to obtain your euros. If in doubt, ask someone in order to avoid waiting in the wrong queue.

For security reasons, most banks have electronic double doors with metal detectors, allowing one person in at a time. Metal objects and bags should first be deposited in lockers situated in the foyer. Press the button to open the outer door, then wait for it to close behind you. The inner door then opens automatically.

If you need to have money sent to you in Italy, banks at home can telex money to an Italian bank, but it takes about a week. American Express, Thomas Cook and Western Union all provide swifter money transfer services.

THE EURO

The euro (€) is the common currency of the European Union (EU). It went into general circulation on 1 January 2002, initially for 12 participating countries. Italy was one of those 12 countries taking the euro in 2002, with lire phased out in February 2002. EU members using the euro as sole official currency are known as the Eurozone. Several EU members have opted out of joining this common currency. Euro notes are identical throughout the Eurozone countries, each one including designs of fictional architectural structures. The coins, however, have one side identical (the value side), and one side with an image unique to each country. Both notes and coins are exchangeable in each of the Eurozone countries.

Bank Notes
Euro bank notes have seven denominations. The €5 note (grey in colour) is the smallest, followed by the €10 note (pink), €20 note (blue), €50 note (orange), €100 note (green), €200 note (yellow) and €500 note (purple). All notes show the 12 stars of the European Union.

5 euros

10 euros

20 euros

50 euros

100 euros

200 euros

500 euros

2 euros   1 euro   50 cents   20 cents   10 cents

5 cents   2 cents   1 cent

Coins
The euro has eight coin denominations: €1 and €2; 50 cents, 20 cents, 10 cents, 5 cents, 2 cents and 1 cent. The €1 and €2 coins are both silver and gold in colour. The 50-, 20- and 10-cent coins are gold. The 5-, 2- and 1-cent coins are bronze.

Using the Telephone

You can find public telephones on the streets of all the main towns in the Veneto, as well as at bars and post offices. In Venice there are public phones in most of the main squares and at virtually every *vaporetto* landing stage. Many of these now accept prepaid phonecards, so it is far easier and more convenient for visitors to make long-distance calls.

Telephone company logo

CALL CHARGES

The cheapest times to phone within Italy are between 6:30pm and 8am from Monday to Friday, after 1:30pm on Saturday and all day on Sunday. International calls worldwide are cheapest between 10pm and 8am Monday to Saturday and all day Sunday. Although Telecom Italia phones are still the most common on the streets of Venice, phones by other companies are slowly creeping in, each with its own pre-paid phonecard, available from tobacconists or newsagents.

In general, it is much cheaper to dial direct for

Telephone sign

international calls from a payphone rather than going through the operator or making collect or credit card calls. Telephoning from hotel rooms is usually expensive and is sometimes marked up by as much as several hundred per cent. In general, it is more expensive to phone abroad from Italy than, for example, from the US or the UK.

TELEPHONE OFFICES

The old-style *Telefoni* (telephone offices) run by the Italian telecommunications companies Telecom Italia and ASST are no longer found in the Veneto. These

operator-assisted, metered telephone booths have been replaced by banks of the same card- and coin-operated public telephones that can be found on the streets of Venice and throughout the Veneto region. Each of the main towns also has a number of centrally located payphones, which can be found at the following addresses:

Venice
Ferrovia Santa Lucia. Map 1 B4.
Piazzale Roma. Map 5 B1.

Verona
Ferrovia Porta Nuova.

Padua
Riviera Ponti Romani 40.

Vicenza
Via Vescovado.

If you want to send a telegram anywhere in Italy or abroad, you can go to any post office or call 186 for assistance.

USING A TELECOM ITALIA CARD TELEPHONE

3 The display shows how much credit is left.

4 Dial the number and wait to be connected.

5 If you still have credit and want to make a second call, press the "follow-on call" button.

1 Lift the receiver and wait for the dialling tone

2 Insert a phonecard in the slot.

To use a card, break off the marked corner and insert, arrow first.

USING PUBLIC TELEPHONES

You can dial long-distance and international calls from public telephones. When making long-distance calls, always make sure that you have plenty of change ready. If you don't put enough coins in to start with, the telephone disconnects you and retains your money. Coin-operated phones are slowly being phased out in favour of pay-phones which take telephone cards (*carta* or *scheda telefonica*). You can buy these from post offices, newspaper kiosks and tobacconists (*tabacchi*) that display the black-and-white T sign.

Tabacchi sign

Any Italian number you dial in Italy must now be prefixed by its area code, even if you are making a local call. When dialling Italian numbers from abroad, do not drop the zero from in front of the area code.

E-MAIL

The Internet has made e-mail a viable and popular way to communicate from abroad. You can e-mail from the following Internet points:

Internet Point
Dorsoduro 3812/A, San Pantalon, Venice. **Map** 6 D2.
Tel 041 71 46 66.
◯ *9:15am–8pm Mon–Fri, 9:15am–7:30pm Sat.*
www.teleradiofuga.com

Internet Point
Galleria La Bottega
Calle delle Botteghe, San Marco 2970, Venice. **Map** 6 F2.
Tel 041 241 30 19. ◯ *10am–10pm daily (until midnight in summer).*

Venetian Navigator
Calle Caselleria, Castello 5300, Venice. **Map** 7 C1. *Tel 041 522 86 49.* ◯ *10am–10pm daily.*
www.venetiannavigator.com
@ vn@venetiannavigator.com

VeNice
Lista di Spagna,149 Cannaregio, Venice. **Map** 2 D4. *Tel 041 275 82 17.* ◯ *9am–11pm daily.*
www.ve-nice.it
@ info@ve-nice.it

REACHING THE RIGHT NUMBER

To ring Italy from the UK, and Ireland dial 00 39 then the number, including the full area code. From the US and Canada, dial 0 11 39 and from Australia, dial 00 11 39.

- Dialling code for
  Venice   041
  Verona   045
  Vicenza   0444
  Padua   049
  Treviso   0422
- International directory
  enquiries   176
- International operator
  assistance   170
- Telegrams and cables in
  Italy and abroad 186

To reach the operator in your own country to place a reverse charge or credit card call dial 172 followed by: 0044 for BT, UK; 0544 for CWC, UK; 1011 for AT&T, US; 1022 for MCI, US; 1001 for Canada; 1061 for Telstra, Australia and 1161 for Optus, Australia.
- *See also* Emergency Numbers, p272.

Sending Letters

The Italian postal service is notoriously inefficient. Expect anything sent abroad to take some time, especially during the August holiday season. Postcards to the UK can take up to a month if sent during the summer, and letters sent within Italy can take up to a week to reach their destination. For urgent or important communications, it is better to use the faster *Posta Prioritaria* system, or the more reliable *Raccomandata* (recorded delivery).

You can buy stamps (*francobolli*) from any tobacconist which has the black-and-white

Post Office sign

T sign, as well as from post offices. Post office hours are usually 8:30am to 2pm, Monday to Friday and 8:30am to noon on Saturday and the last day of the month. Main offices stay open until early evening.

SENDING PARCELS

Sending parcels from Italy can be extremely difficult. Unless certain rules are adhered to, it is unlikely that your package will be sent. Large items must be in a rigid box, wrapped in brown paper and bound with string and a lead seal. You will need to fill in a customs declaration form. Smaller items can be sent as a letter in a padded envelope.

POSTE RESTANTE

Letters and parcels should be sent care of (c/o) Fermo Posta, Ufficio Postale Principale, followed by the name of the town in which you wish to pick them up. Print the surname clearly in block capitals to make sure the letters are filed correctly. To collect your post, you need to show some form of identification and pay a small fee.

MAIN POST OFFICES

Fondaco dei Tedeschi 5554, Venice. **Map** 7 B1.
Tel 041 240 41 49.

Piazza Isolo 13, Verona.
Tel 045 805 03 49.

Piazza Garibaldi, Vicenza.
Tel 0444 33 20 77.

Corso Garibaldi 25, Padua.
Tel 049 877 22 09.

City letters   Other destinations

...lian post box

TRAVEL INFORMATION

The easiest way to reach the Veneto is by air. Direct flights link Venice to major European cities, and there are a few direct intercontinental flights. However, visitors from outside Europe usually transfer at Milan or Rome. Venice's Marco Polo airport, 10 km (6.5 miles) north of the city, receives both domestic and European flights as well as some charter flights. The airport is relatively small, but a new terminal is being built to help it handle the high volume of traffic. Treviso and Verona have their own small airports,

Alitalia aircraft

both of which receive flights from the UK. Car drivers who plan to tour the Veneto must bear in mind toll charges on European motorways. Visitors to Venice itself will have to leave their cars in one of the large car parks on the outskirts of the city because there are no streets for cars in the centre. Parking fees are heavy, and owners run the risk of leaving their cars unattended for the length of their stay. However, the region's rail network is good, and Venice railway station links the city to towns of the Veneto, and major European cities.

The quayside at Venice's Marco Polo airport

ARRIVING BY AIR

Venice is served by two airports: Marco Polo for scheduled flights and Treviso for charter flights. The city is linked to London, Paris and all other major European cities by direct flights. It is now possible to fly direct from New York to Venice with **Delta Airlines**. Alternatively, visitors from outside Europe can take a budget flight to London, Paris, Amsterdam or Frankfurt, and then a connecting flight to Venice from there.

Daily scheduled flights from London to Venice are operated by **British Airways** from Gatwick, and **Alitalia** (not direct) from Heathrow. Low-cost airline **easyJet** offers direct departures from Bristol, East Midlands and London Gatwick. The lowest fares are usually available only to those who avoid peak periods and book well in advance; booking via the Internet also saves money.

Many charter flights operate to Venice (Treviso) as does

low-cost airline **Ryanair** from London Stansted. Ryanair also serves Treviso from Liverpool, Dublin, Shannon, Paris, Rome, Brussels, Barcelona, Frankfurt and Dusseldorf.

If you wish to book flights during your stay, travel agents such as **American Express** or **Agenzia Bucintoro** in Venice offer a good service.

PACKAGE HOLIDAYS

Taking a package holiday to the Veneto is more convenient but not always cheaper than going independently of a tour operator. It is always worth comparing the costs, particularly if you are intending to travel off-season when charter flights are at their cheapest. For visitors who prefer the convenience of a package holiday, Venice is usually offered as a single destination or sometimes as part of a two- or three-centre holiday that includes Florence and Rome. Transfer from the airport on arrival is usually included in the holiday price. Most tour operators tend to

concentrate on Venice as a centre, though some offer packages to Verona or touring trips of the Veneto taking in the popular villas, museums and art galleries.

USEFUL NUMBERS

Alitalia
Venice. *Tel 06 22 22.*
www.alitalia.it

British Airways
Venice. *Tel 199 712 266.*
www.britishairways.com

Delta Airlines
Tel 404 715 26 00 (US only).
www.delta.com

easyJet
www.easyjet.com

Ryanair
www.ryanair.com

American Express
See p269.

Agenzia Bucintoro
See p269.

Airport Information
Venice. *Tel 041 260 92 60.*
www.veniceairport.it
Verona. *Tel 045 809 56 66.*
Treviso. *Tel 0422 31 51 11.*

MARCO POLO AIRPORT (VENICE)

Facilities are limited at the airport, but there is a hotel reservations office and a currency exchange office tha

Verona airport check-in desk

is open all day. There are also several banks, a self-service restaurant and a post office.

The most dramatic entry from the airport into Venice is by boat. The Alilaguna public water launch to San Marco and the Lido departs hourly from 6:10am to around midnight daily. Tickets are available from the office close to the exit of the arrivals hall. The journey to Venice takes about an hour and costs €12 per person. The boat stops near the San Marco, San Zaccaria, Murano, Fondamente Nuove and Lido *vaporetto* stops. Water taxis operating from the airport to San Marco only take 30 minutes but will cost around seven times as much as the public launch. Beware of water taxi touts who will charge you a good deal more than the official fare.

The less spectacular but quicker and cheaper alternative to the lagoon crossing is the ATVO bus to Piazzale Roma. The service meets all scheduled flights and costs around €3. Cheaper still, but stopping along the way, is the public bus to Piazzale Roma, which departs every 30 minutes. There is also a land taxi rank at the front of the airport. The journey takes 15 minutes and the drop-off point is Piazzale Roma.

VISO AIRPORT

a small airport which charter flights from Stansted) twice a change office is flights are in e coach service ma in Venice, with flights,

costs about €5 and takes approximately 45 minutes. Alternatively, you can take the public bus No. 6 which runs to Treviso station, where there is a regular rail service to Venice. For those on package tours the transport to Venice is pre-arranged and normally included in the overall price of the holiday.

VERONA AIRPORT

Verona airport receives flights from London (Gatwick), Frankfurt and Paris. There is a currency exchange office which is open daily. The bus service from the airport to Verona, which links up with scheduled flights, costs about €4.50.

PORTERS IN VENICE

Unless you are staying very close to your arrival point, you will have to take a *vaporetto* to the landing stage nearest to your hotel. Porters are very expensive; you will have to pay for the porter's boat fare, as well as for each piece of luggage – each piece costs the same as an adult. The cost of a porter handling

two suitcases, including your *vaporetto* fare, could amount to nearly €10. If there are no porters available, which is often the case, call your hotel and ask for a porter to meet you.

ARRIVING BY CAR

To drive your own car in Italy you will need an international Green Card (for insurance purposes) and your vehicle registration documentation. EU nationals who do not have the standard pink licence will need an Italian translation of their licence, available from most motoring organizations and Italian tourist offices. Requirements vary for visitors from non-EU countries; check with your insurance company before leaving for Italy. Insurance can always be bought at the border. This is also required to hire a car. (*See also p286.*)

CAR HIRE NUMBERS

In addition to those below, each major car hire company has an office at Venice, Treviso and Verona airports.

Piazzale Roma, Venice
Expressway *Tel 041 522 30 00.*
Avis *Tel 041 522 58 25.*
Hertz *Tel 041 528 40 91.*

Padua Railway Station
Maggiore *Tel 049 875 62 28.*
Avis *Tel 049 864 76 61.*
Hertz *Tel 049 875 22 02.*

Verona Railway Station
Maggiore *Tel 045 803 21 84.*
Avis *Tel 045 800 66 36.*
Hertz *Tel 045 800 08 32.*

Vicenza Railway Station
Maggiore *Tel 0444 54 59 62.*
Avis *Tel 0444 32 16 22.*
Hertz *Tel 0444 23 17 28.*

Boat from Venice's Marco Polo airport into the city

Travelling by Train

Italy's state railway (Ferrovie dello Stato or FS) runs an extensive and efficient rail network throughout the Veneto. Services are regular, trains tend to be punctual and the cost of travel is very reasonable. The variety of trains ranges from the painstakingly slow *locale*, which stops at almost every station, through various levels of fast intercity services to the high-speed Italian Eurostar, which links Venice with Rome and the rest of Italy.

Eurostar – Italy's fastest train

ARRIVING BY TRAIN

Santa Lucia railway station in Venice is the terminus for trains from Paris, Munich, Innsbruck, Vienna, Geneva, Zurich and other European cities. Passengers travelling from London have to change in Paris or Ostend. Fast intercity trains link Venice with Verona, Bologna, Milan, Rome and other major Italian cities.

Europe-wide train passes such as Eurail (US) or InterRail for those under 26 (Europe) are accepted on the FS network. You will have to pay a supplement, however, to travel on Italian Eurostar trains.

SANTA LUCIA STATION, VENICE

Standing at the west end of the Grand Canal, Ferrovia Santa Lucia is a modern, well-equipped station. There are *vaporetti* landing stages below the steps of the station with boats going to San Marco and all stops en route. There is also a water taxi and gondola service. Porters are not so easy to find, however. The bus and coach terminal and the only land taxi rank in Venice are in Piazzale Roma nearby (follow yellow signs).

Automatic ticket machines in the station are easy to use and display instructions in six languages. Notes, coins and some credit cards are accepted. Tickets can be booked free of charge in advance through travelagents.

Multilingual display screens give information on arrivals, departures, costs of travel and details about city services and tours. A tourist office offers to make hotel reservations, but queues are long in summer. There is also a Rolling Venice office (*see p270*), a bank and currency exchange, a left luggage facility, a cafeteria and bar, and a shop that sells international newspapers and magazines. There is also a number of telephones. Another useful facility is the *albergo diurno*. This is a daytime hotel where you can rest in a private room with an en-suite shower.

ORIENT EXPRESS

From March to November the *Venice Simplon Orient-Express* runs between London and Venice with stops at Paris, Düsseldorf, Cologne, Frankfurt,

FS train in Verona station

Zurich, St Anton, Innsbruck and Verona. A one-way journey with cabin from London to Venice can cost ten times the price of a charter flight. However, if you opt for the return trip, ticket prices are more reasonable.

The Orient-Express logo

VERONA STATIONS

Verona lies at the intersection of the main railway lines from Venice to Milan and Bologna to Munich. The main station, Porta Nuova, lies south of the centre, connected to it by frequent bus services. Train information is available at the ticket office and automatic help points give information in English. Other facilities include a left luggage office, a bar, an automatic exchange machine and a newspaper shop which sells bus tickets.

The small Porta Vescova station, serving local stations to the east of Verona, is used mainly by locals.

PADUA STATION

Padua is only 30 minutes b train from Venice. The station is in the north of town (10 minute's walk the centre), and buses centre leave from out station. The main bu with services to Ver other towns of the at Piazzale Bosch utes' walk fro

Santa Lucia station in Venice – gateway to the Veneto

Padua's tourist office is within the station building. There is also a left luggage office, a restaurant, a tobacconist, a counter selling bus tickets and a bureau de change open 9am to noon and 3pm to 5:30pm Monday to Saturday; 9am to noon Sunday.

VICENZA STATION

Vicenza, 55 minutes from Venice, is on the main railway line between Verona and Padua. The station is south of the city centre. Facilities include a bar and offices for left luggage, tickets, information and currency exchange open 8am to 12:30pm and 2pm to 6:30pm Monday to Saturday, 8:30am to noon and 2pm to 6pm Sunday.

TRAIN TRAVEL

If you plan to travel around, there are passes which allow unlimited travel on the FS network for a determined period of time, such as the Italy Rail Card and the Italy Flexi Rail Card. Available only to non-residents, the cards can be purchased from the station. The *biglietto chilometrico* allows up to 20 trips totalling under 3,000 km (1,865 miles) for up to five people over two months. This is available from international and local **CIT** offices and from any travel agent selling train tickets. For more information on passes, visit the FS's website (www.fs-on-line.com).

There are facilities for disabled travellers on some intercity services.

Stamp ticket here

Machine for validating tickets

MACHINES FOR FS RAIL TICKETS

These machines are easy to use, and most have instructions in six languages on screen. They take coins, notes and credit cards.

1 Select your destination.

2 The price is shown on the display.

3 Insert coins, notes, or an American Express, VISA or Diners Club card.

4 Take your ticket and change.

5 You must insert your ticket here to validate it for your journey.

TICKETS

On all intercity trains a supplement is charged, even if you have a rail card. Booking is often obligatory on the Eurostar and some other intercity services, and it is also advisable on other trains if you wish to travel at busy times.

If you are travelling less than 200 km (125 miles), a short-range ticket *(biglietto a fasce chilometriche)* is available. The ticket is stamped with the destination you require and it must then be validated in one of the machines at the entrance to the platforms. Both outward and return portions of a ticket must be used within three days of purchase. Tickets can be bought on the train but these are liable to a flat rate surcharge *and* a supplement based on the ticket price.

RAILWAY INFORMATION OFFICES

Tel 89 20 21. (Use this national number for all rail enquiries in Italy, including bookings.)
www.trenitalia.it

BOOKING AGENTS

CIT
San Marco 182,
Venice.
Tel 041 241 19 22.

3–5 Lansdown Rd,
Croydon CR9 1LL,
United Kingdom.
Tel 020 8686 5533.

Orient Express
c/o R+T Travel Service,
Castello 3476,
Venice.
Tel 041 522 17 46.
www.orient-express.com

TRENI IN PARTENZA										
destinazione	ind.suss.	cat.	ore	rit.	bin.	destinazione	ind.suss.	cat.	ore	rit.	bin.
						MODENA	MANTOVA	REG20.	17.45		11
BOLOGNA C.LE		REG20.	17.29		10	VICENZA		REG20.	17.50		3
MILANO C.LE		DIFF20.	17.38		7	MILANO C.LE		DIFF20.	18.03		6
VENEZIA S.L.		IRFR20.	17.42		4	TRIESTE		IR20.	18.34		4
BOLZANO		REG20.	17.44		12	VENEZIA S.L.		DIFF20.	18.41		3
INFORMAZIONI GENERALI SUSSIDIARIE											

Multilingual information board showing train departures

Getting Around Venice by Boat

For visitors to Venice, the *vaporetti* or waterbuses provide an entertaining form of public transport, although most journeys within the city can usually be covered more quickly on foot. The main route through the city for the *vaporetti* is the Grand Canal, and these waterbuses also supply a useful service connecting outlying points on the periphery of Venice and linking the city with the islands in the lagoon. The best value service from a visitor's point of view is the No. 1. This operates from one end of the Grand Canal to the other and travels sufficiently slowly for you to admire the parade of palaces at the waterside *(see pp56–71)*.

Vaporetto stop at the Giardini Pubblici *(see pp120–21)*

A *vaporetto* or waterbus

The smaller, sleeker *motoscafo*

A two-tier *motonave* boat

THE BOATS

The original *vaporetti* were steam-powered (*vaporetto* means little steamer); today they are diesel-run motor boats. Although all the boats tend to be called *vaporetti*, strictly speaking the word applies only to the large wide boats used on the slow routes, such as No. 1. These boats provide the best views. The *motoscafi* are the slimmer, smaller and faster boats, such as No. 52. Some of them might look old and rusty, but they go at quite a pace. The two-tier *motonavi*, which look huge in comparison to the *vaporetti* or *motoscafi*, are used on routes to outlying islands and the Lido.

TYPES OF TICKET

Tickets for travel on the waterbuses are the same price for any length of journey. This makes the service very easy to use, although there are a huge number of different types of ticket which, if applicable, could gain you a saving over the standard single ticket price.

If you only want to cross the Grand Canal, you can buy a crossing ticket for €2. A 60-minute ticket costs €6.50 and allows travel for one hour from the time of validation.

There are also 12-hour (€16), 24-hour (€18), 36-hour (€23), 48-hour (€28) and 72-hour (€33) tickets that entitle the holder and/or group to unlimited travel on most lines and offer better value.

For visits of more than a few days, you can buy a monthly season ticket (*abbonamento*), available from the Piazzale Roma or San Marco ticket offices. Holders of Rolling Venice cards (see p270) can buy a *Tre Giorni Giovane*, or three-day youth pass, for €18.

Many of the lagoon islands can also be visited with a special ticket, available on the Northern Lagoon Line. Some island services, however, such as Lineablu, Clodia Line and Alilaguna Line, are not covered by any of the special tickets.

HOURS OF SERVICE

The main routes run every 10 to 20 minutes until the early evening. Services are reduced at night, particularly after 1am, when a night-route operates. Details of main lines are given in the ACTV timetable, available at most landing stages.

Sightseeing from a *vaporetto* on the Grand Canal

THE MAIN ROUTES

① This is the slow boat down the Grand Canal, stopping at every landing stage, including the new stop Rialto Mercato. The route starts at Piazzale Roma, travels the length of the Grand Canal, then from San Marco it heads east to the Lido.

② The No. 2 is the faster route down the Grand Canal. The whole route goes in a loop, starting at San Zaccaria, continuing westwards along the Giudecca Canal to Tronchetto and Piazzale Roma, then down the Grand Canal back to San Zaccaria and from there out to the Lido (summer only).

⑤⑦ ⑤② The 51 and 52 skirt the periphery of Venice and have also been extended to the Lido. The circular "Giracittà" route provides a scenic tour of Venice, though to do the whole circuit you have to change boats at Fondamente Nuove.

④① ④② Circular "Giracittà" lines taking in Murano. No. 41 runs anticlockwise, while No. 42 goes clockwise.

⑤ The No. 5 is a tourist route connecting San Zaccaria and Murano.

⑥① ⑥② These "Giracittà" routes take in much of Venice, from the Lido to Piazzale Roma.

⑬ The No. 13 leaves from Fondamente Nove and travels to the "garden" islands, including Vignole and Sant'Erasmo.

ⓛⓝ Departing from the Fondamente Nuove, the LN (Laguna Nord) serves the main islands in the northern lagoon: Murano, Mazzorbo, Burano and Torcello, ending at Punta Sabbioni.

VAPORETTO INFORMATION

ACTV (Information Office)
Piazzale Roma, Venice.
Map 5 B1. *Tel* 041 24 24.
www.actv.it

USING THE VAPORETTI

The service is run by **ACTV** (*Azienda Consorzio Trasporti Veneziano*). The waterbus system is constantly being modified, and thus, while every effort is made to keep the map on the inside back cover of this guide up-to-date, it may not reflect the most recent changes made to the lines. If you are not sure which boat to take to reach your destination, check with the boatman – the *vaporetti* crew tend to be very helpful.

Timetable and routes at a *vaporetto* boarding point

1 Tickets are available at most landing stages, some bars, shops and tobacconists displaying the ACTV sign. The price of a ticket remains the same whether you are going one stop or doing the whole circuit, although a few routes are more expensive. There are also a variety of special tickets available (*see* Types of Ticket).

2 Signs on the landing stage tell you at which end you should board the boat.

3 Tickets should be swiped at the automatic machines on the landing stages before each journey. Inspectors rarely board the boats and this makes it surprisingly easy for tourists (and Venetians) to hop on and off the boats without a validated ticket. However, there are steep fines for passengers without tickets, and there are notices in English to this effect in all the boats.

4 An indicator board at the front of each boat gives the line number and main stops. (Ignore the large black numbers on the side of the boat.)

5 Each landing stage has its name clearly marked on a yellow board. Most stops have two landing stages and it is quite easy, particularly if it is crowded and you can't see which way the boat is facing, to board a boat travelling in the wrong direction. It is helpful to watch which direction the boat is approaching from; if in doubt, check with the boatman on board.

Finding Your Way in Venice

Venice is surprisingly small and most of the sights can be covered comfortably on foot. However, to avoid losing your way in the maze of little alleys, make sure you have the Street Finder *(see pp288–301)* handy. The gondola is the most romantic way to see the city, but prices are high, while the water taxi is the fastest means of travelling through the city and out to the islands.

GONDOLAS

Gondolas are a luxury form of transport used only by tourists (apart from Venetians on their wedding day). There are a number of gondola ranks throughout the city and plenty of gondoliers waiting for business.

Before boarding, check the official tariffs and agree a price with the gondolier. Prices are in the booklet *Un Ospite di Venezia (see p268)* and should also be available at gondola ranks. Official costs are around €60–75 for 45 minutes, rising to €80–95 after 8pm, but Gondoliers are notorious for overcharging; sometimes by double the official price. Try bargaining, whatever the cost quoted. During the low season, or when business looks slack, you may be able to negotiate a fee below the official rate and a journey shorter than the minimum of 45 minutes. Another way of cutting costs is to share a gondola – five is the maximum number of passengers.

Gondoliers all speak a smattering of English and have taken basic exams in Venetian history and art. Do not expect your gondolier to burst into *O Sole Mio*, however; the most you are likely to hear are the low melodious cries of *Oe,*

The romance of an early evening gondola ride

Premi and *Stai* – the warning calls that have been echoing down the canals of Venice for centuries. If you want to go on a serenaded tour, join an evening flotilla with accompanying musicians, organized regularly from May to October. Hiring a gondola independently is more romantic, but will cost considerably more. Details are available from any local travel agent.

Sign for one of the *traghetti* across the Grand Canal

TRAGHETTI

Traghetti are gondola ferries that cross the Grand Canal at seven different points, providing an invaluable service for pedestrians. Surprisingly, few tourists make use of this cheap, constant service. The points where the *traghetti* cross the Grand Canal are marked on the Street Finder maps *(see pp288–301)*. Yellow street signs show the way to the *traghetti*, illustrated with a little gondola symbol.

WATER TAXIS

For those with little time and sufficient funds, the fastest and most practical means of getting from A to B is by water taxi. The craft are sleek, white or polished wood motorboats, all equipped with a cabin. They zip to and from the airport in only 30 minutes. There are 16 water taxi ranks, including one at the airport and at the Lido. Telephone numbers and official tariffs are listed in the booklet *Un Ospite di Venezia (see p268)*. Extra is charged for luggage, waiting, night service and for calling out a taxi. If the *vaporetti* are on strike, which is extremely rare, water taxis are like gold dust.

A water taxi

GONDOLA STANDS

San Marco (Molo)
Tel 041 520 06 85.

Rialto (Riva Carbon)
Tel 041 522 49 04.

Railway Station (San Simeone Piccolo)
Tel 041 71 85 43.

WATER TAXI STANDS (SERVING ALL OF VENICE)

Veneziana Motoscafi Piazzale Roma
Tel 041 71 69 22.

Consorzio Motoscafi Rialto
Tel 041 522 23 03.

Serenissima San Marco
Tel 041 522 85 38.

Crossing the Grand Canal by *traghetto*

WALKING IN VENICE

One of the great pleasures of exploring Venice is walking. In the absence of traffic you soon get used to crossing streets and squares without so much as a glance to left or right. What you do have to contend with is the constant flow of tourists. The narrow alleys, particularly in the *sestiere* of San Marco, become extremely congested. To avoid pedestrian congestion keep to the right and avoid stopping on bridges and in narrow streets. However, the vast majority of tourists never venture beyond San Marco and it will be little more than a matter of minutes before you find yourself with only a few locals for company.

When sightseeing in Venice you will inevitably do a lot of walking, and a day taking in the sights can be extremely tiring. You need to allow only 35 minutes to cross the city from north to south on foot – provided you do not lose your way. Most visitors do, and this is, of course, part of the fun of exploring, but sensible shoes are a must, however short you think your journey may be.

Venice is so compact that you are never very far from the yellow signs that give directions to the key points of the city.

The city has countless *campi*, or squares, which open out

Venice, city of bridges

from the narrow alleys. Most of these are equipped with public benches, and footsore tourists can also sit at an open-air café. However, you will be expected to buy a drink, and drinks are expensive. Many of the main sights are concentrated in the *sestiere* of San Marco, either in Piazza San Marco *(see pp74–5)* or close by. Even the main sights in the *sestieri* beyond San Marco are, for most people, within comfortable walking distance of the main square. Apart from the Accademia and San Marco, the signposting is not very impressive, but the maps in this guide will help you find your way around.

An ornate Venetian door knocker

In July and August, when temperatures are at their highest, it is wise to avoid walking around midday. You should also be prepared,

particularly at this time of year, for nasty smells which waft from some of the canals.

From October there is always the risk of high tides *(acqua alta)*, which cause flooding in the city. The first area to flood is Piazza San Marco. Duck-boards are laid out in the square, however, and along main thoroughfares. If you are not equipped with wellington boots you can always buy cheap knee-high plastic shoe covers from local shops.

ADDRESSES IN VENICE

For any newcomer to the city of Venice, the system of addresses is initially very confusing. All buildings are numbered by the *sestiere* (administrative district) in which they fall rather than by the street. Hence a typical address would merely give the name of the *sestiere* followed by the number of the building, for example San Marco 2517 or Cannaregio 3499.

To locate an address it is, therefore, essential for you to establish the name of the street or square or, failing that, the nearest landmark. The Venetians resort to a book called *Indicatore Anagrafico*, which lists all the numbers in Venice and their corresponding streets. More useable, perhaps, is the more recent publication, *Calli, Campielli e Canali*, which also provides detailed maps of the city and islands.

You will find translations of Venetian words commonly used in place names in the Street Finder *(see p288)*.

A plethora of confusing signs in Cannaregio

Getting Around the Veneto

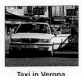

Taxi in Verona

Day trips can be made from Venice by train or bus, and the city centres can be covered easily on foot or by local bus. Although the train and bus networks are excellent, the most practical and pleasant means of travel is by car, allowing total independence to explore the countryside. However, some of the roads between towns tend to be very congested in the summer, city centres are banned to tourist traffic, and the cost of petrol is high.

A city bus in central Verona

ON FOOT AND BY BUS

All the cities of the Veneto are small enough to get around reasonably comfortably on foot. Limited traffic zones means that walking is pleasant and there are plenty of squares where you can sit and watch the world go by.

City buses are cheap and regular. Tickets, which must be bought prior to travel, are available from news-stands, bars, tobacconists and shops which display the bus company sign. There are also ticket vending machines in the streets, usually near stops, which take coins and notes. A flat fee is charged for rides within the city and the suburbs. The ticket becomes valid only when you time-stamp it in the machine at the front or rear of the bus.

It is normally cheaper and quicker to travel between towns by train. In some cases the bus will take twice as long as the train, however, there are a few towns such as Asolo where your only choice of public transport is a bus. In most cases the bus departure point is near the train station. You can usually buy a ticket valid for one, two or more hours of travel.

The city of Venice has excellent rail and bus connections. The most popular routes connect nearby towns such as Mestre, Mira, Marghera and Stra.

TAXIS

Travelling by taxi in the Veneto is not cheap. Meters show a fixed starting charge, then clock up every kilometre. There are extra charges for luggage, trips to the airports and journeys taken between 10pm and 7am, on Sundays and public holidays. Taxi drivers do not necessarily expect a tip – Italians give small tips or none at all.

Take taxis only from the official ranks, not from touts at railway stations and airports. In Venice the taxi rank

Rules of the Road

Drive on the right and, generally, give way to the right. Seat belts are compulsory in the front and back, and children should be properly restrained. You must also carry a warning triangle in case of breakdown. In town centres, the speed limit is 50 km/h (30 mph); on ordinary roads 90 km/h (55 mph); and on motorways 110 km/h (70 mph) for cars up to 1099cc, and 130 km/h (80 mph) for more powerful cars. Penalties for speeding include spot fines and licence points, and there are drink-driving laws as elsewhere in the EU.

One-way street

is in Piazzale Roma; in the Veneto towns of Verona, Vicenza and Padua, taxis can be found at the main piazzas.

CAR HIRE

If you book your car within the Veneto, local Italian firms such as Maggiore (*see p279*) tend to be cheaper than the international ones. Whichever company you choose, make sure that quoted prices include collision damage waiver, theft, breakdown service and IVA (Italian VAT, currently 19 per cent). Insurance against theft is usually an extra. To hire a car you must be over 21 and have held a licence for at least a year. Visitors from outside the EU need an international licence, though in practice hire firms may not insist on this.

DRIVING AND PARKING

Cities in the Veneto have limited traffic zones and normally only residents and taxis can drive into the centre. Visitors can unload at their hotel, but must then park on the outside of town and come in by foot or bus. Some hotels have a limited number of parking permits, but this is no guarantee of a space. Your

Speed limit (on minor road)   **End of speed restriction**

Pedestrianized street – no traffic   **Give way to oncoming traffic**

Give way 320 m (350 yd) ahead   **Danger (often with description)**

Moto Guzzi's classic Gambalunga in the market place at Montagnana

best bet is to telephone in advance and warn the hotel of your arrival.

Official parking areas are marked by blue lines, usually with meters or an attendant nearby. The *disco orario* system allows free parking for a limited period in certain areas. The cardboard discs, which you place on your windscreen, are provided by car hire companies, or can be purchased at petrol stations and also at supermarkets in the cities of the Veneto.

If you have your car towed away, phone the **Polizia Municipale**, or Municipal Police.

Disco orario parking disc

In Venice parking is prohibitively expensive. The closest car parks to the centre are at Piazzale Roma, where space is at a premium. There is a huge car park on the Isola del Tronchetto, linked to Venice

by *vaporetto* and bus. There are cheaper car parks at Fusina and San Giuliano in Mestre.

Many of the main roads are old, with only a couple of lanes, and traffic can be heavy. What looks like a short trip on the map may take much longer than you expect. For more details on road conditions contact **CIS** (Centro Informazione Stradale). *Autostrada* tolls, levied on the motorways, are expensive. Payment can be made in cash or by pre-paid magnetic cards called Viacards. These are available from ACI offices **(Automobile Club d'Italia)** and tobacconists.

PETROL

Motorway service stations are open 24 hours a day. Petrol stations are scarce in the countryside and most do not accept credit cards. Many are closed all afternoon, all day Sunday and the whole of August. However, you will find some self-service petrol stations with automatic pumps that accept notes.

BREAKDOWNS

The **ACI** provides an efficient 24-hour service also available to foreign visitors. The organization has reciprocal arrangements with affiliated associations in other countries such as the AA or RAC in Britain.

The picturesque but hair-raising ardesana *(see p204)*

VENICE STREET FINDER

All the sights, hotels, restaurants, shops and entertainment venues in Venice have map references which refer you to this section of the book. The key map below indicates the areas of the city covered by the Street Finder, and includes the colour coding specific to each area. Following the map section is a complete index of street names *(see pp298–301)*. The standard Italian spelling has been used on the maps throughout this book, but when exploring the city you will find that the street signs are often printed in Venetian dialect. Sometimes this means only a slight variation in the spelling (see the word Sotoportico/Sotoportego below), but some names look completely different. For example, Santi Giovanni e Paolo *(see Map 3)* is often signposted as "San Zanipolo". Major sights are labelled in Italian.

RECOGNIZING STREET NAMES

The signs for street *(calle)*, canal *(rio)* and square *(campo)* will soon become familiar, but the Venetians have a colourful vocabulary for the maze of alleys which makes up the city. When exploring, the following may help.

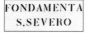

FONDAMENTA S.SEVERO

Fondamenta
A street that runs alongside a canal, often named after the canal it follows.

RIO TERRA GESUATI

Rio Terrà A filled-in canal. Similar to a *rio terrà is a piscina*, which often forms a square.

SOTOPORTEGO E PONTE S.CRISTOFORO

Sotoportico or Sotoportego
A covered passageway.

SALIZADA PIO X

Salizzada A main street (formerly a paved street).

RIVA DEI PARTIGIANI

Riva A wide *fondamenta*, often facing the lagoon.

RUGAGIUFFA

Ruga A street lined with shops.

CORTE DEI DO POZZI

Corte
A courtyard.

RIO MENUO O DE LA VERONA

Many streets and canals in Venice often have more than one name: o means "or".

0 metres   500

0 yards   500

Murano
(Inset on map pages 3 & 4)

3 4

Murano

7 8

RANDE

San Marco *Castello*

KEY TO STREET FINDER

	Major sight
	Place of interest
	Railway station
	Ferry boarding point
	Vaporetto boarding point
	Traghetto crossing
	Gondula mooring
	Coach station
	Tourist information office
	Hospital with casualty unit
P	Parking
	Police station
	Church
	Synagogue
⊠	Post office
=	Railway line

SCALE OF MAP PAGES

0 metres	200
0 yards	200

SCALE OF MURANO INSET

0 metres	500
0 yards	500

Street Finder Index

KEY TO ABBREVIATIONS USED IN THE STREET FINDER

C	Calle	d.	di, del, dell',	R	Rio	Sta	Santa
Can	Canale		dello, della,	R T	Rio Terrà	Sto	Santo'
Cpo	Campo		dei, delle, degli	Rg	Ruga/Rughetta	SS	Santi/Santissimo
Cplo	Campiello	Fmta	Fondamenta	Sal	Salizzada	Stp	Sottoportico
Ct	Corte	Rm	Ramo	S	San/Sant'		

General Index

W

Y

Z

Acknowledgments

Dorling Kindersley would like to thank the many people whose help and assistance contributed to the preparation of this book.

Main Contributors
Susie Boulton studied languages and history of art at the University of Cambridge. She has been visiting Venice for over 20 years and is the author of several guide books on the city.

Christopher Catling has been visiting Italy for over 25 years since his first archaeological dig there while he was a student at Cambridge University. He is the author of several guide books on Italian cities and regions, including *The DK Travel Guide to Florence and Tuscany.*

Additional Contributor
Gillian Price was born in England in 1953 but grew up in Sydney, Australia. She moved to Venice in 1981 and has written nine books on walking in Italy. Gillian has been contributing to Dorling Kindersley's Eyewitness Travel Guide series since 1998.

Sally Roy first got to know Venice while at school in Rome and has been returning to the country ever since. She read medieval history at St Andrew's University, Edinburgh, and has contributed to several books on Italy.

Additional Illustrations
Annabelle Brend, Dawn Brend, Neil Bulpitt, Richard Draper, Nick Gibbard, Kevin Jones Associates, John Lawrence, The Maltings Partnership, Simon Roulstone, Sue Sharples, Derrick Stone, Paul Weston, John Woodcock.

Additional Photography
Ian O'Leary, JoAnn Titmarsh.

Design and Editorial
Deputy Editorial Director Douglas Amrine
Deputy Art Director Gaye Allen
Map Co-Ordinators Simon Farbrother, David Pugh
Production Hilary Stephens
Picture Research Ellen Root
Revisions Beverley Ager, Uma Bhattacharya, Hilary Bird, Michael Blacker, Dawn Brend, Lucinda Cooke, Michelle Crane, Felicity Crowe, Stephanie Driver, Michael Ellis, Gadi Farfour, Anna Freiberger, Vinod Harish, Mohammad Hassan, Irena Hoare, Annette Jacobs, Jasneet Kaur, Steve Knowlden, Vincent Kurien, Erika Lang, Jude Ledger, Carly Madden, Nicola Malone, Ian Midson, Pete Quinlan, Steve Rowling, Simon Ryder, Sands Publishing Solutions, Azeem Siddiqui, Meredith Smith, JoAnn Titmarsh, Janis Utton, Conrad Van Dyk, Lynda Warrington, Fiona Wild.

Research Assistance
Jill De Cet, Hans Erlacher, Paolo Frullini, Oscar Gates, Marinella Laini, Elizabetta Lovato, Fabiola Perer, Alan Ross, Sarah Sole.

Index
Indexing Specialists, 202 Church Road, Hove, East Sussex, UK.

Special Assistance
Comune di Vicenza; Arch. Gianfranco Martinoni at the Assessorato Beni Culturali Comune di Padova; Ca' Macana; Cesare Battisti at the Media Tourist Office, Venice; Curia Patriarcale Venezia; D.ssa Foscarina Caletti at the Giunta Regionale di Venezia; Jane Groom, Brian Jordan; Alexandra Kennedy; Joy Parker; Frances Hawkins, Lady Frances Clarke and John Millerchip of the Venice in Peril Fund; the staff of the APT offices throughout the Veneto, in particular Anna Rita Bisaggio in Montegrotto Terme, Stephano Marchioro in Padua; Anna Maria Carlotto, Virna Scarduelli and Christina Erlacher in Verona, Anselmo Centomo in Vicenza; Heidi Wenyon.

Photography Permissions
Dorling Kindersley would like to thank the following for their kind permission to photograph at their establishments:
Venice: Amministrazione Provinciale di Venezia (Museo dell'Estuario, Torcello); Ca' Mocenigo; Ca' Pesaro; Ca' Rezzonico; Caffè Quadri; Collegio Armeni; Fondazione Europea Pro Venetia Viva, San Servolo; Fondazione Giorgio Cini (San Giorgio Maggiore); Peggy Guggenheim Museum; Hôtel des Bains; Libreria Sansoviniana; Museo Archeologico; Museo Correr; Museo Diocesano d'Arte Sacra; Museo Fortuny; Museo Storia Navale; Museo Storico Naturale; Museo Vetrario, Murano; Arch. Umberto Franzoi and staff at the Palazzo Ducale; Procuratie di San Marco (Basilica San Marco); Santi Giovanni e Paolo; San Lazzaro degli Armeni; Santa Maria Gloriosa dei Frari; Scuola Grande dei Carmini; Scuola Grande di San Rocco.
Veneto: Arena Romano, Verona; Basilica, Vicenza; Caffè Pedrocchi, Padua; Duomo, Padua; Duomo, Vicenza; Giardini Giusti, Verona; Museo Archeologico, Verona; Museo di Castelvecchio, Verona; Museo Civico, Malcésine; Museo Civico, Vicenza; Museo Concordiese, Portogruaro; Museo degli Eremitani, Padua; Museo Lapidario Maffeiano, Verona; Museo del Storia Naturale, Verona; Ossuario di San Pietro, Solferino; Sant'Anastasia, Verona; San Fermo Maggiore, Verona; San Giorgio, Monsélice; San Giorgio in Braida, Verona; San Lorenzo, Vicenza; Santa Maria in Organo, Verona; San Pietro in Malvino, Sirmione; San Severo, Bardolino; San

Malvino, Sirmione; San Severo, Bardolino; San Stefano, Verona; San Zeno Maggiore, Verona; Santuario di Monte Berico, Vicenza; Teatro Olimpico, Vicenza; Università di Padova; Contessa Diamante Luling-Buschette, Villa Barbaro, Masèr; Conte Marco Emo, Villa Emo, Fanzolo di Vedelago.

Picture credits

t = top; tc = top centre; tr = top right; cla = centre left above; ca = centre above; cra = centre right above; cl = centre left; c = centre; cr = centre right; clb = centre left below; cb = centre below; crb = centre right below; bl = bottom left; bc = bottom centre; br = bottom right.

Every effort has been made to trace the copyright holders, and we apologize in advance for any unintentional omissions. We would be pleased to insert the appropriate acknowledgments in any subsequent edition of this publication.

Works of art have been reproduced with the permission of the following copyright holders: *Maiastra* 1912 Constantin Brancusi © ADAGP, Paris and DACS, London 2006 134cr; *Interno Olandese II* c.1928 Joan Miró © Successio Miró/ADAGP, Paris and DACS, London 2006 134c; *Matisse at Venice Biennale* 1992 Larry Rivers © DACS, London/VAGA, New York 2006 256tc.

The publishers are grateful to the following museums, companies, and picture libraries for permission to reproduce their photographs:

ACCADEMIA OLIMPICA, VICENZA: 172tr, 173crb; ACE PHOTO/AGENCY TORE GILL: 254b; ACE/MAURITIUS: 257t; ACTV S.P.A: 282cla, 282clb; ALAMY IMAGES: AA World Travel Library 239cl; CuboImages srl/Bluered 11bl; FAN travelstock/Michael Schindel 264cr; Cris Haigh 239tl; Jon Arnold Images 186; Jon Arnold Images/Demetrio Carrasco 263cr; Michael Juno 238cla; Aguilar Patrice 30tr; Travelshots.com 10tc; travelstock44 10bl; ANCIENT ART & ARCHITECTURE COLLECTION: 38c, 40br, 40tl; APT DEL BRESCIANO: 35b; ARCHIV FÜR KUNST UND GESCHICHTE: 26tl/c/cr, 30bl, 36, 43br, 44crb, 45bl, 45t, 46tl, 46tr, 48cla, 49clb, 50b, 54br, 130b, 131b, 131c, 132b, 133t, 30/31cb; ARCHIVIO RAIMONDO ZAGO 49cl. ARCHIVIO VENEZIANO: Sarah Quill 29br, 51crb, 67cl, 106tr, 144t.

BAUER L'HOTEL: 223tr; Benetton: 51tl; BIBLIOTECA CIVICA DI TRIESTE (FOTO HALUPCA): 119b; BRIDGEMAN ART LIBRARY, LONDON: *Madonna and Child and Saints* (triptych altarpiece) by Giovanni Bellini (c.1431–1516),

Santa Maria dei Frari, Venice 27tl/tr; *The Siege of Antioch* 1098 by William of Tyre. Bibliothèque Nationale, Paris 40cla; *Marco Polo with Elephants and Camels* from Livre des Merveilles, Bibliothèque Nationale, Paris, 42cb; *View of Venice* by Bernardo von Breitenbach, from Opusculum Sanctarum Peregrinationum in Terram Sanctam, Bibliothèque Nationale, PARIS, 8–9; *Family Tree of the Cornaro Family,* Italian School (18th century), Palazzo Corner Ca' Grande, Venice, 69tr; *Salome* by Gustav Klimt (1862–1918) Museo d'Arte Moderna, Venice, 105br; *The Nuns' Visiting Day* by Francesco Guardi (1712–93), Museo Ca' Rezzonico, Venice, 112bl; *St George Killing the Dragon* by Vittore Carpaccio (c.1460/5–1523/6), Scuola di San Giorgio degli Schiavoni, Venice, 118tl; *The Stealing of the Body of St Mark* by Tintoretto (1518–94), Accademia, Venice, 131t; *The Rape of Europa* by Francesco Zuccarelli, Accademia, Venice, 133c; *Marco Polo dressed in Tartar costume* (c.1700) Museo Correr, Venice/Giraudon, 4tr/115br; OSVALDO BÖHM: 20b, 20cl, 29bl, 41crb, 63tl, 79tl, 132c, 132t, 144c.

DEMETRIO CARRASCO: 124b, 139br, 141t, 227tr, 274t; CENTRO EUROPEO MESTIERI: 262br; CEPHAS PICTURE LIBRARY: Mick Rock, 35cra and 238tr; CIGA HOTELS: 70tl; CLAIRE CALMAN: 55cr; GIANCARLO COSTA: 47clb; CORBIS: Ashley Cooper 263tl, William Manning 10cr, royalty-free 146; JOE CORNISH: 15b, 209c, 216bl; STEPHANIE COLASANTI: 56, 195br.

DOLOMITI SUPERSKI: Freddy Planinschek 262tc, 264bl; CHRIS DONAGHUE THE OXFORD PHOTO LIBRARY: 3 (inset), 5tl, 76t, 156br, 280t; MICHAEL DENT: 82b, 252tl; DRAUGHTSMAN: 268tr.

E.T. ARCHIVE: Sala dei Prior Siena, 41tl; Baroque Hall of Mirrors, Palazzo Papadopoli, Venice, 64tl; *The Apothecary's Shop* by Pietro Longhi, Accademia, Venice, 130c; ELECTA, MILAN: 180cr, 181t/cl; ERIZZO EDITRICE SRL: 105clb; MARY EVANS PICTURE LIBRARY: 7 (inset), 9 (inset), 24tl, 39clb, 44bl, 47br, 47t, 53 (inset), 58cra, 58tr, 63c, 64c, 69ca, 143tr, 159 (inset), 221 (inset), 259 (inset), 32c.

FERROVIA DELLO STATO: 272tl.

JACKIE GORDON: 273t; GRAZIA NERI: 41b, 49tl, 50crb, 50tr, 65br, 92tl, 157b, 254t; Marco Bruzzo, 5tr, 32t, 35clb, 40tr, 166t; Cameraphoto 71tr, 115bl, 42/43c; Graziano Arici 100tr; Roberta Krasnig 268bl; PEGGY GUGGENHEIM MUSEUM, VENICE: 134b; THE RONALD GRANT ARCHIVE: 50cla.

HEMISPHERES IMAGES: Maurizio Borgese 16; ROBERT HARDING PICTURE LIBRARY: 216cl; HOTEL

DEUTSCH COLLECTION: 38br, 38tr, 39br, 43clb, 46br, 48bc, 49br, 61tr, 66b, 66cra, 69cl, 101c, 140bl, 181br, 199b.

IMAGE BANK: Guido A. Rossi, 11 (inset); IMAGE SELECT: Ann Ronan, 44cl. LONDRA PALACE: 226br HUGH MCKNIGHT PHOTOGRAPHY: 71tl; MAGNUM PHOTOS/ DAVID SEYMOUR: 48tr; MARKA: 37b, L Baldissin 237bcb; L Barbazza 249br; Roberto Benzi 276cl; Enrico Cerretelli 150bl; Cristina Dogliani 262b; M Motta 277cl; Ubik 237bcla, Ubik/Pizzo 237bcar; MORO ROMA: 30cl, 48/49c; MUSEO ARCHEOLOGICO, VERONA: 38bl; MUSEO CIVICO AGLI EREMITANI: 179t/c/b; MUSEO CIVICO DI ODERZO: 39t; THE MANSELL COLLECTION: 46crb, 47bl.

NEWIMAGE S.R.L.: 33bc; Rolando Fabriani 33bc; NHPA/GERARD LACZ: 217b; NHPA/LAURIE CAMPBELL: 217c; NHPA/SILVESTRIS FOTOSERVICE: 217crb; THE NATIONAL GALLERY, LONDON: 29t.

OLYMPIA/SELECT: 34b, 51br, 51clb, 157t, 255t; OLYMPIA/SELECT/LARRY RIVERS: 256t.

PALAZZO ABADESSA: 223bl; PERFORMING ARTS LIBRARY/GIANFRANCO FAINELLO: 256c.

THE ROYAL COLLECTION ©1994 HER MAJESTY QUEEN ELIZABETH 11: 46/47c.

JOHN FERRO SIMS: 167t; SCALA, FIRENZE: *Madonna di Ca' Pesaro* by Titian (1477/89–1576), S. Maria Gloriosa dei Frari, Venice 27, c/cr; *Ultimi Momenti del Doge Marin Faliero* by Francesco Hayez (1791–1881), Pinacoteca di Brera, Milan, 43t; *Banquet of Antony and Cleopatra* by Giambattista Tiepolo (1692–1770), Palazzo Labia, Venice, 60t; *Ultimi Momenti del Doge*

Marin Faliero by Francesco Hayez (1791–1881), Pinacoteca di Brera, Milan, 68cra; *Crocifissione* by Tintoretto (1518–94), Scuola Grande di S. Rocco, Venice, 106c/cb; *S Michele* by Giambono (15th century), Accademia, Venice, 123b; *Il Trasporto della Santa Casa di Loreto* by Giambattista Tiepolo (1692–1770), Accademia, Venice, 130tr; *Presentazione al tempio* by Titian (1477/89–1576), Accademia, Venice,133b; *Intérieur Hollandais II* by Joan Miró (1928), Museo Guggenheim, Venice, 134c; *Madonna col Bambino* by Filippo Lippi (1406–69), Cini Collection, Venice 134t; *Annunciazione* by Vittore Carpaccio (1460 c.– 1526), Ca' d'Oro, Venice,144b; Pala di San Zeno by Andrea Mantegna (1431–1506), San Zeno, Verona, 200cl; SCIENCE PHOTO LIBRARY: Earth Satellite Corporation, 10 (inset); SETTORE BENI CULTURALI, PADUA: 180t/cla/ clb; SPECTRUM COLOUR LIBRARY: 28b; STUDIO PIZZI: 45cla, 47crb; TONY STONE IMAGES: 214cla, 216t, 50/51c; SUPERSTOCK: Steve Vidler 11tr.

TASTING PLACES: 262cl.

VELA SPA: 283ca, 283cb.

JACKET
Front: OXFORD PHOTO LIBRARY: Chris Donaghue clb; PHOTOLIBRARY: Index Stock Imagery/Froelich Terri main image. Back: John Heseltine bl, clb, tl; ROGER MOSS cla. Spine: DK IMAGES: John Heseltine b; PHOTOLIBRARY: Index Stock Imagery/Froelich Terri t.

All other images © Dorling Kindersley. For further information see: **www.dkimages.com**

SPECIAL EDITIONS OF DK TRAVEL GUIDES

DK Travel Guides can be purchased in bulk quantities at discounted prices for use in promotions or as premiums. We are also able to offer special editions and personalized jackets, corporate imprints, and excerpts from all of our books, tailored specifically to meet your own needs.

To find out more, please contact:
(in the United States) **SpecialSales@dk.com**
(in the UK) **travelspecialsales@dk.com**
(in Canada) DK Special Sales at **general@tourmaline.ca**
(in Australia) **business.development@pearson.com.au**

Phrase Book

In Emergency

Help!	Aiuto!	eye-**yoo**-toh
Stop!	Fermate!	fair-**mah**-teh
Call a doctor.	Chiama un medico	kee-**ah**-mah oon **meh**-dee-koh
Call an ambulance.	Chiama un' ambulanza	kee-**ah**-mah oon am-boo-**lan**-tsa
Call the police.	Chiama la polizia	kee-**ah**-mah lah pol-ee-**tsee**-ah
Call the fire brigade.	Chiama i pompieri	kee-**ah**-mah ee pom-pee-**air**-ee
Where is the telephone?	Dov'è il telefono?	dov-**eh** eel teh-leh-**foh**-noh?
The nearest hospital?	L'ospedale più vicino?	loss-peh-**dah**-leh pee-**oo**vee-**chee**-noh?

Communication Essentials

Yes/No	Sì/No	see/noh
Please	Per favore	pair fah-**vor**-eh
Thank you	Grazie	**grah**-tsee-eh
Excuse me	Mi scusi	mee **skoo**-zee
Hello	Buon giorno	bwon **jor**-noh
Goodbye	Arrivederci	ah-ree-veh-**dair**-chee
Good evening	Buona sera	bwon-ah **sair**-ah
morning	la mattina	lah mah-**tee**-nah
afternoon	il pomeriggio	eel poh-meh-**ree**-joh
evening	la sera	lah **sair**-ah
yesterday	ieri	ee-**air**-ee
today	oggi	**oh**-jee
tomorrow	domani	doh-**mah**-nee
here	qui	kwee
there	la	lah
What?	Quale?	**kwah**-leh?
When?	Quando?	**kwan**-doh?
Why?	Perchè?	pair-**keh**?
Where?	Dove?	**doh**-veh

Useful Phrases

How are you?	Come sta?	**koh**-meh stah?
Very well, thank you.	Molto bene, grazie.	**moll**-toh **beh**-neh, **grah**-tsee-eh
Pleased to meet you.	Piacere di conoscerla.	pee-ah-**chair**-eh dee coh-**noh**-shair-lah
See you soon.	A più tardi.	ah pee-**oo** tar-dee
That's fine.	Va bene.	va **beh**-neh
Where is/are ...?	Dov'è/Dove sono...?	dov-**eh**/doveh **soh**-noh?
How long does it take to get to ...?	Quanto tempo ci vuole per andare a ...?	**kwan**-toh **tem**-poh chee voo-**oh**-leh pair an-**dar**-eh ah ...?
How do I get to ...?	Come faccio per arrivare a ...?	**koh**-meh **fah**-choh pair arri-**var**-eh ah...?
Do you speak English?	Parla inglese?	par-lah een-**gleh**-zeh?
I don't understand.	Non capisco.	non ka-**pee**-skoh
Could you speak more slowly, please?	Può parlare più lentamente, per favore?	pwoh par-**lah**-reh pee-oo len-ta-**men**-teh pair fah-**vor**-eh
I'm sorry.	Mi dispiace.	mee dee-spee-**ah**-cheh

Useful Words

big	grande	**gran**-deh
small	piccolo	**pee**-koh-loh
hot	caldo	**kal**-doh
cold	freddo	**fred**-doh
good	buono	**bwoh**-noh
bad	cattivo	kat-**tee**-voh
enough	basta	**bas**-tah
well	bene	**beh**-neh
open	aperto	ah-**pair**-toh
closed	chiuso	kee-**oo**-zoh
left	a sinistra	ah see-**nee**-strah
right	a destra	ah **dess**-trah
straight on	sempre dritto	**sem**-preh **dree**-toh
near	vicino	vee-**chee**-noh
far	lontano	lon-**tah**-noh
up	su	soo
down	giù	joo
early	presto	**press**-toh
late	tardi	**tar**-dee
entrance	entrata	en-**trah**-tah
exit	uscita	oo-**shee**-ta
toilet	il gabinetto	eel gah-bee-**net**-toh
free, unoccupied	libero	**lee**-bair-oh
free, no charge	gratuito	grah-**too**-ee-toh

Making a Telephone Call

I'd like to place a long-distance call.	Vorrei fare una interurbana.	vor-**ray far**-eh oona in-tair-oor-**bah**-nah
I'd like to make a reverse-charge call.	Vorrei fare una telefonata a carico del destinatario.	vor-**ray far**-eh oona teh-leh-fon-**ah**-tah ah **kar**-ee-koh dell dess-tee-nah-**tar**-ree-oh
I'll try again later.	Ritelefono più tardi.	ree-teh-**leh**-foh-noh pee-oo **tar**-dee
Can I leave a message?	Posso lasciare un messaggio?	**poss**-oh lash-**ah**-reh oon mess-**sah**-joh?
Hold on.	Un attimo, per favore	oon **ah**-tee-moh, pair fah-**vor**-eh
Could you speak up a little please?	Può parlare più forte, per favore?	pwoh par-**lah**-reh pee-**oo for**-teh, pair fah-**vor**-eh?
local call	la telefonata locale	lah teh-leh-fon-**ah**-ta loh-**kah**-leh

Shopping

How much does this cost?	Quant'è, per favore?	kwan-**teh** pair fah-**vor**-eh?
Do you have ...?	Avete ...?	ah-**veh**-teh... ?
I'm just looking.	Sto soltanto guardando.	stoh sol-**tan**-toh gwar-**dan**-doh
Do you take credit cards?	Accettate carte di credito?	ah-chet-tah-teh **kar**-teh dee **creh**-dee-toh?
What time do you open/close?	A che ora apre/ chiude?	ah keh **or**-ah **ah**-preh/kee-**oo**-deh?
this one	questo	**kweh**-stoh
that one	quello	**kwell** oh
expensive	caro	**kar**-oh
cheap	a buon prezzo	ah bwon **pret**-soh
size, clothes	la taglia	lah **tah**-lee-ah
size, shoes	il numero	eel **noo**-mair-oh
white	bianco	bee-**ang**-koh
black	nero	**neh**-roh
red	rosso	**ross**-oh
yellow	giallo	**jal**-loh
green	verde	**vair**-deh
blue	blu	bloo
brown	marrone	mar-**roh**-neh

Types of Shop

antique dealer	l'antiquario	lan-tee-**kwah**-ree-oh
bakery	la panetteria	lah pah-net-tair-**ree**-ah
bank	la banca	lah **bang**-kah
bookshop	la libreria	lah lee-breh-**ree**-ah
butcher's	la macelleria	lah-mah-chell-eh-**ree**-ah
cake shop	la pasticceria	lah pas-tee-chair-**ee**-ah
chemist's	la farmacia	lah far-mah-**chee**-ah
delicatessen	la salumeria	lah sah-loo-meh-**ree**-ah
department store	il grande magazzino	eel **gran**-deh mag-gad-**zee**-noh
fishmonger's	la pescheria	lah pess-keh-**ree**-ah
florist	il fioraio	eel fee-or-ee-**oh**
greengrocer	il fruttivendolo	eel froo-tee-**ven**-doh-loh
grocery	alimentari	ah-lee-men-**tah**-ree
hairdresser	il parrucchiere	eel par-oo-kee-**air**-eh
ice cream parlour	la gelateria	lah jel-lah-tair-**ee**-ah
market	il mercato	eel mair-**kah**-toh
news-stand	l'edicola	leh-**dee**-koh-lah
post office	l'ufficio postale	loo-**fee**-choh pos-**tah**-leh
shoe shop	il negozio di scarpe	eel neh-**goh**-tsioh dee **skar**-peh
supermarket	il supermercato	su-pair-mair-**kah**-toh
tobacconist	il tabaccaio	eel tah-bak-**eye**-oh
travel agency	l'agenzia di viaggi	lah-jen-**tsee**-ah dee vee-**ad**-jee

Sightseeing

art gallery	la pinacoteca	lah peena-koh-**teh**-kah
bus stop	la fermata dell'autobus	lah fair-**mah**-tah dell **ow**-toh-booss
church	la chiesa	lah kee-**eh**-zah
	la basilica	lah bah-**seel**-i-kah
closed for the public holiday	chiuso per la festa	kee-**oo**-zoh pair lah **fess**-tah
garden	il giardino	eel jar-**dee**-no
library	la biblioteca	lah beeb-lee-oh-**teh**-kah
museum	il museo	eel moo-**zeh**-oh
railway station	la stazione	lah stah-tsee-**oh**-neh
tourist information	l'ufficio turistico	loo-**fee**-choh too-**ree**-stee-koh

Staying in a Hotel

Do you have any vacant rooms?	Avete camere libere?	ah-veh-teh kah-mair-eh lee-bair-eh?
double room	una camera doppia	oona kah-mair-ah doh-pee-ah
with double bed	con letto matrimoniale	kon let-toh mah-tree-moh-nee-ah-leh
twin room	una camera con due letti	oona kah-mair-ah kon doo-eh let-tee
single room	una camera singola	oona kah-mair-ah sing-goh-lah
room with a bath, shower	una camera con bagno, con doccia	oona kah-mair-ah kon ban-yoh, kon dot-chah
porter	il facchino	eel fah-kee-noh
key	la chiave	lah kee-ah-veh
I have a reservation.	Ho fatto una prenotazione.	oh fat-toh oona preh-noh-tah-tsee-oh-neh

Eating Out

Have you got a table for …?	Avete una tavola per … ?	ah-veh-teh oona tah-voh-lah pair …?
I'd like to reserve a table.	Vorrei riservare una tavola.	vor-ray ree-sair-vah-reh oona tah-voh-lah
breakfast	colazione	koh-lah-tsee-oh-neh
lunch	pranzo	pran-tsoh
dinner	cena	cheh-nah
The bill, please.	Il conto, per favore.	eel kon-toh pair fah-vor-eh
I am a vegetarian.	Sono vegetariano/a.	soh-noh veh-jeh-tar-ee-ah-noh/nah
waitress	cameriera	kah-mair-ee-air-ah
waiter	cameriere	kah-mair-ee-air-eh
fixed price menu	il menù a prezzo fisso	eel meh-noo ah pret-soh fee-soh
dish of the day	piatto del giorno	pee-ah-toh dell jor-no
starter	antipasto	an-tee-pass-toh
first course	il primo	eel pree-moh
main course	il secondo	eel seh-kon-doh
vegetables	il contorno	eel kon-tor-noh
dessert	il dolce	eel doll-cheh
cover charge	il coperto	eel koh-pair-toh
wine list	la lista dei vini	lah lee-stah day vee-nee
rare	al sangue	al sang-gweh
medium	al puntino	al poon-tee-noh
well done	ben cotto	ben kot-toh
glass	il bicchiere	eel bee-kee-air-eh
bottle	la bottiglia	lah bot-teel-yah
knife	il coltello	eel kol-tell-oh
fork	la forchetta	lah for-ket-tah
spoon	il cucchiaio	eel koo-kee-eye-oh

Menu Decoder

l'acqua minerale gasata/naturale	lah-kwah mee-nair-ah-leh gah-zah-tah/ nah-too-rah-leh	mineral water fizzy/still
l'agnello	lahn-yell-oh	lamb
al forno	al for-noh	baked
alla griglia	ah-lah greel-yah	grilled
l'anguilla	lahng-gwee-lah	eel
l'aragosta	lah-rah-goss-tah	lobster
arrosto	ar-ross-toh	roast
il baccalà	eel bahk-kah-lah	dried salted cod
la birra	lah beer-rah	beer
la bistecca	lah bee-stek-kah	steak
il brodetto	eel-broh-det-toh	fish soup
il burro	eel boor-oh	butter
il caffè	eel kah-feh	coffee
i calamari	ee kah-lah-mah-ree	squid
il carciofo	eel kar-choff-oh	artichoke
la carne	la kar-neh	meat
carne di maiale	kar-neh dee mah-yah-leh	pork
i fagioli	ee fah-joh-lee	beans
il fegato	eel fay-gah-toh	liver
il formaggio	eel for-mad-joh	cheese
le fragole	leh frah-goh-leh	strawberries
il fritto misto	eel free-toh mees-toh	mixed fried fish
la frutta	la froot-tah	fruit
frutti di mare	froo-tee dee mah-reh	seafood
i funghi	ee foon-ghee	mushrooms
i gamberi	ee gam-bair-ee	prawns
il gelato	eel jel-lah-toh	ice cream
l'insalata mista	leen-sah-lah-tah mees-tah	mixed salad
l'insalata verde	leen-sah-lah-tah vehr-day	green salad

il latte	eel laht-teh	milk
i legumi OR i contorni	ee leh-goo-mee ee kon-tor-nee	vegetables
il manzo	eel man-tsoh	beef
la melanzana	lah meh-lan-tsah-nah	aubergine
la minestra	lah mee-ness-trah	soup
il pane	eel pah-neh	bread
il panino	eel pah-nee-noh	bread roll
le patate	leh pah-tah-teh	potatoes
le patatine fritte	leh pah-tah-teen-eh free-teh	chips
il pepe	eel peh-peh	pepper
la pesca	lah pess-kah	peach
il pesce	eel pesh-eh	fish
il pollo	eel poll-oh	chicken
il prosciutto cotto/crudo	eel pro-shoo-toh kot-toh/kroo-doh	ham cooked/cured
il riso	eel ree-zoh	rice
il sale	eel sah-leh	salt
la salsiccia	lah sal-see-chah	sausage
le seppie	leh sep-pee-eh	cuttlefish
secco	sek-koh	dry
la sogliola	lah soll-voh-lah	sole
i spinaci	ee spee-nah-chee	spinach
succo d'arancia/ di limone	soo-koh dah-ran-chah/ dee lee-moh-neh	orange/lemon juice
il tè	eel teh	tea
la tisana	lah tee-zah-nah	herbal tea
il tonno	eel ton-noh	tuna
la torta	lah tor-tah	cake/tart
la trippa	lah treep-pah	tripe
vino bianco	vee-noh bee-ang-koh	white wine
vino rosso	vee-noh ross-oh	red wine
il vitello	eel vee-tell-oh	veal
le vongole	leh von-goh-leh	clams
lo zucchero	loh zoo-kair-oh	sugar
gli zucchini	lyee dzu-kee-nee	courgettes
la zuppa	lah tsoo-pah	soup

Numbers

1	uno	oo-noh
2	due	doo-eh
3	tre	treh
4	quattro	kwat-roh
5	cinque	ching-kweh
6	sei	say-ee
7	sette	set-teh
8	otto	ot-toh
9	nove	noh-veh
10	dieci	dee-eh-chee
11	undici	oon-dee-chee
12	dodici	doh-dee-chee
13	tredici	tray-dee-chee
14	quattordici	kwat-tor-dee-chee
15	quindici	kwin-dee-chee
16	sedici	say-dee-chee
17	diciassette	dee-chah-set-teh
18	diciotto	dee-chot-toh
19	diciannove	dee-chah-noh-veh
20	venti	ven-tee
30	trenta	tren-tah
40	quaranta	kwah-ran-tah
50	cinquanta	ching-kwan-tah
60	sessanta	sess-an-tah
70	settanta	set-tan-tah
80	ottanta	ot-tan-tah
90	novanta	noh-van-tah
100	cento	chen-toh
1,000	mille	mee-leh
2,000	duemila	doo-eh mee-lah
5,000	cinquemila	ching-kweh mee-lah
1,000,000	un milione	oon meel- yoh-neh

Time

one minute	un minuto	oon mee-noo-toh
one hour	un'ora	oon or-ah
half an hour	mezz'ora	medz-or-ah
a day	un giorno	oon jor-noh
a week	una settimana	oona set-tee-mah-nah
Monday	lunedì	loo-neh-dee
Tuesday	martedì	mar-teh-dee
Wednesday	mercoledì	mair-koh-leh-dee
Thursday	giovedì	joh-veh-dee
Friday	venerdì	ven-air-dee
Saturday	sabato	sah-bah-toh
Sunday	domenica	doh-meh-nee-kah

Vaporetto Routes Around Venice

The Vaporetto Routes

The ACTV network runs regular services around the city and out to most of the islands. Some services are circular for part of their route; others extend their routes during the high season. Full details of the different types of vaporetti *and how to use them are given on pages 282–3.*

KEY		
✈ Airport	— Terminal route B	— City centre route 1
🚉 Railway station	— Terminal route O	▬▬ City centre route 2 (part season)
� Car ferry	— Terminal route R	═ City centre route 5 (seasonal)
○ Waterbus stop	═ Terminal route C (seasonal)	═ City centre route 8 (seasonal)
— Terminal route A	— Terminal route F	— City centre route 13